BIOGRAPHICAL
ENCYCLOPEDIA
of
SCIENTISTS

BIOGRAPHICAL ENCYCLOPEDIA of SCIENTISTS

Volume 4
Mach – Schrödinger

Editor
RICHARD OLSON

Associate Editor
ROGER SMITH

Marshall Cavendish
New York • London • Toronto

Project Editor: Tracy Irons-Georges
Research Supervisor: Jeffry Jensen
Acquisitions Editor: Mark Rehn
Photograph Editor: Karrie Hyatt
Production Editor: Cynthia Breslin Beres
Proofreading Supervisor: Yasmine A. Cordoba
Layout: James Hutson

Photograph Researcher: Susan Hormuth, Washington, D.C.

Published By
Marshall Cavendish Corporation
99 White Plains Road
Tarrytown, New York 10591-9001
United States of America

Library of Congress Cataloging-in-Publication Data

Biographical encyclopedia of scientists / editor Richard Olson, associate editor Roger
    Smith.
        p.   cm.
    Complete in 5 v.
    Includes bibliographical references and index.
    1. Scientists—Biography—Encyclopedias. 2. Science—Encyclopedias. 3. Science—
Dictionaries. I. Olson, Richard, 1940-   . II. Smith, Roger, 1953 Apr. 19-   .
ISBN 0-7614-7064-6 (set)
ISBN 0-7614-7068-9 (vol. 4)
Q141.B532 1998
509'.2'2—dc21   97-23877
                                                                                    CIP

First Printing

Contents

As an aid to users of the *Biographical Encyclopedia of Scientists*, guides to pronunciation for profiled scientists with foreign names have been provided with the first mention of the name in each entry. These guides are rendered in an easy-to-use phonetic manner. Stressed syllables are indicated by capital letters.

Letters of the English language, particularly vowels, are pronounced in different ways depending on the context. Below are letters and combinations of letters used in the phonetic guides to represent various sounds, along with examples of words in which those sounds appear and corresponding guides for their pronunciation.

Symbols	Pronounced As In	Spelled Phonetically
a	answer, laugh	AN-sihr, laf
ah	father, hospital	FAH-thur, HAHS-pih-tul
aw	awful, caught	AW-ful, kawt
ay	blaze, fade, waiter	blayz, fayd, WAYT-ur
ch	beach, chimp	beech, chihmp
eh	bed, head, said	behd, hehd, sehd
ee	believe, leader	bee-LEEV, LEED-ur
ew	boot, loose	bewt, lews
g	beg, disguise, get	behg, dihs-GIZ, geht
i	buy, height, surprise	bi, hit, sur-PRIZ
ih	bitter, pill	bih-TUR, pihl
j	digit, edge, jet	DIH-jiht, ehj, jeht
k	cat, kitten, hex	kat, KIH-tehn, hehks
o	cotton, hot	CO-tuhn, hot
oh	below, coat, note	bee-LOH, coht, noht
oo	good, look	good, look
ow	couch, how	kowch, how
oy	boy, coin	boy, koyn
s	cellar, save, scent	SEL-ur, sayv, sehnt
sh	issue, shop	IH-shew, shop
uh	about, enough	uh-BOWT, ee-NUHF
ur	earth, letter	urth, LEH-tur
y	useful, young	YEWS-ful, yuhng
z	business, zest	BIHZ-ness, zest
zh	vision	VI-zhuhn

BIOGRAPHICAL ENCYCLOPEDIA of SCIENTISTS

Ernst Mach

Areas of Achievement: Physics and science (general)

Contribution: Mach did original research in projectile motion. He is also famous for his theory or philosophy of science called positivism. He criticized Sir Isaac Newton's conception of absolute space and time, which had a tremendous impact on the thought of Albert Einstein.

Feb. 18, 1838	Born in Chirlitz-Turas, Moravia (now Chrlice-Turany, Czech Republic)
1855-1860	Attends the University of Vienna, receiving a doctorate in physics
1860-1864	Stays on at the University of Vienna to teach
1864	Accepts a teaching position at the University of Graz
1867	Marries Ludovica Marussig
1867	Accepts a teaching position at Charles University in Prague
1872	Publishes *Die Geschicte und die Wurzel des Satzes von der Erhaltung der Arbeit* (*History and Root of the Principle of the Conservation of Energy*, 1911)
1883	Publishes *Die Mechanik in ihrer Entwickelung historische-kritisch dargestellt* (*The Science of Mechanics*, 1893)
1895	Returns to the University of Vienna
1897	Suffers a stroke
1901	Retires from teaching and serves in the Austrian parliament
Feb. 19, 1916	Dies in Vaterstetten, Germany

Early Life

The Austrian physicist Ernst Mach was born on February 18, 1838, in Chirlitz-Turas, Moravia, in part of the Austro-Hungarian Empire that later became the Czech Republic. His early education took place principally at home by his father.

Mach attended the University of Vienna in 1855, where he studied mathematics, physics, and philosophy. He received his doctorate in 1860. It is interesting to note that Christian Johann Doppler, whose contribution to physics included the discovery of the Doppler effect, had been associated with the university, and his studies of sound waves and moving bodies would determine some of Mach's research interests. Mach stayed on at the university until 1864, when he accepted a position as professor of physics at the University of Graz.

Research in Physics

In 1867, Mach married and accepted a professorship in experimental physics at Charles University in Prague. He worked there for the next twenty-eight years. This was the most produc-

(Library of Congress)

tive time of his career: He published more than one hundred articles in scientific journals.

His primary area of research was the branch of physics known as mechanics. Mach developed and perfected the use of photography to study the motion of projectiles through various media and the resultant wave patterns. The importance of his research in this area was demonstrated in 1931 when the scientific community accepted "Mach 1" as the term for the speed of sound. Mach was also engaged in research concerning the physiology of sensation.

Philosophy and History of Science

Mach was a student of the history of science, which made him keenly aware of what leads to progress in the sciences. He noticed that the best scientific theories were the ones that were based on experiment and observation and that used few, if any, metaphysical concepts. A

Positivism

Although Mach did groundbreaking and original experiments in physics, his greatest contribution is his theory and philosophy about science called positivism.

The theory of positivism has one basic principle: No concept can enter into a scientific hypothesis or theory unless it can be explained completely in terms of observations. In order to appreciate this principle, one needs to place it in a broader context.

Upon reflecting on the history of science, Mach realized that the success of a scientific theory is directly related to the degree to which it is based on observation. In addition, he noticed that some concepts that had no basis in observation had crept into most scientific theories and turned out to be the source of much misunderstanding and confusion.

Mach saw his task and that of subsequent scientists as the removal of these concepts from science, guarding against their return, and assurance that no other concepts except those grounded in observation entered into a scientific theory. In other words, all science must begin and end with observation. Thus, positivism is a theory about how scientific theorizing should take place.

The purpose of scientific theories cannot be to explain human experiences, as traditional scientists had presumed, since these explanations usually involved concepts that could not, even in principle, be detected by the senses. Rather, since observation is the basis for all of science, theories exist merely to describe experiences, to offer some sort of unity to them.

Mach was courageous enough to accept the logical consequences of his position. His views led him to reject such concepts as molecules, absolute space, absolute time, and the ether, for example, because they cannot be observed, experienced, or detected. Theories may use concepts, but they must be tied to and completely reducible to observations. Another consequence of positivism is that, since observation is the basis for all of science, the distinctions among the different sciences are arbitrary and conventional.

Mach's positivism has had a profound influence on many scientists, especially physicists. Although none of his contemporaries was willing to go to the extreme that Mach did, many were open to the spirit of his position. A group of scientists and philosophers who met on a regular basis in Vienna in the 1920's, dubbed "the Vienna circle," instituted a program of scientific methodology that incorporated the key principle of Mach's position. They named their view logical positivism. For them, a concept was meaningful only to the extent that it was observable. They had a broader understanding of what counts as observation, however, which permitted them to acknowledge the existence of molecules, for example.

They also were influenced by Mach's insistence on the arbitrariness of the differences among the sciences, and they set out to merge the various fields in what came to be known as the Unity of Science movement. They envisioned the reduction of all the different branches into one: physics.

Bibliography

The Encyclopedia of Philosophy. Paul Edwards, ed. New York: Macmillan, 1967.

A History of Philosophy. Frederick Copleston. Vol. 8. Garden City, N.Y.: Doubleday, 1989.

Logical Positivism. Alfred J. Ayer. New York: Free Press, 1959.

metaphysical concept is one that cannot, in principle, be observed, detected, proved, or verified by the usual means open to science.

It takes only a short logical step to conclude that the best scientific theories would be those that eliminate all metaphysical concepts, but this is no easy task. Even Sir Isaac Newton, who shared Mach's disdain for things metaphysical, let them sneak into his physics in *Principia Mathematica* (1687). Newton freely spoke of and used the notions of absolute space and absolute time even though they cannot be observed. The observer is always in space and in time and therefore can never be in an objective position to determine their existence experimentally.

Mach's contemporaries were also guilty of metaphysical thinking when it came to the study of light waves. It was a fundamental belief that, since light is a wave, there must be a medium in which these waves travel. Every other wave phenomenon had a medium—air for sound waves, for example. Hence, scientists introduced the concept of the "ether." All experiments to detect it, however, were negative. Mach concluded that the concept of the ether ought to be eliminated from the wave theory of light.

Impact

Mach's writings in this area had a fundamental and profound impact on subsequent physicists and philosophers. For example, his influence on Albert Einstein, as Einstein himself admitted on many occasions, cannot be overestimated. Without Mach's critique of space, time, and the ether, Einstein's theories of special and general relativity may not have been developed.

Logical positivism, a scientific-philosophical program originating from meetings among scientists and philosophers in Vienna in the 1920's and 1930's, took Mach's claims to heart and attempted to banish all concepts from the sciences that could not be verified experimentally.

Later Life

In 1895, Mach came back to the University of Vienna to teach philosophy. He was given the title of professor of history and theory of the inductive sciences. During this time, he saw a number of his works translated into English. He suffered a stroke in 1897 and retired from the university in 1901 to serve in the Austrian parliament.

Mach moved to his son's house in Germany in 1913 and died on February 19, 1916. Einstein wrote his obituary.

Bibliography

By Mach

Die Geschicte und die Wurzel des Satzes von der Erhaltung der Arbeit, 1872 (*History and Root of the Principle of the Conservation of Energy*, 1911)

Die Mechanik in ihrer Entwickelung historische-kritisch dargestellt, 1883 (*The Science of Mechanics: A Critical and Historical Exposition of Its Principles*, 1893)

Beiträge zur Analyse der Empfindungen, 1886 (*Contributions to the Analysis of the Sensations*, 1897)

Populärwissenschaftliche Vorlesungen, 1894 (*Popular Scientific Lectures*, 1895)

Die Principien der Wärmlehre, 1896 (*Principles of the Theory of Heat, Historically and Critically Eludicated*, 1986)

Erkenntnis und Irrtum, 1905 (*Knowledge and Error: Sketches on the Psychology of Enquiry*, 1976)

Die Prinzipien der physikalischen Optik, historisch und erkenntnispsychologisch entwickelt, 1921 (*The Principles of Physical Optics, an Historical and Philosophical Treatment*, 1926)

About Mach

The Age of Ideology. Henry David Aiken. Boston: Houghton Mifflin, 1957.

Ernst Mach. Vol. 6 in *Boston Studies in the Philosophy of Science*, edited by Robert Cohen and Raymon Seeger. Dordrecht, the Netherlands: D. Reidel, 1970.

Ernst Mach: His Life, Work, and Influence. John T. Blackmore. Berkeley: University of California Press, 1972.

(John H. Serembus)

John J. R. Macleod

Areas of Achievement: Chemistry, medicine, and physiology

Contribution: Macleod contributed to a better understanding of respiration and metabolism in human physiology. He was a codiscoverer of insulin, which has benefited millions of diabetic patients.

Sept. 16, 1876	Born in Cluny, Scotland
1893	Enters medical school at the University of Aberdeen
1898	Graduated with degrees in medicine and surgery
1899	Receives a fellowship to study at the University of Leipzig, Germany
1900	Teaches physiology and biochemistry at London Hospital
1903	Marries Mary W. McWalter
1903	Becomes a professor of physiology at Western Reserve University in Cleveland, Ohio
1905	Begins research on carbohydrate metabolism
1913	Publishes a book on diabetes
1918	Becomes a professor of physiology at the University of Toronto
1922	Participates in the first insulin treatment for diabetes
1923	Awarded the Nobel Prize in Physiology or Medicine
1925	Serves as president of the Royal Canadian Institute
1926	Publishes a book on the role of insulin in metabolism
1928	Becomes a professor of physiology at Aberdeen
Mar. 16, 1935	Dies in Aberdeen, Scotland

(The Nobel Foundation)

Early Life

John James Richard Macleod was born in Cluny, a small Scottish village where his father was a minister. His family moved to the city of Aberdeen, where he received his early education.

At the age of seventeen, Macleod entered the University of Aberdeen in order to study medicine. He was a diligent student, being graduated with honors in 1898. He received a fellowship that enabled him to spend a year of further education at the University of Leipzig, Germany.

Macleod's first employer was the London Medical School, where he helped professors to set up classroom demonstrations. After two years, he was appointed a lecturer in biochemistry. Showing early talent as a writer, he coauthored a textbook on physiology for medical students.

Research Publications

In 1903, Macleod was appointed a professor of physiology at Western Reserve University in

The Discovery of Insulin

Diabetes is a disease in which the body is unable to metabolize sugar in the bloodstream. The discovery of insulin, obtained from the pancreases of animals, enabled diabetic patients to control their blood sugar levels through daily injections and a restricted diet.

The word "diabetes" comes from the Greek language, meaning "siphon," because the initial symptom is frequent and urgent urination. Subsequent physical problems may include weight loss, fatigue, high blood pressure, kidney disease, and blindness.

A seventeenth century Swiss physician with an interest in anatomy wanted to determine the function of the pancreas which is a soft organ located behind the stomach. He removed the pancreas of a dog and found that it developed diabetes-like symptoms of frequent urination and great thirst.

In 1869, a German medical student named Paul Langerhans was studying the internal structure of the pancreas under a microscope. He noted the presence of some unique clusters of cells scattered through the pancreas, now called the islets of Langerhans. The function of these cells, however, was a mystery.

In the early twentieth century, autopsies of people who had died of diabetes showed that the islet cells in their pancreases had degenerated. Researchers suggested that islet cells produce an essential hormone for sugar metabolism. They named it insulin, derived form the Latin word for "island."

If insulin could be extracted from the pancreases of animals, it might help patients suffering from diabetes. When this procedure was tried, however, it was not successful. Presumably, digestive enzymes from the pancreas were inactivating the insulin hormone.

A young Canadian surgeon, Frederick Grant Banting, had an idea to overcome this problem. He proposed tying off the ducts from the pancreas to stop the flow of digestive fluids. If the pancreas then stopped producing its enzymes, the insulin would perhaps retain its potency.

Banting needed a well-equipped laboratory to test his idea. He obtained the support of Macleod, who was head of biochemistry at the University of Toronto. In 1921, with the help of student Charles Best, Banting successfully extracted insulin for the first time. The insulin extract was tested on a dog that had been made diabetic by removing its pancreas. The dog was kept alive with daily insulin injections.

The first human patient to receive insulin extract was a fourteen-year-old boy who had been diabetic for two years. He was in critical condition, weighing only 75 pounds. Insulin injections brought his blood sugar level under control. He regained normal weight and lived to maturity.

Diabetes patients worldwide soon benefited from the pioneering work of Banting, Best, and Macleod. Insulin was produced commercially from the pancreases of slaughtered cattle and hogs.

In the 1950's, synthetic insulin became available, but it was too expensive for large-scale manufacture. In the 1980's, a recombinant deoxyribonucleic acid (DNA) technique was developed to synthesize human insulin, making an ample supply available.

Bibliography

Diabetes. Alvin Silverstein. Hillside, N.J.: Enslow, 1994.

Diabetes. Barbara Goodheart. New York: Franklin Watts, 1990.

The Discovery of Insulin. Michael Bliss. Chicago: University of Chicago Press, 1982.

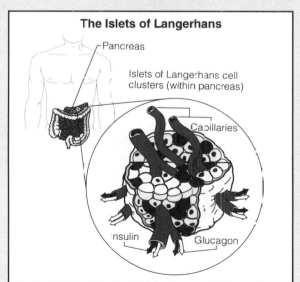

The Islets of Langerhans

Pancreas

Islets of Langerhans cell clusters (within pancreas)

Capillaries

Insulin

Glucagon

(Hans & Cassady, Inc.)

Cleveland, Ohio. During the next fifteen years there, he published numerous research papers and two books. These publications established his international professional reputation.

An area of particular interest to Macleod was the study of carbohydrate metabolism. Normally, starchy foods such as bread or cereal are metabolized into glucose (sugar), which is carried by the bloodstream as a nutrient for cells and to the liver for storage. Diabetic patients are unable to utilize sugar, so it is excreted in their urine.

Macleod wrote a series of twelve papers on glycosuria, which is the medical term for an abnormal amount of glucose in the urine. The presence of glucose in the urine is a key sign of diabetes.

Research in Toronto
In 1918, Macleod moved to the University of Toronto. In his first year there, he coauthored a textbook entitled *Physiology and Biochemistry in Modern Medicine*. This authoritative book of nearly a thousand pages was widely used in medical schools, going through seven editions.

Frederick Grant Banting, a young Canadian surgeon, approached Macleod for help with a research project on insulin. Although reluctant at first, Macleod eventually provided the needed laboratory facilities. He also assigned a student, Charles Best, to assist Banting in his work.

Banting and Best succeeded in 1921 in isolating insulin from the pancreases of dogs. Successful treatment of diabetic animals and human patients soon followed. In 1923, Banting and Macleod were jointly awarded the Nobel Prize in Physiology or Medicine.

Nobel Prize Controversy
Banting believed that Macleod should not have received credit for the discovery of insulin. He described Macleod as someone "never to be trusted . . . selfish, deceptive." Although Banting and Best had done the clinical work on insulin extraction on their own, the Nobel Committee wanted to recognize Macleod for his extensive earlier work on metabolism and diabetes research.

Banting later set up a new laboratory at Toronto for cancer research. Macleod wrote three books on insulin, one being a popularization called *The Fuel for Life* (1928). He returned to his native land in 1928 and died there in 1935. Best, the student member of the research team, completed his medical schooling and became the replacement for Macleod's position at the University of Toronto.

Bibliography
By Macleod
Practical Physiology, 1903
Organic Chemistry, 1907 (with H. D. Haskins)
Diabetes: Its Pathological Physiology, 1913
Fundamentals of Human Physiology, 1916 (with R. G. Pearce)
Physiology and Biochemistry in Modern Medicine, 1918
Insulin and Its Uses in Diabetes, 1925
Carbohydrate Metabolism and Insulin, 1926
The Fuel for Life, 1928

About Macleod
The Discovery of Insulin. Michael Bliss. Chicago: University of Chicago Press, 1982.
Nobel Prize Winners: An H. W. Wilson Biographical Dictionary. Tyler Wasson, ed. New York: H. W. Wilson, 1987.
Sir Frederick Banting. Lloyd G. Stevenson. Toronto: Ryerson Press, 1947.

(Hans G. Graetzer)

Edwin Mattison McMillan

Areas of Achievement: Chemistry, physics, and technology

Contribution: McMillan discovered and named the element neptunium and made other major contributions to understanding the transuranic elements. He also developed synchrotron particle accelerators that attained much higher energies than cyclotrons.

Sept. 18, 1907	Born in Redondo Beach, California
1932	Earns a Ph.D. from Princeton University
1932-1940	Conducts accelerator research with Ernest Orlando Lawrence at the University of California, Berkeley (UCB)
1940	Discovers element 93 and names it neptunium
1941-1942	Conducts radar research at the Massachusetts Institute of Technology (MIT)
1942-1945	During World War II, conducts research on the atomic bomb at Los Alamos, New Mexico
1946-1973	While a professor at UCB, develops a proton synchrotron accelerator
1951	Shares the Nobel Prize in Chemistry with Glenn Seaborg for research on transuranic elements
1958	Appointed the director of the Lawrence Berkeley Laboratory
1963	Shares the Atoms for Peace Prize with Russian V. I. Veksler for developing the synchrocyclotron
1990	Awarded the National Medal of Science
Sept. 7, 1991	Dies in El Cerrito, California

Early Life

Edwin Mattison McMillan was born in Redondo Beach, California, but grew up in Pasadena, where his father established a medical practice. He had an interest in physics as far back as he could remember and started building electronic gadgets and attending public lectures at the California Institute of Technology (Caltech) when he was quite young. After receiving his bachelor's and master's degree from Caltech, he moved to Princeton University, where he received his Ph.D. in 1932.

Following his doctorate, McMillan spent two years on a National Research Council fellowship and then was asked by Ernest Orlando Lawrence to join his newly established Radiation Laboratory at the University of California, Berkeley. The laboratory was built around Lawrence's high-energy cyclotrons, particle accelerators that were beginning to be applied to the study of the radioactive isotopes produced by nuclear disintegration.

Transuranic Elements

In 1940, McMillan, like many other scientists in the world, was studying the fission process

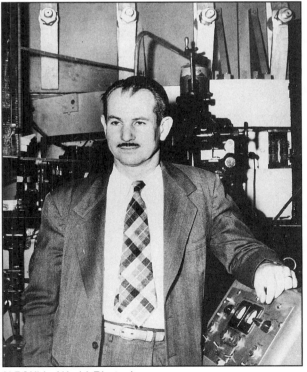

(AP/Wide World Photos)

that had been discovered the year before by Otto Hahn and Fritz Strassman in Germany. He found that after uranium was bombarded with neutrons, an element remained with a half-life of 2.3 days that could not be identified as one of the fission products.

After chemically separating this element, he discovered that it had been produced by the attachment of a neutron to the uranium and subsequent radioactive decay to a new element. Since uranium was named for the planet Uranus, McMillan decided to call the new element neptunium after the planet Neptune, the next planet out in the solar system.

The Development of the Atomic Bomb
After working on radar at the beginning of World War II, McMillan was asked to join the highly secret atomic bomb project at Los Alamos. He organized a series of lectures on nuclear physics so that all the scientists at that laboratory would have the latest information. His main task was the development of the gun-type bomb that fired a subcritical piece of uranium 235 into another mass of the same element in order to produce a chain reaction and a nuclear explosion. This bomb was exploded over the city of Hiroshima, Japan, on August 6, 1945.

High-Energy Accelerator Research
The cyclotron, which had been invented in 1932 by Lawrence, was limited in the energy that it could impart to a proton by the increase in mass caused by relativity. As the mass increases, the proton loses its synchronization with the electrical impulses provided by the cyclotron.

McMillan adjusts the controls of his synchrotron in 1948. (Lawrence Berkeley Laboratory, courtesy of AIP Emilio Segrè Visual Archives)

The Discovery of Element 93

McMillan discovered neptunium, the first transuranic element and the first artificially created one.

When a uranium nucleus is struck by a neutron, either it will split into two fragments, with an accompanying release of energy, or the neutron will attach to the nucleus to form a radioactive isotope. The fission fragments fly apart in opposite directions, sharing the fission energy of 200 million electronvolts, while any new isotope of uranium will remain near its original position.

McMillan used a thin target of uranium so that most of the fission fragments would leave the target and any activity remaining would be attributable to new isotopes of uranium. Two new radioactive species were found in the target after neutron bombardment—one decaying quickly, with a half-life of about twenty-three minutes, and the other decaying more slowly, with a half-life slightly longer than two days.

The shorter-lived activity had been identified earlier as uranium 239, and McMillan guessed that the longer-lived activity might be a new element formed by beta decay of the excited nucleus. Since each element has unique chemical properties, any new element should be separable by chemical processes.

McMillan, using chemical techniques, successfully separated the longer-lived activity from the shorter one and thus proved that he had found element 93.

Bibliography
Lawrence and His Laboratory. J. L. Heilbron and Robert W. Seidel. Berkeley: University of California Press, 1989.
"Radioactive Element 93." Edwin Mattison McMillan and P. H. Abelson. *Physical Review* 97 (1940).

McMillan found a way to keep the accelerating impulses in step with the bunches of particles being accelerated. This made it possible to accelerate the protons to much higher energies, and it is this process that is used in most high-energy accelerators, or synchrocyclotrons, today.

McMillan was given many awards in his career, such as the Nobel Prize in Chemistry in 1951, the Atoms for Peace Prize in 1963, and the National Medal of Science in 1990. He died on September 7, 1991.

Bibliography
By McMillan
"Radioactive Element 93," *Physical Review*, 1940 (with P. H. Abelson)
"The Synchrotron: A Proposed High-Energy Particle Accelerator," *Physical Review*, 1945
Lecture Series in Nuclear Physics, 1947 (with others)
"The Transuranium Elements: Early History" in *Les Prix Nobel en 1951*, 1952
Experimental Nuclear Physics, vol. 3, 1959 (with E. Segrè, G. C. Hanna, M. Deutsch, and O. Kofoed-Hansen)
"The History of the Cyclotron," *Physics Today*, 1959

About McMillan
Current Biography Yearbook. Anna Rothe, ed. New York: H. W. Wilson, 1952.
"Edwin Mattison McMillan." In *The Nobel Prize Winners: Chemistry*, edited by Frank N. Magill. Pasadena, Calif.: Salem Press, 1990.

(Raymond D. Cooper)

Marcello Malpighi

Areas of Achievement: Medicine and physiology

Contribution: Malpighi discovered the anatomical connections between the venous and arterial vessels and confirmed William Harvey's concepts of the circulation. He also studied the small vessels of the kidneys and of other organs and identified the red cell components of blood.

Mar. 10, 1628	Baptized in Crevalcore, near Bologna, Papal States (now Italy)
1646	Enters the University of Bologna and is tutored by Francesco Natali
1649	Studies medicine under Bartolomeo Massari
1653	Earns a doctorate in philosophy and medicine
1656	Moves to Pisa and is influenced by Alfonso Borelli
1660	Returns to Bologna to teach theoretical medicine
1660	Moves to Messina as the first professor of medicine at its university
1666	Returns to Bologna to teach
1669	Elected to the Royal Society of London
1691	Called to Rome to be the personal physician to Pope Innocent XII
Nov. 29, 1694	Dies in Rome, Papal States

Early Life

Marcello Malpighi (pronounced "mahl-PEE-gee") was born in 1628. His first interests were focused on literature, and it was not until his seventeenth birthday that he studied philosophy under the direction of Francesco Natali.

In 1649, dismayed by the death of both of his parents, Malpighi was encouraged by Natali to study medicine and did so under Bartolomeo Massari and Andrea Mariani. He attended dissections of the circulation of animals and of humans carried out by Massari and others.

A Medical Degree and Research Activities

Malpighi received his medical degree in 1653 and achieved such a high reputation in medicine that he was invited to become a professor of medicine in Pisa in 1656. There, he met Alfonso Borelli, with whom he discussed his often-novel ideas and who became a close friend.

It was in this period that Malpighi developed his approach to science as firmly based on observations and experiments rather than philosophical and scholastic considerations, which he judged to be empty of significance. Because his health was failing in Pisa—he blamed the hot and humid climate—he returned to Bologna, where he taught theoretical medicine for two years.

Studies of the Lungs and Kidneys

It was from Bologna that Malpighi reported his fundamental observations on the structures of the lungs and identified the final connections in William Harvey's proposal of the circulation of the blood. His reputation had grown, and he was invited to become the first professor of medicine at the University of Messina, where he stayed for four years.

Malpighi returned to Bologna in 1666 when he published his first report on the kidney and its blood supply. Through his use of the microscope, then a novelty in science, and with skillful injections of ink into blood vessels, he was able to outline the vascular supply and important structures in other organs as well, such as the tongue, the brain, the heart, and various glands.

In the 1670's, he extended his studies to embryology, mostly in the chicken, and to congenital malformations. He also suggested that the development of large cysts in polycystic kidneys could be related to the blockage of urine.

Recognition

Malpighi and his contributions were widely recognized and appreciated. He was elected to

Capillaries and the Microcirculation

Malpighi used a microscope to study the circulation of blood in the lungs and kidneys.

Through careful observations of the direction of the flow of blood in veins and calculations of the amount of blood pumped by the heart per unit time, William Harvey had conceived of the concept that blood is not continuously formed in the body but instead circulates within it. In other words, blood travels through the heart and lungs to various organs and then returns to the heart and lungs. He did not identify, however, the connecting system between the venous and arterial blood vessels. Harvey's theory was a deduction, not a demonstration.

Malpighi, unlike Harvey, used the microscope to study the structure of the lungs. He learned by a variety of techniques, including inflation of the lungs by way of the trachea and injection of ink into blood vessels, that the lungs of the frog consist of small air sacs surrounded by a network of small vessels called the capillaries, about the size of hairs. The network of capillaries, now termed the microcirculation, was eventually discovered to be the pathway for the transport of oxygen in the body.

Malpighi also used the microscope and injection of ink into blood vessels to discover structures in the kidneys now called glomeruli (earlier known as Malpighian corpuscles). Blood reaching the kidney first enters the glomeruli and then leaves to be distributed over contorted, fiber-like structures called the convoluted tubules. No direct connection exists between the blood in the glomeruli and these tubules. Malpighi concluded that urine is formed in the glomeruli and that only the smaller components of blood pass through them in a filtration process.

Bibliography

"Glomerular Filtration." David A. Maddox, William M. Dean, and Barry M. Brenner. In *Renal Physiology*, edited by Erich E. Windhager. Vol. 1, section 8 of *Handbook of Physiology*. New York: Oxford University Press, 1992.

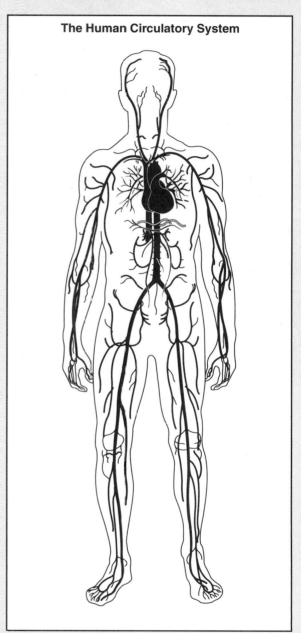

The Human Circulatory System

(Hans & Cassady, Inc.)

The Pathway for Oxygen: Structure and Function in the Mammalian Respiratory System. Ewald R. Weibel. Cambridge, Mass.: Harvard University Press, 1984.

(National Library of Medicine)

the Royal Society of London in 1669. Throughout his scientific career, however, he was often severely criticized because of the radical nature of many of his ideas and because of his intolerance of accepted dogma that was not based on solid observational or experimental evidence.

Final Years
In 1691, at the pinnacle of his scientific career, Malpighi accepted an invitation to become the personal physician of Pope Innocent XII in Rome. Unfortunately, Malpighi himself suffered from ill health—gout, heart palpitations, and probably kidney stones—and died of a stroke on November 29, 1694.

Bibliography
By Malpighi
De pulmonibus observationes anatomicae, 1661 ("About the Lungs," *Proceedings of the Royal Society of Medicine*, 1929-1930)

Epistolae anatomicae de cerebro, ac lingua . . . Quibus anonymi accessit exercitatio de omento, pinguedine et adiposis ductibus, 1665

De Viscerum structura excercitatio anatomica . . . accedit dissertatio eiusdem polypo de cordis 1666 (partial trans. as *Concerning the Structure of the Kidneys*, 1925)

Dissertatio epistolica de formatione pulli in ovo . . ., 1673 ("On the Formation of the Chicken in the Egg" in *Marcello Malpighi and the Evolution of Embryology*, 1966, by Howard B. Adelmann)

About Malpighi
A History of the Life Sciences. Lois N. Magner. New York. Marcel Dekker, 1979.

"Malpighi, Marcello." Luigi Belloni. In *Dictionary of Scientific Biography*, edited by Charles Coulston Gillispie. New York: Charles Scribner's Sons, 1970.

"Malpighi's 'Concerning the Structure of the Kidneys.'" J. M. Hayman, Jr., *Annals of Medical History* 7 (1925).

Marcello Malpighi and the Evolution of Embryology. Howard B. Adelmann. Ithaca, N.Y.: Cornell University Press, 1966.

(Francis P. Chinard)

Benoit B. Mandelbrot

Areas of Achievement: Mathematics and physics

Contribution: Mandelbrot founded fractal geometry, a language to describe forms of nature, such as mountains and coastlines, that are not made up of straight lines, circles, or smooth curves.

Nov. 20, 1924	Born in Warsaw, Poland
1944-1945	Attends the École Polytechique
1948	Earns an M.S. in aeronautics from the California Institute of Technology
1952	Earns a Ph.D. in mathematics from the University of Paris
1953-1954	Invited to the Institute for Advanced Study at Princeton University
1955-1957	Teaches at the University of Geneva
1958	Joins the staff of the IBM Thomas J. Watson Research Center
1960's	Studies stock market fluctuations and the water levels of the Nile River
1973	First uses the term "fractal" to describe a new family of geometric shapes
1982	Publishes *The Fractal Geometry of Nature*
1982	Elected to the American Academy of Arts and Sciences
1985	Given the Barnard Medal for Meritorious Service to Science
1986	Awarded the Franklin Medal
1993	Wins the Wolf Prize for changing how nature is viewed
1993	Officially retires from IBM

Early Life

Benoit B. Mandelbrot (pronounced "MAN-dehl-broht")—the "B." does not stand for anything—was born in Warsaw, Poland, in 1924 to a Lithuanian Jewish family. His father was a clothing wholesaler, and his mother was a dentist. Mandelbrot did not go to school regularly as a child. Instead, he was tutored by his Uncle Loterman; they spent much time playing chess and reading maps.

In 1936, when Mandelbrot was thirteen, the family moved to France. Although he entered school, his schooling was disrupted because of World War II. It was during this time that he was heavily influenced by his Uncle Szolem Mandelbrojt, a mathematician and university professor. Later in life, Mandelbrot recalled only one major disagreement with his uncle. Szolem Mandelbrojt thought that geometry was all right for children but that true mathematicians had to grow out of it.

Formal Education

During World War II, from 1942 to 1944, Mandelbrot moved around and worked, once as a toolmaker for the railroad. After the war, when he was twenty, he began the monthlong examination for admittance into the leading science schools. Although his formal schooling was incomplete, he did well on the examinations. Part of the reason that he did so well was his ability to see shapes and pictures in his mind, and his drawings often led him to the solutions to problems. He was admitted to the École Polytechnique, a famous school in France, and was graduated two years later.

After his graduation, Mandelbrot was recommended for a scholarship to study at the California Institute of Technology (Caltech), where he was graduated with a degree in aeronautics. Returning to France, he spent a year in the air force before attending the University of Paris, where he eventually earned his Ph.D. in mathematics in 1952.

Frequency Distribution

It was while studying in Paris that Mandelbrot became interested in the subject of frequency distribution, which is how things center around an average. For example, if sand is poured out of a bucket, the pile of sand will be tallest in the center and will slope off to each side. The side view of this pile looks like a bell, which accounts for the term "bell-shaped curve" for frequency distribution.

Mandelbrot was interested, however, in those things in the world that did not follow the normal bell-shaped curve. Mathematicians had no way to represent these irregularities, such as the rise and fall of rivers or the price of cotton over the years. The study of statistical irregularities was to be a major focus for the rest of his life.

Teaching and Family Life

Jobs for mathematicians are usually either in teaching or research. For six years after earning his Ph.D. in Paris, Mandelbrot taught at a number of different schools. For the 1953-1954 academic year, he was at Princeton University. From 1955 to 1957, he taught at the University of Geneva.

It was during this time that Mandelbrot married Aliette Kagan; they had two children, Laurent and Didier. In 1957 and 1958, he was junior professor of applied mathematics at Lille University.

A Career at IBM

In 1958, Mandelbrot became a member of the research department of International Business Machines (IBM). He stayed with the company for thirty-five years, until his retirement in

Fractals and Patterns in Nature

The term "fractal" describes the irregular geometry of the world. It provides the base for the branch of science called chaos, which studies the order and patterns of seemingly random things such as earthquakes and the shape of clouds.

Scientists interested in irregularities in nature, such as fern leaves and holes in swiss cheese, want to describe these things mathematically.

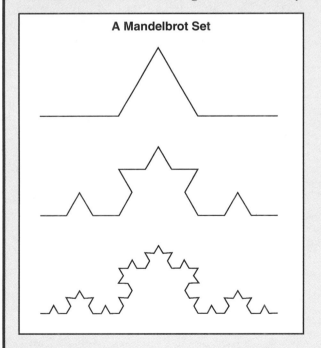

A Mandelbrot Set

Mandelbrot also saw irregularities in other fields, such as medicine (in heartbeats) and economics (in price fluctuations). In attempts to explain how all these subjects fit together, he coined the term "fractal." Always favoring pictures over formulas, he showed how complex patterns could be represented with short equations. If the answer to the equation is fed back into itself, this process occurs over and over, which is known as iteration.

One of the resulting shapes has become known as a Mandelbrot set. If the pattern is looked at closely, magnified a million times for example, baby Mandelbrot sets, sea horses, and other patterns appear. These shapes go on forever and illustrate the concept of infinity. Fractals also demonstrate that very small changes in the original equation make very large differences in the shape of the outcome. This relationship has led some scientists to wonder whether the genetic codes that make up plant and animal life are not necessarily as complex as once thought.

Bibliography

Chaos: Making a New Science. James Gleick. New York: Penguin Books, 1987.

Fractals, the Patterns of Chaos: A New Aesthetic of Art, Science, and Nature. John Briggs. New York: Simon & Schuster, 1992.

Penrose Tiles to Trapdoor Ciphers. Martin Gardner. New York: W. H. Freeman, 1989.

(Hank Morgan/Science Source)

vention of the field of fractal geometry for which he is best known.

Fractal Geometry and Computers

Mandelbrot claimed that he never learned the complete alphabet in school and that he learned the multiplication tables only to five. He had a gift, however, for visualizing pictures. By the 1970's, computers had become powerful enough to do the mathematics needed to turn his equations into graphics, and he used these computers so that others could see the outcome of his work.

Using his simple fractal formulas, computers could generate artificial landscapes that looked real. These fractal landscapes were used in many popular motion pictures produced in the 1980's. Fractal geometry is also used to study such topics as protein structure, acid rain, and the strength of steel.

Bibliography

By Mandelbrot

"How Long Is the Coast of Britain?: Statistical Self-Similarity and Fractional Dimension," *Science*, 1967

Fractals, 1977 (revised as *The Fractal Geometry of Nature*, 1982)

About Mandelbrot

Chaos: Making a New Science. James Gleick. New York: Penguin Books, 1987.

Fractals for the Classroom. H. O. Peitgen. New York: Springer-Verlag, 1989.

"Interview with Benoit Mandelbrot." Monte Davis. *Omni* (February, 1984).

(Tom Hull)

1993. He was known as a mathematical jack-of-all-trades; his interests were varied, and IBM gave him considerable freedom. During his career at IBM, he took temporary positions at several schools in order to follow his interests. He taught economics at Harvard, engineering at Yale, and physiology at the Einstein School of Medicine. He also kept up his study of statistical irregularities; it is for his resulting in-

Guglielmo Marconi

Areas of Achievement: Invention and technology

Contribution: Marconi developed radio wave communication. The legacy of his work includes the radio broadcasting industry, shortwave radio for amateurs, and navigation by radar.

Apr. 25, 1874	Born in Bologna, Italy
1888	Studies physics and chemistry with private tutors
1895	Sets up radio experiments in his attic
1896	Moves to London and receives his first patent for radio telegraphy
1897	Forms the Marconi Wireless Telegraph Company
1898	Demonstrates ship-to-shore radio for Queen Victoria
1900	Tunes radio signals to different frequencies
1901	Transmits the first radio signal from England to Canada
1909	Receives the Nobel Prize in Physics
1912	The sinking of the *Titanic* shows the need for radio on ships
1914	Defends his patent rights in court
1918	Transmits messages from England to Australia
1920's	Develops shortwave radio communication
1932	Directs microwaves with a dish antenna
1934	Demonstrates the use of microwaves for navigation in fog
1935	Proposes television transmission via microwaves
July 20, 1937	Dies in Rome, Italy

Early Life

Guglielmo Marconi was born in 1874 at Bologna, Italy. His father was a wealthy landowner, and his mother came from Ireland. He received home schooling from private tutors and, by the age of fourteen, showed special talent for physics and chemistry.

In 1894, Marconi read an obituary notice of Heinrich Hertz that told about his experiments on transmitting electromagnetic waves across a laboratory room. Marconi had the inspiration that such waves could be useful for communication through space without requiring transmission lines like the telephone and telegraph.

Marconi's parents allowed him to set up an electrical laboratory in the attic of their home. He built an induction coil to produce high-voltage sparks and detected the resulting radiation with a simple loop antenna. Working by himself, he successfully duplicated Hertz's observations.

Improving the Apparatus

To increase the distance at which a signal could be received, Marconi built a more sensitive detector called a "coherer." He connected a battery and electric bell to the coherer to give an audible sound when a signal was received. Marconi stationed his brother in a field some distance from their house. When the spark coil was activated in the attic, the bell would ring up to 200 feet away.

To increase the distance, Marconi constructed a larger induction coil and experimented with antennas. Using the new system, the signal traveled more than a mile, where his brother reported its reception by waving a flag.

Demonstrations of Wireless Telegraphy

Marconi applied to the Italian government for funds to build a bigger transmitter but was turned down. He then went to London and gave demonstrations at several scientific meetings. In 1896, he obtained the first patent for his invention.

To improve the apparatus, Marconi added a telegraph receiver key that produced dots and dashes of Morse code. He gave successful radio demonstrations to the British Post Office and the Royal Navy, and he also sent messages across the English Channel to France.

A Wireless Telegraph System

Marconi's transmitter created radio waves from a high-voltage discharge produced by an induction coil. His receiver detected this radiation by means of a "coherer" connected to a battery and telegraph key.

When electric current from a battery flows through a coil of wire, a magnetic field is created around the coil. If the current is interrupted, the magnetic field collapses and produces high-voltage sparks. This principle is used in the spark coil of an automobile ignition system.

In 1887, Heinrich Hertz observed that electric sparking from a coil generates radiation that can be detected a short distance away. Marconi improved Hertz's transmitter by attaching an overhead antenna to the coil. He also added a telegraph key to the circuit so that current from the battery could be started and stopped easily.

The receiver that Hertz used to detect radio waves was a single loop of wire with a small gap in it. Radiation from the transmitter caused sparks to jump across the gap. These sparks provided visual evidence that radio waves had been received. Marconi verified for himself that the Hertz loop detector worked as described, but he needed a more sensitive, reliable device to receive signals at a greater distance.

Marconi had read about something called a coherer that sounded promising. The coherer is a small glass tube containing two electrodes separated by a thin layer of finely ground metal powder. The powder normally does not conduct an electric current, but electric sparks will cause the metal particles to stick together (or cohere), thus making a good conductor.

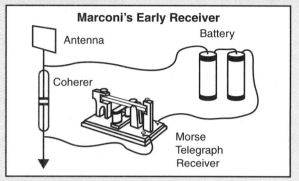

Marconi's Early Receiver

Antenna

Battery

Coherer

Morse Telegraph Receiver

(from Coe's *Marconi, Pioneer of Radio*)

The principle of the coherer had been discovered earlier when engineers were trying to find a lightning protector for cross-country telegraph lines. A wire was connected from the overhead line through a coherer to the ground. When lightning struck, the metal granules clung together to form a path by which the jolt of electricity could pass harmlessly into the ground.

After extensive experimentation, Marconi found that a coherer containing a mixture of 95 percent nickel and 5 percent silver gave the best results. He also improved the sensitivity by making the layer of metallic powder very thin and by pumping the air out of the glass tube.

To indicate when a signal had arrived at the coherer, Marconi connected a battery and telegraph receiver to it. The telegraph would click whenever the coherer was conducting but remained silent at other times. Eventually, the telegraph had a ticker tape attachment to record dots and dashes automatically.

To complete his receiver, Marconi connected an antenna to one terminal of the coherer. In 1895, a radio signal was successfully detected over a mile away from the transmitter in his attic laboratory.

Bibliography

American Science and Invention: A Pictorial History. Mitchell Wilson. New York: Bonanza Books, 1954.

A History of the Marconi Company. W. J. Baker. New York: St. Martin's Press, 1972.

Marconi, Pioneer of Radio. Douglas Coe. New York: J. Messner, 1943.

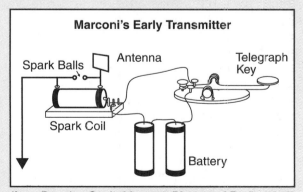

Marconi's Early Transmitter

Spark Balls

Antenna

Telegraph Key

Spark Coil

Battery

(from Douglas Coe's *Marconi, Pioneer of Radio*, 1943)

In 1898, Marconi set up a transmitter on board a ship and reported the progress of a popular yacht race at sea. This event caught the imagination of the general public and made his name famous in England.

The First Transatlantic Radio Signal

Marconi had successfully sent radio waves up to 100 miles, but he was anxious to try for greater distances. He won approval from his financial backers to build a 25,000-watt transmitting station on the west coast of England. Marconi made a voyage across the Atlantic to determine how far the signal would carry. From the transmitter in England, he was able to receive Morse code messages more than 1,000 miles away.

Encouraged by this success, he built a receiving antenna on Cape Cod, hoping to pick up the signal all the way from England. This project was done secretly to avoid unfavorable publicity in case of failure. Unfortunately, the antenna tower blew down in a storm. Marconi then moved his equipment to Newfoundland in eastern Canada. The antenna was mounted on a kite with a long cable. On December 11, 1901, with the kite flying at 400 feet, the prearranged signal of three dots, repeated over and over, was clearly received from England. Although regular message service took two more years, Marconi's vision of transatlantic communication had been fulfilled.

The *Titanic* Disaster

In 1912, the luxury ship *Titanic* collided with an iceberg in the north Atlantic ocean and sunk. More than 1,500 passengers and crew members drowned, and 706 people, mostly women and children, were rescued from lifeboats when the *Carpathia*, sixty miles away, responded to the SOS emergency radio call. More lives could have been saved if another ship, only twenty miles away, had heard the SOS.

The *Titanic* disaster brought international agreement that all oceangoing ships should be required to carry radio equipment. When a passenger ship caught fire in 1913, nearby ships from six different countries responded to the SOS and were able to save most of the people. Newspaper publicity about such rescue operations created widespread public support for radio.

(The Nobel Foundation)

Further Developments

Marconi broke new ground by investigating radio transmission at shorter wavelengths. He found that shortwave radio requires relatively little power because the waves are reflected efficiently by the ionosphere in the earth's upper atmosphere.

In the 1930's, Marconi experimented with microwaves, which are very directional when used with a dish antenna. He demonstrated how a microwave beam could guide a ship in fog. Microwaves later became the basis for radar, which is essential for airplane safety.

Marconi was made a noble by the Italian government in 1929 and given the title "marchese." He died in Rome in 1937 at the age of sixty-three.

Bibliography

By Marconi

"Wireless Telegraphy," *Proceedings of the Institution of Electrical Engineers*, 1899

Improvement in Apparatus Employed in Wireless Telegraphy, 1899

"Transatlantic Wireless Telegraphy," *Proceedings of the Royal Institution of Great Britain*, 1908-1910

"Radio-Telegraphy," *Nature*, 1911

The Progress of Wireless Telegraphy, 1912

Radio Communications, 1925

About Marconi

Marconi, Father of Radio. David Gunston. New York: Thomas Y. Crowell, 1965.

Marconi: The Man and His Wireless. Orrin E. Dunlap. Reprint. New York: Arno Press, 1971.

My Father, Marconi. Degna Marconi. New York: McGraw-Hill, 1962.

(Hans G. Graetzer)

Edme Mariotte

Areas of Achievement: Botany, earth science, physics, and physiology

Contribution: Mariotte, an ingenious experimentalist, determined the laws of elastic collisions, related barometric pressure to winds and the weather, proposed laws for the flow of fluids through pipes, examined certain aspects of human vision, and studied the color of rainbows and the movement of sap in plants.

1620	Born near Dijon, France
1667	Submits studies on movement of sap in plants to the Académie des Sciences, to which he is elected as a physicist
1668	Publishes studies on the blind spot of the eye
1670	Moves to Paris and participates in the activities of the Académie des Sciences
1673	Publishes a treatise on the laws of impact of elastic and inelastic bodies
1679	Reports on the properties of air
1678	Reports on the scientific method
1681	Completes studies on the colors of rainbows
May 12, 1684	Dies in Paris, France
1686	His studies on the movement of water and other fluids are published posthumously

Early Life

Nothing definite is known about the early life of Edme Mariotte (pronounced "mar-YAWT"). He lived and was educated in Dijon, France, and may have taken religious orders as abbott and prior of a small community in Burgundy.

It was from Dijon that he submitted his first

scientific study to the Académie des Sciences in Paris, on the movement of sap in plants. He had already communicated with Christiaan Huygens, the Dutch physicist who had developed a wave theory of light, on one of his own discoveries, the blind spot of the eye.

Approach to Scientific Problems

Following his move to Paris, around 1670, Mariotte became immersed in the affairs of the Académie des Sciences and participated actively in programs concerning physics and mathematics. In these fields, as well as in biological ones, he demonstrated an unusual ability to link observations with experiments and interpretations with data.

He thus used and advocated induction as a method of reasoning based on experiments. He deprecated hypothetical systems not based on more pragmatic approaches. During his career, he showed an independence of thought that often led him to question accepted dogma and to advance novel interpretations at variance with contemporary concepts.

Influence on Other Scientists

Mariotte had considerable influence with members of the academy and on other scientists as well. He collaborated with Philippe de la Hire, a mathematician, on a number of physical problems and with many other members of the academy, such as Huygens, on a variety of experiments.

He also corresponded extensively with scientists elsewhere. One of these was Gottfried Wilhelm Leibniz, a philosopher and mathematician who participated in Mariotte's studies of the atmosphere.

Studies of Hydrodynamics

Mariotte's activities and interests covered a wide range. He examined carefully the collisions of elastic and inelastic bodies, the motion of the pendulum, and the properties of gases. He also studied the atmosphere, the effects of pressure on gases and fluids, and the design of hydraulic systems, particularly those relating to fountains and to the design of paddles for mills.

The Movement of Water and of Other Fluid Bodies

Mariotte's major contributions were on the relationships between pressure and the movement of water and of other fluids such as air in various conduits.

Early on, Mariotte drew an analogy between the circulation of blood, already known to be the result of pressure differences, and the movement of sap in plants. The latter was also the result of hydraulic pressure differences rather than the product of the continuous generation of the fluids as had previously been assumed.

He also examined the resistance of water to penetration by cannon balls, which are noted to bounce or skip if hitting the water at sufficiently small angles. Extending these observations, he described the laws of collisions of elastic and inelastic bodies such as clay, glass, or ivory balls in direct and oblique encounters. He used these experiments to explain the behavior of water as an inelastic and incompressible fluid in contrast to the behavior of compressible gases.

From his experiments with gases, he formulated what is generally referred to as Boyle's law of gases, named after seventeenth century scientist Robert Boyle. The volume occupied by a given quantity of a gas is inversely related to the pressure exerted on that gas. Mariotte also demonstrated that the solubility of air in water is directly related to the pressure on the gas and inversely related to the temperature of the water.

Mariotte applied the results of these and related studies to the problems of jet sizes for fountains and the wall thicknesses of pipes required to prevent bursting. He also studied the frictional losses in flowing systems and the effects of water jets on mill wheel paddles.

His contributions in these fields form the cornerstone of modern hydraulics.

Bibliography
Fundamentals of Physics. D. Halliday and R. Resnick. New York: John Wiley & Sons, 1988.
Phloem Translocation. M. J. Canny. Cambridge, England: Cambridge University Press, 1973.
Textbook of Physiology. A. C. Guyton, 8th ed. Philadelphia: W. B. Saunders, 1991.

(Roger-Viollet)

Later Life and Appreciation

During this period, Mariotte formulated his views of scientific methodology, expressed in a practical manner throughout his scientific career. In effect, he emphasized experiment rather than theory and interpretation rather than broad speculation.

He was highly regarded by his colleagues and by other scientists and praised for his outstanding experimental designs and for their simplicity. His discoveries were recognized and his interpretations, although challenged by some at the time that he introduced them, were generally accepted. In some fields such as hydraulics, his contributions still form their basic foundations.

Mariotte died in 1684 in Paris.

Bibliography

By Mariotte

"La Congéation de l'eau," *Journal des Sçavans*, 1672

Traité de la percussion au choc des corps, 1673

Essai de logique, contenant les principes des sciences et la manière de s'en servir pour faire des bons raisonnements, 1678

De la végétation des plantes, 1679

De la nature de l'air, 1679

De la nature des couleurs, 1681

Traité du mouvement des eaux et des autres corps fluides, 1686 (*The Motion of Water and Other Fluids, Being a Treatise of Hydrostatics . . .*, 1718)

Œuvres de Mariotte, 1717

"Expériences touchant les couleurs" in *Histoire de l'Académie depuis 1666 jusqu'en 1699*, 1733

About Mariotte

"Mariotte, Edme." Michael S. Mahoney. In *Dictionary of Scientific Biography*, edited by Charles Coulston Gillispie. New York: Charles Scribner's Sons, 1970.

(Francis P. Chinard)

Walter E. Massey

Areas of Achievement: Physics and science (general)

Contribution: Massey contributed to the understanding of the properties of materials at very low temperatures. He has also shown leadership in promoting the availability of science education to all students, regardless of race or gender.

Apr. 5, 1938	Born in Hattiesburg, Mississippi
1958	Earns a B.S. from Morehouse College
1966	Awarded M.A. and Ph.D. degrees in physics from Washington University
1966	Becomes a staff physicist at Argonne National Laboratory
1968-1970	Serves on the faculty of the University of Illinois
1970	Named an associate professor of physics at Brown University
1975	Appointed dean of the college at Brown
1979-1984	Serves as the director of Argonne
1979-1993	Teaches physics at the University of Chicago
1984-1991	Acts as vice president for research and for Argonne at the University of Chicago
1988	Named president of the American Association for the Advancement of Science
1991	Becomes the director of the National Science Foundation
1993-1995	Acts as provost and senior vice president for academic affairs for the University of California
1995	Named president of Morehouse College

(AIP Emilio Segrè Visual Archives)

Early Life

A native Mississippian, African American scientist Walter Eugene Massey attended a predominantly black high school and was admitted to college directly from the tenth grade. For someone who had never heard of physics, Morehouse College proved to be a challenge.

Massey admits that he "probably would have flunked out of Morehouse long before graduation—had it not been for a physics teacher there." Such mentors and role models are prominent in his autobiographical notes.

Physics and More Physics

Massey recognized that a B.S. degree in mathematics and physics from Morehouse was not his passport to success, but it did allow him to spend a year teaching physics before graduate study at Washington University in St. Louis, Missouri.

A shock awaited him in the form of a disastrous mathematics examination, but a graduate student helped him survive the program. His mentor, Dr. Eugene Feenberg, would help him while Massey completed his thesis. Although Massey's teachers were white, he acknowledges that they were highly supportive. As a result of his own education, Massey came to believe strongly in the importance of mentors in a student's life. He received both his M.A. and Ph.D. degrees in 1966.

Massey began his scientific career at Argonne National Laboratory. Appointments at the University of Illinois and Brown University brought him recognition in both teaching and research. In 1975, he became dean of the college at Brown.

The Scientist-Administrator

Massey's talents in science and administration produced the unique dual appointment as professor of physics at the University of Chicago and director of the Argonne National Laboratory. In addition to these duties, Massey soon became vice president of the University of Chicago, for research and for Argonne National Laboratory.

The demands of these positions restricted his scientific research. Instead, Massey directed his energies toward becoming a leader in those policy-making organizations where he could influence the direction and spread of opportunities in science. Concerned about fairness, Massey was especially forceful in his support of science and education for women and minorities.

Rising to the Top

Massey could never be content with a static life; only the highest and most demanding positions could make possible the attainment of his goals. In 1991, President George Bush appointed him director of the National Science Foundation, where he was responsible for the distribution of much federal research support. Massey also had greater opportunities to seek support in both political and public forums.

Massey still believed that the United States' educational forces must display more concern and have a greater impact. The opportunity to influence directly one of the country's largest and most visible educational institutions came

Atoms Without Heat

According to very-low-temperature physics, a field in which Massey conducted much research, the mathematical study of helium atoms at temperatures near absolute zero allows the prediction of fundamental properties of both the matter itself and its interaction in solutions.

Helium atoms are unreactive chemically. They usually have two neutrons, but the light helium isotope has only one. Helium liquid never freezes unless pressure is applied; it remains a liquid at any temperature, making for a fascinating study.

Early in the twentieth century, quantum physics showed that all particles have angular momentum like the spin of a top and that protons, electrons, and atoms are allowed only certain energies, called quanta. These notions are applied in cryogenics, the study of the production and effects of very low temperatures.

Elementary particles, such as helium atoms, having spins of one-half are called fermions; those with spins of one are designated bosons. Helium 3 is a fermion since it has an odd number of spins, while the boson helium 4 has an even number of spins. Both are quantum liquids, or fluids behaving like waves. One can observe the properties of either substances or waves, but it is more practical to study them mathematically.

The number of fermions in a given quantum state can only be one, while bosons prefer to have a large number in the same state. These differences illustrate the close relationship between mathematics and the practical innovations of cryogenics.

Bibliography

"Helium Group (Gases)." Florence Stein. In *Kirk-Othmer Encyclopedia of Chemical Technology*. New York: John Wiley & Sons, 1996.

"Low Temperature Physics, Superconductivity, and Superfluidity." Anthony Leggett. In *The New Physics*. New York: Cambridge University Press, 1989.

in 1993 when he was appointed provost and senior vice president for academic affairs for the University of California system.

While leaving that powerful position must have been a difficult decision, in 1995 Massey became the ninth president of Morehouse College. By returning to his intellectual roots, this master scientist hoped to promote his forward-looking vision and to continue to voice his ideals, to the benefit of science and education in the United States.

Bibliography

By Massey
"Ground State of Liquid Helium—Boson Solutions for Mass 3 and 4," *Physical Review*, 1966

"Theory of Dilute Solutions of He³ in Liquid He⁴," *Physical Review*, 1969 (with Chia-Wei Woo and Hing-Tat Tan)

"Science Education in the United States: What the Scientific Community Can Do," *Science*, 1989

"Past Imperfect: A Success Story Amid Decades of Disappointment," *Science*, 1992

About Massey
"At Morehouse, a New Outlook." Gail Hagans Towns. *Atlanta Constitution*, February 16, 1996.

"Man of Energy." Robert Cross. *Chicago Tribune*, November 6, 1985.

"Profile: Walter E. Massey—Scientist, Administrator, Role Model." Tim Beardsley. *Scientific American* (June, 1992).

"Walter E. Massey." David E. Newton. In *Notable Twentieth-Century Scientists*, edited by Emily J. McMurray. New York: Gale Research, 1995.

(K. Thomas Finley)

Antonia Maury

Areas of Achievement: Astronomy and physics

Contribution: Maury created an improved method of classifying stellar spectra and studied the spectrum of Beta Lyrae.

Mar. 21, 1866	Born in Cold Spring, New York
1887	Earns a bachelor's degree from Vassar College
1888-1896	Employed as research assistant at Harvard Observatory
1889	Discovers the second known spectroscopic binary star
1891-1894	Employed as teacher at the Gilman School
1896-1918	Employed as teacher and lecturer at various locales
1897	Publishes the results of her studies of stellar spectra
1918-1935	Returns to Harvard Observatory as a research assistant
1919-1920	Receives the Pickering Fellowship
1933	Publishes the results of her studies of Beta Lyrae
1935-1938	Serves as curator of the Draper Park Observatory Museum
1938-1948	Makes annual visits to Harvard Observatory
1943	Awarded the Annie Jump Cannon Prize
Jan. 8, 1952	Dies in Dobbs Ferry, New York

Early Life
Antonia Caetana De Paiva Pereira Maury was born in Cold Spring, New York, on March 21, 1866. Her father, Mytton Maury, was a clergyman and amateur naturalist. Her mother, Virginia Draper Maury, was the sister of Henry

Classification of Stellar Spectra

The spectra of stars can be organized in ways that reveal patterns of stellar evolution.

Light from a star forms a spectrum when it passes through a prism, just as sunlight forms a rainbow. Soon after Henry Draper made the first photograph of a steller spectrum in 1872, astronomers began classifying spectra based on patterns of bright and dark lines.

The system used by Harvard Observatory divided spectra into groups labeled with the letters of the alphabet. Maury realized that this system did not organize the spectra into a logical sequence. She created her own system using groups labeled with Roman numerals. Spectra within each group were labeled "a" (wide, sharp lines), "b" (wide, blurred lines), or "c" (narrow, sharp lines). The Danish astronomer Ejnar Hertzsprung discovered that all "c" stars were giant stars.

Influenced by Maury's system, the Harvard system was simplified and rearranged into a sequence based on temperature, from hottest to coolest: O, B, A, F, G, K, M. Hertzsprung and the American astronomer Henry Norris Russell independently charted stars on a chart comparing temperature and brightness. These charts, known as Hertzsprung-Russell (H-R) diagrams, reveal three major groups of stars: the main sequence (medium-sized stars ranging from hot and bright to cool and dim), white dwarves (small, hot, dim stars), and red giants (large, cool, bright stars). As a main sequence star ages, it expands into a red giant, then loses its outer layers to become a white dwarf.

Bibliography

The Classification of Stars. Carlos Jaschek. Cambridge, England: Cambridge University Press, 1987.

Stars. James B. Kaler. New York: Scientific American Library, 1992.

Stars and Their Spectra: An Introduction to the Spectral Sequence. James B. Kaler. Cambridge, England: Cambridge University Press, 1989.

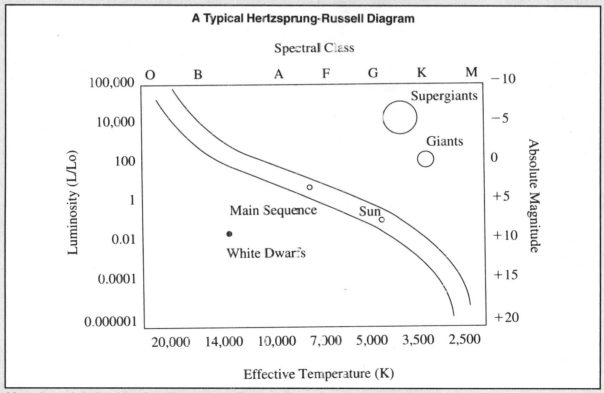

Maury's work helped lead to Hertzsprung-Russell diagrams, charts that classify stars based on their spectra.

Draper, a physician and noted amateur astronomer.

Antonia Maury earned a bachelor's degree from Vassar College in Poughkeepsie, New York, in 1887, with honors in astronomy, physics, and philosophy.

First Years at Harvard

In 1888, Maury began working for Edward C. Pickering, the director of the Harvard College Observatory in Cambridge, Massachusetts. Her work was part of a large project of studying stellar spectra known as the Henry Draper Memorial. Maury's task was to investigate the spectra of bright northern stars. Based on these studies, she decided that the system used to classify stellar spectra was inadequate, and she created her own.

During this time, Maury also studied the spectra of spectroscopic binary stars. These stars appear to be single stars when viewed through a telescope, but they have spectra that reveal them to be double stars. Pickering discovered the first such star, Zeta Ursae Majoris, in 1889. Maury discovered the second, Beta Aurigae, later the same year.

Although Pickering respected Maury's ability, he grew impatient with the slowness of her detailed studies and thought her new classification system unnecessary. Maury was unhappy with Pickering's close supervision of her work. She began teaching science at the Gilman School in Cambridge in 1891 and worked only intermittently at Harvard until 1896. The results of her studies were published in 1897.

Return to Harvard

Maury worked as a teacher and lecturer at various institutions from 1896 to 1918. She returned to Harvard Observatory in 1918, where she received a Pickering Fellowship from 1919 to 1920. Maury investigated the spectra of binary stars, particularly the complex, variable spectrum of Beta Lyrae. Her studies of this star were published in 1933.

Maury left Harvard in 1935 and served as curator of the Draper Park Observatory Museum in Hastings, New York, until 1938. From 1938 to 1948, she visited Harvard Observatory annually to check the accuracy of her predictions of the behavior of the spectrum of Beta Lyrae. Maury received the Annie Jump Cannon Prize from the American Astronomical Society in 1943. She died in Dobbs Ferry, New York, on January 8, 1952.

(Science Photo Library)

Bibliography

By Maury

"Spectra of Bright Stars Photographed with the 11-inch Draper Telescope as a Part of the Henry Draper Memorial and Discussed by Antonia C. Maury Under the Direction of Edward C. Pickering," *Annals of the Astronomical Observatory of Harvard College*, 1897

"The Spectral Changes of β Lyrae," *Annals of the Astronomical Observatory of Harvard College*, 1933

About Maury

The Biographical Dictionary of Scientists: Astronomers. David Abbott, ed. New York: Peter Bedrick Books, 1984.

The Harvard College Observatory: The First Four Directorships, 1839-1919. Bessie Zaban Jones and Lyle Gifford Boyd. Cambridge, Mass.: Harvard University Press, 1971.

Women in Science: Antiquity Through the Nineteenth Century. Marilyn Bailey Ogilvie. Cambridge, Mass.: MIT Press, 1986.

(Rose Secrest)

James Clerk Maxwell

Areas of Achievement: Astronomy, mathematics, and physics

Contribution: One of the creative geniuses of modern theoretical physics, Maxwell introduced statistical methods to the kinetic theory of gases and developed the electromagnetic theory of light. In developing electromagnetic field theory, he unified all the phenomena of electricity, magnetism and optics and predicted the existence of radio waves.

June 13, 1831	Born in Edinburgh, Scotland
1847-1850	Studies at the University of Edinburgh
1850-1854	Studies as an undergraduate at Cambridge University in England
1854-1856	Named a Fellow of Trinity College, Cambridge
1856-1860	Serves as a professor of physics at Marischal College in Aberdeen, Scotland
1861	Elected to the Royal Society of London
1860-1865	Made a professor of physics and astronomy at King's College, London
1871-1879	Serves as a professor of experimental physics at Cambridge
1871	Publishes *Theory of Heat*
1873	Publishes *Treatise on Electricity and Magnetism*
1874	Appointed director of the Cavendish Laboratory
1876	Publishes *Matter and Motion*
Nov. 5, 1879	Dies in Cambridge, England

(Library of Congress)

Early Life

James Clerk Maxwell was born at his family's estate in Dumfrieshire, Scotland, where he spent his first ten years. Although the original family name was Clerk, James's father added "Maxwell" after inheriting the estate from his Maxwell ancestors.

Trained as a lawyer, Maxwell's father never practiced extensively but spent his time studying architecture and tinkering with mechanical gadgets. Since James's youth was spent remote from any school, his education was entirely in his mother's hands. She taught him reading and writing, motivated his curiosity, and encouraged his prodigious memory. In 1839, when Maxwell was eight, she died, abruptly ending his idyllic lifestyle as well as his education. For the next two years, a tutor was employed, but the results were disastrous.

Mr. Maxwell enrolled his ten-year-old son at Edinburgh Academy. Although James did badly at first, he soon began to excel in mathematics, receiving the annual mathematics award at the age of thirteen. The following year, his father began taking him to meetings of the Edinburgh Royal Society. At the age of fourteen, Maxwell discovered a new mathematical method for forming ovals; his results were presented to the society in March, 1846.

A pivotal point in Maxwell's youth was the memorable afternoon in April, 1847, when his uncle took him to visit the private laboratory of physicist William Nicol. Enthralled by the demonstrations of experiments in progress, Maxwell set his course on becoming a physicist. In November of the same year, he enrolled at the University of Edinburgh, where he spent the next three years developing his mathematical skills and writing two more papers for the Royal Society.

Maxwell entered Cambridge University in October, 1850. His brilliance was recognized early by his teachers, and he was elected a scholar at Trinity College after his second year. At Cambridge, the intellectual life was ruled by competition for a high score in the mathematical tripos, a grueling seven-day examination taken during the fourth year. Those aspiring to high honors had to excel in analytical ingenuity, emphasized on the last four days. Maxwell, an excellent mathematician, had prepared diligently; he placed second on the tripos when he took it in January, 1854.

Academic Career

After receiving his undergraduate degree, Maxwell continued his studies at Cambridge, where he was elected a Fellow of Trinity College at the age of twenty-four. As part of his duties, he began to experiment with electricity and magnetism.

In 1860, Maxwell joined the faculty of King's College, London, where he spent the next five years formulating his theory of the electromagnetic field. Maxwell resigned this position five years later to devote more time to writing a treatise on electricity and magnetism and to serve as an examiner for the tripos examinations.

It was Maxwell's profound questions about thermodynamics and about electricity and magnetism that led to changes in the curriculum, in particular to the founding of a physics laboratory for research in these nascent sciences. Because a professor knowledgeable in these fields was needed, the position was offered to Maxwell, who assumed his duties at the new

Cavendish Laboratory in the autumn of 1871.

In addition to his new administrative duties, editing the unpublished papers of the laboratory's namesake, and publishing his treatise, Maxwell had to devote his spare time to caring for his bedridden wife. The constant strain took its toll, and in 1877 Maxwell began to experience stomach pains. He suffered stoically for two years. When he finally consulted a doctor in early 1879, his ailment was diagnosed as stomach cancer. He died November 5 of the same year at the age of forty-eight.

Maxwell's Theory of Electromagnetism

Maxwell showed that light is an electromagnetic wave consisting of varying electric and magnetic fields that propagate through space.

In his study of electric and magnetic forces, Maxwell was concerned with the fundamental question of how electric charges reach across empty space to exert forces on distant charges. Sir Isaac Newton had proposed that forces were exerted across space by "action at a distance," which, lacking a mechanism, provided no explanation at all.

In the nineteenth century, Michael Faraday hypothesized that electrical charges exert forces at a distance by means of fields. Every charge is surrounded by an electric field. When a second charge is introduced into the field, it experiences a force and it exerts a force on the first charge. The field is the mechanism that couples two charges together through a distance. The same argument applies to stationary magnets that create magnetic fields.

When changing in magnitude, electric and magnetic fields create each other: A changing magnetic field creates an electric field, and a changing electric field creates a magnetic field. The strength of the field created is proportional to the rate of change of the creating field.

If a magnetic field is changing at a nonsteady rate, a changing electric field is produced. An electric field, changing at a nonsteady rate, will in turn create a changing magnetic field. A continuous chain of creation is thus possible, in which a varying magnetic field creates a varying electric field that creates a varying magnetic field and so on.

Maxwell realized that he could unite the electric and magnetic fields into a single electromagnetic field by means of a set of equations, now called Maxwell's equations. Using these, Maxwell was able to show that changing electric and magnetic fields, which are perpetually re-creating each other, are also propagating through space as waves of electromagnetic energy. When he calculated the speed of these waves, he obtained 186,000 miles per second—the speed of light. Thus, in 1864, Maxwell concluded that light consists of electromagnetic waves composed of rapidly changing, closely coupled, electric and magnetic fields.

In addition to offering a remarkably original theory of light, which succeeded where others had failed, Maxwell's electromagnetic theory implied that light waves represent only a tiny portion of the possible electromagnetic waves that could be generated. This led to the idea that waves longer than light (radio waves) could be produced in the laboratory. In 1887, twenty-five years after Maxwell's prediction and eight years after his death, the existence of radio waves was experimentally confirmed by Heinrich Hertz in Germany.

The electromagnetic theory of light unified electricity, magnetism, and optics. All are governed by the compact set of equations developed by Maxwell. These equations not only surpassed all previous accounts of these phenomena in explanatory power but also changed the course of physics by articulating a new type of theory: field theory.

Bibliography

Clerk Maxwell and Modern Science. Cyril Domb, ed. London: Athlone Press, 1963.

Conceptual Physics. P. G. Hewitt. Boston: Little, Brown, 1995.

The Contributions of Faraday and Maxwell to Electrical Science. R. A. R. Tricker. London: Pergamon Press, 1966.

James Clerk Maxwell and the Theory of the Electromagnetic Field. J. Hendry. Philadelphia: IOP, 1986.

Bibliography
By Maxwell
Theory of Heat, 1871
Treatise on Electricity and Magnetism, 1873 (2 vols.)
Matter and Motion, 1876
The Scientific Papers of James Clerk Maxwell, 1890 (2 vols.; W. D. Niven, ed.)

About Maxwell
The Demon in the Aether. Martin Goldman. Edinburgh, Scotland: P. Harris, 1983.
James Clerk Maxwell. Ivan Tolstoy. Chicago: University of Chicago Press, 1981.
James Clerk Maxwell, Physicist and Natural Philosopher. C. W. F. Everitt. New York: Charles Scribner's Sons, 1975.
The Life of James Clerk Maxwell. L. Campbell and W. Garnett. London: Macmillan, 1882.

(George R. Plitnik)

Maria Goeppert Mayer

Areas of Achievement: Chemistry and physics

Contribution: Mayer's early work with molecular spectra provides a theoretical basis for important developments in laser physics and molecular orbital calculations. She also developed the shell model of the nucleus.

June 28, 1906	Born in Kattowitz, Upper Silesia, Germany (now Katowice, Poland)
1924	Enters Georgia Augusta University
Jan., 1930	Marries Joseph Mayer
1930	Receives a Ph.D. in physics
1930	Immigrates to the United States
1940	Publishes the textbook *Statistical Mechanics* with her husband
1941	Takes over Enrico Fermi's classes in physics
1945	Named voluntary associate professor of physics at the University of Chicago
1946-1959	Works at Argonne National Laboratory
1947	Proposes, with Edward Teller, a theory for the origin of the elements
1948	Develops the nuclear shell model
1955	Publishes *Elementary Theory of Nuclear Shell Structure* with J. Hans D. Jensen
1959-1972	Takes a paid full professorship at the University of California, San Diego
1960	Suffers a stroke
1963	Wins the Nobel Prize in Physics
Feb. 20, 1972	Dies in San Diego, California

Early Life

Maria Goeppert was born June 28, 1906, in Kattowitz, Upper Silesia, Germany, which is now Katowice, Poland. Her family had been college professors for six generations. When Maria was four years old, her father was given the post of professor of pediatrics at Georgia Augusta University in Göttingen, Germany. She attended private school and eventually entered the university.

Early Career

Goeppert originally intended to study mathematics. Upon meeting Max Born and being introduced to the infant field of quantum mechanics, however, she soon switched to physics. She received her Ph.D. in physics in 1930 for research involving atomic decay processes in which two photons (quanta of light) are emitted.

While at the university, she met Joseph Mayer, an American physical chemist who was

(The Nobel Foundation)

studying there; they married shortly before her graduation and moved to the United States. Joseph accepted a position at The Johns Hopkins University in Baltimore, and Maria pursued a variety of research areas, studying the spectra emitted by molecules, and taught a few classes. While in Baltimore, Maria Goeppert Mayer became a United States citizen and had two children, a girl and a boy.

In 1939, her husband accepted a position at Columbia University, but again no position was available for Mayer. She continued to do research on her own and taught whenever possible. They coauthored *Statistical Mechanics* (1940), which was a standard text for college classes for the next forty years.

At the outbreak of World War II, Enrico Fermi left to take part in the Manhattan Project to design the first nuclear bombs. On twenty-four-hour notice, Mayer took over his classes. She took part in a research group working on the problem of separating uranium isotopes, and, with Edward Teller, she conducted research on isotopic abundances, proposing a "little bang" theory to explain the origin of the elements.

After the War

After World War II, Joseph Mayer was offered a position in chemistry at the University of Chicago. Maria Goeppert Mayer was appointed a voluntary associate professor in physics and was given a part-time position at Argonne National Laboratory.

Mayer brought a fresh outlook to the structure of the nucleus. Her earlier work with her husband in chemistry gave her the ability to look at the "big picture" of a problem. She noticed various trends in the characteristics of nuclei with certain numbers of nucleons that could not be explained by the accepted liquid-drop model of the nucleus. Such trends reminded her of the electronic shells in atoms, leading her to a theory of nuclear shells. Independently, J. Hans D. Jensen came up with a similar model.

San Diego

In 1960, the University of California, San Diego, created a new position in the physics department for Mayer; it was her first full-time position. Although she suffered a stroke shortly after moving to San Diego, she continued to teach and travel widely. In 1963, Mayer shared the Nobel Prize in Physics with Jensen for her nuclear shell model. She remained at the university until her death on February 20, 1972.

Bibliography
By Mayer
"Über Elementarakte mit zwei Quantensprungen," *Annalen der Physik*, 1931
Statistical Mechanics, 1940 (with Joseph E. Mayer)
"On the Origin of the Elements," *Physical Re-*

The Nuclear Shell Model

Mayer studied the arrangement of nucleons—protons and neutrons—in the nucleus of the atom and designed a model that helped explain the abundance of certain configurations.

The nucleus of the atom is composed of two types of particles, called nucleons. The mass of these particles is about two thousand times the mass of an electron. One type of nucleon, the proton, is positively charged; the other type, the neutron, is neutral. The force that holds the nucleus together is the strong nuclear force, the strongest of the four fundamental forces. The strong nuclear force is an attractive force: A proton will be drawn to another proton or to a neutron. It has a very short range; the nucleons must be right next to each other in order to be attracted.

At present, physicists do not totally understand this strong nuclear force or exactly how the nucleons (protons and neutrons) interact inside the nucleus. One still cannot write down a mathematical equation for this force. One model of the nucleus, the liquid-drop model, assumes that each nucleon interacts only with its nearest neighbors. This model has been quite successful in explaining nuclear masses and nuclear fission. Unfortunately, this model does not account for the so-called magic numbers that are observed in the nucleus.

Nuclei that have 2, 8, 20, 28, 50, 82, and 126 neutrons or protons are more abundant than other nuclei with the same total number of nucleons, which suggests that these nuclei are more stable than most. Other evidence also suggests that these magic numbers are significant to nuclear structure. Nuclei with a number of neutrons equal to a magic number have a much larger neutron separation energy (the energy required to remove a single neutron), suggesting that in these nuclei, the neutrons are much more tightly bound to the nucleus, an effect similar to that seen in closed electron shells in atoms.

The shell model of the nucleus is an attempt to explain these magic numbers. The basic assumption in the shell model is that each nucleon interacts predominantly with a force field produced by all the other nucleons. An attractive force can be thought of as a well, trapping the protons and neutrons in it at various levels. In the simplest possible case of this potential well, the shape of the well is assumed to have a square bottom. From this model, the number of nucleons needed to fill each of the energy levels in the well can be calculated. They should correspond to the magic numbers, since the nucleus would be most stable with a full shell. Unfortunately, although the calculations using this shape yielded magic numbers, they were close to but not quite the same as those observed.

Something was missing. The answer was provided by Mayer and J. Hans D. Jensen in 1949, working independently. The nucleons have an inherent spin to them, just as electrons do. Taking into account this spin and applying conservation of angular momentum to the original model results in a splitting of the previous levels. The new magic numbers, which reflect the number of nucleons that can occupy any level, agree with those observed.

Bibliography
The Atomic Nucleus. R. D. Evans. New York: McGraw-Hill, 1955.
Concepts of Modern Physics. Arthur Beiser. New York: McGraw-Hill, 1987.
Elements of Nuclear Physics. Walter Meyerhof. New York: McGraw-Hill, 1967.
Modern Physics. Paul A. Tipler. New York: Worth, 1978.

view, 1949 (with Edward Teller)

"On Closed Shells in Nuclei," *Physical Review*, 1949

"Nuclear Configurations in the Spin-Orbit Coupling Model," *Physical Review*, 1950

"The Structure of the Nucleus," *Scientific American*, 1951

Elementary Theory of Nuclear Shell Structure, 1955 (with J. Hans D. Jensen)

"The Shell Model" in *Nobel Lectures in Physics*, vol. 4, 1972

About Mayer

A Life of One's Own: Three Gifted Women and the Men They Married. Joan Dash. New York: Harper & Row, 1973.

"Maria Goeppert-Mayer." Eugene Wigner. *Physics Today* 25, no. 5 (1972).

"Maria Goeppert-Mayer: Atoms, Molecules, and Nuclear Shells." Karen E. Johnson, *Physics Today* 39, no. 9 (1986).

"Maria Goeppert-Mayer: Two-Fold Pioneer." Roger G. Sachs. *Physics Today* 35, no. 2 (1982).

(Linda L. McDonald)

Sir Peter Medawar

Areas of Achievement: Immunology and science (general)

Contribution: Medawar demonstrated that rejection of transplants is under immunological control. He also wrote many popular books on scientific matters, particularly on the philosophy of science.

Feb. 28, 1915	Born in Rio de Janeiro, Brazil
1935	Receives a bachelor's degree from Madgalen College, Oxford
1938-1944	Serves as a Fellow of Madgalen
1944-1946	Teaches zoology and anatomy at St. John's College, Oxford
1947-1951	Named Mason Professor of Zoology at the University of Birmingham
1949	Made a Fellow of the Royal Society of London
1951-1961	Named Jodrell Professor of Zoology and Comparative Anatomy at University College
1959	Receives the Copley Medal of the Royal Society of London
1960	Awarded the Nobel Prize in Physiology or Medicine
1962-1971	Serves as director of the National Institute for Medical Research
1965	Knighted by Queen Elizabeth II
1969	Suffers a cerebral hemorrhage
1975	Becomes director emeritus
1977	Named a professor of experimental medicine at the Royal Institution
1980	Suffers another stroke
1985	Has a third stroke
Oct. 2, 1987	Dies in London, England

Early Life

Peter Brian Medawar was born in Rio de Janeiro, Brazil, in 1915 to a Lebanese father, who was a naturalized British citizen, and an English mother. When he was young, his family moved to England, where he attended school and lived for the rest of his life. In prepatory school, he knew that he was "hooked on science; no other kind of life would do."

His secondary school studies were at Marlborough, from which he went as an undergraduate to Madgalen College, Oxford University. He studied with the eminent zoologist J. Z. Young. Upon obtaining a first-class degree in zoology, Medawar became a research fellow. He married Jean Shinglewood Taylor in 1937.

The Rejection of Grafts

Early in World War II, Medawar was asked by the Medical Research Council to study why skin taken from one human being would not graft permanently on another human. Injuries caused by the war gave this question particular

(The Nobel Foundation)

relevance, as it was desirable to use skin grafts to treat major wounds and burns. Skin from volunteer donors could not be used permanently for grafts. Medawar studied why skin is rejected if grafted from one person to another.

Medawar's work indicated that the rejection of a skin graft is under immunological control. Previously, rejection of a graft was generally thought to be the result of genetic causes and was therefore considered an insuperable problem. Similar considerations would apply to the transplantation of a kidney or any other organ.

Because of Medawar's work, medicine came a little closer to being able to attempt the heart, lung, and kidney transplantations that would later draw so much publicity, with drugs being used to suppress the immune system and reduce the chance of the transplants being rejected. Medawar thought that his work had provided moral rather than substantive support for work on transplantation, as it greatly encouraged those who hoped that transplantation would be possible.

For his work on immunology, Medawar was awarded the Nobel Prize in Physiology or Medicine in 1960. The Australian scientist Sir Frank Macfarlane Burnet was corecipient with him. Medawar gave his Nobel lecture, "Immunological Tolerance," on December 12, 1960.

Administrator, Researcher, Writer, Lecturer

Medawar was much interested in the philosophy of science, and his thinking on this subject was considerably influenced by the work of Sir Karl Popper. Medawar wrote many very readable books about science and scientific matters for the general public. In 1962, he became director of the National Institute for Medical Research at Mill Hill in London. He did his administrative work and kept two days for his own research. He was knighted in 1965.

In September, 1969, Medawar had a major cerebral hemorrhage. He was in the hospital for months and twice was near death. He returned to work in 1970, although he could not use his left hand, and he retired as director in 1971.

Medawar's output of scientific research decreased after 1969, but his writing did not. In New York in 1980, he had another stroke in the midbrain that affected his speech, swallowing,

Immunological Tolerance

The barrier that usually prevents successful transplantation of tissues between two people is an immunological barrier. When Medawar's work began, it was not apparent that this barrier could be overcome and tissues successfully transplanted between two individuals.

The Australian scientist Sir Frank Macfarlane BurnetMacfarlane] had predicted that an individual might be experimentally altered to be able to accept foreign substances that would otherwise be rejected.

Medawar and his colleagues tested this hypothesis by inoculating mouse embryos in the womb with a foreign substance so that they developed an immunological tolerance to the substance introduced. When grafting was done on these mice after maturation, they accepted not only their own tissue as grafts but also foreign tissue of the same immunologic type as that which was introduced into the embryonic mouse. Immunity was developed in the embryo. This work was done with L. Brent and Rupert Everett Billingham, a student and a former student of Medawar.

In five years' work on a series of outstanding experiments, Medawar showed that rejection was not an insuperable problem. His work demonstrated experimentally that an animal could be prepared so that it could later accept some foreign substance within its body that it would otherwise reject. Medawar called this phenomenon "immunological tolerance."

Medawar's work provided experimental confirmation of Burnet's hypothesis that the ability to produce a specific antibody develops during an animal's lifetime and is not inherited. The immune system learns to distinguish "self" from what is "not self"—these distinctions are not inborn. In contrast to foreign tissue, individuals do not usually mount immune responses to their own tissue. Much research is being done to identify the mechanisms responsible for the maintenance of natural immunological tolerance to constituents of the host's own body. When self-tolerance is lost, the result is often autoimmune disease.

Bibliography

Immunology: A Foundation Text. Basiro Davey. Englewood Cliffs, N.J.: Prentice Hall, 1990.

Immunology: A Synthesis. Edward S. Golub and Douglas R. Green. 2d ed. Sunderland, Mass.: Sinauer Associates, 1991.

Immunology: An Illustrated Outline. David K. Male. New York: Gower Medical Publishers, 1986.

Immunology: An Introduction. Ian R. Tizard. 3d ed. Fort Worth, Tex.: Saunders College Publishers, 1992.

Immunology at a Glance. J. H. L. Playfair. 5th ed. Oxford, England: Blackwell Scientific Publications, 1992.

Immunology: The Making of a Modern Science. Richard B. Gallagher et al., eds. San Diego: Academic Press, 1995.

and walking. Nevertheless, assisted by his wife, Jean, he continued working, writing, speaking, and traveling. In June, 1985, Medawar had a third stroke, and several others followed. He died on October 2, 1987, at the age of seventy-two.

Bibliography
By Medawar

The Uniqueness of the Individual, 1957

The Art of the Soluble: Creativity and Originality in Science, 1967

Recent Advances in the Immunology of Transplantation: Genetics and the Future of Man, 1968

The Hope of Progress: A Scientist Looks at Problems in Philosophy, Literature, and Science, 1972

Advice to a Young Scientist, 1979

Pluto's Republic, 1982

Aristotle to Zoos: A Philosophical Dictionary of Biology, 1983

The Limits of Science, 1984

Memoir of a Thinking Radish: An Autobiography, 1986

The Threat and the Glory: Reflections on Science and Scientists, 1990

About Medawar

"The Art of the Soluble." *Nature* (October 8, 1987).

"Sir Peter Medawar." In *The Nobel Prize Winners: Physiology or Medicine*, edited by Frank N. Magill. Pasadena, Calif.: Salem Press, 1991.

"Sir Peter Medawar." *New Scientist* (April 12, 1984).

"Sir Peter Medawar (1915-1987)." N. A. Mitchison. *Nature* (November 12, 1987).

(*Maureen H. O'Rafferty*)

Lise Meitner

Area of Achievement: Physics

Contribution: Meitner was a codiscoverer of the element protactinium and was the first person to recognize that atoms of uranium can undergo fission, or split, when bombarded by neutrons.

Nov. 7, 1878	Born in Vienna, Austro-Hungarian Empire (now Austria)
1906	Earns a Ph.D. in physics at the University of Vienna
1908	Begins her collaboration with the chemist Otto Hahn
1914-1918	Serves as an X-ray operator with the armed forces during World War I
1918	Publishes her discovery of protactinium
1919	Named a professor at the Kaiser Wilhelm Institute
1933	Participates in the Solvay Congress on nuclear physics
1934	Begins to study transuranic elements
1938	Forced by the Nazi Party's anti-Jewish laws to flee to Sweden
1939	Publishes a paper explaining fission
1946	Serves as a visiting professor at Catholic University, Washington, D.C.
1947	Shares the Planck Medal with Hahn
1959	Lectures at Bryn Mawr College in Pennsylvania
1960	Retires to Cambridge, England
1966	Shares the Fermi Medal with Hahn and Fritz Strassman
Oct. 27, 1968	Dies in Cambridge, England

Early Life

Lise Meitner (pronounced "MITE-nur") was born in Vienna, the third of eight children in a nonobservant Jewish family. Her father was a lawyer who encouraged her early interest in mathematics and physics. Despite the difficulties facing female scholars of her time, she earned a Ph.D. in experimental physics, with highest honors, at the University of Vienna in 1906.

Meitner's postdoctoral work in Vienna included research in the relatively new field of radioactivity. In 1907, she moved to Berlin, where she attended the lectures of Max Planck. She served for a time as his assistant, and he remained her friend and adviser. Meitner found congenial intellectual and social surroundings in a physics community that included Albert Einstein and Max von Laue.

Work with Hahn

In 1908, Meitner met Otto Hahn, who invited her to join him at the Kaiser Wilhelm Institute. For many years, their work focused on identifying the elements involved in radioactive decay series. Hahn's expertise in chemistry was complemented by Meitner's knowledge of mathematics and skill in building and operating equipment such as electroscopes. Her meticulous work gained international recognition through lectures, publications, and participation in prestigious conferences.

When Germany went to war in 1914, Hahn was called for active service. Meitner returned to Austria, where she served as an X-ray operator with the armed forces, treating wounded soldiers. She later returned to her laboratory in Berlin, where she was joined by Hahn whenever he was on leave.

In 1919, Hahn and Meitner published their discovery of the element they named protactinium, element 91 on the periodic table between uranium and thorium.

Scientific and Political Changes

By the 1930's, it was recognized that radioactivity could be artificially induced—for example, by bombardment of stable nuclei by alpha particles. Furthermore, the neutron particle had been isolated. These discoveries extended the realm of radioactivity and opened the field of nuclear physics. Both areas were investigated by Hahn and Meitner, who were joined by a skilled analytical chemist named Fritz Strassman.

More ominous were the political develop-

(Library of Congress)

ments that came with Adolf Hitler's rise to power. Meitner was protected by her Austrian citizenship from Hitler's anti-Jewish policies until 1938, when Austria was taken over by Germany. Her passport became invalid, and she was never issued a German passport. Although she had converted to Protestantism in 1908, she was required to fill out a form listing her ancestry. Her Jewish family history excluded her from continuing research at the Kaiser Wilhelm Institute.

Friends in the international physics community came to Meitner's aid, arranging a post for her at the Nobel Institute in Stockholm, Sweden. Her harrowing escape from Germany, made at night with only two small suitcases and involving illegal border crossings, was made possible by Dutch physicist Dirk Coster.

From Radioactivity to Nuclear Physics

The study of radioactivity contributed to the opening of a new field known as nuclear physics.

Radioactivity involves the spontaneous emission of particles and energy from elements located at the upper end of the periodic table. It was discovered accidentally in 1896 by Antoine-Henri Becquerel. Three different kinds of emission were recognized, designated by the Greek letters alpha, beta, and gamma. Investigation showed the alpha particles to be ionized helium atoms, the beta particles to be electrons, and the gamma radiation to be electromagnetic and similar to X rays.

Prior to the discovery of radioactivity, atoms were considered to be unchangeable, identical components unique to each of the elements that had been organized by Dmitry Mendeleyev into the periodic table, with each element having an atomic number ranging from 1 to 92 and an atomic weight from 1 to more that 230.

With the recognition that the alpha, beta, and gamma emissions came from individual atoms, the concept of elements had to be changed. An alpha particle has a weight (or mass) of 4 units and a positive electric charge of 2. Beta particles have a negligible mass and a negative charge of 1. Gamma particles (or rays) have no mass or charge and represent pure energy.

Careful studies showed that atoms of uranium, the heaviest natural element, emit a series of alpha and beta particles, eventually becoming lead. With the emission of each alpha or beta particle, the atom becomes a different element. The sequence is called a decay series. Its study requires chemists skilled in identifying elements to work out the details in collaboration with physicists skilled in particle identification. This was the kind of work done by Meitner and Otto Hahn.

Occasionally, a new kind of element is recognized that fills in an existing gap in the periodic table, as in the case of the discovery of protactinium by Hahn and Meitner.

The discovery of artificially induced radioactivity, using alpha particles as bullets against targets of lighter-weight elements, plus the discovery of neutrons, greatly enriched scientists' concept of atoms, already recognized as consisting of a nuclei surrounded by electrons, specific in number for each element. Nuclei were thought to be composed of protons (hydrogen ions) and neutrons with roughly the same mass. The atomic number for each element was equal to the number of protons, and the atomic weight was equal to the sum of the number of protons and neutrons. The chemical identity of the atom depends on the number of protons. Sometimes, however, the number of neutrons may vary, giving rise to isotopes.

In the case of uranium, all atoms have 92 protons in the nucleus, but some have 146 neutrons and others have only 143. These different nuclei are known as uranium 238 and uranium 235.

$$n + U\ 235 \rightarrow Ba\ 140 + Kr\ 93 + 3n$$

This equation represents the bombardment of uranium 235 by one neutron, resulting in the fission into barium and krypton, as recognized by Meitner. The release of three neutrons causes a chain reaction, providing more neutrons to split more uranium atoms. It is the net increase in neutrons that causes the chain reaction required for the atomic bomb.

Bibliography
Lise Meitner: A Life in Physics. Ruth Lewin Sime. Berkeley: University of California Press, 1996.

Meitner took Swedish citizenship in 1947 and remained there until her retirement in 1960.

Fission

In late 1938, Meitner's nephew, Otto Robert Frisch, a physicist working with Niels Bohr in Copenhagen, visited her. She had received news from Hahn and Strassman about the results of their neutron bombardment of uranium. They were at a loss to explain their detection of barium, a much lighter element.

Meitner recognized that the uranium atoms must have split into barium and gaseous krypton. Furthermore, energy would have been released in the process. This fission would make possible the atomic bomb that ended World War II in 1945, and Meitner's role in its discovery came to worldwide attention.

Visits and Honors

In 1946, Meitner was visiting professor at Catholic University in Washington, D.C. She met with President Harry S Truman, was named "Woman of the Year" by the Women's National Press Club, and was awarded honorary degrees by several universities.

In 1959, Meitner returned to the United States. At Bryn Mawr, a women's college in Pennsylvania, she gave lectures and inspired the young students, especially those majoring in scientific fields.

Her final visit, in 1964, was marred by a heart attack from which she never fully recovered.

When Hahn was awarded the 1946 Nobel Prize in Chemistry for his discovery of fission, no mention was made of Meitner's contribution. In 1947, however, the Planck Medal was given jointly to Hahn and Meitner. In 1966, the U.S. Atomic Energy Commission gave its Fermi Medal to Hahn, Meitner, and Strassman. By that time, Meitner's advanced age prevented her from accepting the medal in person, so American chemist Glenn Seaborg brought it to her in Cambridge, England.

Final Years

Meitner retired from her position in Sweden in 1960 and moved to Cambridge to be near the Frisch family. She died and was buried there in 1968 a few weeks before her ninetieth birthday. The inscription on her tombstone reads "Lise Meitner: A physicist who never lost her humanity."

Bibliography

By Meitner

"The Status of Women in the Professions," *Physics Today*, 1960

"Looking Back," *Bulletin of the Atomic Scientists*, 1964

About Meitner

"Discovery of Fission and How It Began." O. R. Frisch. *Physics Today* 20 (November, 1967).

Lise Meitner: A Life in Physics. Ruth Lewin Sime. Berkeley: University of California Press, 1996.

Lise Meitner: Atomic Pioneer. Deborah Crawford. New York: Crown, 1969

(Katherine R. Sopka)

Gregor Johann Mendel

Areas of Achievement: Biology and genetics

Contribution: Mendel's experiments demonstrated the manner in which physical traits are inherited from one generation to the next. From his observations were derived two laws that provided the foundation of modern genetics.

July 22, 1822   Born in Heinzendorf, Austria (now Hyncice, Czech Republic)

1840   Begins studies in philosophy at the Olmütz Institute

1843   Enters the Altbrünn Monastery

1845   Begins theological studies at Brünn Theological College

1847   Ordained as a priest

1849   Receives a temporary appointment as a teacher of mathematics and Greek at Znaim High School, but fails the natural science section of the certification examination the next year

1851-1853   Studies physics, chemistry, mathematics, and biology at the University of Vienna

1854   Returns to teaching science in Brünn

1856-1871   Conducts research on inheritance in plants

1867   Sends seed packets to botanist Karl von Nägeli for reproducing his pea experiments

1868   Assumes the position of monastery abbot and gradually ceases his botanical research

Jan. 6, 1884   Dies in Brünn, Moravia, Austria-Hungary (now Brno, Czech Republic)

Early Life

Johann Mendel was born in Heinzendorf, Austria, on July 22, 1822. Since his father was a peasant farmer with horticultural interests, Mendel spent much of his early life tending plants in the garden and helping in the orchard. After demonstrating academic promise in his elementary education, he was sent away to secondary school, where he completed the curriculum despite illness from poverty-induced nutritional deficiencies.

Although Mendel was a top student, his education would have ended at this point if a falling tree had not disabled his father. Unable to continue farming, his father sold the farm, giving the children substantial portions of the profit, and Mendel's sister donated her share to help finance his philosophy studies at the Olmütz Institute.

In 1843, Mendel entered the Augustinian monastery at Brünn, Moravia (later renamed Brno, Czech Republic) and assumed his mo-

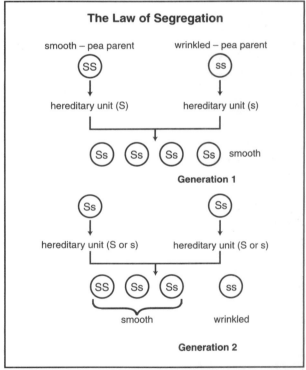

Mendel's law of segregation is demonstrated by an initial cross between true-breeding plants with smooth peas and plants with wrinkled peas. The smooth trait is dominant and the wrinkled trait is recessive. The second generation consists of smooth-pea plants and wrinkled-pea plants produced in a ratio of 3:1.

nastic name of Gregor. He obtained a tempo-rary teaching position at a local secondary school in 1849. Although the qualifying examination for a permanent position was ordinarily taken after several years of university study, Mendel, without the benefit of a university education, attempted to acquire certification to become a regular teacher the following year.

After Mendel failed the examination in the area of natural science, his abbot sent him to the University of Vienna, where he studied science and mathematics until 1853. Upon completion of his studies, Mendel began teaching science at a high school in Brünn, a profession that he continued until his election as abbot of the monastery in 1868. It is interesting to note that Mendel never gained an official teaching certification.

The Laws of Heredity

Mendel mated purebred pea plants having easily observable physical traits such as flower color, shape of pea, or height of plant in order to observe the physical characteristics of the offspring.

After Mendel self-pollinated a plant to see the offspring's physical traits, and he then selected a plant with a particular trait such as shape of pea and artificially mated it with a plant having a different pea shape. He observed that self-pollinated plants with wrinkled peas always bred true (produced offspring with wrinkled peas), while self-pollinated smooth pea plants sometimes bred true and sometimes produced a mixture of smooth-pea offspring and wrinkled-pea offspring.

Crossbreeding a true-breeding smooth-pea plant with a wrinkled-pea plant produced offspring plants that were identical with regard to pea shape, all smooth. This observation led Mendel to propose the law of uniformity, which states that the mating of two different types of plants produces offspring in the next generation that are all alike.

In order to determine what had happened to the hereditary factor controlling the wrinkled-pea trait, Mendel allowed members of this first generation to breed with one another, producing a second generation that consisted of a mixture of smooth-pea offspring and wrinkled-pea offspring. Statistically, there were three plants with smooth peas to every plant with wrinkled peas. The trait of wrinkled peas had not been lost in the first generation, only hidden. This observation led Mendel to propose his law of segregation, which states that the mating of the uniform offspring will not again produce uniformity, but rather will produce offspring segregated into different forms according to a specific mathematical ratio.

Mendel deduced that every pea plant possesses two heredity units (now known as genes) for pea shape. When bred, each parent plant contributes one of these hereditary units for pea shape to the offspring. He determined that the hereditary unit responsible for the smooth pea (symbolized as S) exerted dominance over the unit responsible for the wrinkled pea (symbolized as s). A pea plant possessing two recessive hereditary units (ss) would have wrinkled peas, while a plant with either two dominant units (SS) or one of each type (Ss) would have smooth peas.

Mendel demonstrated that each parent plant contributes a factor (gene) determining a given trait and that the pairs of factors are not averaged in the offspring. He also demonstrated that a gene-determined trait could disappear in one generation because it was not being expressed and reappear in a later generation.

Mendel's well-designed experiments were the first to focus on the statistical relationships of physical traits produced in the breeding of hybrid plants. Although the significance of his work was not recognized during his lifetime, these experiments provided the foundation on which the modern science of genetics is based.

Bibliography

Gregor Mendel's Experiments on Plant Hybrids. Alain F. Corcos and Floyd V. Monaghan. New Brunswick, N.J.: Rutgers University Press, 1993.

Mendel's Principles of Heredity. William Bateson. Cambridge, England: Cambridge University Press, 1913.

The Origin of Genetics: A Mendel Source Book. Curt Stern and Eva Sherwood. New York: W. H. Freeman 1966.

Origins of Mendelism. Robert C. Olby. Chicago: University of Chicago Press, 1985.

Mendel and His Peas

Because Mendel had always been curious about the origin of the colors and shapes occurring in the plant world, he acquired a small plot of land in the monastery garden, which he developed into a scientific laboratory to study these characteristics. He chose peas for his study because they were easy to cultivate, readily fertilized one another, and grew rapidly. He grew twenty-two varieties that displayed differences in shape, size, and color. Over a seven-year period, he bred his peas and observed the characteristics of the offspring produced.

In his experiments, Mendel noticed that when two different types of peas were mated, the members of the next generation would all be alike. He called this phenomenon the law of uniformity. When one of the uniform offspring was mated to another uniform offspring, the peas produced in the next generation, however, were not uniform. They were split into groups possessing different characteristics according to a definite numerical ratio. This phenomenon he termed the law of segregation.

(National Library of Medicine)

His experiments showed that an averaging of parental characteristics does not occur in the offspring; instead, these characteristics retain their identity. He found that some physical traits are dominant (more likely to be seen in the offspring) and other traits are recessive (less likely to be seen).

Mendel concluded that each parent possesses two factors for a particular trait and that one of these factors is passed on to its offspring. When two different factors are inherited, one from each parent, the dominant factor is the observable one. While the recessive characteristic is not observable, it is still present to be passed on to the next generation. When an offspring obtains a recessive factor from each parent, the recessive physical characteristic again becomes observable.

Mendel Reveals His Work

Mendel described his experiments at the February, 1865, meeting of the Brünn Society for the Study of Natural Science and presented his conclusions the following month. This work was formally published in 1866 in the society's proceedings as "Versuche über Pflanzenhybriden" (*Experiments in Plant-Hybridisation*, 1910). Mendel's publication had no immediate impact on biological thought, even though it reached the major libraries of Europe and America.

Beginning in 1866, Mendel tried to establish a collaboration with noted botanist Karl von Nägeli. In 1867, he sent Nägeli 140 packets of seeds for reproducing his experiments with peas, but the work was never attempted.

Later Life

With his elevation to abbot in 1868, Mendel's life became occupied with administrative duties, leaving little time to pursue scientific interests. In 1874, the Austrian government passed a bill imposing taxation on church properties, and Mendel spent the remaining years of his life fighting this taxation. Although many mourned the death of a beloved, obstinate old priest in January, 1884, no one recognized the passing of a great biologist.

In 1900, three European biologists—Carl Erich Correns, Erich Tschermak von Seysenegg, and Hugo de Vries—independently obtained experimental results similar to those published by Mendel thirty-four years earlier. The acknowledgement of his discovery of the basic laws governing heredity came sixteen years after his death.

Bibliography
By Mendel
"Versuche über Pflanzenhybriden," *Verhandlungen des naturforschenden vereins*, 1866 (*Experiments in Plant-Hybridisation*, 1910)

About Mendel
Life of Mendel. Hugo Iltis. New York: Hafner, 1966.
Living Biographies of Great Scientists. Henry Thomas and Dana Lee Thomas. Garden City, N.Y.: Garden City Books, 1959.
Mendel. Vitezslav Orel. London: Oxford University Press, 1984.

(*Arlene R. Courtney*)

Dmitry Ivanovich Mendeleyev

Area of Achievement: Chemistry
Contribution: Mendeleyev recognized the regular variation in the chemical and physical properties of the elements. This periodic law aided in the discovery of new elements and in the prediction of their properties.

Feb. 8, 1834	Born in Tobolsk, Siberia, Russia
1849	Travels to the University of Moscow but is denied admittance
1850	Begins training as a schoolteacher at the Institute of Pedagogy, St. Petersburg
1855	Receives a teaching diploma
1859	Travels on a government grant throughout Europe
1863	Appointed a professor of chemistry at the Technological Institute of St. Petersburg
1866	Appointed a professor of chemistry at the University of St. Petersburg
1868-1871	Publishes the chemistry textbook *Osnovy khimii* (*The Principles of Chemistry*, 1890)
1871	Predicts that the vacant spaces in his periodic table will be filled by yet-to-be-discovered elements
1876	Visits the United States
1890	Resigns his university position in protest
1893	Becomes the director of the Bureau of Weights and Measures
Feb. 2, 1907	Dies in St. Petersburg, Russia

Early Life

Dmitry Ivanovich Mendeleyev (pronounced "mehn-deh-LAY-ehf") was born in Siberia in 1834. Shortly after his birth, his father went blind and had to resign as director of the local high school. Consequently, his mother was forced to seek work in a glass factory to support the family, which included fourteen children.

In 1849, his father died and the glass factory was destroyed by fire. Mendeleyev and his mother hitchhiked to Moscow, so that fifteen-year-old Dmitry could finish his education at the university there. Being Siberian, however, he was not permitted entrance, and again mother and son traveled across country to St. Petersburg.

At the St. Petersburg Institute of Pedagogy, while training to be a teacher, Mendeleyev was instructed by Alexander Woskressensky. Woskressensky's work on inorganic chemistry fascinated Mendeleyev, who was struck by the similarities in the chemical and physical properties of various groups of elements. Mendeleyev's interest in classification was also aroused by classes in zoology, genetics, and mineralogy.

A Career in Academia

After spending a few years as a science teacher at Odessa in the Crimea, Mendeleyev returned to the University of St. Petersburg to obtain a higher degree in chemistry. In 1859, a government grant enabled him to travel through Europe and participate in chemical conferences. As a result, his thoughts once more turned to chemical classification. He recognized the need for classifying the chemical and physical properties of the elements.

After receiving his doctorate, Mendeleyev was appointed a professor of chemistry at the Technological Institute of St. Petersburg in 1863. Three years later, he took a similar position at the University of St. Petersburg. Mendeleyev was required to teach classes in inorganic chemistry, and he soon realized that no suitable textbook existed for this area. Therefore, he began to write his own, a comprehen-

The Periodic Table of the Elements

IA	IIA	IIIB	IVB	VB	VIB	VIIB	VIII			IB	IIB	IIIA	IVA	VA	VIA	VIIA	0
1 H																	2 He
3 Li	4 Be											5 B	6 C	7 N	8 O	9 F	10 Ne
11 Na	12 Mg				←		Transition elements		→			13 A1	14 Si	15 P	16 S	17 C1	18 Ar
19 K	20 Ca	21 Sc	22 Ti	23 V	24 Cr	25 Mn	26 Fe	27 Co	28 Ni	29 Cu	30 Zn	31 Ga	32 Ge	33 As	34 Se	35 Br	36 Kr
37 Rb	38 Sr	39 Y	40 Zr	41 Nb	42 Mo	43 Tc	44 Ru	45 Rh	46 Pd	47 Ag	48 Cd	49 In	50 Sn	51 Sb	52 Te	53 I	54 Xe
55 Cs	56 Ba	57* La	72 Hf	73 Ta	74 W	75 Re	76 Os	77 Ir	78 Pt	79 Au	80 Hg	81 Ti	82 Pb	83 Bi	84 Po	85 At	86 Rn
87 Fr	88 Ra	89† Ac															

*Lanthanoids			57 La	58 Ce	59 Pr	60 Nd	61 Pm	62 Sm	63 Eu	64 Gd	65 Tb	66 Dy	67 Ho	68 Er	69 Tm	70 Yb	71 Lu
†Actinoids			89 Ac	90 Th	91 Pa	92 U	93 Np	94 Pu	95 Am	96 Cm	97 Bk	98 Cf	99 Es	100 Fm	101 Md	102 No	103 Lr

The Periodic Law

Mendeleyev noticed that, when the chemical elements were arranged in order of increasing atomic weights, their properties were repeated in a predictable manner, forming a table of vertical columns (groups) and horizontal rows (periods).

Mendeleyev's early versions of the periodic table were not without their problems, and the table was modified over the years as new research into the fundamental nature of matter was uncovered. When Mendeleyev first formulated his periodic table, the existence of protons, electrons, and neutrons was not known. Consequently, the periodicity of the elements was based on atomic weight, which was a measurable and variable quantity for each element.

One major problem with Mendeleyev's periodic table was that some elements fell into groups in which they obviously did not belong. For example, if arranged in order of increasing atomic weight, iodine did not fall into the same group as bromine and chlorine, elements with which it shared many common properties. Periodicity was eventually found to depend on atomic number, rather than atomic weight as Mendeleyev had thought, and the revised periodic law states that the properties of the elements are a periodic function of their atomic numbers. Switching iodine and tellurium places both elements in their correct groups.

Early in the twentieth century, it was shown that the atomic weight of an element is roughly equal to the sum of protons and neutrons in one of its atoms. The atomic number was shown to be equal to the number of protons. For the lighter elements (the first two dozen or so), the ratio of protons to neutrons is about 1:1. For these elements, either the atomic weight or atomic number can be used to demonstrate the periodicity of the elements. Mendeleyev's periodic table worked quite well for these lighter elements but not as well for the heavier elements, which have more neutrons in proportion to their protons.

Elements in the same group have the same number of electrons in their outer (valence) shells. The number of valence electrons is also related to the group number. Lithium, sodium, and potassium, which all have one valence electron, are found in group 1 and have similar properties. For this reason, they generally show similar chemical and physical properties to one another but quite different properties to many other groups of elements.

Mendeleyev knew nothing about electrons when he first predicted that new elements would be discovered one day to fill the spaces in his periodic table. He recognized, however, that each new element would be found to have similar properties to the other elements in the same group.

Bibliography

Chemical Periodicity. R. T. Sanderson. New York: Reinhold, 1960.
The Periodic System of the Chemical Elements. J. van Sprosen. Amsterdam: Elsevier, 1969.
The Periodic Table of the Elements. R. J. Puddephatt and P. K. Monaghan. Oxford, England: Oxford University Press, 1986.

sive text that eventually was published as *Osnovy khimii* between 1868 and 1871. The book was translated into English as *The Principles of Chemistry* in 1890, as well as into French and German, and it brought Mendeleyev recognition throughout Europe.

Because of his liberal views and sympathies with student grievances, Mendeleyev often found himself battling university administrators and government bureaucracy. Perhaps as a result, he was never elected to the Imperial Academy of Sciences. In 1890, he resigned his university position in protest after another such battle. Three years later, he became the director of the Bureau of Weights and Measures.

The Periodic Law

Mendeleyev's attempt to organize his chemistry textbook in a logical manner led him to the discovery of the periodic law. Unlike the recent successes at classifying carbon compounds, no systematic classification of the other elements and their compounds was then available.

(Library of Congress)

Using a series of cards, Mendeleyev wrote down the properties and atomic weights of the elements (about seventy were known at the time). By arranging and rearranging the cards, he recognized a repeating or periodic relationship between the properties of the elements and their atomic weights: When arranged in order of increasing atomic weights, the properties of the elements were repeated every so often.

While others had noticed the periodicity of the elements with little interest, it was Mendeleyev who recognized the fundamental significance of this arrangement. Elements with similar properties fell into vertical columns (groups) and horizontal rows (periods), which formed a table. Elements within the groups have similar valences (degrees of combining power, according to atomic weights).

Mendeleyev left spaces in his periodic table, and, in 1871, he predicted that they would be filled by elements unknown at that time. He also predicted the properties of these undiscovered elements. Between 1875 and 1886, the elements gallium, scandium, and germanium were discovered, and each fit into its position as predicted by Mendeleyev. As a result, the concept of the periodic law gained universal acceptance.

Mendeleyev died in St. Petersburg in 1907 just before his seventy-third birthday.

Bibliography

By Mendeleyev

"Die periodische Gesetzmässigkeit der chemischen Elemente," *Justus Liebigs Annalen der Chemie, Supplementband VIII*, 1871

"Remarques à propos de la découverte du gallium," *Comptes Rendus*, 1875

"The Periodic Law of the Chemical Elements," *Journal of the Chemical Society*, 1889

Osnovy khimii, 1868-1871 (*The Principles of Chemistry*, 1890)

An Attempt Towards a Chemical Conception of the Ether, 1904

About Mendeleyev

Great Chemists. E. Farber, ed. New York: Interscience, 1961.

"Mendeleev's Periodic System of Chemical Elements." Bernadette Bensaude-Vincent. *British Journal for the History of Science* 19 (1986).

"The Process of Discovery: Mendeleev and the Periodic Law." Don C. Brown. *Annals of Science* 31 (1974).

(Nicholas C. Thomas)

Dorothy Reed Mendenhall

Areas of Achievement: Cell biology and medicine

Contribution: Mendenhall described the abnormal cell that is characteristic of Hodgkin's disease. She also worked to improve health care during pregnancy, childbirth, infancy, and childhood.

Sept. 22, 1874	Born in Columbus, Ohio
1891-1895	Attends Smith College, earning a bachelor's degree
1895-1896	Attends the Massachusetts Institute of Technology (MIT)
1896-1900	Attends the medical school at The Johns Hopkins University, earning an M.D.
1900-1901	Serves an internship at Johns Hopkins
1901-1902	Receives a fellowship in pathology at The Johns Hopkins Hospital
1902	Describes the Reed cell
1902-1903	Serves a residency at the New York Infirmary for Women and Children
1903-1906	Works as a resident physician at Babies Hospital
1906	Marries Charles Elwood Mendenhall
1914-1936	Employed as a field lecturer by the home economics department of the University of Wisconsin
1917-1936	Employed as a medical officer by the U.S. Children's Bureau
July 31, 1964	Dies in Chester, Connecticut

Early Life

Dorothy Reed Mendenhall was born Dorothy Reed in Columbus, Ohio, on September 22, 1874. Her mother was Grace Kimball Reed, and her father was William Pratt Reed, a successful shoe manufacturer. Her father died in 1880, leaving Dorothy in the care of her mother and her maternal grandmother. The family spent summers at the Kimball family home in Talcottville, New York, and made trips to Europe between 1887 and 1900.

After being educated at home by her grandmother, Reed entered Smith College in Northampton, Massachusetts, in 1891. She was graduated with a bachelor's degree in 1895. Although she had first considered a career in journalism, a biology course at Smith inspired her to study medicine. In 1895 and 1896, Reed completed required courses in chemistry and physics at the Massachusetts Institute of Technology (MIT) in Cambridge, Massachusetts. She entered the medical school of The Johns Hopkins University in Baltimore, Maryland, in 1896. She received an M.D. from Johns Hopkins in 1900.

Mendenhall with her husband and dog. (Sophia Smith Collection)

The Reed Cell

Reed served an internship at The Johns Hopkins Hospital from 1900 to 1901 and received a fellowship in pathology at the same hospital from 1901 to 1902. During this fellowship, she conducted research in the pathology of Hodgkin's disease. In 1902, she identified an abnormal cell present in the lymph nodes of patients with this disease. Her description of this cell, later known as the Reed cell, demonstrated that Hodgkin's disease was not a form of tuberculosis, as previously believed. She also described the various stages of Hodgkin's disease.

The discovery of the Reed cell was greeted

Hodgkin's Disease

Hodgkin's disease, once thought to be a form of tuberculosis, is now known to be a cancer of the lymphatic system.

Hodgkin's disease was first described in 1832 by the British physician Thomas Hodgkin. The most common symptom of the disease is swelling of the lymph nodes under the arm, in the neck, or in the groin. Other symptoms include fever, chills, night sweats, fatigue, loss of appetite, weight loss, and itchy skin.

Until the early twentieth century, Hodgkin's disease was often thought to be a form of the infectious disease tuberculosis. In 1902, Dorothy Reed Mendenhall demonstrated that the abnormal cell found in Hodgkin's disease, now known as the Reed cell, is not caused by tuberculosis. Later, it was determined that Hodgkin's disease is actually a malignant lymphoma (a cancer of the lymphatic system). The lymphatic system, which aids the body in fighting infection, includes the lymph nodes and the spleen.

The Reed cell is believed to cause the symptoms of the disease. It is an abnormally large connective tissue cell containing one or two large nuclei. Although it can be found in other diseases, such as mononucleosis, it is most closely associated with Hodgkin's disease.

Hodgkin's disease accounts for about 1 percent of all cancers in the United States and causes about 1,500 deaths per year. It is most commonly seen between the ages of fifteen and thirty-five or in persons over the age of fifty-five. It is somewhat more common in men than in women.

The exact cause of Hodgkin's disease is unknown. There appears to be a genetic factor involved; siblings of persons with the disease have a higher incidence rate than the general population. Other factors that increase the risk of Hodgkin's disease include exposure to radiation and contact with certain chemicals.

Hodgkin's disease exists in four forms, based on the type of cells involved. In the lymphocyte-predominant form, an abnormally high number of lymph cells are found in the lymph node. In the nodular sclerosis form, an abnormally high number of connective tissue cells divide the lymph node into "islands" of lymph tissue. In the mixed cellularity form, the number of lymph cells is variable and white blood cells are found in the lymph node. In the lymphocyte-depleted form, an abnormally low number of lymph cells are found in the lymph node.

Mendenhall was the first to describe the four progressive stages of Hodgkin's disease in detail. In stage 1, only one lymph node is involved. In stage 2, more than one lymph node is involved, but only on one side of the diaphragm (the thin muscle under the lungs that aids in breathing). In stage 3, lymph nodes on both sides of the diaphragm are involved. In stage 4, organs other than the lymphatic system are involved.

Stage 1 and stage 2 Hodgkin's disease are usually treated with radiation. Stage 3 and stage 4 usually require chemotherapy (treatment with drugs that attack cancer cells). If properly treated during its early stages, Hodgkin's disease has a cure rate of about 90 percent.

Bibliography

Hodgkin's Disease. Henry S. Kaplan. Cambridge, Mass.: Harvard University Press, 1980.

Malignant Lymphoma: Biology, Natural History, and Treatment. Alan C. Aisenberg. Philadelphia: Lea & Febiger, 1991.

Malignant Lymphomas, Including Hodgkin's Disease: Diagnosis, Management, and Special Problems. Bruce W. Dana. Boston: Academic Publishers of America, 1993.

with international acclaim. Despite this reception, Reed believed that a woman had little chance of advancing her career at Johns Hopkins. In June, 1902, she began serving a residency at the New York Infirmary for Women and Children. In January, 1903, she became the first resident physician at the newly opened Babies Hospital in New York.

Marriage and the Loss of a Child

Reed left her medical career to marry Charles Elwood Mendenhall on February 14, 1906. She followed her husband to Madison, Wisconsin, where he was a professor of physics at the University of Wisconsin. Dorothy Reed Mendenhall remained at home to rear her children until 1914.

Mendenhall's first child died a few hours after birth in 1907. During this difficult childbirth, she herself was injured and was infected with fever. This tragedy later inspired her to strive to make childbirth less dangerous for both mother and child. Mendenhall's second child, born in 1908, died in 1910 after suffering a fall. Her two other children, born in 1910 and 1912, went on to successful careers in education and medicine.

A Second Career

Mendenhall returned to the profession of health care in 1914, when she accepted a position as a field lecturer in the department of home economics at Wisconsin. She studied infant mortality while lecturing on maternal and infant health care throughout the state. She opened the first infant welfare clinic in Wisconsin in 1915. As a result of her efforts, Madison was declared to have the lowest infant mortality rate of any city in the United States in 1937.

Meanwhile, Mendenhall was also employed as a medical officer in the U.S. Children's Bureau. Beginning in 1917, she served the bureau by studying child nutrition. She helped develop standards for normal heights and weights in children from birth to age six in order to aid in the assessment of their development. She also represented the United States at the International Child Welfare Conference in 1919.

Mendenhall was involved in the development of several publications for the Children's Bureau. One of the most influential of these dealt with the nutritional importance of milk. Others dealt with child health care in general.

In 1926, Mendenhall compared infant and maternal mortality rates in Denmark and the United States. The results of her study, published in 1929, indicated that American mortality rates were higher because of unnecessary interference with the natural childbirth process. Her report advocated educating midwives to assist in childbirth using Danish methods.

Final Years

After her husband died in 1935, Mendenhall began to withdraw from her career. She left her

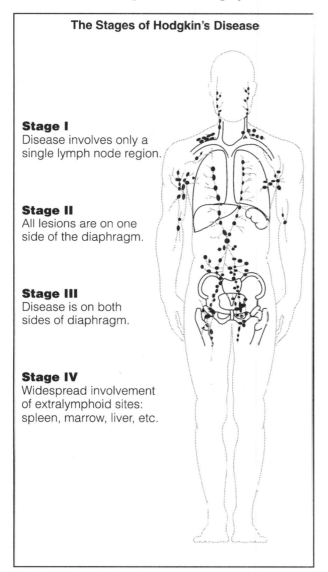

The Stages of Hodgkin's Disease

Stage I
Disease involves only a single lymph node region.

Stage II
All lesions are on one side of the diaphragm.

Stage III
Disease is on both sides of diaphragm.

Stage IV
Widespread involvement of extralymphoid sites: spleen, marrow, liver, etc.

(Hans & Cassady, Inc.)

positions with the University of Wisconsin and the Children's Bureau in 1936. After traveling in Mexico and Central America, she settled in Tryon, North Carolina. She spent the last years of her life in Chester, Connecticut, where she died of heart disease on July 31, 1964.

Bibliography
By Mendenhall

"A Case of Acute Lymphatic Leukaemia Without Enlargement of the Lymph Glands," *American Journal of Medical Science*, 1902

"On the Pathological Changes in Hodgkin's Disease with Especial Reference to Its Relation to Tuberculosis," *Johns Hopkins Hospital Reports*, 1902

"Prenatal and Natal Conditions in Wisconsin," *Wisconsin Medical Journal*, 1917

Milk: The Indispensable Food for Children, 1918

"The Work of the Children's Bureau," *Smith College Quarterly*, 1919

Child Care and Child Welfare: Outlines for Study, 1921 (with others)

"Preventative Feeding for Mothers and Infants," *Journal of Home Economics*, 1924

What Builds Babies?: The Mother's Diet in the Pregnant and Nursing Periods, 1925

Midwifery in Denmark, 1929

About Mendenhall

American Women in Science. Martha J. Bailey. Santa Barbara, Calif.: ABC-CLIO, 1994.

Notable American Women: The Modern Period. Barbara Sicherman and Carol Hurd Green, eds. Cambridge, Mass.: Harvard University Press, 1980.

Women of Science: Righting the Record. G. Kass-Simon and Patricia Farnes. Bloomington: Indiana University Press, 1990.

(Rose Secrest)

Maria Sibylla Merian

Area of Achievement: Zoology

Contribution: Merian was the first scientist to observe the metamorphosis of tropical insects by raising their caterpillars and to make drawings and engravings of them for book illustrations, showing both the insects and the plants on which they feed.

Apr. 2, 1647	Born in Frankfurt am Main, Hessen (now in Germany)
1660	Begins to study silkworm development
1665	Marries painter Johann Andreas Graff
1679	Publishes the first part of her caterpillar book
1681	Moves from Nuremberg to Frankfurt when her stepfather dies
1683	Publishes the second part of her caterpillar book
1685	Enters a Lutheran religious commune in Friesland
1686	Becomes the first European scientist to describe the development of tadpoles into frogs
1691	Moves to Amsterdam, the Netherlands
1699	Travels to Surinam to observe and draw tropical insects
1701	Returns to the Netherlands with collected insects
1705	Publishes a book on the insects of Surinam
1715	Suffers a stroke
Jan. 13, 1717	Dies in Amsterdam, the Netherlands

Early Life

Anna Maria Sibylla Merian (pronounced "MAY-ree-ahn") was born in Frankfurt am Main as the daughter of Germany's most celebrated artist and engraver, Matthäus Merian the Elder, and his second wife, Johanna Catharina Heim.

After her father's death in 1650, her mother married Jacob Marrell, a Dutch flower painter who taught Maria drawing. Marrell's pupil, Abraham Mignon, taught Maria painting and engraving before she was ten. By the time that she was thirteen, she began raising silkworms on mulberry leaves and lettuce in order to observe their metamorphoses. Thus, she had excellent preparation for her future life's work.

(National Archives)

A Young Wife, Artist, and Scientist

At the age of eighteen, Merian married the painter Johann Andreas Graff. After five years in Frankfurt, they moved to Nuremberg, where Merian painted and taught flower painting and embroidery to girls. Her first book, *Florum fasciculus* or *Neues Blumen-buch* (new book of flowers), published in three parts in 1675, 1677, and 1680, contained samples for students to copy for paintings or embroidery.

Merian, who was also rearing two daughters, began work on the first of two books on caterpillars found in the areas of Frankfurt and Nuremberg, *Der Raupen wunderbare Verwandelung und sonderbare Blumen-Nahrung*, published in two volumes in Nuremberg in 1679 and 1683. She painted the stages of metamorphosis of each insect with its host plant on parchment, then engraved the composition on a copper plate. She colored many of the prints herself.

When her stepfather died, Merian and her family moved back to Frankfurt, but, in 1685, her husband returned to Nuremberg and Merian entered a Labadist (a pietist Protestant sect) commune in Friesland with her mother, brother, and daughters. While there, she expanded her interest in development to frogs and became the first European to describe their metamorphosis.

The Insects of Tropical America

In 1690, Merian's mother died, and the next year Merian and her daughters moved to Amsterdam, where all three painted plants and animals in private collections, including the beautiful butterflies and caterpillars brought back from Surinam, a Dutch colony in South America, by Labadist missionaries.

She began to collect, raise, and draw these tropical caterpillars and their butterflies.

At the age of fifty-two, after drawing up her will in preparation for the hazardous voyage, Merian traveled to Surinam with her younger daughter to collect, observe, and draw more tropical insects, aided by a stipend from the Dutch government. They stayed nearly two years, returning home because Merian became ill. Her book *Metamorphosis insectorum surina-*

Studies of Tropical Insects

The Stages of Metamorphosis in the Butterfly

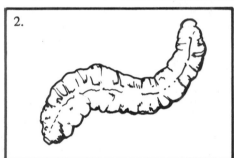

1. Eggs laid by an adult butterfly
2. Butterfly larva
3. A pupa encased in a cocoon
4. An adult butterfly

Merian's most important publication contains sixty engravings with ninety studies of the caterpillars, worms, spiders, ants, lizards, toads, and frogs of Surinam.

Each illustration in *Metamorphosis insectorum surinamensium* (1705) of a caterpillar also portrays its entire metamorphosis: egg, pupa, and adult, winged insect, usually a moth or butterfly. Before Merian, no one had recorded the life histories of tropical insects or painted them from life.

Her drawings revealed to European naturalists for the first time the astonishing diversity of tropical insects and plants. As most of the insects were unknown in Europe—John Ray's *Historia insectorum* was not published until 1710, after his death—and Merian was not a systematist (one who classifies animals or plants), she did not name them but instead placed the insects under the names of their host plants. Even a number of the plants were unknown to scientists in Europe. She did provide full descriptions in her text, including of their colors, in addition to many hand-colored plates.

Merian's original drawings are collected in the Academy of Sciences in St. Petersburg and in the Royal Library at Windsor Castle.

Bibliography

Maria Sibylla Merian in Surinam: Commentary to the Facsimile Edition of "Metamorphosis insectorum surinamensium" (Amsterdam 1705) Based on Original Watercolors in the Royal Library Windsor Castle. E. Rücker and W. T. Stearn. London: Pion, 1982.

"Maria Sibylla Merian, 1647-1717, Entomological and Botanical Artist." W. T. Stearn. Introduction to *The Wondrous Transformation of Caterpillars: Fifty Engravings Selected from "Erucarum ortus"* (1718), by Merian. London: Scolar Press, 1978.

mensium, published in Amsterdam in 1705, has been called one of the most beautiful ever published in the field of natural history.

Scientific Recognition

Merian was criticized as unladylike for traveling to Surinam and searching for insects in the tropics. She was even criticized for the beauty of her plates; although her portrayals of insects and plants were realistic, each was an artistic composition, differing greatly from earlier natural history publications. The famous natural historian Carolus Linnaeus, however, studied her drawings and descriptions carefully and named many of them for the tenth edition of *Systema natura* in 1768. He cited her illustrations for at least a hundred species of insects.

Merian's work has received more attention since the publication of some of her drawings from those collected at Windsor Castle. Her portrait was reproduced on a Dutch banknote in 1991, and a stamp with one of her illustrations was issued in the Netherlands. She died in Amsterdam in 1717.

Bibliography

By Merian

Florum fasciculus, 1675-1680 (3 vols.; also as *Neues Blumen-buch*, 1680; new book of flowers)

Der Raupen wunderbare Verwandelung und sonderbare Blumen-Nahrung, 1679-1683 (2 vols.; the wondrous transformation of caterpillars and their remarkable diet of flowers)

Metamorphosis insectorum surinamensium, 1705

About Merian

Women in Science: Antiquity Through the Nineteenth Century. Marilyn Bailey Ogilvie. Cambridge, Mass.: MIT Press, 1986.

Women on the Margin: Three Seventeenth Century Lives. Natalie Zemon Davies. Cambridge, Mass.: Harvard University Press, 1995.

(Janet Bell Garber)

Albert Abraham Michelson

Areas of Achievement: Astronomy and physics

Contribution: Michelson invented the interferometer, performed a classic experiment trying to measure the earth's motion through the "ether," devised an exact means of determining the speed of light, and measured the diameter of stars.

Dec. 19, 1852	Born in Strelno, Prussia (now Strzelno, Poland)
1869-1873	Attends the U.S. Naval Academy at Annapolis, Maryland
1875	Appointed an instructor of physics at the U.S. Naval Academy
1880-1882	Studies in Berlin and Paris
1882	Appointed an instructor of physics at the Case School of Applied Science in Cleveland, Ohio
1885	Becomes a Fellow of American Academy of Arts and Sciences
1887	With Edward W. Morley, performs ether-drift experiment
1889	Named chair of physics at Clark University in Massachusetts
1894	Appointed chair of physics at the University of Chicago
1899	Elected president of the American Physical Society
1907	Awarded the Nobel Prize in Physics and the Copley Medal of Royal Society of London
1922	Measures the diameter of Betelgeuse with an interferometer
1925-1927	Conducts velocity of light experiments
May 9, 1931	Dies in Pasadena, California

A 20-inch Michelson interferometer on the Hooker telescope. (California Institute of Technology)

Early Life

Albert Abraham Michelson was born in the Prussian town of Strelno (now Strzelno, Poland) in 1852. Within a few years, his parents emigrated to the United States, settling first in California and then in Nevada. They sent him to San Francisco to attend high school, where he lived with the principal and earned three dollars a month keeping the instruments in the science laboratory in order.

Because his family could not afford tuition at a private college or university, Michelson applied for appointment to the U.S. Naval Academy in Annapolis. Because Nevada was allowed a single appointment and it went to the son of a Civil War veteran, so Michelson applied directly to President Ulysses S. Grant, who eventually gave him the appointment. He

was graduated from Annapolis in the spring of 1873 and spent the next two years on naval duty.

A Scientific Career

The Navy recognized Michelson's scientific talent by appointing him an instructor of physics at the academy in September, 1877. That same autumn, as he prepared a lecture on the topic, Michelson became interested in previous methods used to measure the velocity of light. With characteristic experimental insight, he modified the techniques used by earlier European scientists and reported the results of his measurements to the *American Journal of Science* in the spring of 1878. His continuing work on measuring the velocity of light brought him, at the age of only twenty-six, a growing reputation in the United States and abroad as a talented and brilliant physicist.

Sensing the need to enhance his knowledge of physics, especially optics, Michelson took leave of the naval academy for study in Europe from 1880 to 1882. In Berlin and Paris, he studied with such renowned scientists as Hermann von Helmholtz and first devised his famous interferometer, which he used throughout his life to perform precise measurements of a variety of items. With financial backing from inventor Alexander Graham Bell, he tried to measure the relative velocity of Earth and the surrounding "ether" (a light-carrying medium believed to fill space) with his newly created instrument. In 1881, he reported in the *American Journal of Science* that he had not found the so-called ether drift.

Studies of Light

While in Europe, Michelson realized that his strong interest in experimental physics, especially his studies of various aspects of light, needed a supportive research environment, which he did not find at Annapolis. He gladly accepted a position as an instructor in physics at the newly formed Case School of Applied Science in Cleveland, Ohio.

While there, Michelson teamed with Edward W. Morley, a professor of chemistry at

---

The Michelson-Morley Experiment

Between 1886 and 1887, Michelson, joined by Edward W. Morley, improved his experimental efforts to measure the ether's effect on the movement of light. Using his ingenious interferometer, they found no evidence of this effect.

Michelson used his interferometer to measure various aspects of light precisely. In the historically famous experiment of 1887, Michelson and Morley used this apparatus, which split a beam of light in two at *b* so that it could travel in perpendicular paths *d* to *e* and *d'* to *e'*, be reflected by mirrors at each corner of the apparatus (*d, e, d'*, and *e'*), and return to central observation point *f* after the two beams were combined at *b* (see figure). They mounted the apparatus on a stone floating in mercury, rotating it through a full circle to account for any possible effect of position on the earth's surface.

Michelson and Morley made several observations for four days and found no interference pattern attributable to a slowing the speed of light by the ether, the imagined medium in space through which the earth was thought to move. Although they hoped to find such an effect to demonstrate experimentally the existence of the ether, they were unable to do so. Scientists later used this null result to support Albert Einstein's notion in his special theory of relativity that the speed of light is constant; the interferometer experiment would only measure a constant speed of light, not a varying one. Physicists eventually abandoned the ether theory.

The Path of Light Beams in the Interferometer

(from Michelson and Morley's "On the Relative Motion of the Earth and the Luminiferous Ether" in *American Journal of Science*, 1887)

Bibliography

The Ethereal Aether: A History of the Michelson-Morley-Miller Aether-Drift Experiments, 1880-1930. Loyd S. Swenson. Austin: University of Texas Press, 1972.

"Michelson-Morley Experiment." Robert S. Shankland. *American Journal of Physics* 32 (1964).

Western Reserve University, adjacent to Case. In 1887, they repeated, with more precision and refinement, Michelson's earlier interferometer experiment seeking to measure the effect of the ether on the movement of light. As a strong advocate of the ether theory as the mechanism for electromagnetic transmission, Michelson hoped that this carefully crafted experiment would produce evidence of the existence of ether. Once again, the results indicated that the ether had no effect on the movement of light.

This null result compounded the confusion of nineteenth century physicists in their attempts to explain electromagnetic radiation. More important, it eventually led many scientists to use the Michelson-Morley outcome as experimental evidence supporting Albert Einstein's special theory of relativity, which eliminated the need for an ether. Einstein, however, never claimed any direct connection between his formulation of the relativity theory and this classic experiment.

Scientific Legacy

Michelson's superb experimental measurements gained for him growing acclaim in the scientific community. In 1889, he moved from Case to the new Clark University in Worcester, Massachusetts, and, in 1894, he accepted an appointment as chair of the physics department at the University of Chicago. In each of these academic positions, he continued his research work using the interferometer, which gave him a precise means to determine the speed of light, to establish the length of the standard meter using the light waves of cadmium, and to measure the diameter of stars. These well-regarded achievements earned for him the 1907 Nobel Prize in Physics; Michelson was the first American so honored.

When he died on May 9, 1931, in Pasadena, California, Michelson was still involved in measuring the speed of light. The figures that he reported from his work between 1925 and 1927 remained definitive for a generation. This pioneering American physicist left a legacy of precise, accurate experimentation and ingenious techniques that gave the world of science an experimental foundation for relativity and accurate measurements of light and length.

Bibliography

By Michelson
"On a Method of Measuring the Velocity of Light," *American Journal of Science*, 1878
"On the Relative Motion of the Earth and the Luminiferous Ether," *American Journal of Science*, 1887 (with Edward W. Morley)
"Measurement of Jupiter's Satellites by Interference," *Nature*, 1892
"Comparison of the International Meter with the Wavelength of the Light of Cadmium," *Astronomy and Astrophysics*, 1893
Light Waves and Their Uses, 1903
"The Rigidity of the Earth," *Astrophysical Journal*, 1919 (with Henry G. Gale)
Studies in Optics, 1927
"Measurement of the Velocity of Light Between Mount Wilson and Mount San Antonio," *Astrophysical Journal*, 1927

(The Nobel Foundation)

About Michelson

"Biographical Memoir of Albert Abraham Michelson, 1852-1931," Robert A. Millikan. *National Academy of Sciences Biographical Memoirs* 19 (1938).

The Master of Light: A Biography of Albert A. Michelson. Dorothy Michelson Livingston. New York: Charles Scribner's Sons, 1973.

Michelson and the Speed of Light. Bernard Jaffe. New York: Doubleday, 1960.

The Michelson Era in American Science, 1870-1930. Stanley Goldberg and Roger H. Stuewer, eds. New York: American Institute of Physics, 1988.

(H. J. Eisenman)

Robert Andrews Millikan

Areas of Achievement: Astronomy, chemistry, physics, and science (general)

Contribution: In a classic physical experiment, Millikan demonstrated the discrete nature of electric charge and measured the charge of an electron. He provided proof of Albert Einstein's photoelectric equation and studied cosmic rays.

Mar. 22, 1868	Born in Morrison, Illinois
1891	Graduated from Oberlin College
1895	Obtains his doctorate at Columbia University
1896	Appointed by Albert Abraham Michelson as an assistant in physics at the University of Chicago
1910	Becomes a full professor at the University of Chicago
1915	Elected to the National Academy of Sciences
1916	Verifies Einstein's photoelectric equation and determines Planck's constant
1920-1925	Studies and names cosmic rays
1921	Accepts the directorship of the Norman Bridge Laboratory of the California Institute of Technology
1922-1932	Represents the United States on the League of Nations Committee for Intellectual Cooperation
1923	Wins the Nobel Prize in Physics
1945	Retires
Dec. 19, 1953	Dies in San Marino, California

Early Life

Robert Andrews Millikan was born in Morrison, Illinois, in 1868. He was one of five children of a Congregational minister and his wife. Millikan described himself as the grandson of pioneers of good, clean-cut stock.

He was graduated from Oberlin College in 1891 and obtained his Ph.D. from Columbia University in 1895. In 1896, Millikan began work in physics at the University of Chicago, where he became a full professor in 1910.

The Oil-Drop Experiment

In 1909, Millikan's graduate student, Harvey Fletcher, was given the task of improving on the measurement of the electric charge. The first measurements were performed in 1897 in Cambridge, England using small water droplets falling inside a closed chamber. In 1903, the method was improved by using two parallel metal plates with a voltage across them to maintain a charge and an X-ray source to ionize the water droplets.

The Oil-Drop Experiment

Millikan demonstrated the discrete nature of electric charge and measured the charge of an electron by suspending oil drops in an electric field so that the electrostatic charge balanced the gravitational force.

Millikan's apparatus consisted of two accurately machined metal plates, 22 centimeters in diameter, separated by 16 millimeters. The top plate had a hole in it to allow small oil droplets, on the order of 0.001 millimeter, to enter. A radium source provided the means to ionize, or charge, the droplets. A large, steady voltage was applied to the plates.

Previous investigations using water droplets were subject to large experimental errors because the water droplets were always changing size as a result of evaporation. Errors on the order of 100 percent prevented meaningful results from this technique. Millikan considered himself a fool for taking so long to think of using oil since considerable research had gone into developing oils with little volatilization for clock movements.

Millikan observed the droplets by shining light perpendicular to the line of sight of a microscope attachment. The droplets were observed as shiny specks of light. They were too small for their size to be measured accurately, but Millikan was able determine that figure indirectly.

Without an applied voltage, the droplets would fall with a terminal velocity described by Stokes's law. Measurement of the rate of fall of the droplets allowed their mass to be determined. Because only large objects had been studied by Stokes's law and because of the effect of random movement of air molecules, correction factors had to be developed to determine the size of the droplets accurately.

When the voltage was applied to the plates, some of the droplets were suspended because the electrostatic attraction to the top of the plate counteracted the gravitational pull downward; this became known as the suspended drop method. Since the mass of the droplet is determined by Stokes's law and the intensity of the electric field is known, the charge can be calculated.

Millikan observed that the charges calculated for thousands of droplets were, within experimental error, all small integers of a basic unit of charge. He concluded that the unit of charge was the electron and determined its charge to be 4.77×10^{-10} statC; this value is now accepted to be 4.803×10^{-10} statC.

This method not only measured the value of the charge of the electron but also proved that electrons are made up of particles of finite size. Before the work of Millikan, it had not been demonstrated that electrical charges are made up of discrete particles.

Bibliography

Introduction to Atomic and Nuclear Physics. Otto Oldenberg. 3d ed. New York: McGraw-Hill, 1961.

"My Work with Millikan on the Oil-Drop Experiment." Harvey Fletcher. *Physics Today* 44 (June, 1982).

The Pursuit of the Atom. Werner Braunbek. New York: Emerson Books, 1959.

University Physics. Francis W. Sears, Mark W. Zemansky, and Hugh D. Young. 6th ed. Reading, Mass.: Addison-Wesley, 1982.

Millikan and Fletcher bettered the method again by using an improved voltage source of 10,000 volts that could maintain a steady charge for a long period of time. They were surprised to find that all but a few of the droplets would rapidly dissipate when the voltage was switched on, while several drops remained suspended in the field. This was the discovery of the balanced charge method.

The substitution of oil droplets for the water droplets led to a high level of stability in the system, since the oil did not evaporate as the water had. This method shows definitively that electrical charge exists in discrete units and can be measured accurately.

The Photoelectric Equation

In 1910, Millikan became a full professor at the University of Chicago, and in 1915 he was elected to the National Academy of Sciences. In 1916, he verified Albert Einstein's photoelectric equation, which describes the energy of electrons emitted from metallic surfaces bombarded with photons. Others had tried, but accurate measurements required extremely clean metal surfaces.

Millikan's work allowed him to give a relatively accurate value of Planck's constant, h. He determined it as 6.57×10^{-34} joules per sec-

(Library of Congress)

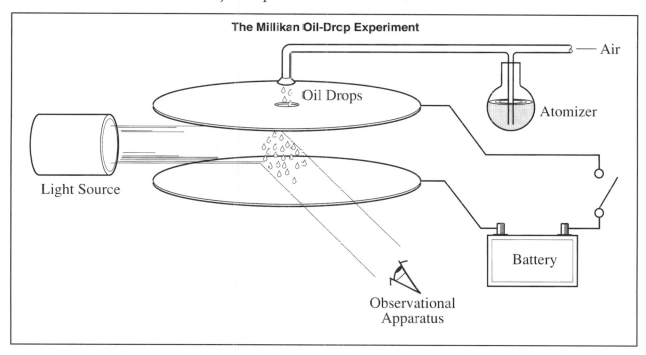

The Millikan Oil-Drop Experiment

Air

Oil Drops

Atomizer

Light Source

Battery

Observational Apparatus

ond; the accepted value is 6.626×10^{-34} joules per second. For both this research and his oil-drop experiments, Millikan was awarded the Nobel Prize in Physics in 1923.

The Study of Cosmic Rays

High-energy radiation, later known as cosmic radiation, was discovered by Swiss physicist Albert Gockel in 1910. Austrian physicist Victor Franz Hess proposed that the radiation was of extraterrestrial origin based on his experiments in a hot-air balloon at various elevations up to 5,200 meters. He showed the intensity of the high-energy radiation to increase with increasing altitude.

Many scientists had doubts, however, as to the true origin of the radiation. Millikan's work on radioactivity led him to investigate this controversy. Using small, unmanned balloons and an electroscope to altitudes of 15,500 meters, Millikan could not duplicate previous results of increasing radiation.

Radiation from radioactive sources known at the time could penetrate only about 2 meters of water, whereas radiation traveling through the atmosphere traveled the equivalent of about 10 meters. In 1925, Millikan and his assistant, George Cameron, used their electroscope in two lakes in California at high elevations. They found that cosmic radiation levels were identical at the surface of the lakes and at depths as much as 6 feet below the surface, indicating rays of very high energy that originated from space.

In 1925, Millikan announced his results to the National Academy of Sciences and called this radiation "cosmic rays." He soon became a popular figure in the press and with the public; his picture was on the cover of the April 25, 1927, issue of *Time* magazine.

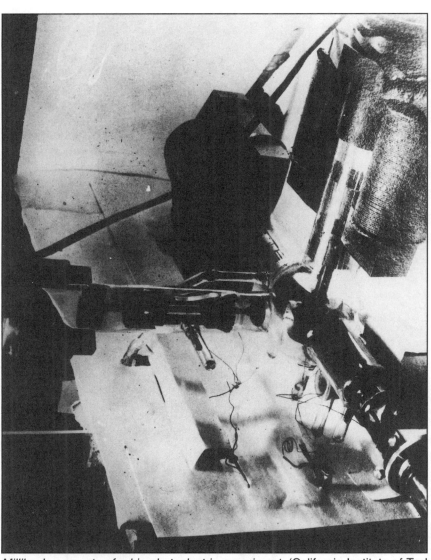

Millikan's apparatus for his photoelectric experiment. (California Institute of Technology)

Later Years

In 1921, Millikan was named the director of the Norman Bridge Laboratory of the California Institute of Technology (Caltech), in Pasadena, California. Between 1922 and 1932, he represented the United States on the League of Nations Committee for Intellectual Cooperation.

Millikan retired in 1945, and he died eight years

later in San Marino, California, at the age of eighty-five.

Bibliography
By Millikan

A First Course in Physics, 1906 (with Henry Gordon Gale)

The Electron: Its Isolation and Measurement and the Determination of Some of Its Properties, 1917, rev. ed. 1924

Evolution in Science and Religion, 1927

A First Course in Physics for Colleges, 1928 (rev. ed.; with Gale)

Time, Matter, and Values, 1932

Electrons (+ and –), Protons, Photons, Neutrons, and Cosmic Rays, 1935

Cosmic Rays, 1939

Electrons (+ and –), Protons, Photons, Neutrons, Mesotrons, and Cosmic Rays: Three Lectures, 1947 (rev. ed.)

Autobiography, 1950

About Millikan

The Physicists: The History of a Scientific Community in Modern America. Daniel J. Kevles. New York: Alfred A. Knopf, 1977.

The Rise of Robert Millikan: Portrait of a Life in American Science. Robert H. Kargon. Ithaca, N.Y.: Cornell University Press, 1982.

"Robert A. Millikan, Physics Teacher." Alfred Romer. *The Physics Teacher* 16 (February, 1978).

"Robert Andrews Millikan." In *The Nobel Prize Winners: Physics*, edited by Frank N. Magill. Pasadena, Calif.: Salem Press, 1989.

(Christopher J. Biermann)

Maria Mitchell

Areas of Achievement: Astronomy and mathematics

Contribution: Mitchell became America's first well-known female astronomer by discovering a comet. She spent her life teaching, traveling, and advancing the causes of women's education and women in science.

Aug. 1, 1818	Born on Nantucket Island, Massachusetts
1835-1836	Opens a school that accepts the children of immigrants and slaves
1836	Begins to assist her father with astronomical observations
Oct. 1, 1847	Observes a new comet
1848	Receives the Frederic VI Gold Medal from the king of Denmark
1848	Voted the first female member of the American Academy of Arts and Sciences
1849	Hired by the U.S. Nautical Almanac Office to compute the positions of Venus
1850	Voted the first female member of the Association for the Advancement of Science
1857	Receives a telescope from a group of prominent U.S. women
1865	Becomes a professor of astronomy at Vassar College
1869	Elected a member of the American Philosophical Society
1873	Founds the American Association for the Advancement of Women
1876	Presides over the fourth session of the Women's Congress, Philadelphia
June 28, 1889	Dies in Lynn, Massachusetts

(Library of Congress)

Early Life

Maria Mitchell grew up on Nantucket Island in a large Quaker family. From her early childhood, she tirelessly investigated her many interests using what books were available on the small whaling island. Her father, William, adhered to the Quaker belief that a girl's education should be comparable to that given boys. Not only did Maria attend the Quaker school on the island, but William made her a part of the astronomical and other scientific work that he did as well. Her father always praised her willingness to work carefully for long hours and her will not to be repressed by the conventional views of women and girls.

Mitchell did have more strong female role models than most American girls, even if they were not scientists. Whaling being a principal concern of the islanders, the men were gone for months, even years, leaving the women to run the town.

Commitment to the Education of Girls

By the time that she was sixteen, Mitchell's accomplished study of science and literature was renowned on the island, and so she became the assistant to the master of the Quaker school.

The following year, she opened her own girls' school and accepted the daughters of slaves and immigrants, as well as Quaker girls. The school had to close after its first year because most of the pupils were poor, but Mitchell continued to believe in the necessity of education for girls.

Librarian by Day, Astronomer by Night

When she was forced to close her school for girls, Mitchell was appointed to the post of island librarian, a position that she held for many years. It was the ideal job for her because she could teach and help visitors while having access to most of the books on the island.

At about the same time, her father was appointed cashier of the island bank. This position came with a house attached to the bank. Fortunately for Mitchell and her father, because of the importance of whaling to their community, a telescope for locating ships at sea was built on the roof of the bank. The stars themselves are also important to navigation at sea, and for this purpose Mitchell and her father spent thousands of nights in their observatory.

Routine Observation and a Big Surprise

Mitchell and her father were hired by the U.S. Coast Guard to make precise maps of the stars for the purposes of navigation at sea. Using their telescope in the night sky, they patiently recorded positions of even the faintest stars.

Over the years, Mitchell came to know the exact locations of the stars and other heavenly bodies. One night, she spotted a star in an unaccustomed place. She recorded her observation and returned the next night to find that the star had moved considerably with respect to the other stars. This was no star—it must have been a new comet. She wrote immediately to an astronomer at Harvard University about her discovery.

Fame for the Lady Astronomer

The comet that Mitchell sighted was observed by other astronomers around the world that same week, but, after some confusion, the authorities decided that Mitchell had seen the comet first. Much excitement and disbelief were generated in the public about a woman making such an impressive discovery—and before men had done so. She received a gold

What the Stars Reveal

Through nightly surveillance of the sky, Mitchell was the first in the world to detect a new comet visiting Earth in 1847. Her lifelong, patient study of the stars helped both navigators and astronomers developing the new field of cosmology, the structure and evolution of the universe.

Humankind has studied the stars since prehistoric times out of wonder and awe of their beauty. Many believed that stories were recorded in the heavenly bodies, and others thought that the stars could foretell destiny. Humankind has also studied the stars in order to know their positions for navigational purposes and to understand them.

On the open sea, there are no landmarks. Early sailors realized that they could navigate by the stars. Accurate maps of the heavens were made for use by sailors working with sextants, compasses, and clocks. Sextants are used for measuring a star or planet's angle above the horizon. A knowledge of when a particular star would rise at a given time of year at a given position on Earth helped a navigator determine the ship's position on the ocean. Today, air and sea navigation are performed with the aid of satellites, but a good navigator still knows the constellations.

Another reason to observe the stars is to determine their chemical makeup. Starlight contains important information about the chemical elements present. Stars are mostly hydrogen and helium, but they contain other elements as well. Stars are the birthplace of the elements. Young stars are almost completely hydrogen. The older a star is, the more elements that it will contain.

When light from one star is focused through a telescope and broken down using a prism, one finds the same rainbow effect obtained from sunlight through a prism. Careful analysis of the spectrum formed, however, shows narrow black lines in some places where color has been removed from the spectrum by a chemical element present in the star.

Each chemical element is capable of absorbing certain known wavelengths of light. If that element is present in the outer regions of a star, it will absorb the appropriate wavelength of light being produced by the interior of the star. This is seen as a black line at a characteristic place in the star's spectrum.

Thanks to the work of the early modern astronomers, scientists now have a thorough understanding of many of the processes occurring in stars. These theories have helped in determining how the universe has progressed from the big bang to the present.

Bibliography

Atoms of Silence: An Explanation of Cosmic Evolution. H. Reeves. Cambridge, Mass.: MIT Press, 1984.
The Historical Supernovae. D. H. Clark and F. R. Stephenson. Oxford, England: Pergamon Press, 1977.
Stars: Their Birth, Life, and Death. I. S. Shklovskii. Translated by R. B. Rodman. San Francisco: W. H. Freeman, 1978.

medal from the king of Denmark and was elected to many scientific societies that previously had excluded women.

Mitchell traveled to Europe and around the United States in the years following her discovery, and she met several prominent male scientists, but not many female ones. She began to use her own prominence to publicize the issues of education for women and the lack of support for female scientists.

A Return to the Education of Women

In the early 1860's, Matthew Vassar was organizing a college for women and was recruiting professors. He tempted Mitchell to join the Vassar College faculty by giving her charge of the new college observatory, which featured the third-largest telescope in the United States at that time. Mitchell was also attracted by the chance to educate young women.

For the next quarter century, Mitchell divided her time between teaching her adoring students and speaking about the importance of women's education. In 1873, she helped to found the American Association for the Advancement of Women. During this time, she said that she believed in women even more than in astronomy. She died in 1889.

Bibliography

By Mitchell

"On Jupiter and Its Satellites," *American Journal of Science and Arts*, 1871

"Astronomical Notes," *Scientific American*, 1876

"The Need of Women in Science" in *Association for the Advancement of Women: Papers Read at the Fourth Congress of Women*, 1876

Maria Mitchell: Life, Letters, and Journals, 1896 (Phebe Mitchell Kendall, ed.)

About Mitchell

Four Nineteenth Century Professional Women. Janet K. Henderson. New Brunswick, N.J.: Rutgers University Press, 1982.

"Maria Mitchell: The Advancement of Women in Science." Sally Gregory Kohlstedt. *New England Quarterly* 51, no. 1 (1978).

Sweeper in the Sky: The Life of Maria Mitchell, First Woman Astronomer in America. Helen Wright. New York: Macmillan, 1949.

(*Wendy Halpin Hallows*)

Peter D. Mitchell

Areas of Achievement: Bacteriology, biology, chemistry, and physiology

Contribution: A pioneer in understanding how living cells make and use energy. Mitchell won the Nobel Prize in Chemistry for his theories that explained how electrical, chemical, and mechanical forms of biological energy are interconverted.

Sept. 29, 1920	Born in Mitcham, Surrey, England
1931	Enters the junior school of Queens College, Tauton
1939	Enters Jesus College, Cambridge University
1943	Receives a B.A. in natural sciences and enters graduate school in biochemistry
1949	Meets Jennifer Moyle, who becomes his lifelong friend and scientific colleague
1950	Receives a Ph.D. in biochemistry
1955	Takes a position in Edinburgh University, Scotland
1958	Marries his second wife, Helen Robertson
1962	Resigns his position at Edinburgh because of poor health
1965	Establishes the Glynn Research Foundation in Cornwall, England
1978	Wins the Nobel Prize in Chemistry
Apr. 10, 1992	Dies at Glynn House, near Bodmin, Cornwall, England

Early Life

Peter Dennis Mitchell was born in Surrey, just outside London, on September 29, 1920. His father, Christopher Gibbs Mitchell, was a talented engineer who, by the end of his life, had designed road systems for about one-fifth of England. His mother, Kate, was a sensitive musician and artist with little knowledge of science. His parents separated when Peter was still young, and he was reared by his mother.

As boys, Peter and his older brother, Bill, had few outside friends. They undertook tasks together, building machines and concocting explosives. Their mother often expressed her pride and appreciation and never scolded the boys when accidents occurred.

Peter's primary schooling was structured and disciplined. He was responsive to praise but sensitive to criticism. Tests taken at the age of twelve indicated that his intelligence quotient (IQ) was only slightly above average. He

---

Mitchell's Chemiosmotic Hypotheses

Mitchell put forth ideas concerning cellular energetics that were so radically new that many scientists of his day considered him crazy. Today, he is recognized as an original and insightful biologist who transformed the conception of vectorial metabolism and energy interconversion in the living cell.

Three so-called chemiosmotic hypotheses account for the phenomena of vectorial metabolism. One explains how oxidative metabolism is used to synthesize adenosine triphosphate (ATP), the chemical energy currency of all living cells. A second explains how cells accumulate nutrients against concentration gradients. A third explains how bacteria swim.

One of Mitchell's primary teachers was Professor David Keilin of Cambridge University. Keilin had discovered cytochromes, electron carriers embedded in the membranes of cells and cell organelles. ATP is synthesized during the oxidation of foodstuffs in animals, and cytochromes facilitate ATP synthesis. Scientists of Mitchell's day postulated that a high-energy chemical intermediate was formed during the oxidation of foodstuffs and that ATP was made from this intermediate. Many scientists tried to find such a chemical intermediate, but all failed.

Mitchell broke new ground by proposing that this postulated high-energy intermediate was not chemical in nature, as most scientists believed, but was instead electrical in nature. He suggested that Keilin's cytochromes transport protons across membranes every time that they are reversibly oxidized. Proton transport generates a proton gradient across the membrane, as well as an electrical field. Mitchell termed this proton electrochemical gradient the "proton motive force" (pmf), by analogy to the electron motive force (emf) of a battery. He suggested that the pmf could be used to drive ATP synthesis.

The pmf, Mitchell further proposed, could be used by living cells for purposes in addition to ATP synthesis. Neutral (noncharged) nutrients such as sugars, amino acids, and vitamins were known to accumulate in cells, but no one knew how. Mitchell suggested that entry of a small nutrient molecule, mediated by a membrane-embedded protein, a transport carrier, is accompanied by the entry of a proton. According to this notion, the pmf provides the driving force for the accumulation of the nutrient because the proton "wants" to flow down its electrochemical gradient. Mitchell's second chemiosmotic hypothesis therefore explains how cells accumulate nutrients.

According to Mitchell's third chemiosmotic hypothesis, bacteria swim by rotating an organelle called a flagellum. Rotation of the flagellum, requiring mechanical energy, drives these small microorganisms in the forward direction. As a consequence, bacteria can swim up concentration gradients of nutrients such as sugars. Mitchell proposed that the pmf drives rotation of the bacterial flagellum because of the flow of protons through the flagellum.

While certain details of Mitchell's ideas were shown to be in error, the essence of his hypotheses always proved to be correct. Mitchell was much ahead of his time. It took the scientific community nearly two decades to accept the ideas that he had formulated when still a young man at Cambridge University.

Bibliography

Biochemistry. Geoffrey Zubay, ed. 3d. ed. Dubuque, Iowa: Wm. C. Brown, 1993.
Enzymes in Metabolic Pathways. Milton H. Saier, Jr. New York: Harper & Row, 1987.

performed so poorly on the Cambridge entrance examinations that his entry into the university was initially denied.

Cambridge Years

Mitchell arrived in Cambridge at the age of nineteen in October, 1939, just after the start of World War II. He joined the Cambridge Natural Science Club and enjoyed the intellectual atmosphere of the group. He received his bachelor of arts degree in 1943 without distinction.

During his graduate studies in biochemistry, Mitchell was influenced by three excellent teachers: Jim Danielli, who worked on cell membranes; David Keilin, who characterized the proteins of the mitochondrial respiratory chain; and Malcolm Dixon, who was an enzymologist. Many of Mitchell's contributions were attributable to his ability to integrate the concepts of these three teachers into a unified picture.

Chemiosmotic Hypotheses

During his last years at Cambridge, and then later in Edinburgh, Scotland, Mitchell formulated his scientific hypotheses. His ideas were radically different from the prevailing thought of the time. The scientific community greeted his notions with skepticism, and Mitchell was branded a crackpot by many prominent scientists. His scientific methods were also questioned. Continual criticism weighed heavily on him, and in 1962 he resigned his post at Edinburgh University as a result of poor health.

Glynn House

Mitchell bought a dilapidated, eighteenth century manor house called Glynn House in Cornwall, England. Together with his colleague, Jennifer Moyle, he established an active research laboratory there, paid for with funds from his own pocket. He and Moyle conducted experiments and established his chemiosmotic hypotheses, in more than a decade of hard work. Mitchell was awarded the Nobel Prize in Chemistry in 1978.

After receiving the Nobel Prize, Mitchell returned to Glynn House, where he continued to publish prolifically. He died on April 10, 1992, of cancer.

Bibliography

By Mitchell

"Coupling of Phosphorylation to Electron and Hydrogen Transfer by a Chemi-Osmotic Type of Mechanism," *Nature*, 1961

"Chemiosmotic Coupling in Oxidative and Photosynthetic Phosphorylation," *Biological Reviews*, 1966

"Vectorial Chemistry and the Molecular Mechanics of Chemiosmotic Coupling: Power Transmission by Proticity," *Transactions of the Biochemical Society*, 1976

"Vectorial Chemiosmotic Processes," *Annual Review of Biochemistry*, 1977

"David Keilin's Respiratory Chain Concept and Its Chemiosmotic Consequences," *Science*, 1979

"Compartmentation and Communication in Living Systems: Ligand Conduction, a General Catalytic Principle in Chemical, Osmotic, and Chemiosmotic Reaction Systems," *European Journal of Biochemistry*, 1979

(The Nobel Foundation)

About Mitchell

"Glynn and the conceptual Development of the Chemiosmotic Theory: A Retrospective and Prospective View." Bruce H. Weber. *Bioscience Reports* 11 (1991).

"The 1978 Nobel Prize in Chemistry." Franklin M. Harold. *Science* (December 15, 1978).

"Peter D. Mitchell." In *The Nobel Prize Winners: Chemistry*, edited by Frank N. Magill. Pasadena, Calif.: Salem Press, 1990.

(Milton H. Saier, Jr.)

Andrija Mohorovicic

Area of Achievement: Earth science
Contribution: Mohorovicic's discovery of the Mohorovicic discontinuity led to the realization that the earth has a thin, brittle crust.

Jan. 23, 1857	Born in Volosko, Istria, Austrian Empire (now in Croatia)
1875	Enrolls at the University of Prague, earning a degree in mathematics and physics
1882	Appointed to the Royal Nautical School in Bakar
1887	Founds the Meteorological Station of Bakar
1891	Appointed professor at the Main Technical School in Zagreb
1892	Becomes the director of the meteorological observatory
1897	Receives his doctorate from the University of Zagreb
1989	Elected to the Yugoslav Academy of Sciences
1909	Discovers the Mohorovicic discontinuity as a result of an earthquake south of Zagreb
1910	Publishes "Das Beben vom 8.X.1909" (the quake of October 8, 1909)
1918-1922	Serves as secretary of the mathematics and science section at the Yugoslav Academy of Sciences
1921	Retires from the Royal Regional Center
Dec. 18, 1936	Dies in Zagreb, Yugoslavia(now in Croatia)

Early Life

Andrija Mohorovicic (pronounced "mah-hahr-ah-VEE-cheech") was born in 1857 in a part of the Austrian Empire that is now Croatia. He was the son of a shipyard carpenter, and his mother died shortly after his birth. He showed his brilliance both in school and by his ability to learn foreign languages, such as English, French, and Italian.

Mohorovicic enrolled at the University of Prague in 1875, studied under physicist Ernst Mach, and earned a degree in mathematics and physics. He was a schoolteacher for seven years before he was appointed to the Royal

Discovering a Discontinuity

Mohorovicic studied seismic waves to provide a picture of the earth's interior.

While it is impossible to see Earth's deepest layers, seismologists can gather much information about the earth's interior by studying the waves generated by earthquakes. These waves are measured with an instrument called a seismograph. Seismographs detect two very different vibrations, called P (primary) waves and S (secondary) waves, which are generated by every quake. P waves travel twice as fast as S waves and so are always detected first by a seismograph.

In 1906, Richard Oldham found that S waves are never detected at the far side of the earth from any earthquake. Since S waves cannot travel through liquid, Oldham postulated that the center of the earth is composed of molten rock. Three years later, Mohorovicic's detailed study of a 1909 Croatian earthquake showed that some P waves traveled faster than others. Knowing that waves can be refracted when they move from one material into another (as when light moves from air into water), he was able to show how some P waves travel faster through a deeper layer of the earth than through the top layer. In doing so, he discovered the boundary between the earth's crust and mantle.

This boundary has since been called the Mohorovicic discontinuity, or Moho. The average depth of the Moho is 21 miles under the continents, while it is only about 3 miles deep under the oceans.

Bibliography

Earthquakes. Bruce Bolt. New York: W. H. Freeman, 1993.

Earthquakes. G. A. Eiby. New York: Van Nostrand Reinhold, 1980.

Earthquakes and Geological Discovery. Bruce Bolt. New York: Scientific American Library, 1993.

Volcanoes and Earthquakes. Jon Erickson. Blue Ridge Summit, Pa.: Tab Books, 1988.

Why the Earth Quakes. Matthys Levy and Mario Salvadori. New York: W. W. Norton, 1995.

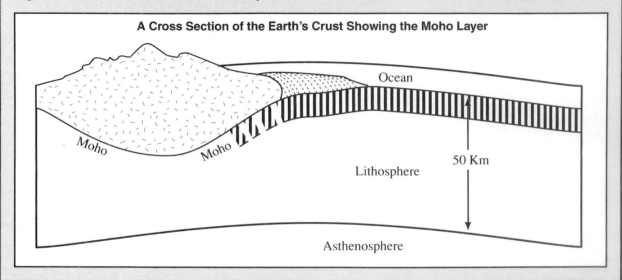

A Cross Section of the Earth's Crust Showing the Moho Layer

Nautical School, where he taught meteorology and oceanography. In 1887, he founded the Meteorological Station of Bakar. In 1891, Mohorovicic was named professor at the Main Technical School in Zagreb and became the director of the meteorological observatory the next year. He received his doctorate from the University of Zagreb in 1897.

In 1900, he was successful in making the Zagreb observatory independent of control from Hungary, and his observatory became the Royal Regional Center for Meteorology and Geodynamics. Despite success in the study of weather, his primary field of interest was soon to become seismology, the study of earthquakes.

In 1901, a strong earthquake was felt in central Croatia. The quake renewed local interest in seismology, and Mohorovicic was able to procure a Italian seismograph for his center. With new equipment and his meticulous work, by 1908 the center had become one of the leading seismological observatories in Europe.

The Mohorovicic Discontinuity

On October 8, 1909, a very destructive earthquake occurred south of Zagreb. From a thorough analysis of seismographs recording this quake, Mohorovicic deduced that some of the seismic waves being recorded were refracted by some discontinuity, or change in density of materials beneath the surface of the earth. He calculated this discontinuity to be approximately 30 miles beneath the surface of the earth.

Other seismologists confirmed his discovery and showed that the discontinuity extended beneath the earth's surface worldwide. This work showed that there are two distinct layers of the earth: an upper layer now called the crust, and a layer below it, called the mantle. The boundary between the two layers is called the Mohorovicic discontinuity—or Moho, for short. The existence of a much-deeper molten core had already been postulated by this time.

Later Work in Seismology

Mohorovicic was responsible for designing a method to determine the exact location of an earthquake's epicenter (the point on the earth's surface directly above the quake itself). He plotted travel times of seismic waves up to 10,000 miles from their epicenter. Being located in a part

(Science Photo Library)

of Europe often hit with major earthquakes, he was extremely interested in the possibility of designing earthquake-proof buildings.

Mohorovicic retired from the Royal Regional Center for Meteorology and Geodynamics in 1921 and died in 1936 at the age of seventy-nine.

Bibliography

By Mohorovicic

"Das Beben vom 8.X.1909" (the quake of October 8, 1909), *Jahrbuch des meteorologischen Observatoriums in Zagreb*, 1910

About Mohorovicic

"Mohorovicic, Andrija." In *Dictionary of Scientific Biography*, edited by Charles Coulston Gillispie. New York: Charles Scribner's Sons, 1980.

"Mohorovicic, Andrija." In *Larousse Dictionary of Scientists*, edited by Hazel Muir. New York: Larousse, 1994.

(Kenneth J. Schoon)

Mario J. Molina

Area of Achievement: Chemistry
Contribution: Molina investigated the effect of chlorofluorocarbons (CFCs) on the atmosphere and found that their decomposition destroys ozone.

Mar. 19, 1943	Born in Mexico City, Mexico
1954	Attends a boarding school in Switzerland
1965	Earns a degree in chemical engineering from the Universidad Nacional Autonoma de Mexico (UNAM)
1965-1967	Conducts postgraduate studies at the University of Freiburg, West Germany
1968	Returns to UNAM as an assistant professor
1972	Receives a Ph.D. in physical chemistry from the University of California, Berkeley
1973	Marries Luisa Tan, a fellow scientist
1973	Begins work with F. Sherwood Rowland at the University of California, Irvine (UCI)
1974	With Rowland, publishes a paper on CFC depletion of ozone
1975-1982	Teaches on the faculty of UCI
1982	Joins the molecular physics and chemistry section of the Jet Propulsion Laboratory (JPL)
1989	Moves to the Massachusetts Institute of Technology (MIT)
1995	Shares the Nobel Prize in Chemistry with Rowland and Paul Crutzen

Early Life

Mario José Molina was born in Mexico City in 1943 to Roberto Molina Pasquel, a lawyer and professor, and Leonor Henriquez de Molina. From an early age, he was attracted to science, and he even converted a bathroom into a laboratory. His aunt, a chemist, helped him conduct advanced experiments. At eleven, Molina was sent to a boarding school in Switzerland in order to expand his view of the world and to learn German.

Molina had already chosen his path—research chemistry—and enrolled in a program in chemical engineering at his father's university, the Universidad Nacional Autonoma de Mexico (UNAM), in 1960. He obtained his undergraduate degree five years later and then returned to Europe, this time to the University of Freiburg in West Germany. After two years of postgraduate work, Molina traveled to Paris and then came home to Mexico, where he set up the first graduate program in chemical engineering at UNAM and joined the faculty as an assistant professor.

A Promising Academic Career

In 1968, desiring to broaden his background, Molina moved to the United States and enrolled at the University of California, Berkeley (UCB). There, he joined a research group headed by George C. Pimentel, his mentor, and met fellow graduate student Luisa Tan, his future wife. Molina completed his Ph.D. in 1972, staying at UCB for another year in order to continue his research in chemical dynamics. He married Tan in 1973; their son, Felipe, would be born in 1977.

Molina's next decision proved to be the most important of his scientific career: He began a collaboration with F. Sherwood Rowland at the University of California, Irvine (UCI). Together, they would study the fate of the chemicals called chlorofluorocarbons (CFCs) in the atmosphere. CFCs, also known as Freons, were widely used in such consumer products as refrigerators, air conditioners, plastic foam, and aerosol cans.

Uncovering an Environmental Threat

Molina and Rowland began their research into CFCs out of scientific curiosity but soon realized the importance of their findings. Although chemically inert, CFCs are harmful to ozone, the naturally occurring rare gas in the upper atmosphere that forms a layer protecting Earth from ultraviolet radiation.

In 1974, Molina and Rowland published their CFC-ozone depletion theory in the journal *Nature* and appealed to the government, the media, and the public to halt this threat to the environment. Their paper attracted attention, and some steps were taken to limit the production of CFCs. The theory did not provoke alarm, however, until the mid-1980's, with the discovery of a large hole in the ozone layer over the Antarctic. The risk was even greater than originally thought. Yet, some scientists continued to doubt that CFCs could have such serious consequences.

Molina, who by that time had formed a research group in the molecular physics and chemistry section of the Jet Propulsion Laboratory (JPL) in Pasadena, California, studied the conditions over this polar region. This group, which included his wife, proved that ice crystals in the stratosphere over the South Pole promote the reaction between CFCs and ozone molecules. Thereafter, the global impact of these chemicals gained broad acceptance, and Molina shared the 1995 Nobel Prize in Chemistry with Rowland and Paul Crutzen.

Molina called himself "heartened and humbled" that his work had contributed to atmospheric chemistry and had a "profound impact on the global environment." A worldwide ban of CFCs, beginning in 1996, was seen by many scientists as offering a solution to the problem of ozone destruction.

Bibliography
By Molina
"Stratospheric Sink for Chlorofluoromethanes: Chlorine Atom-Catalyzed Destruction of Ozone," *Nature*, 1974 (with F. Sherwood Rowland)

As the recipient of one of the prizes, Molina sits next to Princess Lilian of Sweden (left) at the Nobel banquet in Stockholm in 1995. (Reuters/Jan Collsi/Archive Photos)

The Destruction of Ozone

Molina and F. Sherwood Rowland warned that the commonly used, artificial chemicals known as chlorofluorocarbons (CFCs) threaten the crucial layer of ozone molecules surrounding the earth.

CFCs, which were first created in 1928, had found wide application by the 1950's as refrigerants, solvents, and propellants because they are stable, nontoxic, and chemically inert. Scientists began to wonder, however, what becomes of the CFCs that enter the atmosphere.

When broken down by sunlight in the stratosphere, CFCs release chlorine atoms (Cl) and chlorine monoxide (ClO). A single chlorine atom can start a chain reaction that destroys one hundred thousand molecules of ozone, the naturally occurring rare gas in the upper atmosphere. Ozone forms a layer that protects Earth from ultraviolet radiation by filtering out these harmful rays. Without the ozone layer, life on Earth could not exist, and even a small degree of global depletion could increase the rates of skin cancer, cataracts, and immune system damage.

After Molina and Rowland's 1974 article describing the effect of CFCs, the Environmental Protection Agency and the Food and Drug Administration (FDA) in the United States limited the production of these chemicals. The confirmation of a large seasonal reduction of ozone over Antarctica in 1985 prompted great concern and further investigation. Molina and his research group concluded that ice crystals over the South Pole act as catalysts in the chemical reaction involved in ozone destruction. In 1987, the United Nations passed the Montreal Proctocol banning the production of all CFCs worldwide after 1996. It was hoped that compliance with this measure would reverse the damage to the ozone layer.

Bibliography

Between Earth and Sky. Seth Cagin and Philip Dray. New York: Pantheon Books, 1993.

Ozone Crisis. Sharon Roan. New York: John Wiley & Sons, 1989.

"Physical Chemistry of the $H_2SO_4/HNO_3/H_2O$ System: Implications for Polar Stratospheric Clouds," *Science* 1993 (with R. Zhang, P. J. Woolridge, J. R. McMahon, et al.)

"Gas Phase Reaction of Sulphur Trioxide with Water Vapor," *Journal of the American Chemical Society*, 1994 (with C. E. Kolb, J. T. Jayne, D. R. Worsnap, et al.)

"Ozone Depletion: Twenty Years After the Alarm," *Chemical and Engineering News*, 1994 (with Rowland)

About Molina

"Molina, Mario." In *Notable Twentieth-Century Scientists*, edited by Emily J. McMurray, ed. New York: Gale Research, 1995.

(Tracy Irons-Georges)

Jacques Lucien Monod

Areas of Achievement: Bacteriology, biology, genetics, and medicine
Contribution: As an early biochemist and molecular biologist, Monod explained how genes are expressed and how gene expression is controlled.

Feb. 9, 1910	Born in Paris, France
1928	Receives his baccalaureate from the college in Cannes
1931	Receives a B.A. degree from the University of Paris
1936	Studies under Thomas Hunt Morgan at the California Institute of Technology
1941	Receives a D.Sc. degree
1945	Becomes head of a microbial physiology laboratory at the Institut Pasteur in Paris
1954	Becomes head of the cellular biochemistry department at the Institut Pasteur
1959	Named a professor of biochemistry at the University of Paris
1965	Wins the Nobel Prize in Physiology or Medicine jointly with André Lwoff and François Jacob
1967	Appointed a professor of molecular biology at the College de France
1968	Becomes a Fellow of the Salk Institute for Biological Sciences in La Jolla, California
1970	Publishes *Le Hasard et la nécessité* (*Chance and Necessity*, 1971)
1971	Named director of the Institut Pasteur
May 31, 1976	Dies in Cannes, France

Early Life

Jacques Lucien Monod (pronounced "mah-NOH") was born in Paris on February 9, 1910, but the Monod family moved to Cannes, in southern France, when he was seven years old. The family was of Swiss origin, as the family patriarch, a pastor, had emigrated to France from Geneva in 1808. Jacques's mother, Sharlie Todd MacGregor, was an American of Scottish origin, and consequently, the young boy was exposed to different cultural attitudes within the boundaries of his own family. His father, Lucien, was a talented painter and an avid scholar with tremendous admiration for Charles Darwin. He transmitted this appreciation to his young son, thus instilling in him an interest in biology.

Monod's father played an important role in shaping the young boy's education, introducing him first to music and then to biology. He learned to play the cello and thereby gained a love for music. Throughout many of his later years as a molecular biologist, Monod played in a string quartet and directed a Bach choir.

(The Nobel Foundation)

University Education

Until 1928, Monod attended the college at Cannes. In October of that year, he traveled to Paris to begin studies in biology and chemistry. Later, at the biological station at Roscoff, he was influenced by André Lwoff, who showed him the value of microbiology; by Boris Ephrussi, who introduced him to physiological genetics; and by Louis Rapkine, who convinced him that only a molecular description of life can provide an in-depth picture of living organisms.

In 1936, Ephrussi persuaded Monod to accompany him to the California Institute of Technology (Caltech) in Pasadena, California. There, he would study under the great geneticist Thomas Hunt Morgan. During his stay at Caltech, Monod came to appreciate the full

Studies of Bacterial Growth

In his early years as a research scientist, Monod studied bacterial growth, which led him to research into enzyme synthesis.

Monod noted that when two sugars are present in the growth medium, bacterial growth occurs in two phases, separated by a period of no growth. He termed this entire phenomenon diauxy (double growth). He guessed, and later established, that the bacteria use different enzymes to metabolize the two sugars.

During the first phase of growth, one sugar is metabolized by enzymes that are always present. When the first sugar is depleted, the bacteria cease growing, and synthesis of the enzymes necessary for metabolism of the second sugar occurs. Monod termed this latter phenomenon enzyme adaptation. During the latency period, the colony is switching from one metabolic program to another.

Monod then focused his attention on enzyme adaptation in order to determine how bacteria adapt to a changing environment when food sources are scarce. He hypothesized that an inducer molecule might serve as an intracellular signal, indicating the availability of a nutrient.

The signaling molecule, or inducer, could possibly bind to a protein that controls gene expression. Such a protein, a repressor, might prevent gene expression unless the inducer binds to it. Binding of the inducer molecular to the repressor would allow gene expression and hence synthesis of the enzymes necessary for metabolism of the second sugar. These ideas, which evolved slowly as a result of discussions with many scientists, proved in essence to be correct.

In 1954, Monod became director of the department of cell biology at the Institut Pasteur. At the same time, he began his collaborative work with François Jacob. These two scientists, together with their students and associates, began studies to understand enzyme adaptation at the molecular level. They wanted to understand the relationship between environmental signals and the genetic apparatus of a bacterial cell.

Monod and Jacob identified a gene cluster which they called an operon. The operon consisted of a regulatory region at the beginning of a deoxyribonucleic acid (DNA) strand, called an operator, followed by a linear string of structural genes, each coding for a different protein. The repressor protein that Monod had earlier hypothesized proved to bind to the operator, thus preventing expression of the operon.

Availability of the appropriate inducer allowed expression of the genes within the operon. Monod and Jacob postulated that expression of the operon resulted in production of a message that allowed synthesis of the newly needed metabolic enzymes. The message proved to be ribonucleic acid (RNA), an intermediate between the DNA genetic material and the proteinaceous enzymes. It was therefore called messenger RNA (mRNA). Thus, the operonic DNA was transcribed to RNA, and the mRNA was translated to protein.

Bibliography
Microbiology. Lansing M. Prescott, John P. Harley, and Donald A. Klein, eds. 2d ed. Vol. 1. Dubuque, Iowa: Wm. C. Brown, 1990.
Molecular Biology of the Gene. James D. Watson, Nancy H. Hopkins, Jeffrey W. Roberts, Joan Argetsinger Steitz, and Alan M. Weiner, eds. 4th ed. Menlo Park, Calif.: Benjamin/Cummings, 1987.

value of free intellectual exchange in a friendly, rather than a hostile or competitive, environment.

In 1938, Monod married Odette Bruhl, an archaeologist and museum curator. They had two sons—one was to become a geologist, the other a physicist. The death of Monod's wife preceded his own by four years.

World War II Efforts
In 1939, war broke out in Europe. In spite of a medical exemption from military service, which allowed him to retain his academic position in Paris, Monod joined the French resistance movement as an officer, and his laboratory at the Sorbonne served both as an Underground meeting place and as a propaganda print shop.

Although he was captured by the Nazi Gestapo, he managed to escape. Subsequently, he continued his resistance efforts. He helped organize the general strike that ultimately led to the liberation of Paris. He was eventually honored with several military commendations, including the Croix de Guerre, the Legion of Honor, and the American Bronze Star.

Research in Molecular Biology
During his years as a research scientist in Paris, Monod uncovered the molecular nature of the genetic material of living cells. Most important, he collaborated with other scientists to discover how genes are organized, how they code for proteins, and how expression of genes is controlled. This work led to the Central Dogma, which states that deoxyribonucleic acid (DNA) is transcribed to ribonucleic acid (RNA) and that RNA is translated to protein.

The importance of Monod's studies gradually began to be recognized. In 1959, he became a professor of biochemistry at the University of Paris, while retaining his post at the Institut Pasteur. Following his receipt of the Nobel Prize in Physiology or Medicine in 1965, he became director of the Institut Pasteur.

Philosophy
Monod used his fame and influence to bolster the cause of basic research. The French government favored directed research with evident applicability to medicine or industry. Monod pointed out that his basic research activities, conducted with little government support from France, had led to an understanding of heredity and disease. Without support from private sources and the United States, his contributions would have been impossible.

Monod declared that modern science had paved the way to a new moral rationalism based on "logic confronted with experience." In 1970, he published *Le Hasard et la nécessité* (*Change and Necessity*, 1971), which became an immediate best-seller. In this book, he pondered the philosophical implications of discoveries concerning basic life processes. He expressed the opinion that life arose as a result of chance events that were shaped by the need for survival.

Monod concluded that, "Man knows at last that he is alone in the indifferent immensity of the universe. His duty, like his fate, is written nowhere. It is for him to choose between the kingdom and the darkness." He believed that nationalism and war are parts of the "darkness," while universal cooperation and reason are to be found in the "kingdom." Monod died in 1976 at the age of sixty-six.

Bibliography
By Monod
Recherches sur la croissance de cultures bacteriennes, 1942

"Genetic Regulatory Mechanisms in the Synthesis of Proteins," *Journal of Molecular Biology*, 1961 (with François Jacob)

From Biology to Ethics, 1969

Le Hasard et la nécessité: Essai sur la philosophie naturelle de la biologie moderne, 1971 (*Chance and Necessity: An Essay on the Natural Philosophy of Modern Biology*, 1971)

About Monod
"Jacques Lucien Monod." In *The Nobel Prize Winners: Physiology or Medicine*, edited by Frank N. Magill. Pasadena, Calif.: Salem Press, 1991.

"Jacques Monod, 1910-1976." *Nature* (1976).

Origins of Molecular Biology: A Tribute to Jacques Monod. André Lwoff and Agnes Ullmann, eds. Paris: Academic Press, 1979.

(*Milton H. Saier, Jr.*)

Thomas Hunt Morgan

Areas of Achievement: Biology, genetics, and zoology

Contribution: The most famous geneticist of the early part of the twentieth century, Morgan established the fruit fly, *Drosophila melanogaster*, as a preeminent experimental organism. All of the major principles of transmission genetics were developed in his fly laboratory in the period from 1908 to 1926.

Sept. 25, 1866	Born in Lexington, Kentucky
1886	Earns a B.S. from the State College of Kentucky
1890	Awarded a Ph.D. from The Johns Hopkins University
1891	Appointed associate professor of biology at Bryn Mawr College
1904	Appointed professor of experimental zoology at Columbia University
1908	Begins work with *Drosophila* in the laboratory
1927-1928	Serves as president of the National Academy of Sciences
1928	Moves to the California Institute of Technology (Caltech) as head of the biology division
1929	Serves as president of the American Association for the Advancement of Science
1933	Awarded the Nobel Prize in Physiology or Medicine
1939	Receives the Copley Medal of the Royal Society
1942	Retires from Caltech
Dec. 4, 1945	Dies in Pasadena, California

Early Life

Thomas Hunt Morgan was born in Lexington, Kentucky, in 1866, the same year that Gregor Mendel published his observations on inheritance in the garden pea and the new science of genetics was born. The great-grandson of Francis Scott Key, Morgan was a member of a prominent aristocratic family. He developed a passion for the study of living things early in his life through his boyhood nature collections, and he later pursued a four-year program in natural history at the State College of Kentucky.

Morgan began graduate study at The Johns Hopkins University in 1886, and it was there that he developed a lifelong commitment to experimental laboratory research and a hands-on experimental approach to teaching. His research at this time focused on aspects of embryology and regeneration. After receiving his doctorate in 1890, Morgan joined the faculty of Bryn Mawr College as an associate professor of biology.

Bryn Mawr College

While Morgan was not a polished classroom lecturer, he excelled in the research laboratory, where he was always willing to provide instruction to students who were sufficiently adept to keep up with him. Possessing an acute scientific curiosity, Morgan worked with more than fifty different experimental organisms during the course of his professional life. He was one of the first scientists to demonstrate parthenogenesis (the development of an unfertilized egg) in sea urchins, and he studied the regeneration of lost or injured body parts in flatworms, jellyfish, starfish, and other marine organisms.

In 1900, Morgan returned to Naples, Italy, where had previously spent a year as a research scientist. This was just after the rediscovery of Mendel's work, and discussion there among the world's greatest biologists focused on heredity, mutation, and Charles Darwin's views on evolution. From this point on, Morgan's primary research concerns were centered on aspects of genetics and evolution and their relationship to the phenomenon of mutation.

Columbia University and the "Fly Room"

In 1904, Morgan married Lilian Vaughan Simpson, a graduate of Bryn Mawr and an accomplished biologist in her own right. They moved to New York City, where, at Columbia University, he became the country's first professor of experimental zoology. In addition to his interests in genetics and evolution, Morgan still pursued experimental work in development, embryology, and the mechanism of sex determination.

In 1908, Morgan had a graduate student work on what was to be a failed project on eye development in the fruit fly, *Drosophila melanogaster*. Morgan found, however, that the *Drosophila* stocks were easy to maintain in the laboratory, and he began to look for natural variation and new mutant characteristics in this tiny organism.

In May, 1910, Morgan found a striking new fly in his stocks—a white-eyed mutant—startlingly distinct from the other flies with deep red eyes. His elegant and detailed genetic

(Library of Congress)

analysis of the transmission of this mutant trait established the phenomenon of sex-linkage and led to the first assignment of a particular gene (white eye) to a particular chromosome (the X chromosome).

In the following years, dozens of new mutant flies showing variations in wing shape or vein pattern, body shape or color, eye shape or color, and bristle number or pattern were described, and the responsible genes were identified and mapped on one of the four chromosome pairs in *Drosophila*. Morgan coined the terms "linkage" and "crossing-over," and the units of physical distance between genes on chromosome maps are now called "morgans" in his honor.

In 1915, Morgan and three of his former students—Alfred H. Sturtevant, Calvin B. Bridges, and Hermann Joseph Muller—wrote *The Mechanism of Mendelian Heredity*. This work became the classic textbook for the new generation of geneticists and the standard to which subsequent texts ascribed. New observations from the "fly room" emerged regularly over the next decade, resulting in the understanding of other features of transmission genetics, including multiple alleles and nondisjunction.

The California Institute of Technology

In 1928, Morgan left Columbia to become the head of the biology division of the California Institute of Technology (Caltech). His mission was to organize and direct a completely new school of biology, and he did so with a clear focus on basic research, as opposed to teaching or applied research. He emphasized genetics and evolution, along with embryology, physiology, biophysics, and biochemistry, and he successfully recruited one of the most talented groups of biologists ever to work together at a single institution.

In 1933, on the one hundredth anniversary of Alfred Nobel's birth, Morgan was awarded the Nobel Prize in Physiology or Medicine for his work on the chromosome theory of inheritance, the first geneticist to be so honored. He continued his personal research up until the time of his retirement from Caltech at the age of seventy-six. Morgan died three years later in Pasadena, California.

Sex-Linked Genes and Chromosome Maps

Morgan discovered sex-linkage, a pattern of inheritance found only when a gene is located on the X chromosome. Crosses between several different mutant types showing this distinctive inheritance allowed him to construct the first genetic map.

Unlike Gregor Mendel's pea plants, the chromosomes in most animals, including fruit flies and humans, are either sex chromosomes (those involved in sex determination) or autosomes. Fruit flies have one pair of sex chromosomes—two X chromosomes for females and an X chromosome and a Y chromosome for males—and three pairs of autosomes. Genes for body functions or structures unrelated to sex determination can be located on the X chromosome, and the first of these to be described was Morgan's white-eyed (w) *Drosophila* mutant.

When Morgan mated this white-eyed male with a red-eyed female, he found that all the progeny flies were red-eyed. He allowed these progeny flies to interbreed freely and noted that their offspring appeared in an approximate 3:1 ratio, red-eyed to white-eyed. This result was consistent with Mendelian inheritance, except that all the white-eyed flies in this second generation were male. When white-eyed males were crossed with their red-eyed daughters, the progeny consisted of approximately ¼ red-eyed females, ¼ red-eyed males, ¼ white-eyed females, and ¼ white-eyed males.

Morgan interpreted his data by suggesting that the gene for eye color is on the X chromosome and that no equivalent gene exists on the Y chromosome (which is much smaller than the X). Thus, females would have two copies of the gene, whereas males would have only one. A single copy of the white-eye gene will cause the white-eye mutation in males, but females would need two copies of the recessive white-eye gene (one on each of the two X chromosomes) in order to express the trait. The crosses that Morgan performed and his interpretations are shown in the accompanying figure.

Other mutant characters showing sex-linked inheritance were soon discovered, including miniature wing (m) and yellow body (y). Morgan crossed a white-eyed, miniature-winged female with a male showing both of these dominant traits. As expected, all the male progeny showed both mutant traits, while the females had red eyes and large wings. When these were interbred, Morgan found that 63.1 percent of the offspring showed either both mutant traits or both normal traits (parental types). The remaining 36.9 percent, however, showed either white eyes or miniature wings, but not both (recombinant types).

Similar crosses involving flies with the white-eye and yellow-body traits resulted in 98.7 percent parental types and only 1.3 percent recombinant types. Morgan thus concluded that the genes for white eye and yellow body are very close to each other on the X chromosome and are therefore much less likely to be separated by a genetic exchange (cross-over) than are the genes for white eyes and miniature wings, which are separated by a greater physical distance. Morgan constructed the first chromosome map using the X chromosome in *Drosophila*, with the genes w and m separated by 36.9 map units (now called morgans) and w and y separated by only 1.3 morgans.

The discovery of sex-linkage was the conclusive evidence in support of the chromosome theory of heredity. With the procedures developed by Morgan and his colleagues, genetic maps have been constructed for thousands of experimental organisms and they remain one of the most basic and useful tools for genetic analysis.

Bibliography
Genetics. Peter Russell. Boston: Scott, Foresman, 1995.

The Mechanism of Mendelian Heredity. Thomas Hunt Morgan, Alfred H. Sturtevant, Hermann Joseph Muller, and Calvin B. Bridges. New York: Henry Holt, 1915.

Sex-Linked Inheritance in Drosophila. Thomas Hunt Morgan and Calvin B. Bridges. Washington, D.C.: Carnegie Institute, 1916.

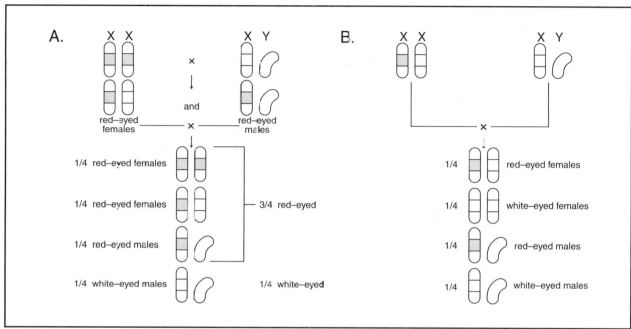

A.: A red-eyed female is crossed with a white-eyed male. The red-eyed progeny interbreed to produce offspring in a 3/4 red to 1/4 white ratio. All the white-eyed flies are male B: A white-eyed male is crossed with its red-eyed daughter, giving red-eyed and white-eyed males and females in equal proportions.

Bibliography

By Morgan

The Development of the Frog's Egg: An Introduction to Experimental Embryology, 1897

Regeneration, 1901

Evolution and Adaptation, 1903

Experimental Zoology, 1907

Heredity and Sex, 1913

The Mechanism of Mendelian Heredity, 1915 (with Alfred H. Sturtevant, Hermann Joseph Muller, and Calvin B. Bridges)

A Critique of the Theory of Evolution, 1916

Sex-Linked Inheritance in Drosophila, 1916 (with Bridges)

The Genetic and the Operative Evidence Relating to Secondary Sexual Characters, 1919

The Physical Basis of Heredity, 1919

Some Possible Bearings of Genetics on Pathology, 1922

The Third Chromosome Group of Mutant Characters of Drosophila Melanogaster, 1923 (with Bridges)

Laboratory Directions for an Elementary Course in Genetics, 1923 (with Muller, Sturtevant, and Bridges)

Human Inheritance, 1924

Evolution and Genetics, 1925

"The Genetics of *Drosophila*," *Bibliographia Genetica,* 1925 (with Bridges and Sturtevant)

The Theory of the Gene, 1926

Experimental Embryology, 1927

What Is Darwinism?, 1929

The Scientific Basis of Evolution, 1932

Embryology and Genetics, 1934

About Morgan

T. H Morgan: The Man and His Science. Garland E. Allen. Princeton, N.J.: Princeton University Press, 1978.

"Thomas Hunt Morgan." In *The Nobel Prize Winners: Physiology or Medicine,* edited by Frank N. Magill. Pasadena, Calif.: Salem Press, 1991.

Thomas Hunt Morgan, Pioneer of Genetics. Ian Shine and Sylvia Wrobel. Lexington: University Press of Kentucky, 1976.

(Jeffrey A. Knight)

Samuel F. B. Morse

Areas of Achievement: Invention and technology

Contribution: An accomplished artist and second-rate politician, Morse is best remembered for inventing the telegraph and the transmission code of dots and dashes that is named after him. This technology ushered in a new age of telecommunications.

Apr. 27, 1791	Born in Charlestown, Massachusetts
1810	Graduated from Yale College
1815	After studying art abroad, returns to New York City and paints miniature portraits
1825	Founds the National Academy of Art and Design
1832	Meets Charles Thomas Jackson and becomes interested in electromagnetism
1833	Demonstrates the first device to send signals over wires
1834	Publishes a political pamphlet arguing that the papacy and Jesuits are conspiring to subvert democracy by promoting Catholic immigration
1836 and 1841	Runs unsuccessfully for mayor of New York City
1837	Patents his telegraph system
1844	Sends the first telegraph message from Baltimore to Washington, D.C.
1854	Morse code is approved by the U.S. patent office
1861	Transcontinental telegraph service links the Atlantic and Pacific coasts
Apr. 2, 1872	Dies in New York, New York

Early Life

Samuel Finley Breese Morse was born into a well-educated and distinguished New England household on April 27, 1791. His father, the Reverend Jedidiah Morse, held national reputations both as America's leading geographer and as an outspoken, anti-Unitarian Calvinistic crusader. Samuel inherited from his father both a keen intellect and a proclivity for controversy.

From infancy, young Morse received the best educational training. Beginning school at the age of four, he later matriculated at the prestigious Phillips Academy, Andover, and then at Yale College. During his youth, however, it was drawing and art—not science and mathematics—that consumed his passion. As a junior at Yale, he began painting, and after his graduation in 1810, he traveled to England to continue his artistic studies.

From Painter to Inventor

After four years abroad, Morse returned to the states. Although gifted with artistic talent, he could not find a patron to support his romantic landscape paintings, so he turned to painting miniature portraits for a living. For Morse, this vocation was tolerable but not fully satisfying. Despite achieving some recognition as an accomplished artist and helping to establish the National Academy of Art and Design, at midlife Morse was still groping to find his genius.

In 1832, the disgruntled, forty-one-year-old painter ventured again to Europe in the hope of igniting his career. His days abroad were uneventful, but, on the return voyage, he met Charles Thomas Jackson, a laboratory scientist returning from his studies in Europe. Their exchange aboard the ship about the recently discovered principles of electromagnetism and its possible uses intrigued Morse. This memorable voyage marked the beginning of Morse's interest in telecommunications and the ending of his life as a painter.

The Birth of the Telegraph

Convinced that pulses of electrical current could convey messages over wires, an inspired and motivated Morse returned to the United States to begin work on what would become his two greatest inventions: the telegraph and

The Rise of Telegraph Technology

Morse's inventions contributed significantly to the improvement in the mode of communicating information by signals through the application of electromagnetism.

Like all great inventors, Morse relied heavily on the work of other scientists before him. In 1819, Hans Christian Ørsted discovered that a wire carrying an electric current could deflect a magnetic needle and that the direction of the deflection could be reversed with a reversal in the flow of current.

Following this discovery, other scientists such as William Sturgeon, Michael Faraday, and Joseph Henry further developed the field of electromagnetism, the branch of physics that deals with the relation between electricity and magnetism. Morse's great contribution was to invent a device that would make practical use of this new technology.

The word "telegraph" comes from the Greek words *tele*, meaning far or distant, and *graphos*, meaning to write or to signal. Telegraphy thus deals with the transmission of signals over long distances. Morse's telegraph was the first instrument to transform messages via coded signals into electrical form and transmit them reliably over long distances.

The original apparatus included a transmitter connected by wire to a receiver. The transmitter included a battery and a key that permitted the operator to connect the circuit for short or longer periods. The earliest receiver used an ink pen attached to an electromagnetic needle and spring to record on paper the messages of dots and dashes. Later, a buzzer was added so that the operator could receive the messages by sound rather than by sight.

For meaningful information to be transmitted, a code that assigned letters of the alphabet to designated patterns of dot and dash signal impulses had to be devised. Part of Morse's genius was his insight to construct a code that assigned the simplest patterns of dots and dashes to the most common letters.

Few inventions have had a profound or as immediate impact on economic, social, and even military developments as the telegraph. One day after Morse demonstrated his system, a telegram was sent from Washington, D.C., to Baltimore and a new commercial age began. Politicians also found quick use for the technology. During the 1844 Democratic Convention in Baltimore, the telegraph enabled delegates to receive immediate feedback from party leaders in Washington, D.C., regarding the nomination of a vice presidential candidate. Overnight, the ability to transmit information by electric current destroyed the tyranny of distance and altered forever the communication patterns of humankind.

Within a decade, the telegraph line expanded as special machines plowed trenches and buried lead pipes containing telegraph wires along the railways that connected America's major cities. The railroad and telegraph partnership was natural, since the railroads needed fast and reliable communication along tracks and telegraph companies needed rights-of-way that were easily and quickly accessible to repair crews.

By the time of the outbreak of the Civil War—the first major war transmitted over telegraph lines— America's railways were wired with more than 23,000 miles of cable. Five years later, a transatlantic cable linked Europe and North America. Suddenly, commercial and diplomatic exchanges, which previously required months of waiting, could be transacted with several strokes of a key.

The decline in the importance of the railroad and telegraph industries has not diminished the historic importance of Morse's invention. The telephone, television, and the Internet "information superhighway" are modern adaptations of Morse's telegraphic technology, a technology that ushered in a new age of telecommunications.

Bibliography

Samuel Morse and the Electronic age. Wilma Hays. New York: Franklin Watts, 1966.

"Technology of the Future." John Steele Gordon. *American Heritage* 44, no. 6 (October, 1993).

The Telegraph: A History of Morse's Invention and Its Predecessors in the United States. Lewis Coe. Jefferson, N.C.: McFarland, 1993.

(Library of Congress)

Morse code. Despite his minimal knowledge of electricity, Morse's work moved forward at a rapid pace. By 1837, he had developed a functional telegraph.

After spending several years perfecting the devise, Morse was ready to demonstrate it to the world. He ran cable from the nation's capital to the railroad depot in Baltimore. On May 24, 1844, Morse sent, via wire, a coded message: "What hath God wrought." His business partner, Alfred Vail, received and decoded the message and returned it to Morse. With this transmission, a new electronic age was born.

Morse the Politician
This American technological giant also contributed, although in a less commendatory way, to the political life of the nation. A vehement na-tionalist, Morse wrote numerous tracts that expressed the nativist position that Catholic immigration was threatening the American way of life. He fought fiercely to restrict Catholic immigration to the United States and even ran on the Native American ticket for the mayor of New York City.

Morse also was an outspoken antiabolitionist who lobbied against the emancipation of slaves. Fortunately, his political ideologies did not have the same impact on the course of history as did his technological inventions. Morse died in 1872 just before turning eighty-one.

Bibliography
By Morse
Foreign Conspiracy Against the Liberties of the United States, 1835
Imminent Dangers to the Free Institutions of the United States Through Foreign Immigration, and the Present State of the Naturalization Laws, 1835
An Argument on the Ethical Position of Slavery in the Social System and Its Relation to the Politics of the Day, 1863
Examination of the Telegraphic Apparatus and the Processes in Telegraphy, 1869
Samuel F. B. Morse: His Letters and Journals, 1914

About Morse
The American Leonardo: A Life of Samuel F. B. Morse. Carleton Mabee. New York: Alfred A. Knopf, 1943.
Samuel F. B. Morse. Paul J. Staiti. Cambridge, Mass.: Cambridge University Press, 1989.
Samuel F. B. Morse. William Kloss. New York: H. N. Abrams/National Museum of American Art, Smithsonian Institution, 1988.
Samuel F. B. Morse and American Democratic Art. Oliver W. Larkin. Boston: Little, Brown, 1954.

(Terry D. Bilhartz)

Rudolf Ludwig Mössbauer

Areas of Achievement: Chemistry and physics

Contribution: At a quite young age, Mössbauer was awarded the Nobel Prize in Physics for developing the technique that allows resonance absorption of gamma rays to be studied. This method bears the name Mössbauer spectroscopy.

Jan. 31, 1929	Born in Munich, Germany
1952	Earns a bachelor's degree from the University of Munich
1955	Earns a master's degree at Munich while teaching mathematics there
1957	Discovers the Mössbauer effect while at the Max Planck Institute for Medical Research in Heidelberg
1958	Receives a doctoral degree from Munich
1960	Wins the Science Award of the Research Corporation of America
1961	Awarded the Röntgen Prize of the University of Giessen
1961	Receives the Elliot-Gressen Medal of the Franklin Institute
1961	Awarded the Nobel Prize in Physics
1961-1964	Joins the faculty of the California Institute of Technology (Caltech)
1965-1971	Becomes part of the faculty of the University of Munich
1972-1977	Serves as director of the Institut Laure-Langevin in Grenoble, France
1977	Returns to the faculty of the University of Munich

Early Life

Rudolf Ludwig Mössbauer (pronounced "MURS-bow-ur") was born in Munich, Germany, on January 31, 1929, to Ludwig and Erna (Ernst) Mössbauer. His father was a photo technician, and, upon his completion of high school in 1948, Mössbauer worked at the Rodenstock Optics Factory. This time evidently convinced him that further education would be valuable, and he entered the University of Munich, from which he was granted a bachelor of science degree in 1952, a master's in technical physics in 1955, and a doctorate in physics in 1958.

While working on his master's degree, Mössbauer served as an instructor of mathematics. During the course for his doctorate, he developed the system of measurement now known as the Mössbauer effect. The time period between 1955 and 1957 found Mössbauer, still under the eye of his mentor Heinz Maier-

(AP/Wide World Photos)

One of the Most Precise Measurements Ever Made

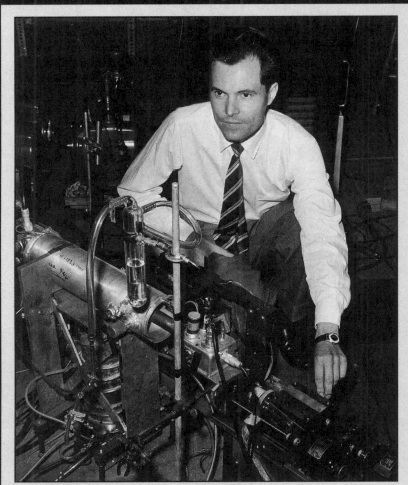

Mössbauer displays an automatic counter that records data from a velocity spectrometer, used to study the Mössbauer effect with rare earth elements. (AP/Wide World Photos)

bauer's discovery paved the way.

Mössbauer realized that the difficulty in matching the frequencies was caused by the recoil of the emitting nucleus. The energy was divided between the gamma ray and the recoiling nucleus, so there was not one frequency of the emitted gamma ray but many. This change in frequency caused by the gamma ray is called the Doppler effect. In order to obtain recoilless emission, Mössbauer used a heavy iridium nucleus in a solid and cooled the sample to the temperature of liquid air (–185 degrees Celsius). Under these conditions, he was able to limit the motion of the atoms and to obtain recoilless emission from about 1 percent of the nuclei.

Although the Mössbauer effect is small, it is measurable by moving the detector toward or away from the sample at a velocity of a few millimeters per second until the resonant condition is observed. Applications of this method range from its use in environmental studies to its assistance in archaeology as well as its use in theoretical studies.

The extreme sharpness of the transition and the accuracy in observing small energy differences make the Mössbauer effect an important tool to study the solid state.

When a radio is tuned correctly, the frequency of the emitted radiation and that of the receiver are exactly matched. Such a match occurs when the source and the receiver are in resonance. The resonance absorption of radiation from lower energy segments of the electromagnetic spectrum has been studied since the late nineteenth century. The same basic techniques applied to gamma radiation failed, however, until Möss-

Bibliography

Applications of Mössbauer Spectroscopy to Environmental and Geochemical Studies. Takeshi Tominga and Yoshitaka Minai. Newark, N.J.: Gordon & Breach, 1984

Chemical Mössbauer Spectroscopy. R. H. Herber, ed. New York: Plenum Press, 1984.

Industrial Applications of the Mössbauer Effect. Gary J. Long. New York: Plenum Press, 1987.

Mössbauer Spectroscopy. N. N. Greenwood and T. C. Gibb. London: Chapman and Hall, 1971.

Mössbauer Spectroscopy and Its Applications. T. E. Crenshaw et al. New York: Cambridge University Press, 1986.

Leibnitz from the University of Munich, serving as a research assistant at the Max Planck Institute for Medical Research in Heidelberg. It was in this setting that he worked with the Mössbauer effect.

The Nobel Prize

Seldom in the history of the Nobel Prizes has the award been made to a person as young or for work accomplished as recently as in the case of Mössbauer. He shared the 1961 prize in physics with Robert Hofstadler when he was only thirty-two years old and for a piece of scientific discovery that he had made only four years previous to that date. Both of these factors clearly indicate the special significance of this scientist's life.

Atomic scientists thought that Mössbauer was wrong when he first published his results, but soon others confirmed and reproduced the effect. In 1960, a meeting of about a hundred scientists was called to discuss the possible applications of this new knowledge to a wide variety of fields. Included in these applications was the first verification of one of the basic postulates of Albert Einstein's general theory of relativity.

Continuing Activity

For decades, Mössbauer remained active at the University of Munich, with the exception of two relatively short periods. Budget cuts and administrative obstacles prompted him to join the California Institute of Technology (Caltech) as a research associate and guest professor of physics between 1961 and 1964. The year 1965 found Mössbauer back at home at Munich, however, where he continued until leaving in 1972 to become the director of the Institut Laure-Langevin in Grenoble, France.

Mössbauer again returned to Munich in 1977 and remained there. He actively conducted physics research and lived in Munich with his wife, Elizabeth, whom he married in 1956; the couple had two children.

Bibliography

By Mössbauer

"Recoilless Nuclear Resonance Absorption of Gamma Radiation," *Science*, 1962

"General Aspects of Nuclear Hyperfine Interactions in Salts of the Rare Earth" in *Proceedings of the Third International Conference on the Mössbauer Effect, Ithaca, New York*, 1963

"Gamma-Resonance and X-Ray Investigations of Slow Motions in Macromolecular Systems," *Hyperfine Interactions*, 1987

About Mössbauer

"Rudolf L. Mössbauer." In *Current Biography Yearbook: 1962*, edited by Charles Moriwitz. New York: H. W. Wilson, 1962.

"Rudolf L. Mössbauer." In *Nobel Prize Winners: An H. W. Wilson Biographical Dictionary*, edited by Tyler Wasson, ed. New York: H. W. Wilson, 1987.

"Rudolf L. Mössbauer." Robert L. Weber. In *Pioneers of Science: Nobel Prize Winners in Physics*. London: Institute of Physics, 1987.

(Kenneth H. Brown)

Sir Nevill Mott

Areas of Achievement: Mathematics and physics

Contribution: Drawing on the laws of quantum mechanics, Mott increased immeasurably the knowledge about solid-state physics. His work on conduction in solids contributed to microelectronics.

Sept. 30, 1905	Born in Leeds, West Yorkshire, England
1928	Earns a B.A. in mathematics from Cambridge University
1928	Studies physics under Niels Bohr in Copenhagen
1933	Appointed Professor of Theoretical Physics at Bristol
1936	Elected a Fellow of the Royal Society of London
1948	Becomes chair of the physics department at Bristol
1948	Appointed director of the Henry Herbert Wills Physical Laboratories at Bristol
1950	Named president of the International Union of Pure and Applied Physics
1954	Appointed Cavendish Professor of Physics at Cambridge
1962	Knighted
1972	Awarded the Copley Medal of the Royal Society of London
1974	Named Emeritus Cavendish Professor of Physics
1977	Awarded the Nobel Prize in Physics
1994	Receives an honorary doctorate in science from Cambridge
Aug. 8, 1996	Dies in Milton Keynes, Buckinghamshire, England

Early Life

Influenced greatly by his parents, Nevill Francis Mott decided early in life to be a physicist. Educated as physicists, both of his parents had worked in the Cavendish Laboratory at Cambridge University under Sir Joseph John Thomson, the discoverer of the electron. When Mott was born in Leeds, England, in 1905, his father switched to a career in science education and his mother became involved in social causes.

Mott always wanted to be a theoretical physicist, but understanding the importance of mathematics to that professsion, he received a scholarship in mathematics from Cambridge. After earning his B.A. in 1928, he studied at Copenhagen University under the great quantum physicist Niels Bohr. Mott's closest friend during his year in Copenhagen was George Gamow, the brilliant Russian nuclear physicist.

Although Mott never received a doctorate, his burning desire to be a physicist—coupled

(The Nobel Foundation)

Defects in Crystals

A theory of solids requires that the crystal form of any solid matter may be deduced from the properties of its individual atoms. Mott contended that atomic disorientations in ionic crystals greatly influence their electrical conductivity.

The atoms of solid material such as ionic crystals arrange themselves in a regular geometric pattern if they are perfect. The resulting structure is known as the crystal lattice. Assuming that all ions occupy their proper places in the lattice, the basic atomic pattern replicates itself throughout the molecular structure of the crystal.

Perfect crystals do not exist. Lattice defects are always present in both the natural and processed state. Defects within the lattice show up as nonuniform shapes and arrangements.

Mott contended that imperfect ionic crystals are better electrical conduits than ideal crystals. He stated that the energy levels required for conduction in ionic crystal are significantly influenced by the number of lattice defects, including not only the absence of atoms (vacancies) or the presence of interstitial atoms but also the density of dislocations.

He showed that when a crystal is deformed under a sufficiently large applied strain, some deformation remains after the strain is removed. The result is that the crystal has been plastically deformed. Just as folding a carpet once reduces the effort required to pull it across a floor, so is it easier to affect conduction in a crystal when a dislocation occurs on one side of a crystal and moves through it. The fold in the carpet is like the dislocation in the crystal.

Mott's theory of dislocations demonstrated that this sliding process, referred to as a slip, results in a plastic deformation that is not homogeneous—only a relatively few of the total amount of atoms take part in the slip process—compared to elastic deformation, which affects all atoms in a crystal. A crystal deformed elastically returns to its original state when the applied strain is removed.

Mott showed that the atomic interpretation of plastic flow cannot be explained on the basis of a perfect lattice. Plastic deformation is not an extension of the theory of elasticity. The dislocation density of a crystal influences significantly its electrical properties. Electron mobility depends partially on how the electrons are scattered by the concentration of dislocation lines. Despite the fact that only a relatively few atoms are involved, concentrations may amount to more than 100 million per square centimeter in ionic crystals.

Bibliography

Crystals, Electrons, Transistors. Michael Eckert and Helmut Schubert. New York: American Institute of Physics, 1990.

Solid State Physics. A. J. Dekker. Englewood Cliffs, N.J.: 1957.

Structure. William G. Moffat, George W. Pearsall, and John Wulff. Vol. 1 in *The Structure and Properties of Materials.* New York: John Wiley & Sons, 1964.

with the good fortune to be associated with brilliant physicists early in life—contributed to his prolific scientific output. Mott was only twenty-five when his first book was published. By the age of thirty, he had written two more books.

Before the War

After returning from Copenhagen, Mott accepted a position as a theoretical physicist at Manchester University, where he worked for a year under Sir Lawrence Bragg, a Nobel laureate. From 1930 to 1933, Mott continued his research at Cambridge into the nature and behavior of atomic and subatomic particles in solids. He usually tried to summarize his research by writing a book. *Theory of Atomic Collisions*, published in 1934, summed up his work at Cambridge University.

Mott left Cambridge in 1933 to spend the next twenty-one years, except for the war years, at Bristol University, where he played a central role in the development of solid-state physics. His work on the properties of metal and electronic processes in crystals contributed greatly to the advancement of semiconductor technology during a period when the transistor was invented. Mott tried to develop a unified interpretation of the principal processes in electronics in order that science could become a useful tool for electronic technologists.

In 1938, Mott published a seminal paper on semiconductors, "Note on the Contact Between a Metal and an Insulator or Semiconductor" in *Proceedings of the Cambridge Philosophical Society*. In 1939, he continued his preoccupation with metal contacts in the paper "The Theory of Crystal Rectifiers" in *Proceedings of the Royal Society*. In 1948, with N. Cabrera, Mott published "Theory of Oxidation of Metals" in *Report on Progress in Physics*, describing how certain nonmetallic materials exhibit metallic behavior when under sufficient pressure. This type of transition became known in scientific circles as the "Mott transition."

The War Years
From 1939 to 1945, Mott worked as a civilian for the British military. Although he was a scientist, he became an engineer when given problems to solve in radar and ordnance technology. When Germany surrendered, the Soviet Academy of Science invited Mott and other leading British scientists to Moscow for a victory celebration.

Back to Bristol
In 1945, Mott returned to Bristol University and began spending less time on research and more time on educational administration. He became interested in the social control of nuclear energy and was chosen in 1946 to be the first president of the newly formed Atomic Scientist's Association. It was also at this time that he developed his lifelong interest in scientific publishing.

Return to Cambridge
Mott returned to Cambridge University in 1954 to become Cavendish Professor of Physics and director of the Cavendish Laboratory. Mott's three immediate predecessors were Thomson, Ernest Rutherford, and Bragg, all Nobel Prize winners. Holders of the Cavendish Chair represented the best of Britain's scientists.

Field of Research
In 1965, Mott started research in a new solid-state field, amorphous semiconductors. Using his earlier work on metal-insulator transitions, his pioneering research on the behavior of noncrystalline or glassy semiconductors led to major contributions in solar energy. Mott received the Nobel Prize in Physics in 1977 for this work. Two books summed up his research, *Electronic Processes in Non-Crystalline Materials* in 1971 and *Metal-Insulator Transitions* in 1974.

Mott was knighted in 1962. He died in 1996 at the age of ninety.

Bibliography
By Mott
An Outline of Wave Mechanics, 1930
The Theory of Atomic Collisions, 1934 (with H. S. W. Massey)
The Theory of the Properties of Metals and Alloys, 1936 (with Harry Jones)
"Note on the Contact Between a Metal and an Insulator or Semiconductor," *Proceedings of the Cambridge Philosophical Society*, 1938
"The Theory of Crystal Rectifiers," *Proceedings of the Royal Society*, 1939
Electronic Processes in Ionic Crystals, 1940 (with R. W. Gurney)
Wave Mechanics and Its Applications, 1948 (with I. N. Sneddon)
"Theory of Oxidation of Metals," *Report on Progress in Physics*, 1948 (with N. Cabrera)
Elements of Wave Mechanics, 1952
Atomic Structure and the Strength of Metals, 1956
Electronic Processes in Non-Crystalline Materials, 1971, rev. ed. 1979 (with E. A. Davis)
Elementary Quantum Mechanics, 1972
Metal-Insulator Transitions, 1974
A Life in Science, 1986
Sir Nevill Mott: Sixty-five Years in Physics, 1995 (as editor, with A. S. Alexandrov)

About Mott
McGraw-Hill Modern Scientists and Engineers. 3 vols. New York: McGraw-Hill, 1980.
"The 1977 Nobel Prize in Physics." Martin L. Cohen and L. M. Falicov. *Science* (November 18, 1977).
"Sir Nevill Mott." In *The Nobel Prize Winners: Physics*, edited by Frank N. Magill. Pasadena, Calif.: Salem Press, 1989.

(Philip N. Seidenberg)

Hermann Joseph Muller

Areas of Achievement: Biology, cell biology, and genetics

Contribution: Muller discovered the phenomenon of mutagenesis and designed an experiment that proved that new genetic mutations could be induced by radiation (X rays).

Dec. 21, 1890	Born in New York, New York
1910	Earns a B.A. from Columbia University
1915	Awarded a Ph.D. from Columbia
1915	Serves as assistant professor of biology at the William Marsh Rice Institute in Houston, Texas
1918	Named assistant professor of zoology at Columbia
1920	Moves to the University of Texas in Austin
1932	Awarded a Guggenheim Fellowship for study in Berlin
1933	Takes a position as a research scientist at the Institute of Genetics in Leningrad, Soviet Union
1937	Moves to the Institute of Animal Genetics at the University of Edinburgh
1940	Returns to United States to teach at Amherst College
1945	Named a professor of zoology at Indiana University
1946	Receives the Nobel Prize in Physiology or Medicine
1949	Acts as president of the American Society of Human Genetics
1964	Retires from Indiana University
Apr. 5, 1967	Dies in Indianapolis, Indiana

Early Life

Growing up in a middle-class neighborhood of German immigrants in Manhattan, Hermann Joseph Muller developed an inquiring, scientific mind. He excelled as an undergraduate at Columbia University and was handpicked by the renowned geneticist Thomas Hunt Morgan to pursue graduate work in his laboratory.

As a member of the group studying the fruit fly (*Drosophila melanogaster*) in Morgan's "fly room," Muller became a major contributor to the chromosome theory of heredity, and he was a coauthor of the first great textbook of modern genetics, *The Mechanism of Mendelian Heredity* (1915), with Morgan, Alfred H. Sturtevant, and Calvin B. Bridges.

Muller's early work with fruit flies was on "chief" genes and modifiers. These are more complex examples of Mendelian inheritance, involving two or more genes for a single trait. His careful elucidation of the inheritance patterns helped to restore faith in Darwinism, since it provided a genetic basis for the small fluctuations in character variation necessary to serve as the raw material for natural selection.

Mutation Studies

In 1920, Muller accepted a position as assistant professor of zoology at the University of Texas in Austin. He believed that the major problems in transmission genetics had been solved, since the chromosome theory and Mendelism had successfully merged. He believed that the future of genetics lay in a new direction—a focus on the nature of the gene and the nature of mutation.

Muller began working with radium and X rays, and he developed an international reputation in 1927 when he presented his work on X-ray-induced mutations at the Fifth International Congress of Genetics in Berlin, Germany. He showed not only that single gene mutations were induced by radiation but that macrolesions (chromosome breaks and rearrangements) could result as well.

To the U.S.S.R. and Back

Muller developed a social idealism as a youth that led to his acceptance of communism under Vladimir Ilich Lenin as an effective approach for addressing poverty, racial prejudice, and worker exploitation. Depressed by a failing marriage, conflicts with his colleagues in Texas, and harassment by the Federal Bureau of Investigation (FBI), Muller left Texas in 1932 to study in Berlin on a Guggenheim Fellow-

ship. He moved to the Institute of Genetics in Leningrad the following year and remained in the Soviet Union until 1937.

Witnessing at first hand the horrors of the police state under Joseph Stalin and the de-

The Induction of Mutations by X Rays

Muller demonstrated that X rays could alter genes permanently, resulting in the production of new, heritable mutations. Radiation was the first physical or chemical mutagen to be discovered.

Muller performed three quite different experiments using three distinct genetic strategies in the fruit fly, *Drosophila melanogaster*, to demonstrate the mutagenic effects of X rays. One of these is shown in some detail in the accompanying diagram.

Muller took male flies exhibiting the sex-linked recessive trait of bobbed bristles and sub-

jected them to varying doses of X radiation. These flies were mated to females showing three different sex-linked recessive mutations. As expected, all the female progeny were nonmutant in appearance. The sons of many such females were then closely examined.

If the X rays had induced a recessive lethal mutation somewhere on the X chromosome in the sperm cells of the irradiated males, then no males showing bobbed bristles should result in the final mating. Conversely, if there were a spontaneous lethal mutation in the maternally derived X chromosome, all the males from the final mating should show bobbed bristles. Muller found that as the X-ray dosage increased, so too did the mutation frequency, and essentially all the new mutants were of paternal origin.

The change in mutation frequency was dramatic—a 15,000 percent increase over spontaneous rates when X rays were used. The X rays were also shown to induce many new visible mutations. From 1910 to 1926, about two hundred different mutations had been found by all *Drosophila* workers combined; using X rays, Muller found half that number by himself in less than two months.

Muller's outspoken warnings concerning the mutagenic dangers of radiation were instrumental to the more conservative use of X rays in medicine and ultimately to the development of the international nuclear test ban treaty.

sc=scute bristles; v=vermillion eye; f=forked bristles
bb=bobbed bristles; +=nonmutant

If, for a given fly and its descendants, an induced or spontaneous lethal mutation occurs in the paternal X chromosome (shaded), no third-generation males of type B will result. If a spontaneous lethal mutation occurs in an original maternal X chromosome, then no third-generation males of type A will result.

Bibliography
"Artificial Transmutation of the Gene." Hermann Joseph Muller. *Science* 66 (1927).

Genes, Radiation, and Society: The Life and Work of H. J. Muller. Elof Axel Carlson. Ithaca, N.Y.: Cornell University Press, 1981.

An Introduction to Genetic Analysis. Anthony Griffiths, J. H. Miller, D. T. Suzuki, R. C. Lewontin, and W. M. Gelbart. New York: W. H. Freeman, 1993.

struction of the study of genetics in the Soviet Union with the rise to power of Trofim Lysenko, Muller left in despair in 1937. He renounced communism as a political system, and, after brief stints at the University of Edinburgh and Amherst College in Massachusetts, he settled into what would be his most permanent position as professor of zoology at Indiana University.

The Nobel Prize

Muller continued his studies on mutation and mutagenesis and in 1946 won the Nobel Prize in Physiology or Medicine for his work on X rays as a mutagen (mutation-causing agent). He was committed to the social implications and applications of his work, and he used his fame as a Nobel laureate to educate the public about the dangers of radiation.

In other areas of social reform, Muller met with mixed success. He championed sexual equality, day care, and positive eugenics, advocating sperm banks and artificial insemination as voluntary reproductive options. He was an atheist and a humanist who believed that humans had the right to plan their own destiny.

Muller retired from Indiana University in 1964 and died in 1967 in Indianapolis at the age of seventy-six.

Bibliography

By Muller

The Mechanism of Mendelian Heredity, 1915 (with Thomas Hunt Morgan, Alfred H. Sturtevant, and Calvin B. Bridges)

"Artificial Transmutation of the Gene," *Science*, 1927

"The Production of Mutations by X-Rays," *Proceedings of the National Academy of Sciences*, 1928

Out of the Night: A Biologist's View of the Future, 1935

Bibliography on the Genetics of Drosophila, 1939

Genetics, Medicine, and Man, 1947 (with C. C. Little and L. H. Snyder)

"The Nature of the Genetic Effects Produced by Radiation" and "The Manner of Production of Mutations by Radiation" in *Radiation Biology*, 1954 (A. Hollaender, ed.)

(The Nobel Foundation)

"Radiation and Human Mutation," *Scientific American*, 1955

Studies in Genetics: The Selected Papers of H. J. Muller, 1962

About Muller

Biological Effects of Radiations. D. S. Grosch and L. E. Hopwood. New York: Academic Press, 1979.

Genes, Radiation, and Society: The Life and Work of H. J. Muller. Elof Axel Carlson. Ithaca, N.Y.: Cornell University Press, 1981.

"Hermann Joseph Muller." In *The Nobel Prize Winners: Physiology or Medicine*, edited by Frank N. Magill. Pasadena, Calif.: Salem Press, 1991.

Nobel Lectures in Molecular Biology, 1933-1975. New York: Elsevier, 1977.

(Jeffrey A. Knight)

Robert S. Mulliken

Areas of Achievement: Chemistry and physics

Contribution: One of the first scientists to apply quantum physics to the study of chemical bonds in molecules, Mulliken won the Nobel Prize in Chemistry for his development of the molecular orbital method.

June 7, 1896	Born in Newburyport, Massachusetts
1921	Earns a Ph.D. in chemistry from the University of Chicago
1921	Named a National Research Fellow at the University of Chicago
1923	Becomes a National Research Fellow at Harvard University
1926	Joins the faculty of the physics department at New York University
1928	Becomes a professor of physics at the University of Chicago
1930, 1932-1933	Visits Europe on a Guggenheim Fellowship
1932-1935	Publishes a series of papers on the electronic structures of polyatomic molecules and valence
1936	Elected to the National Academy of Sciences
1942-1945	Directs the information division of the Manhattan Project at the University of Chicago
1952-1954	Appointed a Fulbright Scholar at Oxford University
1955	Named science attaché to the U.S. embassy in London, England
1966	Wins the Nobel Prize in Chemistry
Oct. 31, 1986	Dies in Arlington, Virginia

(The Nobel Foundation)

Early Life

Robert Sanderson Mulliken, the son of a chemist, was reared in the colonial seaport town of Newburyport, Massachusetts. He expressed an early interest in science generally and chemistry in particular. With a scholarship from the Wheelwright Fund, he studied chemistry at the Massachusetts Institute of Technology (MIT), graduating in 1917.

Mulliken took a wartime job at the American University in Washington, D.C., studying poison gases under the supervision of James B. Conant, but a laboratory accident cut short this work. He was employed briefly at the New Jersey Zinc Company following the war.

Mulliken began graduate studies in chemistry at the University of Chicago in 1919. He worked with William Harkins on problems of isotope separation and, after receiving his Ph.D. in 1921, continued this investigation with a National Research Council Fellowship. In order to study isotope effects in the spectra of molecules, Mulliken went to Harvard University in 1923. There, he became proficient in the experimental techniques of spectroscopy and in the new theoretical advances in quantum physics.

In 1925, he made his first trip to Europe, where he met many of the leading physicists and chemists of the day. He made another trip to Europe in the summer of 1927 and returned twice as a Guggenheim Fellow in the early 1930's. This exposure to the newest advances in quantum science helped Mulliken to develop his own important ideas about the nature of molecular bonding.

Research and Professional Activities

From 1926 to 1928, Mulliken was an assistant professor of physics at New York University. In 1928, he returned to the University of Chicago as a member of the physics department. Mulliken's movement from chemistry to physics and back again reflects the special nature of his research interests, which used physical techniques to investigate chemical problems.

Mulliken's study of the behavior of electrons in molecules produced a particularly important series of papers published from 1932 to 1935 that set out Mulliken's major contribution to the development of the molecular orbital theory. This theory, along with a rival model

known as the valence bond theory, attempted to use quantum mechanics to explain molecular structure.

During World War II, Mulliken suspended his scientific research to assume the post of director of the information division for the Manhattan Project, a group of scientists trying to develop an atomic bomb. In this role, Mulliken was involved in some of the earliest evaluations by scientists of the prospects for the future uses of nuclear weapons and nuclear power.

Mulliken continued to work in the field of molecular science into the 1980's, publishing more than two hundred papers during his career. He received most of the major awards in his field, including the Nobel Prize in Chemistry in 1966.

Personal Activities

Mulliken married Mary Helen Von Noé in 1929. They had two daughters, Lucia Maria and Valerie Noé. He maintained a strong interest in the role of science in society, demonstrated by his active participation in the American Association of Scientific Workers during the 1930's and his role as the science attaché to the U.S. embassy in London in 1955.

Mulliken died in 1986 in Virginia at the age of ninety.

Molecular Orbitals

The molecular orbital model helps to explain the behavior of electrons in molecules.

Mulliken was one of several scientists to advance the molecular orbital model, which tries to explain the behavior of electrons and atoms in molecules using the methods of quantum physics. A rival theory, advanced about the same time by Linus Pauling and others, was called the valence bond theory.

The valence bond theory treated molecules as made of interacting but individual atoms, each maintaining its own electrons. The molecular orbital theory treats the electrons of a molecule as spread out in wave functions, or orbitals, over all the atoms in the chemical bonds of a molecule.

In molecular orbital theory, each state of the molecule is characterized by an electron configu-

ration giving the number and kind of molecular orbitals and how many electrons are in each one. Molecular orbitals each have a particular mathematical form, which can be classified according to the symmetries of a molecule.

The molecular orbital theory became increasingly valuable to scientists as computers made the solution of its complex mathematical equations possible.

Bibliography

The Modern Structural Theory of Organic Chemistry. Lloyd N. Ferguson. Englewood Cliffs, N.J.: Prentice Hall, 1963.

"Molecular Orbitals." Robert S. Mulliken. *Encyclopedic Dictionary of Physics* 4 (1962).

"Spectroscopy, Molecular Orbitals, and Chemical Bonding." Robert S. Mulliken. *Science* (1967).

Bibliography
By Mulliken
"Electronic Structures of Polyatomic Molecules and Valence," *Physical Review*, 1932-1933 (parts 1-4)
"Electronic Structures of Polyatomic Molecules and Valence," *Journal of Chemical Physics*, 1933-1935 (parts 5-14)
Selected Papers of R. S. Mulliken, 1975 (D. A. Ramsay and J. Hinzel, eds.)
Life of a Scientist: An Autobiographical Account of the Development of Molecular Orbital Theory, 1989 (Bernard J. Ransil, ed.)

About Mulliken
Nobel Laureates in Chemistry, 1901-1992. Laylin K. James, ed. Washington, D.C.: American Chemical Society, 1993.
"Robert S. Mulliken." In *The Nobel Prize Winners: Chemistry*, edited by Frank N. Magill. Pasadena, Calif.: Salem Press, 1990.

(Loren Butler Feffer)

Karl Wilhelm von Nägeli

Areas of Achievement: Botany and cell biology
Contribution: Nägeli made important discoveries about anatomy and cell structure in plants.

Mar. 27, 1817	Born in Kilchberg, near Zurich, Switzerland
1840	Earns a doctorate in botany from the University of Geneva
1842	Works with Matthias Jakob Schleiden
1844	Discovers the sexual cells of ferns
1845	Commences a study of apical growth in plants
1845-1852	Works at the University of Zurich as a privatdozent (untenured lecturer) and an assistant professor
1852	Named a full professor at the University of Freiberg
1857	Accepts the chair in botany at the University of Munich
1858	Demonstrates the importance of the sequence of cell divisions in determining plant forms
1858	Presents his micelle theory of starch grain structure
1861	Reports that starch grains and cell walls assume new positions as a result of external stimuli
1884	Publishes *Mechanisch-physiologische Theorie der Abstammungslehre* (mechanical-physiological theory of evolution)
1890	Celebrates the fiftieth anniversary of his doctorate
May 10, 1891	Dies in Munich, Germany

Early Life

Karl Wilhelm von Nägeli (pronounced "NAY-guh-lee"), the son of a physician, grew up near Zurich, Switzerland, and attended school there, both at the Zurich Gymnasium and at the University of Zurich.

Initially a medical student, Nägeli gave up the study of medicine in 1839 and transferred to the University of Geneva to study botany under Alphonse de Candolle. In 1840, he received his doctorate.

After his graduation, he spent the summer semester at the University of Berlin, where he studied the philosophy of Georg Wilhelm Friedrich Hegel. Although Nägeli later claimed that he had not been influenced by Hegel's thought, his work is characterized by a search for universally applicable laws very much characteristic of Hegel's philosophy.

Early Research

In the autumn of 1842, Nägeli traveled from Berlin to the University of Jena, where he worked with Matthias Jakob Schleiden. Together, they published a short-lived scientific journal.

Under Schleiden's influence, Nägeli sought to define certain philosophical truths about the nature of science and its reliance on universal laws over the accumulation of data. This perspective, however, made his early work on cell division more difficult.

Nevertheless, Nägeli did make the discovery that during cell division, the cell wall that forms between two resulting daughter cells is the result of the division, not the cause.

Studies in Plant Anatomy

Starting in 1845 at Jena and ending in 1858 at the University of Munich, Nägeli studied apical growth and tissue formation in plants. In these studies, he introduced the concept of the meristem, a group of plant cells always capable of division. From this, he deduced the significance of the apical cells (those at the point of initial growth). Nägeli demonstrated the importance of the sequence of cell division in determining the form of a plant's parts. He was able to represent this pattern mathematically, an expression of his belief in universal natural laws.

Extending these insights, Nägeli made the distinction between the formative tissues of plants, which actively multiply, and the structural tissues, which no longer multiply.

Apical Cells and Plant Growth

All cells in a plant derive from a single source, the foundation cell. Nägeli investigated the formation of tissues in the stems and roots of plants, using mosses because of their simple structures.

In his study of growth in plants, Nägeli examined apical cells (those found in roots and stems), which are the parts of plants that are actively growing. Nägeli traced all the various tissue and organs in a cell lineage to an apical cell.

Extending these studies to vascular plants and flowering plants, he made the distinction between formative tissues—which he divided into cambia (a layer of formative cells between the wood and the bark in dicotyledonous plants) and meristems (undifferentiated plant tissue consisting of actively growing and dividing cells that give rise to various tissues)—and structural tissues, which were no longer growing.

In the stems and roots of plants, Nägeli found a line of cells that did not change during growth and development. He traced these cells back to the zygote of the plant. These primordial cells were unaltered during the course of the plant's life and represented its original inheritance from its parents.

This research was a major contribution to plant anatomy and had a profound impact on contemporary botanists.

Bibliography

Anatomy of the Dicotyledons: Leaves, Stem, and Wood in Relation to Taxonomy, with Notes on Economic Uses. C. R. Metcalfe. Oxford, England: Oxford University Press, 1950.

Botanical Microtechnique. John Eugene Sass. Ames: Iowa State College Press, 1958.

Plant Anatomy. A. Fahn. 4th ed. Oxford, England: Pergamon Press, 1990.

Later Life

In 1858, Nägeli made a significant contribution to the knowledge of the microscopic structure of cells with his micelle theory of cell structure. This theory founded a tradition of investigating the ultrastructure of plants in Germany and Switzerland and sparked debates that lasted into the early twentieth century.

In 1884, Nägeli published *Mechanisch-physiologische Theorie von Abstammungslehre*, in which he developed the idea that the nutritive trophoplasm and the hereditary idioplasm found in developing embryos are different substances. He noted that spermatozoa are almost completely lacking in trophoplasm, while egg cells contain a considerable amount of it. Since paternal and maternal characteristics are passed on equally, the idioplasm must carry hereditary information. Other biologists, notably August Weismann and Oscar Hertwig, developed this idea in detail.

It was to Nägeli that Gregor Mendel sent his paper "Verusche über Pflanzenhybriden" (1864; "Experiments on Plant Hybrids," 1966), which contained Mendel's laws of heredity. Nägeli, who believed that science operated through universal laws, thought Mendel's statistical details to be of empirical value only, with little utility to science. Nägeli did not, as is often claimed, recommend that Mendel stop experimenting with peas and start working with hawkweed, a plant unsuited to his experiments.

Nägeli celebrated the fiftieth anniversary of his doctoral degree a year before he died, an active scientist and theoretician until the end.

Bibliography

By Nägeli

Das Mikroskop: Theorie und Anwendung desselben, 1867 (2 vols.; with S. Schwendener; *The Microscope in Theory and Practice*, 1887)

Mechanisch-physiologische Theorie der Abstammungslehre, 1884

Die Hieracien Mittel Europas: Monographische Bearbeitung der Piloselloiden mit besonderer Berücksichtigung der mitteleuropaischen Sippen, 1885-1889 (2 vols.; with A. Peters)

"Die Micellartheorie von Carl Nägeli: Auszüge aus den grundlegenden Originalarbeiten Nägelis, Zusammenfassung und kurze Geschichte der Micellartheorie" in *Ostwald's Klassiker der exakten Wissenschaften*, 1908 (Albert Frey, ed.)

About Nägeli

"Carl Wilhelm von Nägeli." D. H. Scott. *Nature* 44 (1891).

"Naegeli, Carl Wilhelm von." Robert Olby. In *Dictionary of Scientific Biography*. Charles Coulston Gillispie, ed. Vol. 9. New York: Charles Scribner's Sons, 1974.

(Christopher S. W. Koehler)

(National Library of Medicine)

Yoichiro Nambu

Area of Achievement: Physics

Contribution: An influential theoretical physicist, Nambu made major contributions to the Standard Model, which accounts for the fundamental interactions between elementary particles.

Jan. 18, 1921	Born in Tokyo, Japan
1942	Earns a B.S. at the University of Tokyo
1950	Becomes a professor of physics at Osaka City University
1952	Earns a Ph.D. in physics at Tokyo
1952-1954	Joins the Institute for Advanced Study in Princeton, New Jersey
1956-1991	Serves as a professor at the University of Chicago
1970	Awarded the American Physical Society's Dannie Heineman Prize
1971	Named Distinguished Service Professor at Chicago
1971	Elected to the National Academy of Sciences and the American Academy of Arts and Sciences
1976	Receives the University of Miami's J. Robert Oppenheimer Prize
1978	Named to the Order of Culture by the Japanese government
1982	Given the National Medal of Science
1984	Becomes an honorary member of the Japan Academy
1985	Wins the Max Planck Medal of the German Physical Society
1986	Awarded the P. A. M. Dirac Medal of the International Center for Theoretical Physics in Trieste, Italy
1994	Wins the Wolf Prize in Physics

(University of Chicago)

Early Life

Yoichiro Nambu spent his youth in Fukui, a small city in Japan, where his father was a teacher of English and literature at a girls' school. The family moved there from Tokyo in 1923 after a huge earthquake had leveled the city. As a child, Nambu read widely in his father's extensive library, subscribed to a popular science magazine, and built his own radio.

Nambu had good teachers in middle school, but he detested the militaristic and nationalistic atmosphere prevalent in Japan in the 1930's. In 1937, he began to attend a prestigious junior college near the University of Tokyo. Students wore uniforms and were kept under military-type discipline. From there, he graduated to the university.

In 1942, Nambu was drafted into the Japanese army as a private, rising to become a liaison officer between army, industry, and university researchers. At the war's end, Nambu returned to the University of Tokyo for three years to work on his Ph.D. In those desperate times, he lived in his office and combed the countryside for food. In 1949, he became a professor at the newly founded Osaka City University.

Research in Japan

Nambu's first original research was in solid-state physics, stimulated by discussions with his officemates in Tokyo. The paper was published in the English-language journal *Progress*

Spontaneous Symmetry Breaking

The fundamental equations of physics and their solutions, the physical states, can be transformed mathematically without changing the physical system that they describe. That feature, called symmetry, can in many cases be hidden; it is then said to be spontaneously broken.

In 1959, Nambu submitted for publication an article explaining a paradox in a theory of superconductivity that had been proposed in 1956 by John Bardeen, Leon N Cooper, and J. Robert Schrieffer, known as the BCS theory. Superconductivity occurs in many metals at sufficiently low temperature and is characterized by zero electrical resistance and expulsion of all magnetic fields.

Although the BCS theory was very successful, earning a Nobel Prize in Physics for its authors in 1972, it appeared to violate a fundamental principle of the theory of electricity and magnetism called gauge invariance, which guarantees the conservation of charge. Nambu explained that this symmetry is present, although hidden. It was restored by the presence in the superconducting state of a new type of particle-like oscillations of the metal atoms, referred to as plasmons. Nambu's mechanism is called spontaneous symmetry breaking.

Nambu and his associate Giovanni Jona-Lasinio then wrote two papers entitled "A Dynamical Model of Elementary Particles Based on an Analogy with Superconductivity." In this case, the broken symmetry is that between the clockwise and counterclockwise spin of certain massless elementary particles. Pairs of these spinning particles are assumed to be combined into three types of spinless particles called pions, which are responsible for the main part of the nuclear force. In this case, spontaneous symmetry breaking results in the observed masses of the pions.

Nambu and Jona-Lasinio's work was done before knowledge of the quark. The same mechanism may well be responsible, however, for the masses of the elementary particles that are made of quarks, and perhaps even for the masses of the quarks themselves. A mechanism closely related to Nambu's plasmons that appeared in the superconductor plays an important role in the electroweak sector of the Standard Model.

The unified electroweak theory combines electricity, magnetism, and the weak nuclear force that is responsible for a type of nuclear radioactivity and other effects in elementary particle physics. This theory has four force-carrying fields or particles. One of these is the massless photon, the quantum of ordinary light, but the other three particles (two charged, one neutral) acquire very large masses as a result of spontaneous symmetry breaking.

The Standard Model has enjoyed great success since it came to be recognized in the mid-1970's. No experiments contradict it, and, when it is eventually unified with the theory of gravitation and a suitable explanation is found for the masses of its fundamental particles, it may close the book on the type of physics that tries to reduce phenomena to the interactions of a small number of basic objects through a small number of fields.

Bibliography

Fearful Symmetry: The Search for Beauty in Modern Physics. A. Zee. London: Macmillan, 1986.

Quarks. Yoichiro Nambu. Translated by R. Yoshida. Philadelphia: World Scientific, 1985.

Superconductivity. A. W. B. Taylor. London: Wykeham, 1970.

Superfluidity and Superconductivity. D. R. Tilley and J. Tilley. 2d ed. Bristol, England: Adam Hilger, 1986.

"A Unified Theory of Elementary Particles and Forces." *Scientific American* (April, 1981).

of Theoretical Physics, founded in 1947 in Kyoto by Hideki Yukawa, who won a Nobel Prize in Physics in 1949.

In bombed-out Tokyo, during and after the war, Shin'ichiro Tomonaga led a group that made revolutionary progress in quantum electrodynamics (QED) that earned for him a Nobel Prize in Physics in 1965. After returning to Tokyo, Nambu worked beside Tomonaga, publishing fourteen papers on QED and related subjects in Yukawa's journal before leaving for the United States.

Research in America Until 1959

Nambu spent two years at the Institute for Advanced Study in Princeton, New Jersey, a private, nonprofit research foundation where Albert Einstein also worked. During his second year there, he was joined by his wife, Cheiko, and their young son. He collaborated with another Japanese theorist, Toichiro Kinoshita, on the treatment of nuclear matter, the highly condensed substance in the interior of heavy atomic nuclei.

Nambu accepted a research position at the University of Chicago. Several promotions later, he became Distinguished Service Professor in 1971 and served for three years as chair of the physics department. His research until 1959 was mainly on the mathematical physics of elementary particles, using methods known as dispersion theory to predict the behavior of the elementary particles. The number of these particles that had been identified was beginning to increase in an explosive manner. In 1957, Nambu predicted the existence of the first of the new massive particles known as vector mesons by analyzing experiments done at Stanford University.

Major Research After 1959

Nambu's most important research began in 1959 with an article on a paradox that arose in the theory of superconductivity, a metallic state with zero electrical resistance. He applied the same method to develop a successful theory of the pion, or pi-meson, the main carrier of the strong forces holding the particles in the nucleus together.

Nambu's mechanism, called spontaneous symmetry breaking, was later adopted by Abdus Salam and Steven Weinberg. Together with Sheldon L. Glashow, Salam and Weinberg formulated the unified theory of electricity, magnetism, and the weak nuclear interaction that is responsible for a type of radioactivity. This so-called electroweak theory forms one of the two parts of the Standard Model of fundamental particle interactions.

The other part of the Standard Model, called quantum chromodynamics, comprises the theory of color quarks, proposed by Nambu in 1966. Quarks, introduced in 1963 by George Zweig and by Murray Gell-Mann, have either one-third or two-thirds the charge of an electron. Three of them are combined to make up the building blocks of the nucleus, the proton and the neutron.

In order to explain the forces that hold quarks together, Nambu proposed that each quark can be of three types, now called colors (but bearing no relation to the ordinary concept of color), which serve as the sources of eight massless particles, called color gluons, which provide the force that "glues" quarks together.

In 1970, Nambu published a paper on the quantum theory of stringlike objects. String theory has drawn the attention of many mathematical physicists and promises a fully unified theory of fundamental interactions, including gravity. If successful, it would be a major step beyond the Standard Model.

Bibliography
By Nambu
Kwoku, 1981 (*Quarks: Frontiers in Elementary Particle Physics*, 1985)
Broken Symmetry: Selected Papers of Y. Nambu, 1995 (T. Eguchi and K. Nishijima, eds.)

About Nambu
"Yoichiro Nambu." In *Notable Twentieth-Century Scientists*, edited by Emily J. McMurray. New York: Gale Research, 1995.
"Yoichiro Nambu: The First Forty Years." Laurie M. Brown. *Progress of Theoretical Physics Supplement No. 86* (1986).

(Laurie M. Brown)

Louis-Eugène-Félix Néel

Areas of Achievement: Earth science, invention, physics, technology

Contribution: Néel proposed a fourth state of magnetism called antiferromagnetism (in addition to dia-, para-, and ferromagnetism). He studied magnetism in rocks, recording the history of Earth's magnetic field.

Nov. 22, 1904	Born in Lyons, France
1924	Studies at the École Normale Supérieure in Paris
1928	Graduated as an Agrégé des Sciences Physiques
1928	Hired as an assistant at the Faculty of Sciences of the University of Strasbourg
1932	Earns a doctorate
1937	Serves as a professor in the Faculty of Sciences at Strasbourg
1945	Serves as a professor in the Faculty of Sciences at the University of Grenoble
1948	Awarded the André Blondel Medal
1952	Works as a scientific counselor to the French navy
1953	Elected a member of the Académie des Sciences
1954	Named director of the Polytechnic Institute of Grenoble
1956	Appointed director of the Centre d'Études Nucléaires de Grenoble
1965	Given the Gold Medal of the Centre National de la Recherche Scientifique
1970	Awarded the Nobel Prize in Physics
1971	Named president of the National Polytechnic Institute of Grenoble
1971	Wins the Grand Gold Medal of Electronics

(The Nobel Foundation)

Early Life

Louis-Eugène-Félix Néel (pronounced "nay-EHL") was born in Lyons, France. His mother was a musician and artist, and his father was a tax collector posted during his career to numerous places in France and North Africa.

Louis was educated at the Lycée du Parc, in Lyons, and the Lycée Saint Louis, in Paris. His university training was at the École Normale Supérieure, from which he was graduated as an Agrégé des Sciences Physiques in 1928. By his own admission, in his university years he was more interested in bridge and billiards than in his studies. He then went to the University of Strasbourg, where he served as assistant to the magnetician Pierre Weiss and continued with graduate studies, receiving his doctorate in 1932. Néel succeeded Weiss in 1937 as professor of physics at Strasbourg. He married Hélène Hourticq in 1931; they had one son and two daughters.

The War Years

During World War II, many of the faculty at Strasbourg, including Néel, removed to the

University of Grenoble, where they remained throughout the war. At the end of the war, Néel elected to join the faculty at Grenoble rather than to return to Strasbourg. During the war years, he worked, among other things, on the degaussing of ships (which he called neutralization) to protect them against magnetic mines.

Professional Career

In 1945, Néel was named director of the Laboratire d'Électrostatique et de Physique du Métal at Grenoble and began a career in research management that was as illustrious as his role as an individual contributor in the field of magnetism. During his career, he served as adviser to the Centre National de la Recheche Scientifique (CNRS), as director of the Polytechnic Institute of Grenoble, as director of the Centre d'Études Nucléaires, as director of the Laboratory of Magnetism at Grenoble, and as president of the National Polytechnic Institute at Grenoble.

His major contributions in the field of magnetism were the discovery of the phenomenon of antiferromagnetism and the associated ferri-

---

Antiferromagnetism and Ferrimagnetism

In 1932, Néel postulated that if in a crystal the dominant exchange constant between near-neighbor pairs of ions with identical magnetic moments is negative, an antiparallel arrangement occurs, resulting in no net magnetization (antiferromagnetism). In 1948, he suggested that if the magnetic moments on the two sublattices differ in magnitude or number, they do not cancel each other out and a net magnetization results (ferrimagnetism).

Néel's predictions were verified indirectly in 1938 and directly by neutron diffraction studies in 1949. Upon heating, the magnetic ordering is ultimately destroyed at a temperature now known as the Néel temperature, and the antiferromagnet becomes paramagnetic (a low, positive, temperature-dependent susceptibility).

The occurrence of antiferromagnetism and ferrimagnetism depends not only on the identity of the two interacting species but also on their spatial separation. Metallic manganese (Mn), for example, is antiferromagnetic, but upon alloying with elements that expand the Mn lattice, increasing the average Mn-Mn distance, ferromagnetism results.

Magnetocrystalline anisotropy (noncoincidence of magnetization direction and crystalline axes) occurs in antiferromagnets just as for ferromagnets and arises from several sources. More complicated structures have also been realized that still derive from the basic concepts of antiferromagnetism: modulated (noncollinear) structures and spin glasses in disordered magnetic alloys.

The consequence of this broad understanding of antiferromagnetism has been the development of a wide variety of magnetic ferrites (spinels and garnets) that combine ferromagnetic-like properties with electrical conductivities on orders of magnitude lower than ferromagnetic metals. These properties are advantageously exploited in high-frequency transformer cores and inductors; in permanent magnets for motors, loudspeakers, and refrigerator door seals; and in computer "bubble" memories and magnetic tapes.

Bibliography

"Anti-ferromagnetism." T. Nagayima, K. Yosida, and R. Kubo. *Advances in Physics* 4 (1955).

Ferrite Materials: Science and Technology. B. Viswanathan and V. R. Murthy. New York: Springer-Verlag, 1991.

Introduction to Magnetism and Magnetic Materials. D. Jiles. New York: Chapman and Hall, 1991.

Paleomagnetism: Magnetic Domains and Geologic Terranes. R. F. Butler. Boston: Blackwell Scientific Publications, 1992.

Physics of Magnetism. S. Chikazumi and S. H. Charap. Reprint. Melbourne, Fla.: R. E. Krieger, 1978.

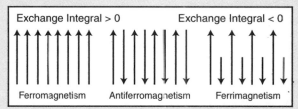

A comparison of magnetic spin ordering in the ferromagnetic, antiferromagnetic, and ferrimagnetic states.

magnetism; studies of the remanent magnetism in the earth's rocks, relevant to magnetic dating; and the synthesis of new oxide ferrites, which are useful for computer memories, magnetic tapes, motors, and transformers.

Recognition

Néel received much recognition over the years, including scientific medals and prizes, honorary doctorates from many universities, foreign memberships in several academies of science, and election to the presidency of the French Physical Society and the presidency of the International Union of Pure and Applied Physics. These honors culminated in the 1970 Nobel Prize in Physics, shared with Hannes Alfvén of Sweden. Néel had more than two hundred publications, including five patents; for all but thirty-two of them, he was the sole author.

Néel was much interested in history and in woodworking and pursued these two hobbies throughout his long life. In 1997, he was still living in Meudon, France, at the age of ninety-two.

Bibliography

By Néel

"Influence des fluctuations du champ moléculaire sur les propriétés magnétiques des corps," *Annales de Physique*, 1932

"Propriétés magnétiques du manganèse et du chrome en solution solide étendue," *Journal de Physique et le Radium*, 1932

"Propriétés magnétiques de l'état métallique et énergie d'interaction entre atomes magnétiques," *Annales de Physique*, 1936

"Théorie du paramagnétisme constant: Application au manganèse," *Comptes rendus hebdomadaires des séances de l'Académie des Sciences*, 1936

"Propriétés magnétiques des ferrites: Ferrimagnétisme et antiferromagnétisme," *Annales de Physique*, 1948

"Essai d'interprétation des propriétés magnétiques du sesquioxyde de fer rhomboèdrique," *Annales de Physique*, 1949

"L'inversion de l'aimantation permanente des roches," *Annales de Géophysique*, 1951

"Antiferromagnetism and Ferrimagnetism," *Physical Society*, 1952

"Confirmation expérimentale d'un mécanisme d'inversion de l'aimantation thermorémanente," *Comptes rendus hebdomadaires des séances de l'Académie des Sciences*, 1952

"Some Theoretical Aspects of Rock Magnetism," *Advances in Physics* (quarterly suppl. of *Philosophical Magazine*), 1955

"The Rare Earth Garnets," *Progress in Low Temperature Physics*, 1964 (with R. Pauthenet and B. Dreyfus)

"Magnetism and the Local Molecular Field," *Science*, 1971

Œuvres scientifiques de Louis Néel, 1978 (*Selected Works of Louis Néel*, 1988)

Un Siècle de physique, 1991

About Néel

The Cambridge Dictionary of Scientists. David Millar et al., eds. Cambridge, England: Cambridge University Press, 1996.

Larousse Dictionary of Scientists. Hazel Muir, ed. Edinburgh, Scotland: Larousse, 1994.

"Nobel Laureates for 1970: Hannes Alfvén and Louis Néel." *Physics Today* (December, 1970).

(Jack H. Westbrook)

Walther Hermann Nernst

Areas of Achievement: Astronomy, chemistry, physics, and technology

Contribution: Nernst made fundamental contributions to electrochemistry, thermodynamics, and photochemistry, which form the foundation of modern physical chemistry.

June 25, 1864	Born in Briesen, West Prussia (now Wabrzezno, Poland)
1887	Becomes an assistant to Wilhelm Ostwald at Leipzig University
1887	Establishes the field of physical chemistry with Ostwald, Jacobus van't Hoff, and Svante Arrhenius
1889	Explains the theory of galvanic cells
1890	Joins the physics department of the University of Göttingen
1894	Becomes the first professor of physical chemistry
1905	Joins the Physicochemical Laboratory, University of Berlin
1906	Presents his heat theorem
1912	Erroneously uses the second law of thermodynamics to "prove" the unattainability of absolute zero
1918	Announces his photochemical atom chain reaction theory
1920	Wins the Nobel Prize in Chemistry
1924	Directs the Institute for Experimental Physics at Berlin
1932	Elected to the Royal Society of London
1933	Retires to his country estate
Nov. 18, 1941	Dies in Bad Muskau, Prussia (now Germany)

(The Nobel Foundation)

Early Life

Walther Hermann Nernst, the son of a judge, was born in Briesen, West Prussia, in 1864. During his rigorous secondary education, he had ambitions of being a poet, but he also carried out scientific experiments in his basement.

Nernst was educated at universities of Zurich, Graz, and Würzburg, where he obtained his doctorate. He conducted work at Graz under the direction of A. von Ettinghausen in the study of the electrification of heated metals placed in a magnetic field. Later, he discovered an electric lamp made of zirconium oxide. His lamp had widespread use, replacing the carbon fiber filament, but it was soon replaced by the use of tungsten filaments. Nernst "glowers" are still used, however, in infrared spectrophotometers.

Contributions to Electrochemistry

Nernst became an assistant to Wilhelm Ostwald at Leipzig University in 1887. While there, he also worked with Jacobus van't Hoff

Heat Theorem

Nernst's heat theorem, known as the third law of thermodynamics, shows that the maximum amount of work obtained from a process can be calculated from the heat given off at temperatures near absolute zero.

In 1900, Theodore William Richards studied the Gibbs free energy of reactions as a function of temperature. Nernst remarked that this data showed that the slope of the change in the Gibbs free energy as a function of temperature of a chemical reaction approaches zero as the temperature approaches absolute zero.

In 1907, Nernst postulated that, at constant pressure, the change in the Gibbs free energy of a reaction is zero at absolute zero. This means that the entropy of a reaction is zero at absolute zero. While Nernst believed this to be valid for any process, it was later shown to be valid only for reactions involving pure substances in internal equilibrium. For example, this theorem does not apply to supercooled liquids.

Older work had ignored the effect of temperature when calculating equilibrium conditions. Nernst's work added a higher level of refinement to earlier work and allowed precise calculations of equilibrium conditions.

Bibliography

Basic Chemical Thermodynamics. Eric Brian Hill. 3d ed. Oxford, England: Clarendon Press, 1982.

The Evolution of Chemistry: A History of Its Ideas, Methods, and Materials. Eduard Farber. 2d ed. New York: Ronald Press, 1969.

Thermodynamics: An Introduction to the Physical Theories of Equilibrium Thermostatics and Irreversible Thermodynamics. Herbert Callen. New York: John Wiley & Sons, 1960.

and Svante Arrhenius to establish the independent field of modern physical chemistry.

In 1889, Nernst presented his theory of galvanic cells based on the new dissociation theory of ions proposed by Arrhenius. The voltage of electrochemical cells is calculated using the Nernst equation. In this same year, Nernst derived equations for the solubility products of ionic materials. These equations predict the conditions under which materials will precipitate from solutions.

The Third Law of Thermodynamics

In 1907, Nernst set forth the third law of thermodynamics, which shows that the maximum amount of work in a process can be calculated by the heat given off by the process at temperatures near absolute zero. Nernst won the 1920 Nobel Prize in Chemistry for his heat theorem.

Nernst erroneously used the second law of thermodynamics to "prove" the unattainability of absolute zero in 1912. Albert Einstein later pointed out the fallacy of Nernst's argument.

Photochemical Atom Chain Reaction

In 1918, Nernst explained his photochemical atom chain reaction theory. He theorized that the energy of a photon produces free radicals that can, in turn, react with other molecules to produce other free radicals. These reactions can continue to occur even after the source of light is removed. This theory explained previous observations that had been unexplained.

Nernst retired from his position as director of the Institute for Experimental Physics at the University of Berlin in 1933. He died in 1941, at the age of seventy-seven.

Bibliography

By Nernst

Theoretische Chemie vom Standpunkte der Avogadroschen Regel und der Thermodynamik, 1893 (*Theoretical Chemistry from the Standpoint of Avogadro's Rule and Thermodynamics*, 1895)

Experimental and Theoretical Applications of Thermodynamics to Chemistry, 1907

Die theoretischen und experimentellen Grundlagen des neuen Wärmesatzes, 1918 (*The New Heat Theorem: Its Foundations in Theory and Experiment*, 1918)

About Nernst

Great Chemists. Eduard Farber. New York: Interscience, 1961.

"Nernst Memorial Lecture." James Riddick Partington. *Journal of the Chemical Society* 3 (1953).

"Walther Hermann Nernst." In *The Nobel Prize Winners: Chemistry*, edited by Frank N. Magill. Pasadena, Calif.: Salem Press, 1990.

The World of Walther Nernst: The Rise and Fall of German Science. Kurt Mendelssohn. Pittsburgh: University of Pittsburgh Press, 1973.

(Christopher J. Biermann)

Sir Isaac Newton

Areas of Achievement: Astronomy, mathematics, and physics

Contribution: One of the greatest thinkers in history, Newton literally changed the way in which the world is viewed with his development of three laws of motion and the law of gravity, his discovery of the calculus, his advances in thermodynamics, and his invention of the reflecting telescope.

Dec. 25, 1642	Born in Woolsthorpe, Lincolnshire, England
1661	Enters Trinity College, Cambridge University
1665	Graduated from Trinity and receives a position as chair
1665-1666	Trinity College closes because of the bubonic plague
1667	Elected a Fellow of Trinity
1671	Elected to the Royal Society of London
1671	Presents a paper on optics to the Royal Society of London
1687	Publishes *Philosophiae Naturalis Principia Mathematica* (*Mathematical Principles of Natural Philosophy*, 1729)
1689	Elected a Member of Parliament from Cambridge
1696	Appointed Warden of the Mint
1701	Resigns his chair at Trinity
1703	Elected president of the Royal Society of London
1703	Publishes *Opticks*
1705	Knighted by Queen Anne
Mar. 20, 1727	Dies in London, England

Early Life

Isaac Newton was born prematurely on Christmas Day, 1642—according to the Julian calendar, or January 4, 1643, by the current Gregorian calendar—in Woolsthorpe, Lincolnshire, England, and was not expected to live. His father, the lord of the manor of a small estate, died before Isaac was born.

Newton attended the village school but showed little to indicate his great intellect. When he was twelve, he began attending the King's School in nearby Grantham. After four years, his mother took him out in order to manage the farm, but two years of mediocre performance persuaded her to allow him to return to school and prepare for college. In 1661, Newton entered Trinity College at Cambridge University.

Shortly after arriving at Cambridge, Newton came to the attention of the mathematician Isaac Barrow. Under Barrow's tutelage, Newton began to display his enormous genius. He would win a mathematical scholarship in 1664, and, when he was graduated in 1665, Barrow resigned his chair in favor of his pupil.

The Plague Years

The year 1665 saw the bubonic plague reach Cambridge. The school was closed and the population dispersed to help control the spread of the disease. Newton returned to Woolsthorpe and remained there until the end of March, 1666. This period gave him months of uninterrupted thought and allowed him to complete work on some of the most revolutionary scientific achievements in history.

The advances that Newton made during this period include his discovery of the calculus, the law of gravity, his three laws of motion, several properties of optics, and the invention of the reflecting telescope.

(Library of Congress)

The Royal Society of London

News of Newton's work in optics reached the preeminent Royal Society of London, and he was elected a member. He was also invited to present his findings in a paper. He presented not only the paper but also his reflecting telescope, which remains one of the most prized possessions of the society.

Robert Hooke, a member of the society, claimed that Newton stole the ideas from him. Hooke was a bright theorist, but he lacked the mathematical and experimental skills needed to investigate his thoughts. As a result, he often speculated on many ideas without providing any supporting evidence for them. His claim began a feud that would last until Hooke's death more than thirty years later. Newton was enraged and nearly withdrew from the society. Although persuaded to remain a member, he would not submit any more of his findings.

Newton's *Principia*

Newton sequestered himself at Cambridge until 1684, when astronomer Edmond Halley approached him with a question concerning gravity. Much to his surprise, he found that Newton had found the answer to his question nearly twenty years earlier during the plague years.

Halley encouraged Newton to put this and other research into a book and even offered to pay for its publication. Newton accepted the offer and began work on *Philosophiae Naturalis Principia Mathematica* (*Mathematical Principles of Natural Philosophy*, 1729), generally known as the *Principia*, perhaps the greatest scientific book of all time.

Newton applied himself to writing the *Principia* with vigor, frequently forsaking food and sleep. In an exceptional exhibition of intellectual effort, he completed the task in fifteen months. Published in 1687, the work is a monument to human genius. Nearly all advances in science and technology since the seventeenth century can be traced to the *Principia*.

The Laws of Motion

The motion of all objects in the universe, large and small, can be explained with three simple laws. These laws remain valid except when the velocity becomes large compared to the speed of light.

After Galileo Galilei showed that the philosophies of Aristotle were invalid, there remained a void in the understanding of how things moved. Newton filled this void by showing that all motion can be described with three simple laws.

The first law states that a body at rest will remain at rest and that a body in motion will remain in motion in a straight line and at a constant velocity, until acted on by an unbalanced outside force. The second law states that the force exerted by an object is equal to the mass of the object multiplied by the acceleration experienced when the force is applied. The third law states that for every action, there is an equal, but opposite, reaction.

The first law is also known as the principle of inertia, where inertia is defined as the tendency of a mass to remain in uniform motion, or at rest, and is measured by mass. The more mass an object has, the more inertia it has. For example, it takes more work to start a bowling ball rolling than a tennis ball. Likewise, once moving, it is harder to stop the bowling ball than the tennis ball.

The velocity of an object will not change on its own. In order to change an object's velocity, some unbalanced force must be applied. The size of this force can be found with Newton's second law. The combination of speed and direction is called velocity. Acceleration is the process of changing an object's velocity, either by changing its speed or by changing its direction of motion. The amount of force needed to cause this acceleration is equal to the amount of acceleration multiplied by the amount of mass. The more mass an object has, the more inertia it has, and the harder it is to accelerate it.

If a force is being applied, there must be something to apply it. Newton's third law states that if one object exerts a force on a second object, the second object must exert a force on the first object that is equal in magnitude, but in the opposite direction. This law explains the interaction between all objects. Normally, one is not consciously aware of this reaction because one object is frequently much larger than the other, and, by Newton's second law, the larger object experiences less acceleration from the same amount of force. This law explains how rockets are able to work even in a vacuum. By pushing gases out with some force, the gases exert an equal and opposite force on the rocket, making it accelerate.

With the exception of very high velocities, which is covered by Albert Einstein's theory of relativity, these three simple statements explain all facets of motion. By applying these laws, humans have been able to improve dramatically the understanding of the universe.

Bibliography

Motion, Sound, and Heat. Isaac Asimov. Vol. 1 in *Understanding Physics.* New York: Barnes & Noble Books, 1993.

Physics. Paul E. Tippen. Westerville, Ohio: Glencoe/McGraw-Hill, 1995.

The great effort to produce the *Principia* led to a nervous breakdown, however, and Newton was never the same again.

Later Life

Newton turned his attention to politics and was elected to Parliament from Cambridge in 1689. In 1696, he was appointed Warden of the Mint and was involved with the recoinage of the currency, as well as the apprehension of counterfeiters—two jobs at which he excelled. Unfortunately, the position took up much of his time and slowed his scientific pursuits considerably.

With Hooke's death in 1703, Newton was elected president of the Royal Society of Lon-

Physics and the Calculus

The mathematics of change and motion, calculus provides a language for expressing the laws of physics in precise mathematical terms.

During his period in Woolsthorpe during the plague, Newton wished to investigate some phenomena of nature and found the current mathematics available to him inadequate for the task. Being one of the most capable mathematicians in history, he invented the mathematics that was required. What he called "fluxions" is now known as the calculus, from the Latin *calculus*, meaning a stone or pebble used in reckoning.

The calculus is the branch of mathematics that deals with change and motion by treating a continuously changing function as if it consisted of small incremental changes. As the size of the incremental changes becomes infinitely small, one finds that the value of the function approaches a particular value. This value can then be used either as an endpoint or for further calculations. The two forms of the calculus are differential and integral.

Differential calculus finds the rate at which a known variable is changing. For example, if one knows the mathematical expression for the velocity of an object, one can use differential calculus to find its acceleration (the rate of change of velocity) at any given moment.

Integral calculus works in the opposite direction and finds the function when the rate of change is known. For example, if one knows the expression for the acceleration of an object, integral calculus will give the expression for the velocity.

Furthermore, one can perform both operations over a definite interval (with precisely defined values) or over an indefinite interval (without defined values). The definite interval will yield a definite, numerical value for an answer, while the indefinite interval will yield an expression that defines the behavior of the function in general. Both have their uses.

The calculus provides a means of expressing physical laws with great precision and with great ease. For example, astronomer Johannes Kepler, a very able mathematician, spent more than twenty years deriving his three laws of planetary motion. By using the calculus and Newton's law of gravity, Kepler's laws can be found very quickly.

Although Newton was the first to discover the mathematics of the calculus, he was characteristically reluctant to publish his work. As a result, the world did not learn of his discovery until much later. In the meantime, Gottfried Wilhelm Leibniz discovered the calculus independently of Newton and is normally listed as the codiscoverer. The notation used in the calculus today was developed by Leibniz.

As a tool, the usefulness of the calculus transcends science. While it is used to calculate the orbits of planets and satellites, weather patterns, and ocean currents, it is also used to make calculations in economic and sociologic theories. The calculus was such a major advancement in mathematics that its discovery is enough by itself to ensure a place in history for both Newton and Leibniz.

Bibliography

Calculus and Analytic Geometry. George B. Thomas, Jr. Reading, Mass.: Addison-Wesley, 1972.

Calculus: Graphical, Numerical, Algebraic. Ross L. Finney, George B. Thomas, Franklin Demana, and Bert K. Waits. Reading, Mass.: Addison-Wesley, 1995.

don. That same year, he published *Opticks*, which consisted of his work in that field from thirty years earlier.

Newton was knighted by Queen Anne in 1705, becoming the first scientist to be so honored for his work. Sir Isaac Newton died on March 20, 1727—or March 31, according to the Gregorian calendar—in London, at the age of eighty-four, as a result of a blocked bladder. He was buried in Westminster Abbey.

Bibliography
By Newton
Philosophiae Naturalis Principia Mathematica, 1687 (*Mathematical Principles of Natural Philosophy*, 1729)
Opticks, 1704
Arithmetica Universalis, 1707 (*Universal Arithmetick*, 1720)

About Newton
In the Presence of the Creator. Gale E. Christianson. New York: Free Press, 1984.
Never at Rest. Richard S. Westfall. New York: Cambridge University Press, 1982.
Six Great Scientists. J. G. Crowther. New York: Barnes & Noble Books, 1995.

(Christopher Keating)

Marshall W. Nirenberg

Areas of Achievement: Biology, cell biology, chemistry, and genetics
Contribution: Nirenberg was the scientist most responsible for deciphering the genetic code.

Apr. 10, 1927	Born in New York, New York
1948	Earns a B.S. from the University of Florida, Gainesville
1952	Receives an M.S. in biology from Florida
1957	Earns a Ph.D. in biochemistry from the University of Michigan, Ann Arbor
1957	Begins research at the National Institutes of Health (NIH) in Bethesda, Maryland
1960	Appointed a research biochemist at NIH
1961	Marries Brazilian biochemist Perola Zaltzman
1964	Announces a transfer RNA-binding technique for deciphering the genetic code
1965	Presented with the National Medal of Science by President Lyndon Johnson
1966	Appointed Chief of Biochemical Genetics at the National Heart, Lung, and Blood Institute of NIH
1967	Elected to the National Academy of Sciences
1968	Awarded the Nobel Prize in Physiology or Medicine
1992	Becomes a signatory to the World Scientists' Warning to Humanity, concerning dangers to the natural environment from human activity

Early Life

Marshall Warren Nirenberg was born in New York City in 1927. When he was ten years old, however, his family moved to Orlando, Florida. Nirenberg soon came to consider himself a Floridian.

In 1944, he enrolled at the University of Florida, studying zoology and botany, subjects that had long interested him. While still an undergraduate, he worked as a laboratory assistant and even as a teaching assistant. While working in the nutrition laboratory, he was introduced to biochemistry, little studied then at the undergraduate level. He learned how to use

The Genetic Code

Nirenberg found that the structures and properties of proteins are controlled by the sequence of bases in deoxyribonucleic acid (DNA) and ribonucleic acid (RNA).

Proteins are very large, complex molecules that direct the vast array of chemical reactions occurring within living organisms and that constitute the life of those organisms. Many structural components of organisms are also proteins. The DNA in any living thing determines what kinds of proteins its cells can make, and thus what kind of organism it is: ant or oak tree, man or woman, and so on.

All protein molecules consist of very long chains of simple components called amino acids. There are only twenty types of amino acids in proteins, but the different orders in which they can be arranged in the chain give rise to many sorts of proteins, with very different biochemical properties. DNA contains the instructions, in coded form, for assembling amino acids into proteins in the right order, but DNA does not control protein production directly. When needed, its code is copied into a related substance called RNA. This comes in three forms: ribosomal RNA (rRNA), which forms ribosomes, the intracellular bodies where proteins are actually assembled; transfer RNA (tRNA), which carries the amino acids to the ribosomes; and messenger RNA (mRNA), which carries the actual instructions for protein assembly.

RNA, like DNA, is itself a long chain molecule, and it is the order of the components called bases in the mRNA chain that codes for the order of amino acids in the protein. The bases may be considered as the letters in which the code is written, but there are only four types of bases: adenine (A), guanine (G), cytosine (C), and uracil (U). Therefore, it takes a "word," or codon, consisting of three bases, in a particular order, to specify a particular amino acid.

This much was suspected, if not yet proven, when Nirenberg began his work, but it was not known which codons specified which particular amino acids. When Nirenberg and J. Heinrich Matthaei added an artificial mRNA containing only the base uracil to their bacterial extract—containing ribosomes, tRNA, free amino acids, and other necessary components—they found that an unnatural protein chain was produced containing only the amino acid phenylalanine. Thus, UUU is the code word for phenylalanine.

Further experiments followed with other artificial mRNAs, but it was not then known how to make long artificial RNA chains with different bases in a particular order, so it was impossible to solve much of the code in this way. Nirenberg and Philip Leder found, however, that RNA chains only three base units long (single codons, in effect), which could be made with bases in a specific order, would cause tRNA carrying the appropriate amino acid to stick fast to the ribosomes. These ribosomes were then filtered out, and the particular amino acid stuck to them could be identified by standard radioactive isotope techniques. The entire code was quickly deciphered.

Bibliography

The Genetic Code. Carl R. Woese. New York: Harper & Row, 1967.

"The Genetic Code: II." Marshall Nirenberg. *Scientific American* (March, 1963).

The Molecular Biology of the Gene. James D. Watson. 4th ed. Menlo Park, Calif.: Benjamin/ Cummings, 1987.

radioactive isotopes to follow the course of biochemical reactions, a technique that was to prove vital to his later research.

Nirenberg was graduated in 1948 but stayed on for graduate studies in biology, continuing to work in the nutrition laboratory. His master's thesis dealt with the classification and ecology of caddis flies, but, in 1952, he began doctoral study in biochemistry at the University of Michigan. His doctoral thesis concerned the uptake of sugars by cancer cells, and he afterward received a fellowship from the American Cancer Society for research at the National Institutes of Health (NIH), in Be-

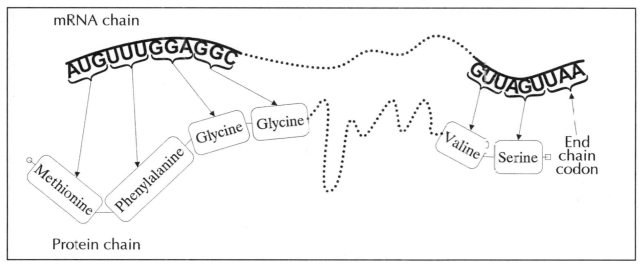

Figure 1. *Protein synthesis is directed by messenger RNA (mRNA). The order of the amino acids in the protein chain is controlled by the order of the bases in the mRNA chain. It takes a codon of three bases to specify one amino acid.*

The Full Genetic Code					
second row → first row ↓	U	C	A	G	third row ↓
U	Phenylalanine Phenylalanine Leucine Leucine	Serine Serine Serine Serine	Tyrosine Tyrosine END CHAIN END CHAIN	Cysteine Cysteine END CHAIN Tryptophan	U C A G
C	Leucine Leucine Leucine Leucine	Proline Proline Proline Proline	Histidine Histidine Glutamine Glutamine	Arginine Arginine Arginine Arginine	U C A G
A	Isoleucine Isoleucine Isoleucine Methionine	Threonine Threonine Threonine Threonine	Asparagine Asparagine Lysine Lysine	Serine Serine Arginine Arginine	U C A G
G	Valine Valine Valine Valine	Alanine Alanine Alanine Alanine	Aspartic Acid Aspartic Acid Glutamic Acid Glutamic Acid	Glycine Glycine Glycine Glycine	U C A G

Figure 2. *The amino acid specified by any codon can be found by looking for the wide row designated by the first base letter of the codon shown on the left, then the column designated by the second base letter along the top, and finally the narrow row marked on the right, in the appropriate wide row, by the third letter of the codon. Many amino acids are represented by more than one codon. The codons UAA, UAG, and UGA do not specify an amino acid but instead signal where a protein chain ends.*

thesda, Maryland. In 1960, he was appointed to the regular staff there.

Cracking the Code

Shortly after this appointment, Nirenberg began to collaborate with German scientist J. Heinrich Matthaei. They prepared an extract from bacterial cells that could make protein even when no intact living cells were present. Adding an artificial form of ribonucleic acid (RNA), polyuridylic acid, to this extract caused it to make an unnatural protein composed entirely of the amino acid phenylalanine. This provided the first clue to the code through which RNA—and, ultimately deoxyribonucleic acid (DNA)—control the production of specific types of protein in living cells.

Nirenberg announced these results at the Fifth International Congress of Biochemistry in Moscow in August, 1961. As an unknown scientist with an obscurely titled paper, his initial talk was very poorly attended. He was asked to repeat it, however, for the final session of the

(The Nobel Foundation)

full congress. Some listeners recall being "electrified" by what they heard, although others (apparently) slept through it.

Over the next few years, many similar experiments were done, by Nirenberg and others, using different forms of synthetic RNA to stimulate protein production. Only modest further progress could be made, however, in deciphering the code by such methods. In 1964, Nirenberg announced that he and Philip Leder had devised a new, more powerful decoding technique. Within a year, the genetic code was fully deciphered.

After the Code

A shy, unassuming man, Nirenberg gained a reputation for total dedication to his science. In 1966, he was appointed Chief of Biochemical Genetics at the National Heart, Lung, and Blood Institute. In 1968, he shared the Nobel Prize in Physiology or Medicine with Har Gobind Khorana and Robert Holley. He has continued to work on the very complex problems of understanding how genetic information controls the development and metabolism of living organisms.

Bibliography
By Nirenberg
"The Dependence of Cell-Free Protein Synthesis in *E. coli* upon Naturally Occurring or Synthetic Polyribonucleotides," *Proceedings of the National Academy of Sciences of the United States*, 1961 (with J. Heinrich Matthaei)
"The Genetic Code: II," *Scientific American*, 1963
"RNA Codewords and Protein Synthesis: The Effect of Trinucleotides upon the Binding of sRNA to Ribosomes," *Science*, 1964 (with Philip Leder)

About Nirenberg
The Eighth Day of Creation: The Makers of the Revolution in Biology. Horace Freeland Judson. New York: Simon & Schuster, 1979.
"Marshall W. Nirenberg." In *The Nobel Prize Winners: Physiology or Medicine*, edited by Frank N. Magill. Pasadena, Calif.: Salem Press, 1991.
"Nirenberg, Marshall W(arren)." In *Current Biography Yearbook*. New York: H. W. Wilson, 1965.

(Nigel J. T. Thomas)

Alfred Nobel

Areas of Achievement: Invention and technology

Contribution: Nobel became a major figure in the explosives industry with his development of dynamite. A philanthropist in his later years, he stipulated in his will that prizes should be awarded to those whose work benefits humankind.

Oct. 21, 1833	Born in Stockholm, Sweden
1841-1842	Attends St. Jakob's Higher Apologist School
1843-1850	Privately tutored by Russian and Swedish teachers
1863	Develops the Nobel detonator for the safer use of nitroglycerin
1865	Nitroglycerin Ltd., managed by Nobel, becomes the first factory to produce nitroglycerin
1865	The headquarters of the company are established in Hamburg
1867	Patents dynamite
1870	Moves his headquarters and laboratory to Paris, France
1875	Develops blasting gelatin, a colloid of nitrocellulose in nitroglycerin
1887	Produces a nearly smokeless blasting powder called ballistite
1895	Writes his last will and testament, leaving his fortune to the Nobel foundation as a benefit to humankind
Dec. 10, 1896	Dies in San Remo, Italy

(The Nobel Foundation)

Early Life

Alfred Bernhard Nobel was born in Stockholm in 1833. His father, Immanuel, was an inventor and industrialist. Nobel received little formal education. Although he spent several years attending school in Stockholm, he and his brothers received most of their schooling between 1843 and 1850 from Russian and Swedish tutors hired by their father. Much of his youth was spent living in St. Petersburg, Russia.

During his late teens, Nobel had the opportunity to travel extensively, visiting North America and much of Europe. During this time, he became fluent in several languages. His aptitude for invention and his natural understanding of the fields of chemistry and management were strongly encouraged by his father.

When Nobel returned from his travels in 1852, he joined his father in business, providing war materials for the Russian czar. Russia's entrance into the Crimean War in 1853 resulted in financial success for the Nobel factory. With the war's end in 1856, however, Nobel's business suffered bankruptcy.

Much of the family dispersed throughout Europe, though Alfred remained in Russia with his brother Ludwig. The Nobel brothers developed a business manufacturing drilling

The Invention of Dynamite

Nobel's invention of dynamite revolutionized the explosives industry. Although composed of explosive nitroglycerin, dynamite was a form that could be handled relatively easily.

Prior to the 1860's, most explosives were based on the liquid substance nitroglycerin. The explosive had been discovered in 1847 and had been extensively utilized for both military and industrial purposes. Nitroglycerin was dangerously unstable, however, and was unsafe in both its manufacture and its use. Nobel's brother, Emil, along with four others, had themselves been killed in a nitroglycerin explosion.

Nobel was determined to develop a way in which the explosive could be handled in a safer manner. He reasoned that if liquid nitroglycerin could be mixed with other, more inert materials, its inherent instability might be lessened.

He carried out numerous experiments in which the explosive was mixed with varying amounts of highly absorbent materials. Among these materials was a diatomaceous earth called kieselguhr, a very porous material that absorbed shock. By absorbing the nitroglycerin, the kieselguhr mixture, which Nobel called dynamite, became a solid that could be easily, and more safely, handled.

Nobel's invention of dynamite transformed nitroglycerin into a more useful explosive. It could be manufactured, shipped, and used with significantly less danger to its handlers.

Bibliography

The Amazing Story of Explosives. Melvin Cook. Salt Lake City: University of Utah Press, 1952.

History of the Explosives Industry in America. Arthur Pine Van Gelder and Hugo Schlatter. New York: Columbia University Press, 1927.

The Life of Albert Nobel. Henrik Schuck and Ragnor Sohlman. London: Heinemann, 1927.

tools. Alfred Nobel's industrial abilities would return dividends, as their investments in the Baku oilfields eventually became as successful as those in the explosives area.

An Inventor and Industrialist

During the early and mid-1860's, Nobel revolutionized the explosives industry. In 1862, he returned to Sweden with his father and began work with nitroglycerin.

His first major invention was the Nobel detonator, a new form of fuse in which detonation of the charge of nitroglycerin was caused by an initial, smaller charge in a cap containing mercury fulminate. Thus, the charge was based on a shock instead of on heat. The device allowed for safer detonation of nitroglycerin. Eventually, this device became known as the "Nobel lighter." The use of a percussion detonator to control the explosion of a larger device was to form the basis for all industrial explosives.

In 1864, Nobel's brother was killed in an industrial accident. The death devastated his father and eventually resulted in the moving of the factory.

In 1865, Nobel, now managing director of the company, established Nitroglycerin Limited, the world's first factory for the manufacture of nitroglycerine. Eventually, he established similar factories through much of the world. His desire for a more controlled explosive led to the development and patenting of dynamite in 1867. The development of dynamite allowed nitroglycerin to be made in a safer form, one more easily handled.

In 1875, Nobel discovered that kieselguhr, an inert material, could reduce the explosive power of nitroglycerin, rendering it even safer for industrial use. He also found that when nitroglycerine was gelatinized with collodion cotton (nitrocellulose), it produced a plastic mass that remained a powerful explosive but lacked the instability inherent in nitroglycerin. Nobel referred to this substance as "blasting gelatin."

Nobel's last major invention was ballistite, developed in the late 1880's in his laboratory in San Remo, Italy. Ballistite represented the earliest form of smokeless powder. At the time, it was used to replace black powder used in small-arms ammunition.

Philanthropy

Nobel's inventions earned for him a considerable fortune. In addition to 355 patents, established in a variety of countries, he also carried out work in electrochemistry, optics, and biology. His work led to later discoveries in the silk and rubber industries. Toward the end of his life, however, Nobel became disillusioned with the applications of many of his inventions toward the aims of war.

It is ironic that Nobel was as much a humanitarian as an industrialist. Although not a formal member of a church, he made frequent donations to the Swedish church in Paris. By comparison with other industries, his employees had high pay and good benefits. Nobel had a strong desire for world peace, even to the point of wishing that all guns could be "sent to hell."

In his last will and testament, written in 1895, Nobel directed that his fortune—the equivalent of 9 million dollars at the time and approximately 100 million dollars by the standards of late twentieth century—be used to benefit humankind. Foundations would be established to award yearly prizes in the areas of physics, chemistry, physiology or medicine, literature, and peace. The first Nobel Prizes were awarded in 1901.

Bibliography
By Nobel
On Modern Blasting Agents, 1875

About Nobel
Alfred Nobel: A Biography. Kenne Fant. Waltham, Mass.: Little, Brown, 1993.

Alfred Nobel, the Man and His Work. Erik Bergengren. London: Nelson, 1962.

Nobel: A Biography of Alfred Nobel. Nicholas Halasz. London: Robert Hale, 1960.

The Nobel Prize. Peter Wilhelm. London: Springwood Books, 1983.

(*Richard Adler*)

John Howard Northrop

Areas of Achievement: Biology, cell biology, chemistry, technology, and virology

Contribution: A prolific scientist, Northrop is best known for his study of enzymes. He won the Nobel Prize in Chemistry for crystallizing pepsin and trypsin and for proving that enzymes are proteins.

July 5, 1891	Born in Yonkers, New York
1915	Earns a Ph.D. in chemistry from Columbia College
1915	Begins working for Jacques Loeb at the Rockefeller Institute
1917-1919	Commissioned a captain in the U.S. Army
1919	Begins his study of pepsin and trypsin
1924	Elected as a full member of the Rockefeller Institute
1929	Crystallizes pepsin
1930	Proves that enzymatic action is a function of the crystallized protein
1935	Begins to research the chemical nature of viruses
1942-1945	Serves as a consultant and official investigator to the National Defense Research Committee
1946	Awarded the Nobel Prize in Chemistry jointly with Wendell Meredith Stanley and James Batcheller Sumner
1949	Begins work at the University of California, Berkeley
1970	Retires
May 27, 1987	Dies in Wickenberg, Arizona

Early Life

John Howard Northrop was born into a scientific family. His father held a Ph.D. in zoology and was an instructor at Columbia College in New York. His mother was a naturalist and an instructor at Normal College (now Hunter College). Sadly, his father died in a fire at Columbia nine days before Northrop's birth.

Northrop was graduated from Yonkers High School in 1909 and entered Columbia College. While majoring in biochemistry, he took as many science and mathematics courses as the school would allow. He was also a member of championship fencing, rifle, and pistol teams and enjoyed other essentially individual sports, such as tennis and golf. Encouraged by his mother, Northrop continued his studies at Columbia, earning his master's and doctorate degrees.

The Rockefeller Institute

Upon his graduation from Columbia, the college awarded him a traveling fellowship, but World War I made it impossible for him to study in Europe. Instead, he applied to work with Jacques Loeb at the Rockefeller Institute for Medical Research (now Rockefeller University) in New York.

Under Loeb, Northrop began investigations of the effect of environmental factors on the lifespan and heredity of fruit flies. During his research, he developed a way to grow fruit flies that were completely free of microorganisms.

World War I

The U.S. entry into World War I in 1917 caused shortages of critical chemicals. Northrop developed a process for making acetone, which was needed to make explosives, from molasses. The Army made Northrop a captain in the Chemical Warfare Service. He oversaw construction of a new plant that would make acetone using his process, but the war ended before the plant was finished.

Prize-Winning Work

Northrop returned to Rockefeller in 1919 and began independent research. In 1924, he was elected to full membership in the institute. He gathered his own research staff at the institute's branch in Princeton, New Jersey, and ad-

Proof That Enzymes Are Proteins

Northrop isolated pepsin by crystallization, then exhaustively tested the isolated enzyme and proved that it is a protein.

Enzymes are organic catalysts that speed up the rate of particular reactions but are not used up in those reactions. The existence of enzymes and their effects on other chemicals had been well known before Northrop's research, but disagreement existed over the chemical nature of enzymes. Enzymes had been identified in samples containing protein. Some scientists believed that the proteins were enzymes, while others believed that other molecules contained in the sample were the real enzymes.

When molecules of the same chemical stack very closely, they form a crystal. Molecules that are different do not stack the same way and thus do not form part of the crystal. James Batcheller Sumner was the first to purify an enzyme using this principle. Northrop knew of this work and used Sumner's methods to crystallize pepsin, an enzyme that he had been studying for many years.

Northrop conducted many experiments in an effort to separate pure pepsin from the protein. Every test failed, which proved that pepsin is a protein. He then conducted similar experiments with trypsin, another digestive enzyme, and obtained the same results. Sumner, Northrop, and Wendell Meredith Stanley shared the 1946 Nobel Prize in Chemistry for their related work in purifying and identifying enzymes and viruses as proteins.

Bibliography

Discovering Enzymes. David Dressler and Huntington Potter. New York: W. H. Freeman, 1991.

"John Howard Northrop." Roger M. Herriott. *Journal of General Physiology* 77 (June, 1981).

Nobel Prize Winners in Chemistry: 1901-1961. Eduard Farber. New York: Abelard Schuman, 1963.

(The Nobel Foundation)

dressed himself to more thorough examination of his previous work.

Northrop had begun experimenting with enzymes in 1920 but was unable to determine their composition. After James Batcheller Sumner announced his method for crystallizing urease, Northrop used that method to crystallize pepsin and trypsin, and he succeeded in proving that enzymes are proteins. For this work, he shared the 1946 Nobel Prize in Chemistry with Sumner and a colleague from Rockefeller, Wendell Meredith Stanley.

Not Finished Yet

War again interrupted Northrop's work. Through World War II, he and his staff worked for the Office of Scientific Research and Development. He succeeded in producing a very sensitive gas detector and also a highly portable model for use by soldiers in the field.

After the war, Northrop resumed his studies of enzymes and viruses. In 1949, the Rockefeller Institute closed its Princeton location. He elected to take a position with the University of California, Berkeley, but still received support from the institute.

Northrop continued working until he was forced to retire in 1970. A year later, he moved to Arizona, where he remained active and full of curiosity until his death in 1987.

Bibliography

By Northrop

"The Mechanism of Agglutination" in *The Newer Knowledge of Bacteriology and Immunology*, 1928 (Edward O. Jordan and I. S. Falk, eds.)

"Pepsin, Trypsin, Chymo-trypsin" (with Kunitz) in *Handbuch der biologichen Arbeitsmethoden*, 1936 (Emil Abderhalden, ed.)

"Die kristallisierten Proteinasen" in *Die Methoden der Fermentforschung: Unter mitarbeit von Fachgenossen*, 1938 (Eugen Bamann and Karl Myrbäck, eds.)

Crystalline Enzymes: The Chemistry of Pepsin, Trypsin, and Bacteriophage, 1938

"Die Chemie der kristallisierten Enzyme" in *Handbuch der Enzymologie*, 1940 (F. F. Nord and R. Weidenhagen, eds.)

Crystalline Enzymes, 2d ed., 1948 (with Moses Kunitz and Roger M. Herriott)

"Enzymes and the Synthesis of Proteins" in *The Chemistry and Physiology of Growth*, 1949 (Arthur K. Parpart, ed.)

About Northrop

"A Biographical Sketch of John Howard Northrop." Roger M. Herriott. *The Journal of General Physiology* 45 (March, 1962).

A History of the Rockefeller Institute: 1901-1953. George W. Corner. New York: Rockefeller Institute Press, 1964.

"John Howard Northrop." Frederick C. Robbins. *Proceedings of the American Philosophical Society* 135, no. 2 (1991)

(Laurence M. Burke II)

George A. Olah

Area of Achievement: Chemistry
Contribution: An organic chemist and Nobel laureate who developed synthetic methods, Olah shaped the modern concept of carbocations and pioneered superacid chemistry.

May 22, 1927	Born in Budapest, Hungary
1949	Earns a Ph.D. from the Technical University of Budapest
1949-1954	Serves as a professor at the Technical University of Budapest
1954-1956	Named associate scientific director of the Central Chemical Research Institute of the Hungarian Academy of Sciences
1957-1965	Works as a research scientist with the Dow Chemical Company
1964	Wins the American Chemical Society Award in Petroleum Chemistry
1965-1977	Named chair and Mabery Professor at Case Western Reserve University
1972 and 1988	Awarded J. S. Guggenheim Foundation Fellowships
1976	Elected to the U.S. National Academy of Sciences
1977	Becomes Loker Professor at the University of Southern California
1977	Given a Centenary Lectureship from the British Chemical Society
1992	Receives the Richard C. Tolman Award and the Mendeléev Medal
1993	Wins the Pioneer of Chemistry Award from the American Institute of Chemists
1994	Awarded the Nobel Prize in Chemistry

Early Life

George Andrew Olah was born in 1927 to Julius and Magda (Krasznai) Olah in Budapest, Hungary. His passion for science began during undergraduate and later graduate work at the Technical University of Budapest. He received a doctorate in organic chemistry under Geza Zemplén in 1949, then accepted a faculty position and married Judith Lengyel.

In 1954, Olah joined the Central Chemical Research Institute of the Hungarian Academy of Sciences as associate scientific director and head of the organic chemistry department. Following the abortive Hungarian uprising against Soviet rule in October, 1956, however, the Olahs fled Hungary for London with their young son and much of the research group, subsequently moving to Canada by the spring of 1957.

Emigrating to America

Olah was employed by Dow Chemical Company first at its subsidiary Dow Chemical Canada Ltd., in Sarnia, Ontario, where a second son was born, and then at Dow's Eastern Research Laboratory in Framingham, Massachusetts.

In 1965, Olah became chair of the chemistry department of Western Reserve University in Cleveland, Ohio, and continued as chair after its merger with Case Institute until 1969, when he was appointed Charles F. Mabery Distinguished Research Professor. Then, in 1977, he settled in Los Angeles as the Donald P. and Katherine B. Loker Distinguished Professor of Organic Chemistry and director of the Loker Hydrocarbon Research Institute at the University of Southern California (USC).

Olah obtained naturalized U.S. citizenship in 1970 and often includes the following sentiment in his otherwise formal biographical abstract: "America still is offering a new home and nearly unlimited possibilities to the newcomer who is willing to work hard for it. It is also where the 'main action' in science and technology remains."

Research Both Fundamental and Practical

Some organic chemists are mainly concerned with chemical synthesis. Others are physical organic chemists who study how chemical reactions work. Olah applied physical organic concepts to develop new synthetic methods and reagents. This research includes hydrocarbon chemistry, superacids, ionic intermediates and complexes, and organic fluorine and phosphorous compounds.

His early work on aromatic alkylations and other electrophilic reactions contributed to later discoveries of previously unknown substitution reactions under superacid conditions for the controlled functionalization of alkanes and related chemical processes such as high-octane gasoline production, the condensation of methane to yield liquid hydrocarbons, and the depolymerization of heavy oils and coal.

By the late 1990's, Olah had published more than one thousand scientific papers and monograph chapters, had written or coauthored at least fourteen books, and held more than a hundred patents. This was in addition to his role as general editor for the Wiley-Interscience series "Reactive Intermediates in Organic Chemistry" and "Monographs in Organic Chemistry," together with positions on the editorial boards of the *Journal of Organic Chemistry*, *Index Chemicus*, and *Current Abstracts*.

Olah was awarded the Nobel Prize in Chemistry in 1994.

Bibliography
By Olah
Einfuhrüng in die Theoretische Organische Chemie, 1960
Friedel-Crafts and Related Reactions, 1963-1965 (4 vols.; as editor)

Olah explains the formula for hydrocarbon. (Reuters/Fred Prouser/Archive Photos)

Superacids Stabilize Carbocations

Superacids provide a medium in which unstable carbocations are prepared and preserved long enough for their structure and other properties to be studied.

Many chemical reactions of organic compounds proceed through transient intermediates called carbocations, which are the positive ions of carbon compounds. Carbocations are electrophilic (electron-deficient) species that ordinarily are too fleeting for direct observation. Kinetic, stereochemical, and product studies since the 1920's, however, support their presence.

Highly polar solvents that are chemically inert toward electrophiles ("electron-loving" substances) were needed for carbocations to become stable, long-lived species. Olah first used the Lewis acid antimony pentafluoride (SbF_5) for this purpose in 1962 and later employed fluoroantimonic acid ($HF—SbF_5$) magic acid ($FSO_3H—SbF_5$), and other mixtures to confirm the existence of alkyl carbocations with nuclear magnetic resonance (NMR) and other spectroscopic methods. Such media are referred to as superacids because they are more acidic than 100 percent sulfuric acid.

Superacid solutions promote a variety of acid-catalyzed reactions that have potential importance for industrial chemistry. Olah also developed solid superacids for use as heterogeneous catalysts.

Bibliography

Carbocation Chemistry. Pierre Vogel. Amsterdam: Elsevier, 1985. "George Olah and the Chemistry of Carbocations." Barry Thomas. *Chemistry Review* 5 (November, 1995).

"My Search for Carbocations and Their Role in Chemistry." George A. Olah. *Angewandte Chemie International Edition in English* 34 (1995).

"Spectroscopic Observation of Alkylcarbonium Ions in Strong Acid Solutions." George A. Olah and Charles U. Pittman. *Advances in Physical Organic Chemistry* 4 (1966).

Superacids and Acidic Melts as Inorganic Chemical Reaction Media. Thomas A. O'Donnell. New York: VCH, 1993.

Carbonium Ions, 1968-1976 (5 vols.; as editor, with Paul von R. Schleyer)

Friedel-Crafts Chemistry, 1973

Carbocations and Electrophilic Reactions, 1973

Halonium Ions, 1975

Superacids, 1985 (with G. K. Surya Prakash and Jean Sommer)

Hypercarbon Chemistry, 1987 (with Prakash, Robert E. Williams, Leslie D. Field, and Kenneth Wade)

Nitration: Methods and Mechanisms, 1989 (with Ripudaman Malhotra and Subhash C. Narang)

Cage Hydrocarbons, 1990 (as editor)

Electron Deficient Boron and Carbon Clusters, 1991 (as editor, with Wade and Williams)

Chemistry of Energetic Materials, 1991 (as editor, with David R. Squire)

Synthetic Fluorine Chemistry, 1992 (as editor, with Richard D. Chambers and Prakash)

Hydrocarbon Chemistry, 1995 (with Árpád Molnár)

About Olah

"The Disputed Charge Account." Linda Garmon. *Science News* 124 (August 13, 1983).

"George A. Olah." In *The Nobel Prize Winners: Chemistry*, edited by Frank N. Magill. Pasadena, Calif.: Salem Press, 1990.

"George Olah Reflects on Chemical Research." Rudy Baum. *Chemical and Engineering News* 73 (February 27, 1995).

"U.S. Chemist Is Awarded Nobel Prize." M. W. Browne. *New York Times Biographical Service* 25 (October, 1994).

(Martin V. Stewart)

Wilhelm Olbers

Areas of Achievement: Astronomy and medicine

Contribution: An ophthalmologist by profession, Olbers contributed much to modern astronomy, notably the discovery of numerous comets and asteroids, a streamlined method for calculating cometary orbits, and an explanation as to why the night sky is dark and not fully illuminated by the myriad stars in space.

Oct. 11, 1758	Born in Arbergen, near Bremen, Germany
1777	Begins his medical studies at the University of Göttingen
1779	Observes Bode's comet and calculates its orbit
1780	Discovers a comet
1781	Visits Vienna and uses the observatory there to study the newly discovered planet Uranus
1797	Publishes a book on a new method for calculating cometary orbits
1802	Confirms the existence of Ceres, the first of several asteroids to be discovered between Mars and Jupiter
1815	Discovers a comet similar to Halley's comet
1820	Retires from his medical practice to pursue astronomy exclusively
1823	Publishes an article explaining the paradox of darkness at night
Mar. 2, 1840	Dies in Bremen, Germany

Early Life

Heinrich Wilhelm Matthäus Olbers was born into a large family, the eighth child of a Protestant clergyman who fathered a total of sixteen children. He was given a humanistic education in Bremen but became interested in the field of astronomy and taught himself mathematics so as to pursue the subject

At the age of sixteen, Olbers attempted to compute the course of the solar eclipse that occurred in that year, 1774. In 1777, he entered the University of Göttingen to study medicine and was graduated in 1780 with a dissertation on involuntary changes in the shape of the eye, *De oculi mutationibus internis.*

After something akin to a hospital residency in Vienna in 1781, during which he also visited the university's observatory at night, Olbers returned to Bremen to practice medicine. He was interested in what would now be called public health policy, and he was largely responsible for the introduction of the practice of inoculation in Germany.

Astronomy as an Avocation

Olbers made his astronomical observations in his spare time from an observatory in his house. As is sometimes the case, the enthusiasm of the amateur is more intense even than

(National Library of Medicine)

Comets and a Paradox

Olbers' observations of comets and his explanation for the darkness of the night sky helped pave the way for modern astronomy.

Olbers is known for his modern view that a comet's cloud is composed of matter that is repelled by the sun, creating a "tail" directed away from the solar radiation as the body approaches and moves around the center of the solar system. He formed this theory in 1811.

His observations confirmed the orbit, proposed by Carl Friedrich Gauss, of Ceres, an asteroid once presumed to be a new planet. Olbers thought that the second asteroid discovered by him, Pallas (the first was Vesta), might be the remnant, along with Juno, of an earlier, larger planet. It is now believed, however, that most asteroids were formed the same way that the planets were, by the aggregation of "dust." Olbers rejected the contemporaneous idea that meteorites might be stones expelled from the volcanoes of the moon, citing their extreme speed on impact with Earth. The comet that bears his name was discovered by Olbers in 1815.

While Olbers was not the first to propose a modern solution to the paradox of the darkness of the night sky, his explanation of 1823 is surely the most famous. The paradox that bears his name is hardly apparent to the layperson, but, if one considers the universe to be uniform and infinite and space to be transparent, then billions of suns burning in space should fill the night sky with light.

That this is not the case can be explained by positing sufficient interstellar, nontransparent matter to absorb a portion of the light of distant stars. Modern observations have gone beyond Olbers' paradox to confirm the existence of vast areas of so-called dark matter in outer space.

Bibliography

Comet. Carl Sagan and Ann Druyan. New York: Random House, 1985.

The Paradox of Olbers' Paradox: A Case History of Scientific Thought. Stanley L. Jaki. New York: Herder and Herder, 1969.

that of the professional, and Olbers was soon in active correspondence with many of the foremost German astronomers of the day, including J. H. Schröter, F. X. von Zach, and the famous mathematician Carl Friedrich Gauss.

On von Zach's recommendation, Olbers published in 1797 his treatise on the best way to calculate the parabolic orbits of comets, a work that met with much professional acclaim and established his reputation.

Personal Life

Olbers was married twice. His first wife, Dorothea Köhne, died during a difficult childbirth in 1786, after a marriage of only a year. Their daughter would be reared by Olbers' second wife, Anna Adelheid Lurson, whom he married in 1789. The couple had one son. Beginning with the death of his daughter in 1818, a tragedy that was followed by his second wife's death two years later, Olbers withdrew from practical affairs to a large extent.

Still, public life would not allow him to remain inactive, and he continued to be consulted by physicians seeking his help with difficult medical cases and astronomers seeking his scientific counsel. On two occasions during the French occupation under Napoleon, Olbers was sent to Paris as an official representative of the government of the city-state of Bremen.

Most of his life, Olbers enjoyed robust health and was known to have slept only four hours nightly, allowing his extensive astronomical observations. Not only his untiring efforts in the field of astronomy but also his generosity and collegiality set him apart. It may be seen as another of his many permanent contributions to science that he recognized and encouraged the young Friedrich Wilhelm Bessel, who would go on to become one of the great astronomers of the nineteenth century. Olbers died on March 2, 1840, at the age of eighty-one.

Bibliography

By Olbers

Abhandlung über die leichteste und bequemste Methode, die Bahn eines Cometen Zu einigen Beobachtungen zu berechnen, 1797 (concerning

the easiest method of calculating the trajectory of a comet from several observations)
"Über die Durchsichtigkeit des Weltraums" in *Berliner astronomisches Jahrbuch für das Jahr 1826*, 1823 (concerning the transparency of the universe)

About Olbers

"Heinrich Wilhelm Matthias Olbers." Lettie S. Multhauf. In *The Dictionary of Scientific Biography*, edited by Charles Coulston Gillispie. Vol. 10. New York: Charles Scribner's Sons, 1974.
"Olbers, Heinrich Wilhelm Matthäus." Isaac Asimov. In *Isaac Asimov's Biographical Encyclopedia of Science and Technology*. New York: Avon Books, 1976.

(Mark R. McCulloh)

Lars Onsager

Areas of Achievement: Chemistry and physics

Contribution: Onsager made important discoveries in statistical mechanics and was a pioneer in the field of nonequilibrium thermodynamics.

Nov. 27, 1903	Born in Kristiania (now Oslo), Norway
1926-1928	Serves as a research assistant for Peter J. W. Debye in Zurich
1928	Accepts a position as a teaching associate at The Johns Hopkins University
1928	Transfers to Brown University
1931	Publishes two papers in *Physical Review* on reciprocal relationships
1935	Awarded a doctorate from Yale University
1942	Finds an exact solution to the two-dimensional Ising model
1951-1952	Takes a sabbatical as a Fulbright professor at Cambridge University, England
1953	Awarded Rumford Medal of the American Academy of Arts and Sciences
1968	Given the National Medal of Science
1968	Awarded the Nobel Prize in Chemistry
1971	Moves to the University of Miami's Center for Theoretical Study
Oct. 5, 1976	Dies in Coral Gables, Florida

Early Life

Lars Onsager was born in Kristiania (now Oslo), Norway, in 1903. His family was middle class, and he grew up in comfortable surroundings. Following his graduation from secondary school, Onsager enrolled at the Norwegian Technical School in Trondheim, where he studied chemical engineering.

It soon became clear that Onsager had a talent for science. In 1925, he traveled to Zurich, Switzerland, to discuss with noted physical chemist Peter J. W. Debye a correction that Onsager had found to Debye's theory of electrolytes in solution. Debye decided to take Onsager on as a research assistant. After two years in Switzerland, Onsager emigrated to the United States, where he had landed a job as an instructor in freshman chemistry at The Johns Hopkins University. Shortly thereafter, he moved to Brown University, where he continued to teach while conducting research.

Reciprocal Relationships

Onsager remained at Brown from 1928 to 1933. During this period, he worked on the problem of reciprocal relationships. Examples of these types of relationships had been known for more than a hundred years, but Onsager was able to develop a general theory that provided a systematic description for such relationships.

Onsager's theory on reciprocal relationships was outlined in two papers published in 1931. He showed that for small departures from equilibrium, simple relationships can be found to describe the approach to equilibrium.

Onsager's work soon found a variety of applications in nonequilibrium thermodynamics (the study of heat). Onsager himself used his theory to analyze thermal diffusion as a means for isotope separation. In the early 1940's, this work formed the basis for one separation method used to isolate the uranium 235 isotope in the development of the atomic bomb.

Other Scientific Work

In 1933, Onsager moved from Brown to Yale University, where he was to remain for nearly forty years. While at Yale, he continued his work in statistical mechanics. His most important discovery concerned the Ising model, a method used to describe systems, such as magnets, consisting of regular arrays of spinning particles. Onsager announced in 1942 that he had found an exact solution for the partition

An Exact Solution to the Two-Dimensional Ising Model

Onsager discovered an exact solution for the partition function for a two-dimensional Ising model and applied the result to the order-disorder phase transition.

Phase transitions play an important role in the behavior of substances. For interacting particles, a common method used to investigate phase transitions is the Ising model, which consists of particles arranged in a lattice in one, two, or three dimensions. The particles have two states, commonly called spin up and spin down, and interact only with neighboring particles.

Early researchers showed that no phase transition occurs in the one-dimensional Ising model. In 1942, Onsager derived an exact solution for the partition function for the two-dimensional Ising model, from which values for thermodynamic functions can be obtained.

Onsager found T_c, the temperature at which the order-disorder phase transition occurs, and showed that the phase transition is of the second order. Onsager also determined the dependence of spontaneous magnetization on temperature in the vicinity of the critical temperature. Onsager's results were later confirmed experimentally.

The Ising model continues to be used to discuss phase transitions in systems. While approximate solutions to the three-dimensional model had been determined by the mid-1990's, an exact solution to the model analogous to the two-dimensional result found by Onsager had not been obtained.

Bibliography

Exactly Solved Models in Statistical Mechanics. Rodney J. Baxter. New York: Academic Press, 1982.
Introduction to Modern Statistical Mechanics. David Chandler. New York: Oxford University Press, 1987.
Statistical Mechanics and Dynamics. Henry Eyring, Douglas Henderson, Betsy Jones Stover, and Edward M. Eyring. 2d ed. New York: John Wiley & Sons, 1982.

(The Nobel Foundation)

work on the electrical properties of superconductors.

Onsager was awarded the Nobel Prize in Chemistry in 1968. Three years later, after reaching the mandatory retirement age at Yale, he moved to Florida, where he joined the Center for Theoretical Studies at the University of Miami. He continued to work there until his death in 1976.

Bibliography
By Onsager
"Reciprocal Relations in Irreversible Processes," *Physical Review*, 1931 (parts 1 and 2)

"Electric Moments of Molecules in Liquids," *Journal of the American Chemical Society*, 1936

"Theory of Isotope Separation by Thermal Diffusion," *Physical Review*, 1939 (with W. H. Furry and R. Clark Jones)

"Crystal Statistics," *Physical Review*, 1942

"Bose-Einstein Condensation and Liquid Helium," *Physical Review*, 1956 (with Oliver Penrose)

"Magnetic Flux Through a Superconducting Ring," *Physical Review Letters*, 1961

About Onsager
"Autobiographical Commentary of Lars Onsager." Lars Onsager. In *Critical Phenomena*, edited by R. E. Mills. New York: McGraw-Hill, 1971.

"Lars Onsager." H. Christopher Longuet-Higgins and Michael E. Fisher. *Biographical Memoirs of Fellows of the Royal Society* 24 (1978).

"Lars Onsager." In *The Nobel Prize Winners: Chemistry*, edited by Frank N. Magill. Pasadena, Calif.: Salem Press, 1990.

function for the two-dimensional Ising model. He used his result to describe the phase transition occurring between ordered and disordered states in the model.

Onsager continued to be productive in research throughout his life. In 1949, in discussing the behavior of vortices in two dimensions, he developed the concept of negative absolute temperature. This idea was applied a decade later to describe the operation of lasers. In 1960, he proposed a theory for electrical conductivity in ice. In the early 1960's, he also published

(Jeffrey A. Joens)

Jan Hendrik Oort

Area of Achievement: Astronomy
Contribution: Oort's theoretical and observational work established the structure, size, mass, and motion of the Milky Way. He also postulated the existence of the Oort cloud, which is widely accepted as the source of most comets.

Apr. 28, 1900	Born in Franeker, Friesland, the Netherlands
1924	Appointed an astronomer at Leiden Observatory
1926	Receives a doctorate from the University of Groningen
1927	Calculates the mass and size of the Milky Way
1935	Made a professor of astronomy at Leiden University
1935	Elected the general secretary of the International Astronomical Union
1942	Receives the Bruce Medal for his achievements in astronomy
1945	Made the director of Leiden Observatory
1950	Proposes the existence of the Oort cloud
1951	With Hendrik Van de Hulst, discovers 21-centimeter radiation from neutral hydrogen in space
1956	With Theodore Walraven, discovers synchrotron radiation from the Crab nebula
1958	Elected president of the International Astronomical Union
1970	Retires as director of Leiden Observatory
Nov. 5, 1992	Dies in Leiden, the Netherlands

(AP/Wide World Photos)

Early Life
The son of a doctor, Jan Hendrik Oort (pronounced "ahrt") was born in the Netherlands on April 28, 1900, in the town of Franeker, Friesland. He completed his education at the University of Groningen, where he studied under Jacobus Cornelius Kapteyn, from whom he acquired an interest in galactic structure and motion.

After completing his doctorate in 1926, Oort worked briefly at Yale University before returning to the Netherlands and the University of Leiden, where he remained for the rest of his career.

The Shape of the Galaxy
In 1927, Oort was able to confirm and modify the theories of Bertil Lindblad concerning the structure of the Milky Way. Two years earlier, Lindblad had advanced the theory that the Galaxy rotates in its own plane about its center. Oort, by measuring the velocities of a number

of stars in the Milky Way relative to Earth's solar system, was able to verify this theory and to produce estimates for the size and mass of the Galaxy. Eventually, he was able to estimate its rate of rotation and the direction and the distance of the galactic core from the solar system.

Much of this work was made possible by Oort's pioneering research in radio astronomy. Because radio waves pass through the dust particles that obscure the inner parts of the Galaxy from optical observation, they can be used to study the galactic core directly. After World War II, new radio and microwave technologies produced a rapid expansion in radio astronomy, and Oort is credited with establishing the radio observatories at Dwingeloo and Westerbork. These facilities brought the Netherlands to the forefront of this exciting and productive new research area.

In 1951, Oort and his student Hendrik Van de Hulst discovered 21-centimeter microwave radiation emitted by neutral hydrogen in space. This radiation travels freely through dust clouds and is emitted from regions near stars, which made it possible for Oort and Van de Hulst to produce the first maps of the Galaxy, showing the sizes and positions of the spiral arms with respect to Earth.

A Cloud of Comets
As a second area of research, Oort took up the study of comets. In 1950, he proposed what has become known as the Oort cloud.

He suggested that the solar system is surrounded by a cloud of perhaps as many as 10 trillion small icy bodies, at a distance extending to about 1.5 light-years from the sun. Gravitational forces from passing stars occasionally change the orbits of some of these bodies, sending them toward the inner solar system to become comets. This hypothesis accounts for the observed trajectories of comets and has come to be widely accepted.

A Distinguished Senior Scientist
Oort's later career was marked by many honors as a renowned and well-liked researcher. From 1958 to 1961, he served as president of the International Astronomical Union. He retired in 1970 and died in Leiden on November 5, 1992.

The Structure of the Galaxy

The solar system to which Earth belongs is part of a rotating spiral galaxy approximately thirty kiloparsecs across, with a mass 150 billion times that of the sun.

Around the beginning of the twentieth century, it became apparent that the structure of the Milky Way must be similar to that of the spiral nebulas and that these nebulas themselves must be galaxies composed of many stars.

Oort measured the motions of stars relative to Earth to confirm Bertil Lindblad's theory that the Galaxy must rotate. Oort and other researchers continued to refine their observations, using optical and then radio astronomy to penetrate deeper into the galactic disk. The following overall structure has now emerged. The Galaxy rotates faster near the center than toward the edge. Earth's solar system, which is 8.7 kiloparsecs—about 28,000 light-years or 2.7×10^{17} kilometers—from the center, completes a rotation about that center every 200 million years.

Increasingly precise observations and dynamic analyses of this and other spiral galaxies have made it clear that the masses of the stars and other objects visible cannot account for the rotational speeds observed. Much additional mass must exist outside the visible disks of the galaxies. In addition, most current theories about the origin, structure, and evolution of the universe require the existence of more mass than can be directly observed. These anomalies of galactic motion provide evidence that at least some of this mass must exist, but its nature is undetermined.

Bibliography
The Origin and Evolution of Galaxies. B. J. T. Jones and J. E. Jones. Dordrecht, the Netherlands: D. Reidel, 1983.

Structure and Evolution of Galaxies. J. Lequeux. New York: Gordon and Breach, 1969.

Bibliography
By Oort
"Radio Astronomical Studies of the Galactic System," *Proceedings of the Vetlesen Symposium*, 1966

About Oort
"An Appreciation of Jan Hendrik Oort." B. Streomgren. In *Galaxies and the Universe*. New York: Columbia University Press, 1968.
Oort and the Universe: A Sketch of Oort's Research and Person— Liber Amicorum Presented to Jan Hendrik Oort on the Occasion of His Eightieth Birthday, 28 April 1980. H. van Woerden, W. N. Brouw, and H. Van de Hulst, eds. Boston: D. Reidel, 1980.

(Firman D. King)

Aleksandr Ivanovich Oparin

Areas of Achievement: Cell biology and chemistry

Contribution: Oparin is best known for formulating the hypothesis that life originated on Earth by the synthesis of complex organic compounds from simple inorganic chemicals.

Mar. 2, 1894	Born in Uglich, Russia
1917	Graduated from Moscow State University
1922	Proposes a hypothesis of the origin of life on Earth
1924	Publishes a description of his hypothesis
1936	Publishes *Vozniknovie zhini na zemle* (*The Origin of Life on Earth*, 1951)
1946-1980	Appointed head of the Bahk Institute of Biochemistry, Moscow
1953	His hypothesis is supported by research by University of Chicago scientists Harold Urey and Stanley Miller
1957	Organizes the first international meeting on the origin of life
1960	Publishes *Zhizn': Ee priroda proiskhozhdenie i raevitie* (*Life: Its Nature, Origins, and Development*, 1961)
1963	Convenes a second conference on the origin of life
1964	His seventieth birthday is honored with a volume on evolutionary and industrial biochemistry
1970	Elected president of the International Society for the Study of the Evolution of Life
Apr. 21, 1980	Dies in Moscow, Soviet Union

Life from Nonlife

Given the proper mix of simple chemicals, water, and a source of energy, complex reproducing organic compounds can be formed.

Oparin was intrigued by the basic question of how life originated on Earth. The Bible describes a miraculous event, and believers in spontaneous generation (for example, that living frogs can form in inert mud) accepted that explanation. Oparin's research in biochemistry led him to propose a "natural" method.

He proposed a primitive Earth atmosphere rich in hydrogen, methane, ammonia, and water vapor. With the input of high energy from, for example, a lightning stroke, these chemicals might be transformed into complex organic compounds capable of using energy sources from their environment in order to grow and reproduce—to live. This proposal was later supported by independent laboratory research in the United States.

The explanation of how a first lifelike system might originate and reproduce began a new field in biochemistry and an understanding of the possible origin of life on Earth.

Bibliography

"How Did Life Start?" Peter Redetsky. *Discover* 13 (November, 1992).

Origin of Life. Bernard Hagene and Charles Lenay. Translated by Albert V. Carozzi and Marguerite Carozzi. New York: Barron's, 1987.

"The Origin of Life on the Earth." Leslie E. Orgel. *Scientific American* 271 (October, 1994).

Early Life

Aleksandr Ivanovich Oparin was born in Uglich, a small village near Moscow. When he was nine, his parents moved to Moscow because there was no secondary school in their village.

Oparin matriculated at Moscow State University, where he majored in plant physiology. His mentor, K. A. Timiryazev, had known Charles Darwin, and Darwin's theory of evolution indirectly influenced Oparin's thinking. Russian botanist A. N. Bakh further helped shape Oparin's concepts.

Early Research

Although he is widely recognized today for his scientific contributions to the origins of life, much of Oparin's research was in applied biochemistry. He was particularly interested in enzymology, the action of complex organic compounds produced by living cells (for example, digestive enzymes) that cause chemical changes in other organic substances, such as proteins and some foods.

Many of these studies led to his work in a related field, industrial biochemistry. Oparin conducted experiments in changing raw agricultural crops such as potatoes, wheat, and beets into consumer products, including table sugar, bread, and wine.

The Origin of Life

Oparin's applied biochemical research served a valuable purpose in the Soviet Union. His work would enable the Communist govern-

(AP/Wide World Photos)

ment to turn the basic agricultural society of pre-Soviet Russia into the workers' paradise expounded by Karl Marx, Vladimir Ilich Lenin, and Joseph Stalin. His research also led him into the theoretical biochemical field surrounding the origin of life on Earth.

Much of the world accepted a divine origin of life. A natural origin of life, however, would better serve atheistic Communism. In 1922, at a meeting of the Russian Botanical Society, Oparin first introduced his concept of a "protobiont," a hypothetical first form of earthly life. Protobionts (also called "eobionts") were viewed as having developed in the rich chemical soup of the primitive world ocean. They were believed to be large molecules capable of taking energy from their environment and, most important, reproducing.

This concept had been independently arrived at a few years earlier by a British biologist, J. B. S. Haldane. The natural origin of life assumption is often referred to as the Oparin-Haldane hypothesis.

Honors and Recognition
Oparin was highly regarded by his peers and especially by the government of the Soviet Union. His awards included the Order of Lenin, the Bakh Prize, the Kalinga Prize, and the Metchnikoff Gold Medal. In addition, he was named a Hero of Socialist Labor. He served as director of the Bakh Institute of Biochemistry until his death in 1980.

Bibliography
By Oparin
Proiskhozhedenie zhini, 1924 (*The Origin of Life*, 1938)

Vozniknovenie zhini na zemle, 1936 (*The Origin of Life on Earth*, 1951)

Zhizn': Ee priroda proiskhozhdenie i razvitie, 1960 (*Life: Its Nature, Origins, and Development*, 1961)

Vozniknovenie i nachal'noe razvitie zhizni, 1966 (*Genesis and Evolutionary Development of Life*, 1968)

About Oparin
"Alexandr Ivanovich Oparin." In *Great Lives from History: Twentieth Century Series*, edited by Frank N. Magill. Pasadena, Calif.: Salem Press, 1990.

The Origin of Life and Evolutionary Biochemistry. K. Dose et al., eds. New York: Plenum Press, 1974.

The Origins of Prebiological Systems and Their Molecular Matrices. Sidney W. Fox, ed. New York: Academic Press, 1965.

(Albert C. Jensen)

J. Robert Oppenheimer

Areas of Achievement: Invention, physics, and technology

Contribution: Oppenheimer was key in establishing the University of California, Berkeley, and the Institute for Advanced Study at Princeton as international centers for theoretical physics. He is known principally, however, for his role in the development of the atomic bomb during World War II.

Apr. 22, 1904	Born in New York, New York
1922	Enters Harvard University
1927	Receives a Ph.D. from the University of Göttingen
1929	Joins the faculty at the California Institute of Technology and the University of California, Berkeley
1934	Postulates the existence of neutron stars
1942	Placed in charge of the Los Alamos Laboratory for the Manhattan Project
1947	Serves as chair of the general advisory committee to the Atomic Energy Commission (AEC)
1947	Joins the Institute for Advanced Study at Princeton
1949	Opposes the development of the hydrogen bomb but is overruled by President Harry S Truman
1953	Declared a security risk by the AEC
1963	Receives the Fermi Award for his contribution to nuclear research
Feb. 18, 1967	Dies in Princeton, New Jersey

(AP/Wide World Photos)

wide-ranging interests at an early age. His parents enrolled him in the Ethical Culture School in New York City. In 1922, he enrolled in Harvard University, majoring in chemistry; he completed the undergraduate curriculum in three years, being graduated with a B.A. in 1925.

The following year, Erwin Schrödinger proposed a new wave theory for the hydrogen atom, and Oppenheimer wrote his Ph.D. thesis in physics at the University of Göttingen, in Germany, applying Schrödinger's equation to the photoelectric effect in hydrogen and for X rays.

In 1929, Oppenheimer accepted a joint faculty position in physics at the University of California, Berkeley (UCB), and the California Institute of Technology (Caltech) in Pasadena. At UCB, he developed the preeminent center for theoretical physics in the United States, attracting the best graduate students and postdoctoral fellows.

Early Life

Born on April 22, 1904, Julius Robert Oppenheimer demonstrated a keen intellect and

Research in Theoretical Physics

The general public is more aware of Oppenheimer's involvement in the development of the

The Manhattan Project

Oppenheimer's successes as a physicist are greatly overshadowed by his involvement in the Manhattan Project to create an atomic bomb during World War II.

Prior to the initiation of the Manhattan Project, based on experimental evidence that suggested the possibility of using nuclear energy for a bomb of unprecedented destructive power, Oppenheimer organized a small working group of eminent physicists in the summer of 1942 to investigate the theoretical aspects of assembling an atomic weapon. At that time, the U.S. development effort was fragmented and disjointed, and it is now known to have been significantly behind the German effort. The United States was also aware that Japan was working on the development of atomic weapons.

In that year, 1942, General Leslie Groves of the U.S. Army was placed in charge of organizing the development of the atomic bomb. As a result of visiting the various laboratories and interviewing numerous scientists, he decided on Oppenheimer to be the civilian director for bomb design and assembly. In an effort to balance the military criterion of "need to know" only with the need for open discussion by the scientific community, Oppenheimer decided to set up a single, isolated laboratory for the Manhattan Project.

This laboratory was located in a remote region of New Mexico at the site of the Los Alamos Boy's Academy and is now known as the Los Alamos National Laboratory. Initially conceived as a center of research for forty to fifty scientists, Los Alamos swelled to a population of more than seven thousand scientists, engineers, technicians, support staff, and their families—all of whom were completely cut off from the rest of the world for the duration of the project.

Recognizing that there were two isotopes with potential for use in an atomic weapon, Oppenheimer's team developed two types of bombs, one using the isotope uranium 235 and one using the isotope plutonium 239. Each type required radically different engineering approaches to bomb designs, yet both were successfully developed by July, 1945. These bombs were then dropped on the cities of Hiroshima and Nagasaki, Japan, thus bringing an end to World War II.

Oppenheimer did not achieve a research status characteristic of those scientists awarded the Nobel Prize. Nevertheless, he is recognized for his leadership in developing in the United States an internationally respected tradition in theoretical physics. Even the critics of his role in the development of the atomic bomb concede that his keen insight, quick recognition of the relevant scientific and technical issues, superior grasp of the physics involved, and surprising administrative expertise led to the particular success of the Manhattan Project in so brief a period of time.

Bibliography

The Advisors: Oppenheimer, Teller, and the Superbomb. Herbert F. York. Stanford, Calif.: Stanford University Press, 1989.

The Making of the Atomic Bomb. Richard Rhodes. New York: Simon & Schuster, 1986.

Robert Oppenheimer: Letters and Recollections. Alice K. Smith and Charles Weiner, eds. Cambridge, Mass.: Harvard University Press, 1981.

Robert Oppenheimer: The Man and Theories. Michel Rouzé. Translated by Patrick Evans. New York: P. S. Eriksson, 1964.

atomic bomb than of his more scholarly accomplishments. He made important contributions to various areas of pure theoretical physics, however, prior to assuming his position as director of the Los Alamos Laboratory for the Manhattan Project.

After P. A. M. Dirac proposed a relativistic wave equation that included negative energy-state solutions, it was Oppenheimer who showed that Dirac's proposal that the negative energy states were protons was in error; Oppenheimer proved that these negative energy states must have the same mass as the electron. This led to the theoretical prediction of the positron, which was discovered experimentally by Carl David Anderson two years later.

Oppenheimer and M. Plesset published the first paper on the production of pairs of electrons and positrons. It was under Oppenheimer's direction that his school of theoretical physics at UCB developed a highly respected theory of shower production from cosmic rays, which accounted for most of the observed phenomena and has remained fundamentally unchanged. Oppenheimer was among the first physicists to recognize the possibility of the existence of neutron stars, decades before they were experimentally observed.

In 1942, Oppenheimer was asked to be the director of the Los Alamos Laboratory for the Manhattan Project, the top-secret project dedicated to the development of atomic weapons during World War II. As is well known, this effort was successful, whereas the efforts of Germany and Japan to develop similar weapons were not.

In 1947, he was offered the position as director of the Institute for Advanced Study at Princeton University. Under his direction, the institute became the world's center for the development and advancement of high-energy physics and field theory. The students, postdoctoral fellows, and doctoral physicists who worked under Oppenheimer at UCB, Caltech, and Los Alamos reads as a "Who's Who" of twentieth century theoretical physics. This list includes Julian Schwinger, Murray Gell-Mann, Robert Serber, Freeman Dysan, Richard P. Feynman, and Abraham Pais, as well as many others.

Questioning His Loyalty

After his work at Los Alamos, Oppenheimer, fearing an uncontrolled arms race, opposed further development of atomic weapons. In particular, he was at odds with Edward Teller, who was determined to develop what Teller called "the super bomb"—a thermonuclear fusion bomb, otherwise known as a hydrogen bomb.

In 1949, under Oppenheimer's direction, the Board of Scientific Advisors of the Atomic Energy Commission (AEC) rejected a proposal to initiate a program for the manufacture of the hydrogen bomb. This rejection was overridden by President Harry S Truman.

In 1953, as a result of his opposition to devel-

opment of the hydrogen bomb, his sharp tongue (which was quite effective at alienating others), and his position of power within the AEC, Oppenheimer became a victim of the tide of anticommunist McCarthyism. Under the bogus accusation that his loyalty was in question, the Security Hearing Board and the Atomic Energy Commission revoked his security clearance—thus blocking Oppenheimer from having any future official influence or control over policies regarding the development of nuclear weapons. It is believed that Teller's testimony at these hearings weighed heavily in swaying the board. This episode created a long-lasting schism in the scientific community.

It was not until 1963 that the government attempted to redress the humiliation of labeling him a security risk by bestowing upon Oppenheimer the AEC Fermi Award for contributions to nuclear research—ironically, in the year following Edward Teller's receipt of the award.

Bibliography

By Oppenheimer
"Note on the Theory of the Interaction of Field and Matter," *Physical Review*, 1930
"On Massive Neutron Cores," *Physical Review*, 1939 (with G. M. Volkoff)
"On Continued Gravitational Contraction," *Physical Review*, 1939 (with H. Snyder)
The Open Mind, 1955
Some Reflections on Science and Culture, 1960
Robert Oppenheimer: Letters and Recollections, 1980 (Alice K. Smith and Charles Weiner, eds.)

About Oppenheimer
"J. Robert Oppenheimer." Hans Bethe. In *The Road from Los Alamos*. New York: American Institute of Physics, 1991.
J. Robert Oppenheimer, Shatterer of Worlds. Peter Goodchild. Boston: Houghton Mifflin, 1981.
The Oppenheimer Case. Philip Stern. New York: Harper & Row, 1969.

(Stephen Huber)

Hans Christian Ørsted

Areas of Achievement: Chemistry and physics

Contribution: Ørsted, sometimes called the founder of electromagnetism, demonstrated that electric currents can produce magnetic effects.

Aug. 14, 1777	Born in Rudkøbing, Langeland, Denmark
1794	Begins studies at the University of Copenhagen
1797	Receives a pharmacology degree with honors
1798	Joins the editorial staff of a small philosophical journal
1799	Receives a Ph.D. in natural philosophy from Copenhagen
1801-1804	Travels in Germany and France
1805	Offered an unpaid teaching position by Copenhagen
1806	Appointed extraordinary professor of physics
1817	Promoted to ordinary professor of physics
1820	Demonstrates a relationship between electricity and magnetism
1822	Awarded the Copley Medal of the Royal Society of London
1824	Founds the Society for the Diffusion of Physical Science in Denmark
1825	Prepares aluminum chloride and isolates metallic aluminum
1829	Helps establish the Polytechnic Institute and is named its director
1849	Finishes writing *Aanden i naturen* (*The Soul in Nature*, 1852)
Mar. 9, 1851	Dies in Copenhagen, Denmark

Early Life

Hans Christian Ørsted (pronounced "EHR-stehd" and often spelled "Oersted") was born in 1777 as the son of a pharmacist in Rudkøbing, Denmark. Ørsted did not have a formal early education; rather, he was educated by various people in his hometown. In 1788, he began helping his father at his pharmacy.

Ørsted and his brother went to Copenhagen to study at the university there in 1794. Ørsted received his degree in pharmacology with honors in 1797 and his Ph.D. in natural philosophy in 1799. During his studies, he became a devoted student of Immanuel Kant's philosophical ideas. In 1798, Ørsted joined the editorial staff of a short-lived journal promoting Kantian philosophy. Kant's concepts of opposing forces in nature became the basis of Ørsted's view of nature and dominated his scientific investigations for the rest of his life.

Journey Abroad

Following Count Alessandro Volta's creation of a galvanic pile (electrical battery) for producing electricity on demand, Ørsted became

(National Library of Medicine)

Electromagnetism

Electricity and magnetism are interrelated effects. Electric current can produce magnetic fields, and varying magnetic flux can produce electric fields.

Ørsted's Kantian philosophy led him to suspect a connection between electric forces and magnetic forces. Ørsted thought that all forces resulted from a tension between attraction and repulsion. Although he was correct in his belief that there is a relationship between electricity and magnetism, he was wrong as to the basis of that relationship.

Following his discovery that electric current produces an effect on magnetic needles, Ørsted conducted other experiments with electric current and magnetic needles. He showed that the deflection is in opposite directions above and below the wire and that the direction of deflection reverses with a reversal of current. This result showed that the magnetic field lines form circles around a current-carrying wire.

Upon hearing about Ørsted's experiments, Dominique-François-Jean Arago performed his own experiments with electric currents in 1820. Arago showed that current-carrying wires also attract iron filings, in the same way that magnets do. Arago thus proved that the current-carrying wire indeed produces a magnetic effect.

In 1831, Michael Faraday showed that not only can electricity produce magnetism but magnetism can produce electricity as well. He found that changing magnetic fields produce an electrical voltage. It is through the application of Faraday's law that electricity today is made in power plants and in automobile alternators, in which rotating loops of wire produce changes in magnetic fields.

By 1879, André-Marie Ampère had shown the magnetic fields of current-carrying wires interact with one another. Parallel wires with current flowing in the same direction are attracted to one another, and parallel wires with current flowing in opposite directions are repelled. Ampère also determined a way to calculate the intensity of the magnetic field caused by a current-carrying wire.

Finally, in 1865, James Clerk Maxwell put all of the previous work together to develop a set of four equations. These so-called Maxwell's equations form the heart of the modern understanding of electromagnetism. They show that time-varying electric fields produce magnetic fields and that time-varying magnetic fields produce electric fields. The most important aspect of Maxwell's equations is that they can be solved to show that coupled varying electric and magnetic fields propagate as waves, which demonstrated that light is a form of electromagnetic radiation.

Maxwell's Equations

$$\oint_S \mathbf{E} \cdot \hat{n} dA = \frac{Q}{\varepsilon_o} \qquad \oint_C \mathbf{B} \cdot d\mathbf{l} = \mu_o I + \mu_o \varepsilon_o \frac{d}{dt} \int_S \mathbf{E} \cdot \hat{n} dA$$

$$\oint_S \mathbf{B} \cdot \hat{n} dA = 0 \qquad \oint_C \mathbf{E} \cdot d\mathbf{l} = -\frac{d}{dt} \int_S \mathbf{B} \cdot \hat{n} dA$$

Bibliography

The Feynman Lectures on Physics. Richard P. Feynman, Robert Leighton, and Matthew Sands. Reading. Mass.: Addison-Wesley, 1964.

A History of Electricity and Magnetism. Herbert W. Meyer. Cambridge. Mass.: MIT Press, 1971.

Light, Magnetism, and Electricity. Isaac Asimov. Vol. 2 in *Understanding Physics.* New York: Walker, 1966.

---

interested in electrical studies. In 1801, he began a journey through France and Germany that lasted more than two years, visiting many laboratories and lectures in science and philosophy.

During this trip, he became acquainted with Johann Ritter and with Ritter's ideas regarding a relationship between chemistry and electricity. Ørsted eventually incorporated these ideas with his own Kantian philosophy.

Educational Interests

Upon his return to Copenhagen, Ørsted was unable to obtain a position at the university, so he took a job running a pharmacy. He began giving lectures in physics and chemistry, which became extremely popular. The university officials took notice and offered him an unpaid teaching position in 1805. By 1806, he was appointed extraordinary professor of physics, and he was promoted to ordinary professor in 1817.

Ørsted enjoyed teaching and believed strongly in the importance of education. He was committed not only to teaching at the university but also to sharing natural science with all people. He wrote many essays about natural science for laypeople and several textbooks for students. He never lost interest in teaching.

In 1824, Ørsted founded the Society for the Diffusion of Physical Science in Denmark. With his help, the society founded the Polytechnic Institute in Copenhagen, and Ørsted was named its director, a position that he held for the rest of his life.

The Discovery of Electromagnetism

For most of Ørsted's early years teaching at the university, he was either unpaid or paid very little. Consequently, his time was divided between teaching and working at the pharmacy, and he had little time for research other than that associated with his classes.

His Kantian philosophy led Ørsted to believe that all forces originated from the same root causes and must, therefore, be related. This idea, in turn, led him to believe in a connection between electrical forces and magnetic forces.

In April, 1820, Ørsted was lecturing on the similarities between electrical forces and magnetic forces. During the lecture, he sent electrical current through a wire suspended over a compass needle. The needle quivered slightly when the current was applied. Ørsted saw the tiny deflection and thus discovered that electrical current can produce magnetic effects. The connection between electricity and magnetism is now known as electromagnetism.

While often portrayed as an accidental breakthrough during a classroom lecture, Ørsted's discovery of electromagnetism was a direct result of his belief in the relationship between electricity and magnetism. He found the connection because he was looking for it.

Other Studies

While Ørsted is most famous for his discovery of electromagnetism, that field was not his sole area of research. Another major emphasis was the study of the compressibility of gases and liquids. A major goal of this research was to show a correlation between pressure and compression. Ørsted did not accept the atomic theory of matter, which stated that incompressible atoms would limit how small a sample of material could be compressed. He wished to show that there was no pressure at which a gas or liquid could not be compressed further. Ørsted was unable to create enough pressure in his experiments to reach this limit.

With his pharmacological background, Ørsted was also interested in chemistry. In 1825, he succeeded in preparing aluminum chloride and isolating metallic aluminum. He also studied the connection between chemistry and electricity. Ørsted died in Copenhagen in 1851 at the age of seventy-three.

Bibliography

By Ørsted

"Ueber die Art, wie sich die Electricitat fortpflanzt," *Neues allgemeines Journal der Chemie*, 1806

"Bemerkungen hinsichtlich auf Contactelectricitat," *Journal fur Chemie und Physik*, 1817

Experimenta circa effectum conflictus electrici in acum magneticum, 1820 ("Experiments on the Effect of a Current of Electricity on the Magnetic Needle," *Annals of Philosophy*, 1820)

Aanden i naturen, 1850 (*The Soul in Nature*, 1852)

Naturvidenskabelige Skrifter, 1920 (Kristine Meyer, ed.)

About Ørsted

Great Experiments in Physics. Morris H. Shamos. New York: Holt, Rinehart and Winston, 1959.

"Hans Christiaan Oersted: Scientist, Humanist, and Teacher." J. Rud Nielson. *American Physics Teacher* 7 (1939).

Romanticism and the Sciences. Andrew Cunningham and Nicholas Jardine. Cambridge, England: Cambridge University Press, 1990.

(Raymond D. Benge, Jr.)

Paracelsus

Areas of Achievement: Chemistry, medicine, and pharmacology

Contribution: Paracelsus, working in the tradition of alchemy, sought rational approaches to the chemical treatment of disease. His method of pharmacology turned out to be an important step in the direction of modern chemistry.

Nov. 11 (or Dec. 17), 1493	Born in Einsiedeln, near Zurich, Swiss Confederation
1510	According to tradition, receives a medical degree from the University of Vienna
1516	According to tradition, receives a doctoral degree at the University of Ferrara in Italy
1527	Appointed a professor of medicine at the University of Basel
1527	Publicly burns the books of respected eleventh century physician Avicenna
1528	Dismissed from his professorship at Basel after the death of his patron, Frobenius
1530	Publishes *Paragranum* (*Against the Grain*, 1894)
1530	Publishes a clinical account of syphilis
1531	Publishes *Opus paramirum*
1536	Publishes *Grosse Wundarzney* (*Great Surgery Book*, 1894)
1537-1538	Publishes *Astronomia magna* (*Great Astronomy*, 1894)
Sept. 24, 1541	Dies in Salzburg, Austria

Early Life

Philippus Aureolus Theophrastus Bombastus von Hohenheim, who later took the name Paracelsus (pronounced "pahr-uh-SEHL-suhs"), was the only son of William von Hohenheim, a physician and instructor in chemistry at the Bergschule, at Villach, in the Austrian Tyrol. Paracelsus' mother died, probably by suicide, when he was quite young. His father educated him in a variety of scientific areas, including mineralogy and botany.

Paracelsus was a student at the Bergschule, which had been founded by the wealthy Fugger family to provide managers and technicians for their mining and ore-refining enterprises. He may also have been a student of Abbot Johannes Trithemius, a famous alchemist.

The knowledge of his subsequent education is somewhat incomplete, as his own accounts seem rather unreliable. In his late teens, he probably traveled to a number of German and Swiss universities, such itinerant scholarship being a common practice at that time. He claims to have received his medical degree from the University of Vienna in 1510 and his doctorate at the University of Ferrara, Italy, in 1516, but university records are missing in both cases. Then, he apparently spent several years

(Library of Congress)

wandering about Europe, absorbing knowledge about alchemy and medicine. He served as a Venetian army surgeon, traveling as far as Scotland, Arabia, and Egypt.

The Iconoclast

After many adventures, Paracelsus established a promising medical practice in Strasbourg. In 1526, he was summoned to Basel, where he

---

From Alchemy to Pharmacology

Coming from a tradition that treated disease with a mixture of folk remedy and magic, Paracelsus employed chemical therapy based on rationality and observation.

Paracelsus' writings contain many lucid descriptions of diseases, most unambiguous enough for modern physicians to concur with his diagnoses. He was the first to describe congenital syphilis and differentiate it from similar disorders. He also described goiter and cretinism and correctly connected them with the lead content of drinking water. He considered "miner's disease" to be the result of breathing metal particles and not the work of malicious spirits. He attributed neurological symptoms, such as manias and choreas, to genuine diseases and not demonic possession.

He rejected the ancient theory of the four humors, which held that all disease was produced by an imbalance of blood, yellow bile, black bile, and phlegm. He maintained instead that diseases were specific entities, each the result of distinct and external causes, and that the causes were actual substances, such as salts or airborne poisons. Particular diseases had specific targets in the body and their own individual rules of pathogenesis (origin and development). Although harmful bacteria had not yet been discovered, they would have fit wonderfully with Paracelsus' theory.

Just as diseases had specific, material causes, each could be treated with specific, material remedies. Rather than trying to alter humoral imbalances with general remedies such as purging or bloodletting, therapy should address the specific cause. For example, Paracelsus used precise doses of mercury salts to treat syphilis, a therapy that was rediscovered in the twentieth century. He was vilified by other physicians for using this unorthodox treatment, even though it was more successful than the accepted remedies.

Often, Paracelsus' therapeutic rationale exposes a more mystical side to his thinking. For example, he advocated the "doctrine of signatures," which held that the form of a plant contained divine clues about its proper therapeutic use. Yellow plants are identified by their color as specific for liver disease, bile being yellow. The liver-shaped leaves of *Hepatica* identify its use, as reflected in its name (*hepat-* is the Latin prefix meaning "liver").

Paracelsus' choice of particular salts for particular illnesses is considerably more arcane, being based for the most part on alchemical theory, with its mixture of Neoplatonism, hermetic lore, and astrology. He considered the effectiveness of chemical drugs to be mediated by "spirits," the nature of which determined their specificity. Knowledge of these spirits could be obtained through astrological theory.

Paracelsus believed in an instructive correspondence between microcosm (an individual human) and macrocosm (the universe). A disturbance in the heavens produces human disharmony, and vice versa. Therefore, a human disease exists in a strict relationship with astrological events and healing must take this relationship into account. Because specific drugs exist in the same sort of heavenly relationship via their spirits, drug therapy must be understood in astrological terms. Paracelsus, like his contemporaries, understood medical matters chiefly in these terms. His genius was the ability to impose the added criterion of his own observations when devising therapies.

Bibliography

The Chemical Philosophy. Allen G. Debus. 2 vols. New York: Science History Publications, 1977.

The French Paracelsians. Allen G. Debus. Cambridge, England: Cambridge University Press, 1991.

Paracelsus, Magic into Science. Henry M. Pachter. New York: Henry Schuman, 1951.

successfully treated the famous publisher Frobenius for a leg ailment that had resisted the efforts of other physicians. He also treated the humanist Erasmus of Rotterdam, who was a guest of Frobenius at the time. On the basis of such successes (or such connections), he was named city physician and professor of medicine at Basel—at which point, trouble began.

For one thing, Paracelsus was scornful of pomposity, whether ecclesiastical or academic, and he immediately made enemies. He refused to take the oath required for the professorship and instead wrote a denunciation of traditional medical practice. Paracelsus advocated a new therapeutic strategy based not on ancient authority but on direct experience.

Soon after, he publicly burned Avicenna's *Canon of Medicine*, an eleventh century Arabic medical treatise of great authority. At about the same time, he invented the pseudonym "Paracelsus," implying that his knowledge surpassed even that of Celsus, the first century Roman encyclopedist. He further annoyed the Basel academic community by lecturing in local Swiss-German, instead of the customary Latin.

When his protector, Frobenius, died suddenly, Paracelsus was forced to relinquish his professorship. He spent the remainder of his life traveling from city to city—treating patients, writing copiously, and everywhere making enemies through his arrogance and combative behavior. In 1541, he died, possibly violently, in Salzberg, Austria, where his grave soon became a mecca for the sick.

Bibliography

By Paracelsus

Paragranum, 1530 (*Against the Grain*, 1894)

Opus paramirum, 1531

Grosse Wundarzney, 1536 (*Great Surgery Book*, 1894)

Astronomia magna, 1537-1538 (*Great Astronomy*, 1894)

The Hermetic and Alchemical Writings of Aureolus Philippus Theophrastus Bombast of Hohenheim, Called Paracelsus the Great, 1894, reprinted 1976 (2 vols.)

About Paracelsus

Four Treatises of Theophrastus of Hohenheim. H. E. Sigerist et al., trans. Baltimore: The Johns Hopkins University Press, 1941.

Paracelsus. 2d ed. Walter Pagel. Basel, Switzerland: S. Karger, 1982.

(*John L. Howland*)

Louis Pasteur

Areas of Achievement: Bacteriology, chemistry, immunology, and medicine

Contribution: Pasteur discovered the role of microorganisms in fermentation and invented the food preservation process known as pasteurization. One of the founders of bacteriology, he was the first to inoculate animals and humans against infectious disease successfully.

Dec. 27, 1822	Born in Dôle, Jura, France
1843-1847	Studies chemistry and physics at the École Normale Supérieure in Paris
1848	Teaches chemistry at the University of Strasbourg
1854	Appointed a professor of chemistry at the University of Lille
1857	Suggests that fermentation is caused by living microorganisms
1857	Becomes assistant director of the École Normale Supérieure
1862	Elected to the Académie des Sciences
1864	Invents pasteurization as a way to prevent wine from spoiling
1867	Proves that diseases of silkworms are caused by bacteria
1868	Suffers a stroke, resulting in partial paralysis
1881	Successfully inoculates sheep against anthrax
1882	Elected to the Académie Française
1885	Cures a child of rabies
1888	Founds the Institut Pasteur, serving as its director
Sept. 28, 1895	Dies in Villeneuve-l'Étang, near Saint Cloud, France

Early Life

Louis Pasteur (pronounced "pahs-TEWR") was born in 1822 in Dôle, a small town in eastern France near Dijon, to Jean-Joseph Pasteur, a tanner operating his business from the family home, and Jeanne Roqui Pasteur. Louis attended primary school in Arbois and studied for the *baccalauréat* at Besançon.

Pasteur entered the École Normale Supérieure in Paris in 1843, where he studied chemistry and physics and specialized in crystallography, a field in which he made his first original scientific discovery, molecular asymmetry. After earning a doctorate, he accepted a position as professor of chemistry at the University of Strasbourg in 1848. In 1849, he married Marie Laurent, the daughter of a local academic, who bore five children: Jeanne, Jean-Baptiste, Cécile, Marie-Louise, and Camille.

Early Studies in Microbiology

Pasteur received a membership in the Legion of Honor in 1853 for his research on tartaric acid and rose rapidly through the academic

(Library of Congress)

ranks, becoming professor of chemistry and dean of the faculty of the University of Lille in 1854. In 1857, he returned to Paris to accept an appointment as assistant director of the École Normale Supérieure.

Pasteur continued his studies of fermentation and putrefaction in Paris and, at the request of French winemakers, began to examine the causes of alterations in the flavor of wine. He had earlier studied the production of beer

Fermentation and Microbiology

Pasteur proved that fermentation is an organic process caused by microscopic living things.

Conventional wisdom in the nineteenth century held that fermentation, like other transformations of organic material such as the souring of milk or the decay of meat, was a chemical process. For example, brewers thought that beer was produced chemically when malts came into contact with the wooden barrels in which it was produced. Although they knew that yeast was present during fermentation, they considered it a by-product with no real role in the process.

In 1853, a local brewer asked Pasteur to discover the cause of spoilage that frequently occurred during fermentation. He accepted the challenge and, by examining fermenting juices under a microscope, discovered that yeasts play the central role in transforming sugar into alcohol. He used the same techniques to study the souring of milk and again concluded that microorganisms are responsible. In 1857, Pasteur published a report in which he argued that microorganisms cause souring and fermentation. In many ways, this paper marks the beginning of modern bacteriology.

In 1859, he began to study spontaneous generation, the idea that living things emerge from nonliving matter. Most scientists believed in spontaneous generation, the idea that living things could emerge from nonliving organic matter, such as during the process of fermentation or decay. Pasteur rejected this position and devised many elegant experiments to prove that organic material does not ferment or decay unless it has been exposed to outside influences such as atmospheric air.

His experiments led to a public address at the Sorbonne in 1864 describing experiments showing that neither fermentation nor putrefaction can take place in a solution of organic material that had been sterilized by heat. Pasteur attrib-uted this phenomenon to the absence of living microorganisms in a sterilized medium. Although severely criticized by traditionalists, Pasteur's laboratory work played a major part in destroying the idea of spontaneous generation and proved that all living things must have parents.

Pasteur found a practical application for his discoveries when French winegrowers asked him to find ways to keep wine from spoiling during fermentation and storage. Pasteur thought that the alteration of fermenting wine (such as its tendency to produce vinegar) and its spoilage during storage resulted from the presence of microorganisms in the wine. He verified this theory through microscopic examination and determined that wine could be preserved from alteration if unwanted microorganisms could be eliminated.

Pasteur first tried to kill the microorganisms by adding chemical disinfectants. These experiments failed, but he soon discovered that heating wine to 55 degrees Celsius kills the microorganisms without damaging the wine's flavor. Pasteur's process of partial sterilization, now commonly known as pasteurization, is widely used to prevent spoilage in milk and other foods.

Bibliography

Pasteur and Modern Science. René Dubos. Madison, Wis.: Science Tech Publishers, 1988.

The Pasteurization of France. Bruno Latour. Cambridge, Mass.: Harvard University Press, 1988.

"Pasteur's Study of Fermentation." James Bryant Conant. *Harvard Case Histories in Experimental Science.* Vol. 2. Cambridge, Mass.: Harvard University Press, 1957.

"Science, Politics, and Spontaneous Generation in Nineteenth-Century France: The Pasteur-Pouchet Debate." John Farley and Gerald L. Geison. *Bulletin of the History of Medicine* 48 (1974).

for northern French brewers and suspected that microorganisms caused wine to sour, just as they caused beer to spoil. In 1864, he devised a way to prevent spoilage by heating wine, a process now known as pasteurization.

Contagious Diseases in Animals

In 1865, the French government asked Pasteur to study two diseases of silkworms that were harming the French silk industry. He quickly discovered that microorganisms were causing

The Germ Theory of Disease

Pasteur, along with Robert Koch of Germany, proved the central role of germs in causing many diseases. Pasteur's main contribution lay in demonstrating the efficacy of immunization.

Before the last half of the nineteenth century, it was widely believed that disease could not be transmitted directly from one person or animal to another. Instead, most physicians thought that epidemic diseases were caused by nonliving agents called "miasma" produced by the decomposition of organic materials. In essence, the miasmatic theory of disease stated that bad smells caused epidemic diseases such as typhoid fever and cholera. Physicians counseled their patients to avoid coming near such things as decaying vegetation, manure, and carcasses. If this was not possible, they suggested overwhelming the foul odors with camphor and sweet-smelling spices.

By the 1870's, Pasteur's research into fermentation and putrefaction had led him to conclude that all transformations of organic materials are caused by microorganisms. From this point of view, disease is simply another transformation of organic material.

His studies of the microbial causes of human and animal diseases were preceded by a study of disease in insects. In 1865, the French government had asked Pasteur to study two diseases of silkworms called *pébrine* and *flâcherie* that were devastating the French silk industry. He began research at Alais, in southern France, and quickly discovered that microorganisms caused the diseases.

In 1877, Pasteur began to study anthrax, a disease that mainly affects sheep and cattle. Although Koch had explained the etiology of anthrax in an 1876 study, many scientists thought that the disease killed animals by producing a chemical poison. Pasteur discovered that animals contract anthrax by grazing in fields where contaminated blood from dead infected animals has soaked into the soil. The spores of anthrax,

Pasteur showed, are brought to the surface of the soil by earthworms.

Pasteur's main contribution to the germ theory of disease lay not in the discovery of disease-causing organisms but in devising ways to confer immunity. In 1879, he began to study chicken cholera, a disease unrelated to human cholera. Pasteur identified the causative microbe and began experimenting with cultures of different virulence. He accidently injected laboratory chickens with a sample of culture that had been stored for several weeks. These chickens injected suffered few ill effects and later survived an otherwise lethal dose of virulent culture.

This experiment led to one of the most important discoveries in the history of medicine. Pasteur immediately understood that the chicken cholera microbes had been weakened, but not killed, by being placed in storage. These weakened microbes could cause illness, but not death, and animals injected with them gained immunity from the disease.

In 1881, Pasteur conducted a dramatic public experiment to demonstrate the efficacy of his anthrax vaccine. He inoculated twenty-five sheep with attenuated anthrax microbes. Two weeks later, he injected these sheep and twenty-five others with fresh, active microbes. All twenty-five inoculated animals survived; all those not inoculated perished. Pasteur's critics left the field convinced. The ability of germs to cause disease and the effectiveness of immunization could no longer be questioned.

Bibliography

Germ Theory and Its Applications to Medicine and Surgery. Louis Pasteur. H. C. Ernst, trans. Buffalo, N.Y.: Prometheus Books, 1996.

The History of Bacteriology. W. Bulloch. New York: Dover, 1977.

A History of Medical Bacteriology and Immunology. W. D. Foster. London: William Heinemann, 1970.

the diseases and suggested the destruction of infected silkworms.

In 1877, he began to search for the microbiological origin of animal and human diseases and decided to study anthrax, a disease of sheep and cattle. Two years later, Pasteur began studying chicken cholera. In the case of both diseases, he discovered methods of immunization. The chicken cholera studies were especially important because Pasteur discovered that chickens that had been injected with an aged culture could survive injection with virulent cultures.

This experiment led to one of the most important discoveries in the history of medicine. Pasteur loved the saying "chance favors the prepared mind," and he immediately understood that the chicken cholera microbes had been weakened by being placed in storage. In 1880, Pasteur published an article in which he described the process whereby animals gain immunity to disease when injected with attenuated (weakened) microbes.

Immunization

Pasteur had many professional enemies who rejected his theories about the role of microorganisms in disease despite his writings and arguments. He decided to win them over by a public demonstration. In 1881, he invited his detractors to witness an inoculation at a farm near Pouilly-le-Fort, a town near Melun, southeast of Paris. There, Pasteur showed that sheep inoculated with attenuated anthrax microbes could survive later inoculation with active microbes.

Pasteur's success in inoculating animals prompted him to begin experiments on rabies, a disease that brought certain death to infected humans. Pasteur cultured the rabies virus in the spinal cords of rabbits and discovered ways to bring it to a high state of virulence and then attenuate it by drying the spinal cords in the presence of oxygen. In 1884, he successfully inoculated dogs against the disease.

The next year, Pasteur achieved his greatest triumph as a microbiologist. The parents of a young boy who had been bitten by a rabid dog came to Pasteur and asked for help. Although Pasteur had never inoculated a human before, he knew that the boy certainly would die without treatment. He inoculated him with successively stronger doses of attenuated microbes. Pasteur's experiment succeeded: The boy, Joseph Meister, survived.

Recognition

Unlike many scientists, Pasteur received ample recognition during his lifetime. His colleagues elected him to the Académie des Sciences in 1862 and to the Académie du Médecine in 1873, although he had never received any medical training. In 1882, he won election to the Académie Française, France's most prestigious scholarly organization. His career culminated in 1888 with the opening of the Institut Pasteur, a research institute devoted to combating infectious diseases.

When Pasteur died of kidney disease in 1895, he was universally recognized as one of the preeminent scientists of his age.

Bibliography
By Pasteur

"Mémoire sur les corpuscules organisés qui existent dans l'atmosphère, examen de la doctrine des générations spontanées," *Annales des sciences naturelles,* 1861

Études sur le vin: Ses maladies, causes qui les provoquent, 1866

Études sur la maladie des vers à soie: Moyen pratique assuré de la combattre et d'en prévenir le retour, 1870 (2 vols.)

Études sur la bière: Ses maladies, causes qui les provoquent, procédé pour la rendre inaltérable, avec une théorie nouvelle de la fermentation, 1876 (*Studies on Fermentation: The Diseases of Beer, Their Causes, and the Means of Preventing Them,* 1879)

"Charbon et septicémie," *Comptes rendus,* 1877 (with J. F. Joubert)

Oeuvres de Pasteur, 1922-1939 (Pasteur Vallery-Radot, ed.)

Correspondance, 1940-1951 (4 vols.; Vallery-Radot, ed.; *Correspondence of Pasteur and Thuillier Concerning Anthrax and Swine Fever Vaccinations,* 1968)

About Pasteur
The Life of Pasteur. René Vallery-Radot. Trans. by Mrs. R. L. Devonshire. 2 vols. New York: Doubleday, 1923.

Louis Pasteur: Free Lance of Science. René Dubos. Boston: Little, Brown, 1950.

Pasteur: A Great Life in Brief. Pasteur Vallery-Radot. Trans. by Alfred Joseph. New York: Alfred A. Knopf, 1966.

Pasteur: The History of a Mind. Émile Duclaux. Trans. by Erwin F. Smith and Florence Hedges. Philadelphia: W. B. Saunders, 1920.

The Private Science of Louis Pasteur. Gerald L. Geison. Princeton, N.J.: Princeton University Press, 1995.

(C. James Haug)

Wolfgang Pauli

Area of Achievement: Physics

Contributions: Pauli discovered the exclusion principle that bears his name, using it and the atomic theory of Niels Bohr to explain the periodicity of the chemical elements.

Apr. 25, 1900	Born in Vienna, Austria
1921	Receives a Ph.D. summa cum laude in theoretical physics from the University of Munich
1921-1922	Works in Göttingen as an assistant to Max Born
1922	Moves to Copenhagen at the invitation of Niels Bohr
1924-1925	Formulates his exclusion principle
1928	Becomes a professor of theoretical physics at the Federal Institute of Technology in Zurich
1930	Receives the Lorentz Medal
1931	Proposes the existence of a new subatomic particle later named the neutrino
1933	Publishes "Die allgemeinen Prinzipien der Wellenmechanik" (general principles of wave mechanics)
1940-1946	Becomes a visiting faculty member at the Institute for Advanced Study in Princeton, New Jersey
1945	Awarded the Nobel Prize in Physics
1952	Receives the Franklin Medal
1958	Receives the Max Planck Medal
Dec. 15, 1958	Dies in Zurich, Switzerland

Early Life

Wolfgang Ernst Pauli was born on April 25, 1900, in Vienna, Austria. His father, Wolfgang

Joseph Pauli, was a physician who became a well-known biochemist at the University of Vienna. His mother, Bertha, was a writer who had many friends in the worlds of the theater and the press. Young Wolfgang's second name was given in honor of Ernst Mach, the noted professor of theoretical physics who was his godfather.

During World War I, Pauli was a pupil in the Gymnasium of Dobling in Vienna and was recognized as a child prodigy in physics and mathematics. His father frequently obtained from Mach titles of physics and mathematics articles and books for Wolfgang to read. By the time of his graduation from the gymnasium, he was prepared to write three papers on relativity theory, which were published in 1919.

Pauli chose to study theoretical physics with Arnold Sommerfeld in Munich. Sommerfeld

(The Nobel Foundation)

recognized and nourished the budding genius of his pupil. He asked Pauli, who was then nineteen years old, to write in his place an encyclopedia article on relativity theory, which was published in 1921. This article established Pauli's reputation and remains a valid account of the subject. He received his doctorate the same year summa cum laude from the University of Munich.

The Exclusion Principle

In 1921, Pauli joined the University of Göttingen as an assistant in theoretical physics to Max Born. The renowned physicist Niels Bohr gave a series of lectures there, and Bohr invited Pauli to come to Copenhagen as his assistant for one year. Pauli joined him in 1922 to assist in the preparation of Bohr's works for German publication.

Once in Copenhagen, Pauli became engrossed in the problem of the anomalous Zeeman effect. As early as 1896, Pieter Zeeman had noticed that the application of a magnetic field to an atom emitting energy split the spectral lines into multiplets, generally into triplets but sometimes not. Bohr, Sommerfeld, and Alfred Lande all believed—particularly for the alkali metals—that the atomic core around which the valence electron moves possessed an angular momentum that caused this magnetic anomaly.

Pauli proposed that the magnetic anomaly results from properties of the valence electron, not the core. To the already known quantum numbers n, l, and m, he added a fourth, which became known as s, the spin quantum number. He further stated that no two electrons in an atom can possess the same four quantum numbers, a theorem known as the Pauli exclusion principle.

New Quantum Mechanics

After the year in Copenhagen with Bohr, Pauli lived in Hamburg until 1928, when he began his professorship in theoretical physics at the Federal Institute of Technology in Zurich, Switzerland. Except for the World War II years, Pauli remained at the institute for the rest of his career.

Partially as a result of Pauli's conviction that electrons did not travel in orbits around the nucleus, Werner Heisenberg invented the ma-

The Pauli Exclusion Principle

Pauli proposed that no two electrons in an atom can have the same set of four quantum numbers.

Atoms of an element are composed of a nucleus, containing neutrons and a specified number of protons, and of electrons moving about in the space outside the nucleus. According to the Bohr model of the atom, a semiclassical model, the electrons move on orbits that have quantized values of angular momentum.

The model of the atom described by quantum mechanics is based on the solution of the Schrödinger wave equation. (An alternative but mathematically equivalent formalism is the matrix-mechanics method of Werner Heisenberg.) The solutions to the Schrödinger wave equation yield three integral quantum numbers whose allowed values are related.

The principal quantum number, n, gives the approximate distance from the nucleus at which the electron is likely to be found. The values of n can be from one to infinity. For atoms in their ground state, n does not exceed seven.

The second quantum number, l, gives values for the angular momentum of the electron. This number has generally been related to the shape of the region occupied by the electron. For a given electron, the value of l must always be lower than the value of n.

The third number, m, is called the magnetic quantum number since it gives the orientation of the angular momentum vector in a magnetic field. Its values range from negative l to positive l. Therefore, for each value of l there are $2l + 1$ allowed values of m.

These three quantum numbers are insufficient, however, to explain the arrangement of chemical elements in the periodic table. Historically, this arrangement was introduced because of periodicity in the properties of the various elements. Elements were listed in order of increasing mass and, when similar properties were found, a new row was started. The number of elements in succeeding rows is found to be two, eight, eighteen, thirty-two, and fifty. These three quantum numbers allow atomic orbitals corresponding to the rows in the periodic table of one, four, nine, sixteen, and twenty-five.

Pauli explained the situation by introducing a fourth quantum number, s, which represents the spin of the electron. It can have only two values, one representing a clockwise spin and the other a counterclockwise spin. The Pauli exclusion principle states that two electrons in an atom cannot have the same set of four quantum numbers. In effect, this allows each of the orbitals described by the first three quantum numbers to be occupied by a maximum of two electrons, having opposite spins.

The exclusion principle implies that the energy state of each electron can be defined by giving a unique set of values to the four quantum numbers. It accounts for the periodicity in properties that is observed in the chemical elements.

Bibliography

"Exclusion Principle and Quantum Mechanics." Wolfgang Pauli. Translated by R. Schlapp. In *Writings on Physics and Philosophy*, edited by C. P. Enz and K. von Meyenn. Berlin: Springer-Verlag, 1994.

"Remarks on the History of the Exclusion Principle." Wolfgang Pauli. *Science* 103 (February 22, 1946).

trix mechanics formalism of quantum mechanics in 1925. Pauli used this formalism to produce a brilliant solution to the hydrogen atom problem. He published a review article in 1933 in which he presented the physical and mathematical foundations of quantum mechanics.

The Neutrino

Pauli's early years at Zurich were marred by personal troubles. He entered into a short-lived marriage with Kathe Deppner, a dancer. When they divorced, less than a year later, he began to smoke and drink. His father recommended that he consult with famed psychoanalyst Carl Jung. Pauli did so, thus beginning a long association between the two men. After his treatment was completed, Pauli married Franca Bertram, with whom he shared a happy marriage.

During this time, Pauli first proposed the existence of the neutrino in response to an energy deficit in the beta decay of radon. Pauli was unwilling to sacrifice the concept of energy conservation, which he considered a cornerstone of physics. The formal presentation of his proposal was made at the Seventh Solvay Congress in 1933. Experimental verification of the existence of the neutrino did not come until the 1950's.

Pauli was awarded the Nobel Prize in Physics in 1945, the Franklin Medal in 1952, and the Max Planck Medal in 1958. He died in Zurich, Switzerland, on December 15, 1958, at the age of fifty-eight.

Bibliography
By Pauli
"Relativitätstheorie," *Encyklopädie der Mathematischen Wissenschaften*, 1921 ("Theory of Relativity," 1958)

"Quantentheorie," *Handbuch der Physik*, 1926

"Allgemeine Grundlagen der Quantentheorie des Atombaues," *Müller-Pouillets Lehrbuch*, 1929

"Die allgemeinen Prinzipien der Wellenmechanik," *Handbuch der Physik*, 1933

"The Connection Between Spin and Statistics," *Physical Review*, 1940

"Remarks on the History of the Exclusion Principle," *Science*, 1946

"On the Conservation of the Lepton Charge," *Nuovo cimento*, 1957

Writings on Physics and Philosophy, 1994 (C. P. Enz and K. von Meyenn, eds.; R. Schlapp, trans.)

About Pauli
The Creation of Quantum Mechanics and the Bohr-Pauli Dialogue. J. Hendry. Dordrecht, the Netherlands: D. Reidel, 1984.

From X-Rays to Quarks: Modern Physicists and Their Discoveries. E. Segrè. San Francisco: W. H. Freeman, 1980.

"Personal Memories of Pauli." V. F. Weisskopf. *Physics Today* 38 (December, 1985).

Theoretical Physics in the Twentieth Century: A Memorial Volume to Wolfgang Pauli. M. Fierz and V. F. Weisskopf, eds. New York: Interscience, 1960.

(Grace A. Banks)

Linus Pauling

Areas of Achievement: Biology, chemistry, immunology, medicine, and physics

Contribution: Pauling, one of the greatest chemists of the twentieth century, made the structure of molecules a principal theme of his work in structural chemistry, molecular biology, and molecular medicine. His theory of the chemical bond dominated science for several decades.

Feb. 28, 1901	Born in Portland, Oregon
1917-1922	Majors in chemical engineering at Oregon Agricultural College
1922-1926	Conducts graduate and postdoctoral work at the California Institute of Technology
1926-1927	Named a Guggenheim Fellow
1937	Appointed director of the Gates Laboratory and chair of the Division of Chemistry and Chemical Engineering
1939	Publishes *The Nature of the Chemical Bond*
1947	Publishes *General Chemistry*, a textbook that revolutionizes the teaching of college chemistry
1949	Announces that sickle-cell anemia is a molecular disease
1951	Publishes a series of papers on protein structure
1954	Wins the Nobel Prize in Chemistry
1958	With Ava Helen Pauling, presents a petition to halt nuclear bomb tests to the United Nations
1963	Receives the Nobel Peace Prize for his campaign against nuclear testing
1970	Publishes *Vitamin C and the Common Cold*
Aug. 19, 1994	Dies in Big Sur, California

Early Life

Linus Carl Pauling was born in Oregon in 1901. His father, a pharmacist, guided the reading of his inquisitive young son, but his death in 1909 left the family economically and emotionally devastated. Linus studied mathematics and chemistry at Washington High School in Portland, but what convinced him to become a chemist was a dramatic experiment performed by a classmate in his bedroom laboratory.

Pauling's educational career at Oregon Agricultural College was interrupted by financial difficulties, but, through persistence and hard work, he managed to graduate with highest honors in 1922. During his graduate studies at the California Institute of Technology (CIT or Caltech), he married Ava Helen Miller; their marriage resulted in three sons and a daughter. Pauling received his doctorate in 1925.

Following a period of postdoctoral studies, he accepted a Guggenheim Fellowship in 1926 to study the application of the new quantum mechanics to chemical problems. He spent most of his time in Europe at Arnold Sommerfeld's Institute for Theoretical Physics in Munich, Germany. He returned to California in 1927 and began his long career as a teacher and researcher at CIT. He was prodigiously successful, becoming a full professor in 1931 and head of the Division of Chemistry and Chemical Engineering in 1937.

Structural Chemistry and Molecular Biology

Structure was the chief theme of Pauling's scientific work. In his early research, he used the X-ray diffraction technique to determine the structures of such crystals as molybdenite (his first scientific paper) and various silicates and sulfides. In 1930, he began using the electron-diffraction technique for exploring the structures of such molecules as benzene and cyclohexane.

As X-ray and electron diffraction gave Pauling experimental tools for discovering the structures of molecules, so quantum mechanics provided him with a theoretical tool. In 1931, he used quantum mechanics to account for the equivalency of the four bonds around the carbon atom by introducing the idea of hybrid orbitals. In 1939, he integrated many of his structural discoveries into *The Nature of the Chemical Bond*, one of the most influential scientific books of the twentieth century.

In the mid-1930's, Pauling's interest began to shift to molecules contained in living things. His studies of the hemoglobin molecule, a protein, led naturally to his general studies of protein structure. While an Eastman Professor at Oxford University, he used a paper on which he had drawn a chain of linked amino acids to discover a cylindrical coil-like configuration, later called the alpha helix. The most significant element of Pauling's structure was its nonintegral number of amino acids per turn of the helix.

Following an initial announcement of his discovery in 1950, Pauling and his collaborators published a series of eight articles on the alpha helix, the pleated sheet, and the structure of hair, muscle, collagen, hemoglobin, and other proteins.

Molecular Medicine

In the late 1930's, Pauling's work centered increasingly on molecules of medical interest. In 1940, he published his first paper on the structure of antibodies, and, during World War II, he worked on various immunological problems. By the end of the war, he had become involved with sickle-cell anemia, which, in 1949, he showed to be a molecular disease caused by an abnormal hemoglobin molecule.

Capitalizing on his reputation as a great scientist—he won the Nobel Prize in Chemistry in 1954—Pauling, in the 1950's, began to devote his attention to humanitarian issues connected with science. For example, he became involved in the debate over radioactive fallout from nuclear bomb tests. In 1958, he and his wife presented a petition against nuclear testing signed by more than eleven thousand scientists from around the world to Dag Hammarskjöld at the United Nations. In that same year, he wrote a book, *No More War!*, in which he tried to make people aware of the horrifying dangers of nuclear weapons. He received the 1962 Nobel Peace Prize in 1963, when the Partial Nuclear Test Ban Treaty went into effect.

Pauling's later career centered on a particular molecule: ascorbic acid (vitamin C). From published evidence, he concluded that vitamin C, provided it is taken in large enough quanti-

Pauling's Discoveries on the Nature of the Chemical Bond

Pauling's work on the chemical bond helped establish the modern science of molecular structure. By using the tools of X-ray and electron diffraction, he was able to determine the detailed architecture of minerals and metals, and he used the ideas of quantum mechanics to understand these structures through a new theory of the chemical bond.

When Pauling first studied chemistry in high school, valence (the combining power of atoms) was crudely represented by a model of hooks and eyelets. For example, the valence 2 oxygen atom had two eyelets, and the valence 1 hydrogen atom had a single hook. When the two hydrogens were hooked to the oxygen, the formula of water, H_2O, was made reasonable in terms of the two hydrogen-to-oxygen bonds.

In college, Pauling came across the scientific papers of Gilbert Newton Lewis, who became his inspiration and later his friend. Lewis described the chemical bond as a shared pair of electrons. For example, in the hydrogen molecule, made up of two hydrogen atoms, each with a proton and an electron, Lewis depicted the configuration as H:H, where the H's represent the positively charged protons and the dots represent the two negative electrons that are shared between them. These electrons are the "glue" holding the molecule together.

Pauling used X rays to probe inside crystals to discover precisely where atoms are located in relation to neighboring atoms in the substance. For example, in the mineral molybdenite, he found that each molybdenum atom is surrounded by six sulfur atoms arranged in a trigonal prism. He naturally wondered why atoms arranged themselves in these characteristic structures. He discovered the answer in a new field of physics, quantum mechanics, which explained how electrons behaved in atoms.

According to this new theory, electrons in atoms can only exist in certain specific energy states. Furthermore, electrons in and between atoms have to be understood not as particles but as waves. Instead of orbits of electron particles around nuclei, quantum mechanics uses "orbitals" to describe specific regions where electrons are most likely to be found (some scientists envisioned these orbitals as "electron clouds").

Before Pauling's work, physicists could not explain how a carbon atom could form four equivalent bonds, since quantum mechanics describes carbon as having two kinds of outer electron orbitals: an s orbital, which is spherically shaped, and p orbitals, which have a two-lobed shape able to be oriented up and down, side to side, and back to front (that is, in the x, y, and z directions). Pauling showed how the interchange (or resonance) energy of two electrons could lead to the mixing or hybridizing of the two pure s and p orbitals into new ones.

In the case of certain compounds of carbon, the carbon atom can form four equivalent tetrahedral bond orbitals, each a hybrid of one s and three p orbitals. This idea of hybridization allowed Pauling to explain not only the structural and chemical properties of carbon compounds but even the magnetic properties of certain complex inorganic substances as well.

A central idea in Pauling's theoretical treatment of the chemical bond was resonance, in which the true state of a chemical system is neither of the component quantum states but some intermediate one, caused by an interaction that lowers the energy. This idea of resonance was a major factor in Pauling's development of the valence bond theory, in which he proposed that a molecule could be described by an intermediate structure that was a resonance combination or hybrid of other structures. His classic study *The Nature of the Chemical Bond* (1939) provided a unified summary of his experimental and theoretical studies, and it was responsible for the dominance of valence bond theory in chemistry in the 1940's and 1950's.

Bibliography

The Architecture of Molecules. Linus Pauling and Roger Hayward. San Francisco: W. H. Freeman, 1964.

The Chemical Bond. J. J. Lagowski. Boston: Houghton Mifflin, 1966.

The Chemical Bond: A Brief Introduction to Modern Structural Chemistry. Linus Pauling. Ithaca, N.Y.: Cornell University Press, 1967.

The Marvels of the Molecule. Lionel Salem. New York: VCH, 1987.

A Valency Primer. J. C. Speakman. London: Edward Arnold, 1968.

ties, has a beneficial effect in helping the body fight off colds and other diseases. The outcome of this work was a pair of books, *Vitamin C and the Common Cold* (1970) and *Cancer and Vitamin C* (1979).

These books and the many papers and speeches that Pauling gave initiated a controversy about the relative benefits and dangers of treating illnesses with large doses of vitamin C (megavitamin therapy). Large amounts of vitamin C did not prevent his wife from getting cancer, although Pauling claimed that these megadoses helped prolong her life for five years; she died on December 7, 1981.

Philosophy of Science

Pauling's basic approach to science was interdisciplinary, and he made many of his greatest discoveries in fields where scientific disciplines overlap: between chemistry and physics, chemistry and biology, chemistry and medicine.

As an atheist and reductionist, he deeply believed that the universe comprises solely matter and energy and that the structures of moleculars can explain all physical, biological, and even psychological phenomena. He interpreted the death of his wife in this way, as he did the prostate cancer that progressed to his colon and finally to his liver, causing his death on August 19, 1994.

Bibliography

By Pauling

The Structure of Line Spectra, 1930 (with Samuel Goudsmit)

Introduction to Quantum Mechanics, with Applications to Chemistry, 1935 (with E. Bright Wilson, Jr.)

The Nature of the Chemical Bond, and the Structure of Molecules and Crystals: An Introduction to Modern Structural Chemistry, 1939

General Chemistry, 1947

College Chemistry: An Introductory Textbook of General Chemistry, 1950

No More War!, 1958

The Architecture of Molecules, 1964 (with Roger Hayward)

The Chemical Bond, 1967

(The Nobel Foundation)

Vitamin C and the Common Cold, 1970
Chemistry, 1975
Cancer and Vitamin C, 1979 (with Ewan Cameron)
How to Live Longer and Feel Better, 1986

About Pauling

Force of Nature: The Life of Linus Pauling. Thomas Hager. New York: Simon & Schuster, 1995.

Linus Pauling: A Life in Science and Politics. Ted Goertzel and Ben Goertzel. New York: Basic Books, 1995.

Linus Pauling in His Own Words. Barbara Marinacci, ed. New York: Simon & Schuster, 1995.

Linus Pauling: Scientist and Advocate. David E. Newton. New York: Facts on File, 1994.

Linus Pauling: Scientist and Crusader. Florence Meiman White. New York: Walker, 1980.

(*Robert J. Paradowski*)

Ivan Petrovich Pavlov

Areas of Achievement: Medicine, physiology, and psychiatry

Contribution: Pavlov's research on the circulation of the blood, digestion, and the central nervous system, as well as his new methodology, profoundly enriched physiology and the natural sciences.

Sept. 26, 1849	Born in Ryazan, Russia
1870-1875	Attends St. Petersburg University
1875	Attends the Military Medical Academy in St. Petersburg to study medicine
1875	Attends the Veterinary Institute to study digestion and circulation
1877	Travels to Breslau, Germany, to study digestion
1878-1890	Organizes and heads the physiology laboratory of Sergei Botkin
1879	Receives a medical degree from the Military Medical Academy
1881	Marries Seraphima Vasilievna Karchevskaya
1883	Receives a gold medal for his doctoral dissertation
1890	Becomes director of the physiology section of the Institute for Experimental Medicine
1895	Becomes chair of the physiology department at St. Petersburg
1904	Awarded the Nobel Prize in Physiology or Medicine
1907	Elected an academician of the Russian Academy of Sciences
1924	Resigns his chair of physiology at the Military Medical Academy
Feb. 27, 1936	Dies in Leningrad, Soviet Union

Early Life

Ivan Petrovich Pavlov (pronounced "PAV-lawf") was born in Ryazan, Russia, in 1849. His father was on Eastern Orthodox priest, and his mother was from a family of clergymen. He had ten brothers and sisters, six of whom died in childhood. Pavlov was expected to join the clergy and so, at the age of eleven, attended Ryazan Ecclesiastical High School. In 1864, he began attending Ryazan Ecclesiastical Seminary. While at the seminary, he became interested in science, particularly physiology, which studies the functions of living matter such as organs, cells, and tissue.

Pavlov's research can be divided into three major sections. From 1874 to 1883, he focused on the circulation of blood, particularly the nerve mechanisms that regulate blood pressure. From 1879 to 1897, he studied the physiology of digestion and developed new techniques to study the action of the digestive tract. From 1902 to 1936, Pavlov focused on the

(The Nobel Foundation)

Conditioned Reflexes Theory

Pavlov believed that behavior could be explained in terms of observable, measurable physical reactions.

While conducting experiments on digestion, Pavlov noticed that laboratory dogs would salivate in response to the sight or smell of food. He called this reaction an unconditioned (or original) reflex; that is, one that required no training. The dogs would also salivate, however, when they saw or heard Pavlov or another caretaker. Pavlov realized that the dogs were physically responding to some stimulus other than the food itself.

Pavlov trained the dogs to stand on a table in a harness, connected to an apparatus that collected their saliva. The dogs faced a window through which they could see food dropped into a bowl. At the start of the experiments, a sound such as a bell or buzzer would ring before the food dropped into the bowl. At first, the dogs had no salivary response to the sound. After several tests, the dogs would salivate at the sound in anticipation of the food that would soon appear.

Pavlov varied the experiments, using a light or object. The dogs learned to associate the sound, light, or object with the arrival of food. Pavlov called these responses conditioned (or learned) reflexes. He proposed that new pathways were created in the cortex of the brain because of the conditioning process. Pavlov believed that responses were enveloped throughout the life of an organism and that the conditioned reflex was a mechanism of individual adaptation to a changing environment. He suggested that behavior development and learning were affected by conditioned nervous responses. He believed that humans learned complex behavior patterns such as language through conditioning.

Pavlov also showed that behavior could be "unlearned," a phenomenon that he called extinction. If the stimulus is presented without the reinforcement, the response weakens and disappears. In the experiments, if the bell or buzzer sounded and no food was presented, the dogs eventually stopped salivating at the sound.

Some of Pavlov's theory was soon disproven by Karl Lashley, a psychologist who removed parts of the cortex of rats and proved that the ability to learn was not stored in a physical part of the brain. Even so, the laws of conditioning became an important addition to psychology.

Pavlov's ideas had a significant impact on Russian psychology until the 1950's. His work was largely unknown elsewhere until *Conditioned Reflexes*, an English translation of his work, appeared in 1927. Behaviorist psychologists readily adopted Pavlov's research methods and incorporated his ideas. Conditioned reflex theory became popular in psychiatry, psychology, and education. Practical applications of the theory include the formation of positive or negative attitudes. Conditioning is used in advertising and political propaganda to form positive or negative associations. It can also be used to explain how some people learn phobias.

Bibliography

"Conditioning." Eli C. Minkoff. In *Magill's Survey of Science: Life Science Series*, edited by Frank N. Magill. Pasadena, Calif: Salem Press, 1991.

Conditioning: An Image Approach. Donald L. King. New York: Gardner Press, 1979.

The Story of Psychology. Morton Hunt. New York: Doubleday, 1993.

physiology of the brain and higher nervous activity. He was especially interested in the effects of the brain on learned behavior.

Blood Circulation and Digestion

Pavlov entered St. Petersburg University in 1870 to study natural science. He was strongly influenced by Élie de Zion, a professor of physiology, and followed Zion to the Military Medical Academy in St. Petersburg to begin his study of medicine. In 1875, he began studying digestion and circulation at the Veterinary Institute.

In 1877, Pavlov went to Breslau, Germany (now in Poland), in order to study digestion with the specialist Rudolf Heidenhain. After receiving a gold medal for his doctoral dissertation on digestion in 1883, Pavlov was awarded a government scholarship for postgraduate study abroad. He returned to Germany to work on cardiovascular physiology and blood circulation with Carl Ludwig and Sergei Botkin.

While in Germany, Pavlov directed an experimental physiology laboratory and became interested in the influence of the central nervous system on reflexes. Upon his return to St. Petersburg University in 1890, he continued his pioneering research on digestion, which earned for him worldwide recognition and the 1904 Nobel Prize in Physiology or Medicine.

Conditioned Response

Pavlov earned a professorship at the Military Medical Academy and then became chair of the physiology department there. During this time, he became most famous for his study of conditioned responses of the central nervous system. This research was the result of his work on the nervous system's effect on digestion.

Pavlov's theory of conditioned response has been applied to the psychology of humans, the treatment of psychiatric patients, and the learning process in education. Pavlov proposed that conditioned reflexes are developed throughout the life of a living creature. The reflexes are provoked by stimuli—influences on the activity of the creature. The reflexes change in response to changes in the environment of the organism. Living creatures consciously learn to adapt.

Although Pavlov's work on the nervous system and digestion was overshadowed by other researchers, his experiments influenced biological research. He developed a new methodology and method because he viewed the living organism as a complex system. His method of long-term experimentation, or continuous method, was a new concept and led to changes in how research was conducted. Among the laboratory techniques that he advanced were the perfection of surgical procedures to prevent infections, long-term experiments on the same animal, and minimization of the animal's pain.

After the Revolution

After the Bolshevik Revolution in 1917, Pavlov became a strong critic of the new Soviet government. By this time, he already had an international reputation for his research. He had also organized several major research centers and created a large research school that employed up to three hundred physiologists and physicians.

In 1924, he resigned his chair in physiology in protest when the Military Medical Academy expelled all clergymen's sons. Since the communist government considered Pavlov a favored scientist, Vladimir Ilich Lenin granted him special privileges not extended to other scientists. Pavlov was given considerable personal freedom and the right to continue his research and attend church.

In 1935, the government built a laboratory for Pavlov's research in conditioned responses, hoping to use the results for political purposes. Although Pavlov praised the government's efforts in education and science, he remained critical of the socialist practice of government. Pavlov continued his research until his death in 1936.

Bibliography

By Pavlov

O nervakh, zavedyvayushikh rabotoyv podzhelu-dochnoy zheleze, 1875 (with M. I. Afanasiev; on the nerves that govern the pancreas)

O tsentrobezhnykh nervakh serdtsa, 1883 (on the efferent nerves of the heart)

Lekstii o rabotie glavnykh pishchevaritl'nykh zhelez, 1897 (The Work of the Digestive Glands, 1902)

Lekstii o rabote bol'shikh polusharii golovnogo mozga, 1927 (Conditioned Reflexes: An Investigation of the Physiological Activity of the Cerebral Cortex, 1927)

Dvadtsatiletnii opyt obektivnogo izucheniia vysshei nervoi deuatel'nosti zhivotnykh, 1923 (Lectures on Conditioned Reflexes, 1928)

About Pavlov

Ivan Pavlov: The Man and His Theories. Hilaire Cuny. London: Souvenir Press, 1964.

"Ivan Petrovich Pavlov." David Petechuk. In Notable Twentieth-Century Scientists, edited by Emily J. McMurray. Washington, D.C.: Gale Research, 1995.

Pavlov. Jeffrey Alan Gray. New York: Viking Press, 1980.

Pavlov: A Biography. Boris P. Babkin. Chicago: University of Chicago Press, 1949.

(Virginia L. Salmon)

Cecilia Payne-Gaposchkin

Area of Achievement: Astronomy
Contribution: A leader in stellar astrophysics, Payne-Gaposchkin made numerous contributions to the study of stars and their structure. In her 1925 doctoral dissertation, she was the first to propose that stars are composed mainly of hydrogen and helium.

May 10, 1900	Born in Wendover, England
1919	Enters Newnhan College, Cambridge University
1919	Attends an astronomy lecture by Sir Arthur Eddington
1923	Enters Radcliffe College and conducts research at Harvard Observatory
1925	Receives a Ph.D. from Radcliffe with a groundbreaking dissertation on the composition of stars
1936	Nominated to the National Academy of Sciences
1938	Receives an appointment to the Harvard Corporation and becomes a faculty member at the university
1943	Marries Sergei Gaposchkin
1956	Becomes the first woman to be made a full professor at Harvard and is appointed head of the astronomy department
1977	Awarded the Henry Norris Russell Prize from the American Astronomical Society
Dec. 6, 1979	Dies in Cambridge, Massachusetts

(AP/Wide World Photos)

Early Life

Cecilia Payne-Gaposchkin (pronounced "PAYN gah-PEHSH-kyihn") was born Cecilia Helena Payne in rural Wendover, England, in 1900. Her father died when she was four, and she was reared by her mother, who ensured that her daughter received an education.

As a young girl, Cecilia became fascinated with the sciences and was determined to pursue a career as a scientist. Schools in England at the time did not educate girls in the sciences, however, so her early science instruction was mainly self-taught, using whatever few textbooks she could locate.

Payne also had to overcome the stated opposition of many of her teachers. The principal at one school, a churchwoman, told Payne that she was "prostituting her gifts" by going into science. She overcame these difficulties, however, and entered Newnhan College at Cambridge University in 1919.

Astronomy

In 1919, Payne attended a lecture by noted astronomer Sir Arthur Eddington. She later wrote that she was able to recall the entire speech. It was as a result of this lecture that she decided to pursue a career in astronomy and enrolled in as many astronomy courses as she could.

While at Newnhan, she met Harlow Shapley, the director of the Harvard Observatory. Shapley told Payne to seek him out when she graduated, but he did not expect to hear from her again. After finishing her degree at Newnhan, however, she contacted Shapley and went to America.

Harvard Observatory

Payne did her graduate work in astronomy at Radcliffe College. She became the first person to receive a doctorate in astronomy from either Radcliffe or Harvard and the first person to receive a Ph.D. for work performed at Harvard Observatory.

In her dissertation, she argued that stars are made primarily of hydrogen and helium. This theory was counter to the beliefs of the day and was quickly rejected by leading astronomers. Within a few years, however, these same astronomers would acknowledge that Payne was correct. Her dissertation has been called "the most brilliant Ph.D. thesis ever written in astronomy."

Harvard University

Payne continued on at Harvard Observatory and began to teach at the university. The president of Harvard was opposed to allowing women to be faculty members, and she was paid as a technical assistant to one of the male faculty members. She finally received an appointment to the Harvard Corporation in 1938 and became a faculty member, but her courses would not be listed in the school catalog until 1945.

Another obstacle to Payne's advancement was her marriage in 1943 to Sergei Gaposchkin, a fellow scientist. Women at this time were expected to sacrifice their careers for their husbands. Payne-Gaposchkin continued to pursue her career as a scientist, often working with her husband, while also pursuing a life as a wife and mother.

Finally, in 1956, she was appointed a full professor and made the head of the astronomy department at Harvard University, becoming the first female full faculty member.

In 1977, Payne-Gaposchkin received the prestigious Henry Norris Russell Prize from the American Astronomical Society. During her career, she wrote or cowrote nearly 350 scien-

The Composition of Stars

Payne-Gaposchkin argued that the apparent variation in the composition of stars was attributable to differing temperatures, not a differing abundance of elements. She correctly deduced that stars are made of mostly hydrogen and helium, with all other elements present only in small amounts.

Breaking sunlight into its individual colors with a prism produces a rainbow of colors called a spectrum. The emission of light from an individual element creates not a rainbow but a set of colored lines that is unique to that element and acts like a fingerprint. Differing stars have different spectra.

Prior to Payne-Gaposchkin's work, it was believed that all stars had the same surface temperature and that any differences among them resulted from the presence of different elements. Payne-Gaposchkin, through her intensive study of spectra, deduced that these differences exist

because some stars have different surface temperatures. She claimed that the relative abundance of heavy elements in the sun, such as nitrogen and oxygen, are the same as on Earth but that the light elements hydrogen and helium are more than a million times more abundant. This conclusion was initially rejected as being impossible, but it was accepted as fact only a few years later.

Payne-Gaposchkin's ideas quickly led to major advances in the understanding of stars, including the understanding of the power source of stars, fusion. Today, her work is the cornerstone of much work in astronomy.

Bibliography
Astronomy: Journey to the Cosmic Frontier. John D. Fix. St. Louis: C. V. Mosby. 1995.

Astronomy Today. Eric Chaisson and Steve McMillan. Englewood Cliffs, N.J : Prentice Hall, 1996.

tific papers and several books. She died on December 6, 1979, of lung cancer and donated her body to science.

Bibliography

By Payne-Gaposchkin

Stellar Atmospheres: A Contribution to the Observational Study of High Temperature in the Reversing Layers of Stars, 1925 (Ph.D. dissertation)

Variable Stars and Galactic Structure, 1954

Introduction to Astronomy, 1954 (with Katherine Haramundanis)

Stars and Clusters, 1979

Cecilia Payne-Gaposchkin: An Autobiography and Other Recollections, 1984 (Haramundanis, ed.)

About Payne-Gaposchkin

"The Ladies of Observatory Hill." George Greenstein. *The American Scholar* (Summer, 1993).

Notable Twentieth-Century Scientists. Emily J. McMurray, ed. New York: Gale Research, 1995.

(Christopher Keating)

Petrus Peregrinus de Maricourt

Areas of Achievement: Astronomy and physics

Contribution: Initiator of experimental investigation of the magnet and the compass in the West. Produced one of the best observational and experimental treatises in the Middle Ages.

c. early 13th century	Born, probably in Maricourt (or Méhaircourt), Picardy, France
1267	Referred to in Roger Bacon's treatise *Opus tertium*
1268-1269	Involved in the siege of Lucera, Italy, probably as a military engineer
Aug. 8, 1269	Completes *Epistola Petri Peregrini de Maricourt ad Sygerum de Foucaucourt, militem, de magnete* (*Epistle of Petrus Peregrinus de Maricourt, to Sygerus of Foucaucourt, Soldier, Concerning the Magnet*, 1902)
c. late 13th century	Dies, place unknown

Life

Petrus Peregrinus (pronounced "PEH-trus pehr-uh-GRINE-us") de Maricourt—also known as Peter the Pilgrim, Peter of Maricourt, and Pierre Le Pèlerin de Maricourt—was the founder of the science of magnetism in the West. He produced *Epistola Petri Peregrini de Maricourt ad Sygerum de Foucaucourt, militem, de magnete* (1269; *Epistle of Petrus Peregrinus de Maricourt, to Sygerus of Foucaucourt, Soldier, Concerning the Magnet*, 1902), commonly called *Epistola de magnete* or *Letter on the Magnet*, which was arguably the best and most systematic analysis of observations in medieval science. (The only work that is the equal of Petrus' treatise on the lodestone is the "Treatise on the Rainbow" by Theodoric of Freiburg.)

All that is known for certain about Petrus is to be found in his treatise itself—the name of the author and the exact date of the treatise, August 8, 1269—and in a passage praising Petrus written by Roger Bacon, the great medieval advocate of technology and experimentation.

Petrus Peregrinus was born or lived in Maricourt (or Méhaircourt) in Picardy, France. His designation "Peregrinus"—variously translated as "the pilgrim," "the traveler," "the wayfarer," and "the stranger"—suggests his travels. Unfortunately, the only one of his travels that is known for sure is his involvement in the siege of Lucera, Italy, likely as a military engineer; the date of his treatise is on the eve of the battle of Lucera. Because the compass first appeared in China and apparently traveled to Europe via a land route in Central Asia, and later by a sea route around the Middle East, Petrus' title of "the pilgrim" or "the traveler" may suggest travels to the Middle East as a pilgrim in the Holy Land. The title of "pilgrim," however, was also given to participants in the Crusades, even if the war was fought in Europe.

Scientific Reputation

As to the quality of Petrus' scientific work, in addition to the treatise is the extraordinary praise of Roger Bacon. A note attributed to Bacon calls "Master Peter" one of the two best mathematicians. If this is indeed Petrus, then he earned a master arts degree. In *Opus tertium* (1267), Bacon claimed for Master Peter superiority in observation of the natural world to all of his contemporaries. Bacon, who must have met Petrus in the 1260's, mentions Petrus' work on burning mirrors, and Petrus himself refers to a planned or written treatise on mirrors in *Letter on the Magnet*. Bacon also refers to Petrus' knowledge of metallurgy, agriculture, military matters, surveying, and all sorts of experiments and devices. William Gilbert[William)], whose text *De magnete, magneticisque corporibus, et de magnete tellure* (1600; *On the Magnet, Magnetic Bodies Also, and on the Great Magnet the Earth*, 1860) initiated early modern experimental investigation of magnetism, makes much use of Petrus' work.

Several other works attributed to Petrus can be found in the lists of holdings of medieval libraries. Some of these works appear to be

---

The Magnet and the Compass

Petrus described many aspects of magnetism, including the concept of poles of a magnet.

In a series of short chapters in his work *Epistola de magnete* (1269), Petrus explains how to identify a magnet, how to induce magnetism in a piece of iron, how to reverse its poles, and how to make small magnets out of a large magnet. He describes the repulsion of like poles and the induction of iron to the opposite pole of a lodestone or magnet against which it is rubbed.

Petrus was the first person to offer a method for determining the north and south poles of a magnet and was the first known to call them "poles." He made a little spherical lodestone to be a model of the heavens. Moving a needle on the surface of the lodestone, and tracing lines in the direction of the needle, one finds the poles at the intersections of these lines.

Petrus correctly points out that the North Star is not at magnetic north. He erroneously thought, however, that the compass points to the celestial pole, not to the earth's pole. Petrus criticized the idea that the compass pointed to a large deposit of iron at the North Pole of the earth, and he also refuted the notion that a magnet points to the mine in which it originated.

He also devises several instruments based on the magnet. He gave two designs for an astrolabe for locating the angles of stars and planets in the sky. The magnet identifies the north direction, and the astrolabe measures the angle of a heavenly body from north.

Bibliography

Driving Force: The Natural Magic of Magnets. James D. Livingston. Cambridge, Mass.: Harvard University Press, 1996.

Introduction to Magnetic Materials. B. D. Cullity. Reading, Mass.: Addison-Wesley, 1972.

Magnetism: An Introductory Survey. E. W. Lee. New York: Dover, 1970.

sections of the treatise published under other titles, but one of them is a separate treatise on astronomy.

Bibliography
By Petrus Peregrinus
Epistola Petri Peregrini de Maricourt ad Sygerum de Foucaucourt, militem, de magnete, 1269 (*Epistle of Petrus Peregrinus de Maricourt, to Sygerus of Foucaucourt, Soldier, Concerning the Magnet*, 1902)

About Petrus Peregrinus
Hidden Attraction: The Mystery and History of Magnetism. Gerrit Verschuur. New York: Oxford University Press, 1993.
Medieval and Early Modern Science. A. C. Crombie. New York: Doubleday/Anchor Books, 1959.
"Peter Peregrinus." Edward Grant. In *Dictionary of Scientific Biography*, edited by Charles Coulston Gillispie. Vol. 10. New York: Charles Scribner's Sons, 1974.

(Val Dusek)

Jean-Baptiste Perrin

Areas of Achievement: Chemistry and physics
Contribution: Perrin won the Nobel Prize in Physics for developing an experimental proof for the existence of atoms.

Sept. 30, 1870	Born in Lille, France
1895	Publishes a paper demonstrating that cathode rays are negatively charged
1897	Receives a Ph.D. from the École Normale Supérieure, Paris
1903	Writes a textbook on physical chemistry, *Traité de chimie physique*
1908	Publishes the first of his experimental proofs of the existence of atoms
1910	Appointed to a position at the Sorbonne in Paris
1911	Invited to the First International Solvay Conference
1913	Publishes a popular science book on the existence of atoms, *Les Atomes* (*Atoms*, 1916)
1918	Serves as army officer in World War I
1923	Elected to the Académie des Sciences
1926	Awarded the Nobel Prize in Physics
1939	Helps establish the Centre National de la Recherche Scientifique (CNRS) in Paris
1940	Emigrates to the United States because of his antifascist views
Apr. 17, 1942	Dies in New York, New York

Early Life
Jean-Baptiste Perrin (pronounced "peh-RAN") grew up in a modest home, reared along with

Proving the Existence of Atoms

The like patterns of motion of small particles of unlike substances show the physical reality of chemical "atoms."

Throughout the nineteenth century, the existence of atoms and molecules had been only theoretically inferred, largely from the simple ratios in which different substances combined. Units of different gases, or different "atoms," seemed to combine in relatively stable structures, or "molecules." Amadeo Avogadro proposed in 1811 that like volumes of different gases, at the same temperature and pressure, must contain the same number of molecules.

Perrin applied that principle to the study of emulsions. He used the slit ultramicroscope to observe emulsion particles as small as .0001 of a millimeter as they randomly danced across a narrow column viewing field, a sight not unlike watching dust float across a shaft of light in a darkened room.

Perrin determined that the variation in the size of particles vertically within the instrument column was in a definite, not random pattern. From the size and distribution, he calculated the number of particles that would form one unit of the substance, not in grams but in molecular weight. The number, 6×10^{23}, was the first experimentally observed measurement of Avogadro's number. Later, Perrin discovered that Albert Einstein had arrived at a similar number in a purely statistical analysis of such random particle, or Brownian, motion in 1905.

Bibliography

The Evolution of Chemistry: A History of Its Ideas, Methods, and Materials. Eduard Farber. New York: Ronald Press, 1952.

Investigations on the Theory of the Brownian Movement. Albert Einstein. New York: Dover, 1961.

The Rise of the New Physics. A. d'Abro. New York: Dover, 1951.

two sisters by his mother. He attended high school in Lyons and Paris, France, then left for service in the army. Within a year, however, Perrin's skill in mathematics enabled him to gain university admittance to the École Normale Supérieure.

Perrin was among the first students in a new study called physical chemistry. Physical chemists wished to organize into general laws, like those used in physics, the array of descriptive statements that chemists had made about individual compounds and their reactivities. Most physical chemists thought that the best path to this end was thermodynamics, the study of the transfer of energy in chemical reactions, because energy changes could be quantified and measured.

A Chemist's View of Physics

Such a strategy, however, ignored analysis of the individual molecules and atoms that chemists since John Dalton in the early nineteenth century had assumed were the building blocks of individual substances. Perrin's interest in attacking the problems of physical chemistry from this "atomistic" standpoint can be seen in

his first published paper in 1895, in which he demonstrated that cathode rays are negatively charged by collecting and recording their presence within a wired metal cylinder. Perrin coupled this study with experiments on the newly discovered X rays in his Ph.D. thesis in 1897.

Perrin married shortly after receiving his degree. The young scholar was asked to develop a course in physical chemistry, largely thermodynamics, for the leading French university, the Sorbonne. His interest in measuring chemical building blocks, however, would soon reappear.

"Seeing" Atoms and Molecules

Perrin finished his textbook on physical chemistry, *Traité de chimie physique: Les Principes*, in 1903, the same year in which an instrument called the slit ultramicroscope made possible observations of particles closer to the size of hypothetical molecules than ever before. In 1908, Perrin published the first in a series of papers describing the nonrandom distribution of what appeared to be randomly moving small particles in solution.

Perrin's calculations, attributing the motion

(The Nobel Foundation)

His standing in this work was greatly aided by his receipt of the Nobel Prize in Physics in 1926. By the late 1930's, he had helped establish in Paris the Centre National de la Recherche Scientifique (CNRS). In 1940, his antifascist opinions made it necessary that he leave Nazi-occupied France. Although he died in exile, after the war Perrin's remains were reburied in the Pantheon, the resting place of the great leaders of French culture.

Bibliography

By Perrin

Rayons cathodiques et rayons de Röntgen: Étude expérimentale, 1897
Traité de chimie physique: Les Principes, 1903
Peut-on peser un atome avec précison?, 1908
Brownian Movement and Molecular Reality, 1910
Sur les preuves de la réalité moléculaire: Étude spéciale des émulsions, 1912
Les Preuves de la réalité moléculaire, 1913
Les Atomes, 1913 (*Atoms*, 1916)
Les Élémentes de la physique, 1929
La Recherche scientifique, 1933
Grains de matière et de lumière, 1935
L'Organisation de la recherche scientifique en France, 1938
À la surface des chose, 1940-1941
L'Âme de la France éternelle, 1942
Pour la liberation, 1942
Œuvres scientifiques, 1950

About Perrin

The Development of Modern Chemistry. Aaron J. Ihde. New York: Dover, 1984.
Molecular Reality: A Perspective on the Scientific Work of Jean Perrin. Mary Jo Nye. New York: Macmillan, 1972.
Physical Chemistry from Ostwald to Pauling: The Making of a Science in America. John W. Servos. Princeton, N.J.: Princeton University Press, 1990.

(*J. Eric Elliott*)

of such particles to the observable action of still unseen but now measurable molecules, brought him acclaim. In 1910, he was appointed to a chair in physical chemistry at the Sorbonne. In 1913, he wrote a book for general audiences on the impact of his work, *Les Atomes* (*Atoms*, 1916).

A Patriot and an Internationalist

Perrin served as an army officer during World War I. After the war, however, he was concerned with building up scientific institutions to keep France connected with her neighbors and away from peace-threatening nationalism and isolationism.

Max Ferdinand Perutz

Areas of Achievement: Biology, chemistry, and medicine

Contribution: Perutz won the Nobel Prize in Chemistry for his use of X-ray crystallography to determine the molecular structure of the protein hemoglobin.

May 19, 1914	Born in Vienna, Austria
1939	Receives a Rockefeller Foundation Grant
1940	Earns a Ph.D. from Cambridge University
1945	Awarded an Imperial Chemical Industries Research Fellowship
1947	Named director of the Molecular Biology Unit of the Medical Research Council
1960	Publishes a report on the structure of hemoglobin
1962	Awarded the Nobel Prize in Chemistry
1962	Becomes chair of the Medical Research Council Laboratory of Molecular Biology
1963	Named Commander of the Order of the British Empire
1963-1969	Chairs the European Molecular Biology Organization
1971	Awarded the Royal Medal by the Royal Society of London
1974-1979	Serves as Fullerian Professor of Physiology at the Royal Institution in London
1979	Awarded the Copley Medal by the Royal Society of London
1979	Retires from Cambridge University

Early Life

Max Ferdinand Perutz (pronounced "peh-REWTZ") was born and reared in Vienna, Austria. His family was well established in the textile manufacturing industry. Although his parents expected him to study law and join the family business, Perutz became intrigued with chemistry in secondary school. He entered the University of Vienna in 1932 to pursue this interest.

Perutz began doctoral studies at Cambridge University in England in 1936 as a research student at the Cavendish Laboratory. There, he learned the techniques of X-ray crystallography from John Bernal and Isidor Fankuchen. Felix Haurowitz, a protein chemist and Perutz's cousin by marriage, persuaded Perutz to investigate hemoglobin, the protein in red blood cells responsible for oxygen transport. Perutz received his Ph.D. in 1940 for the

(The Nobel Foundation)

X-Ray Crystallography of Proteins

Proteins are composed of chains of amino acids folded into complicated shapes. These shapes can be derived from the pattern formed by X rays deflecting off protein crystals.

Perutz used X-ray crystallography to determine the structure of the respiratory protein hemoglobin. He grew hemoglobin crystals extracted from horses in solution and passed X rays through the solution. The X rays scattered when they hit a crystal, creating a pattern of dots on the photographic film behind the crystal solution.

Perutz produced thousands of these diffraction patterns, focusing on different parts of the molecule. He also added organic mercury to the hemoglobin. This changed the diffraction patterns, giving more clues about the shape of the molecule. He compiled the extensive data using a computer.

Perutz analyzed the data to produce a three-

dimensional model of hemoglobin. Hemoglobin is made of four chains, each of which can bind with oxygen. Perutz also determined that hemoglobin changes shape when it interacts with oxygen.

The explanation of biological functions based on molecular structure is a chief goal of molecular biology. The possibility of treating diseases caused by structural changes in proteins is being investigated.

Bibliography

Introductory Biochemistry. Stuart Edelstein. San Francisco: Holden-Day, 1973.

"The Three-Dimensional Structure of a Protein Molecule." John C. Kendrew. *Scientific American* 205 (December, 1961).

The Use of X-Ray Diffraction in the Study of Protein and Nucleic Acid Structure. K. C. Holmes and D. M. Blow. New York: Wiley-Interscience, 1965.

analysis of X-ray diffraction patterns from hemoglobin crystals.

World War II

Perutz's promising career was interrupted by World War II. In 1940, he was arrested as an "enemy alien" and was interned in Canada, where he and other intellectuals started a camp university. His family's property in Vienna was seized by the National Socialists (Nazis), leaving Perutz without financial resources.

Perutz returned to England in 1941. He contributed to Great Britain's war effort by studying the possibility of using ice floes as aircraft landing sites. In 1942, he married Gisela Peiser, with whom he had two children.

The Structure of Hemoglobin

In 1945, Perutz returned to Cambridge. The next year, he and John Kendrew founded the Medical Research Council Unit for Molecular Biology. Perutz continued to analyze hemoglobin, while Kendrew studied the muscle protein myoglobin.

In 1953, Perutz experienced a breakthrough in his techniques. He started using isomorphous replacement, the addition of heavy metal atoms to the hemoglobin, which gave

additional points of reference in the X-ray diffraction patterns. In 1959, Perutz derived the molecular structure of hemoglobin.

At the same time, Kendrew applied these techniques to the simpler molecule, myoglobin. Perutz and Kendrew published their findings in the journal *Nature* in 1960. In 1962, they received the Nobel Prize in Chemistry for their contribution to the understanding of the structure of globular proteins.

After the Nobel Prize

Perutz continued to use X-ray crystallography to examine the relationship between hemoglobin's structure and its function in oxygen transport. In 1963, he and Hilary Muirhead identified the structural change in the hemoglobin molecule associated with oxygenation. From 1963 to 1969, he chaired the European Molecular Biology Organization. He directed the Medical Research Council Laboratory of Molecular Biology at Cambridge from 1962 until his retirement in 1979.

The contribution of Perutz's meticulous work to the field of molecular biology has been widely recognized. He was elected a Fellow of the Royal Society of London and an honorary member of the National Academy of Sciences, the French Académie des Sciences, and the Academie dei Lincei in Rome.

Bibliography
By Perutz
"Structure of Haemoglobin," *Nature*, 1960 (with M. G. Rossman, Ann F. Cullis, Hilary Muirhead, Georg Will, and A. C. T. North)

Proteins and Nucleic Acids: Structure and Function, 1962

"Structure of Haemoglobin," *Nature*, 1963 (with Muirhead)

Atlas of Haemoglobin and Myoglobin, 1981 (with G. Fermi)

Is Science Necessary?: Essays on Science and Scientists, 1989

Mechanisms of Cooperativity and Allosteric Regulation in Proteins, 1990

Protein Structure: New Approaches to Disease and Therapy, 1992

About Perutz
"Max Ferdinand Perutz." In *The Biographical Dictionary of Scientists*, edited by Roy Porter. New York: Oxford University Press, 1994.

"Max Ferdinand Perutz." In *The Nobel Prize Winners: Chemistry*, edited by Frank N. Magill. Pasadena, Calif.: Salem Press, 1990.

Nobel Prize Winners: An H. W. Wilson Biographical Dictionary. Tyler Wasson, ed. New York: H. W. Wilson, 1987.

(Amy England-Beery)

Max Planck

Area of Achievement: Physics

Contribution: Planck determined the formula for the energy density of a blackbody. In order to do so, he became the first scientist to introduce the idea of the quantum of energy.

Apr. 23, 1858	Born in Kiel, Schleswig (now Germany)
1879	Receives a Ph.D. from the University of Munich, joining the faculty the next year
1885	Appointed a professor at Kiel University
1889	Named a professor of physics at the University of Berlin
1897	Begins work on the problem of blackbody radiation
1900	Proposes the concept of the quantum of energy
1900	Determines values for Planck's constant and the Boltzmann constant, from them deriving values for Avogadro's number and the charge of the electron
1918	Awarded the Nobel Prize in Physics
1926	Retires from Berlin
1930	Named president of the Kaiser Wilhelm Society
1937	Forced to resign for opposing Adolf Hitler's policy toward Jews
1944	His son is implicated in an assassination plot against Hitler and is later executed
1945	Rescued by U.S. forces and reinstated as president of the Kaiser Wilhelm Society (renamed the Max Planck Society)
Oct. 4, 1947	Dies in Göttingen, West Germany

Early Life

The son of a distinguished professor of civil law, Max Karl Ernst Ludwig Planck (pronounced "plawnk") was born into a family with a tradition in law and the Protestant ministry. The Planck family had a reputation for honesty, integrity, and devotion to duty—and, correspondingly, somewhat of a stiffness of character. Max Planck shared these characteristics as he broke family tradition and pursued a career as a physicist.

His first exposure to physics came after his family moved to Munich when he was nine years old. He attended the Gymnasium at Munich, where he was introduced to physics by his professor, Hermann Müller. In addition to his talent in physics, he had avocations in music, where he was considered of a professional level, and mountain climbing, which he pursued throughout most of his adult life.

Planck continued his studies in physics at the University of Berlin during his college years. At Berlin, he studied under Hermann von Helmholtz, who had a reputation for lack of preparation; Gustav Robert Kirchhoff, who had a reputation for perfectly polished lectures that tended to put students to sleep; and Rudolf Clausius, whose research in thermodynamics particularly inspired Planck.

An admirer of Clausius' work, Planck chose to work on reversible transformations in thermodynamics for his doctoral dissertation. Although, his thesis seemed to generate only a mild interest, he was subsequently to be recognized as a truly preeminent thermodynamicist.

In 1880, Planck received an appointment to the faculty at the University of Munich and after five years received an appointment at Kiel University. After Kirchhoff died in 1887, the University of Berlin invited Ludwig Eduard Boltzmann to replace him. Boltzmann declined the position, and in 1889 it was offered to Planck, who accepted.

The Berlin Years

In 1897, at the age of thirty-nine, Planck began working on the problem of the spectral distribution of light emitted by a blackbody radiator—an ideal object that glows emitting radiant energy with a color that is a consequence of its temperature only. As a present-day example, an incandescent light bulb is a nearly perfect blackbody radiator.

In 1900, Planck found a formula that agreed with experiments at all measured wavelengths, including the infrared. In order to derive this formula, however, the mathematics required that the radiation be emitted in discrete chunks, which he called quanta. These quanta of energy (ε) were proportional to the frequency (f) with the constant of proportionality subsequently being dubbed Planck's constant (h).

Planck used this relationship, $\varepsilon = hf$, as a mathematical gimmick to derive his result and at first assumed that his result would remain valid as the value of ε approached zero. This result would agree with the classical idea that radiant energy is emitted continuously by the glowing object. He later was forced to conclude, however, that these quanta were not merely mathematical tricks but rather a fundamental characteristic of nature and that blackbodies—and, indeed, all material objects—radiate energy in discrete chunks.

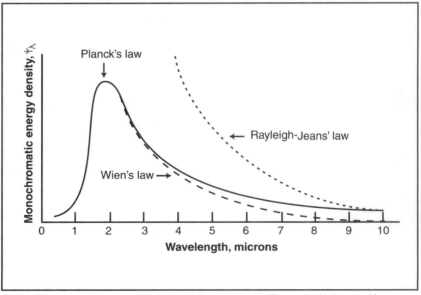

(from *Physics of the Atom*, 4th ed., 1984, by M. Russell Wehr et al.)

Planck's Law for Blackbody Radiation

A blackbody radiates light with a distribution of frequencies (or wavelengths) that is a function of the object's temperature, but independent of its material content.

A perfect mirror reflects all light incident upon it. On the other hand, a material such as carbon (or "lamp black") does not reflect light, but rather absorbs nearly all light incident upon it—hence the term "blackbody." Blackbody radiators in thermodynamic equilibrium, however, must reemit this radiant energy that it has absorbed and will do so characteristic of its temperature. At sufficiently high temperatures, the blackbody will glow. A good example of a blackbody in thermal equilibrium is an object inside a pottery kiln while it is being fired.

Previous efforts to explain the spectral distribution of a blackbody were made by Wilhelm Wien and by the collaboration of Lord Rayleigh and Sir James Hopwood Jeans.

Rayleigh's result was derived directly from classical electromagnetic theory and agreed with experimental measurements for emitted light of long wavelengths (infrared). His result predicted, however, the unrealistic behavior that the emitted energy would approach infinity as the emitted wavelength approached zero—in stark contrast to experiment.

On the other hand, Wien's result, which contained less theoretical justification, adequately described the distribution at short (ultraviolet) wavelengths where the energy per wavelength approached zero as the wavelength approached zero. Wien's result became erroneous, however, at long wavelengths.

The blackbody spectrum had been carefully studied and measured at the Physikalisch Technische Reichsanstalt of Berlin and elsewhere. Neither theoretical effort satisfactorily agreed with the experimental results. Both solutions are shown in the figure (on facing page), along with the blackbody spectrum.

Planck first arrived at the correct solution by what he called "lucky guesswork": He stumbled on a formula that agreed perfectly with the experimental results. Yet, he was unable to derive his formula from classical electrodynamics. Furthermore, when he studied the Rayleigh-Jeans derivation, he could find no errors in their analysis. This situation suggested that perhaps a fundamental problem existed with assumptions regarding classical electrodynamics itself.

Planck was able to derive his formula if he assumed that the blackbody emitted radiant energy in discrete chunks known as quanta, with the energy (ε) proportional to its frequency (f), rather than as a continuous flow of energy as assumed by classical electrodynamics. Mathematically, if he let $\varepsilon = hf$, where h is Planck's constant (6.63×10^{-34} joules per second), then he could correctly derive his formula.

Initially, Planck used this assumption as a mathematical trick to obtain his result. Subsequent attempts to merge his discrete chunks into a continuous flow of energy, however, met with failure. He was forced to accept that these quanta of energy were central and fundamental to the analysis.

The explanation of the photoelectric effect by Albert Einstein in 1905 showed that light (radiant energy) is also absorbed in the same discrete chunks of energy given by $\varepsilon = hf$. Subsequent work by Niels Bohr in 1913 showed that atomic spectra can be described if electrons occupy discrete energy levels in atoms.

It is the idea of the quantum of energy, reluctantly proposed by Planck, that initiated the age of quantum theory that revolutionized the understanding of the world of the atom.

Bibliography

The Feynman Lectures on Physics. Richard P. Feynman, Robert B. Leighton, and Matthew L. Sands. 3 vols. Reading, Mass.: Addison Wesley, 1963-1965.

From X-Rays to Quarks: Modern Physicists and Their Discoveries. Emilio Segrè. San Francisco: W. H. Freeman, 1980.

Fundamentals of Modern Physics. Robert Martin Eisberg. New York: John Wiley & Sons, 1961.

It is this concept of the quantum of energy that proved to be the genesis for the development of quantum mechanics. Planck's research in this area was of such critical importance to the development of theoretical physics and to the understanding of nature in general that in his lifetime his reputation was second only to that of Albert Einstein. In 1918, Planck was awarded the Nobel Prize in Physics for his successful work on the blackbody problem and his discovery of the quantum of energy.

A Life Filled with Courage and Sorrow

Although Planck was highly regarded as a theoretical physicist, his personal life was marred by grievous tragedies. His first wife died in 1909, and three of their four children died during or just after World War I—the older son in combat and two daughters in childbirth. Their fourth child, the younger son, was put to death by the Nazis in 1945 for allegedly conspiring in a plot against the life of Adolf Hitler.

Planck himself was victimized by the Nazi tide. He was not swayed by Hitler's propaganda, and at no time did he use his reputation to support the Nazi regime. He even met with Hitler to argue against his policies but was rebuffed. Indeed, Planck was forced to resign the presidency of the Kaiser Wilhelm Society in 1937 because of his efforts to aid Jewish colleagues.

Immediately after World War II, Planck was reinstated as president of the (former) Kaiser Wilhelm Society, the name of which was changed to the Max Planck Society. This society remains one of the most respected research institutes in the world. Planck died in 1947 at the age of eighty-nine.

Legacy

According to Armin Hermann's *The Genesis of Quantum Theory* (1971), when Planck was asked in 1931 how he came upon the quantum theory, he responded: "It was an act of desperation. For six years I had struggled with the blackbody theory. I knew the problem was fundamental and I knew the answer. I had to find a theoretical explanation at any cost, except of the inviolability of the two laws of thermodynamics."

Today, it may be difficult to appreciate the courage that it took for Planck essentially to abandon some of the fundamental tenets underlying what is now called classical mechanics and classical electrodynamics, to be an unwilling revolutionary, in order to solve the blackbody problem. The solution required a rethinking of the fundamental pillars of science and ultimately led to a complete revolution in the understanding of nature.

(Library of Congress)

Bibliography
By Planck
Das Princip der Erhaltung Energie, 1887
Vorlesungen über Thermodynamik, 1897
Acht Vorleungen über theoretische Physik, 1910
Das Wesen des Lichts, 1920
Kausalgesetz und Willensfreiheit, 1923
Physikalische gesetzlichkeit im lichte neuer forschung, 1926
Das Weltbild der neuen Physik, 1929
The Universe in the Light of Modern Physics, 1931
    (combined trans. of *Physikalische gesetzlichkeit im lichte neuer forschung* and *Das Weltbild der neuen Physik*)

Where Is Science Going?, 1932

Introduction to Theoretical Physics, 1932-1933 (5 vols.)

Wege zur Physikalischen Erkenntnis, 1933 (*The Philosophy of Physics*, 1936)

Die Physik im Kampf um die Weltanschauung, 1935

Wissenschaftliche Selbstbiographie, 1948 (*Scientific Autobiography and Other Papers*, 1949)

Physikalische Abhandlungen und Vortrage, 1958

The New Science, 1959 (combined ed. of *The Universe in the Light of Modern Physics*, *Where Is Science Going?*, and *The Philosophy of Physics*)

About Planck

From X-Rays to Quarks: Modern Physicists and Their Discoveries. Emilio Segrè. San Francisco: W. H. Freeman, 1980.

"The Genesis and Present State of Development of the Quantum Theory—Max Planck." Jefferson Hane Weaver. In *The World of Physics*. Vol. 2. New York: Simon & Schuster, 1987.

The Genesis of Quantum Theory. Armin Hermann. Cambridge, Mass.: MIT Press, 1971.

(Stephen Huber)

Rodney Robert Porter

Areas of Achievement: Biology, chemistry, and immunology

Contribution: Porter contributed to the determination of the chemical structure of antibodies and also unraveled the way that the body's complement system destroys antigens.

Oct. 8, 1917	Born in Newton-le-Willows, Lancashire, England
1939	Earns a degree in biochemistry at Liverpool University
1939-1945	Serves in the Royal Engineers
1945	Begins his work with Frederick Sanger at Cambridge University
1948	Awarded a Ph.D. from Cambridge
1949-1960	Investigates antibody structure at the National Institute for Medical Research in Mill Hill, London
1960	Named a professor of immunology at St. Mary's Hospital Medical School, London University
1967	Wins the Ciba Medal of the Biochemistry Society
1967	Becomes Whitley Professor of Biochemistry at Oxford University
1972	Wins the Nobel Prize in Physiology or Medicine jointly with Gerald M. Edelman
1973	Awarded the Royal Medal of the Royal Society of London
Sept. 7, 1985	Dies in an automobile accident in Winchester, Hampshire, England

Early Life

Rodney Robert Porter, the son of a railway clerk, claimed that no interest in science ran in his family. Nevertheless, from a very early age, he was fascinated by chemistry and medicine.

The Structure of Antibodies

Antibodies or immunoglobulins are serum proteins that bind to foreign materials (antigens) in the body and protect against disease. Porter and Gerald M. Edelman, working independently but cooperatively, determined the structure of these compounds.

Porter initially used the enzyme papain, which splits proteins in specific places, to divide antibodies taken from rabbits into three parts. Two of the sections were found to be identical and were the units to which antigens bind; these segments are designated "Fab." The third section crystallized and is referred to as "Fc" (fragment crystalline). The fact that this section crystallizes indicates that it is somewhat uniform or constant in its composition.

While Porter was investigating these aspects of antibodies, Edelman determined that immunoglobulin G (IgG), the main antibody fraction in blood serum, is composed of four polypeptide chains, two short or light chains (L) and two longer or heavy chains (H). Combining their work, Porter and Edelman developed a Y-shaped model for the structure of the antibody.

Porter's work in the determination of antibody structure provided a major impetus to the greater understanding of the immune system. Research on autoimmune diseases, transplantation, and cancer immunotherapy has built on Porter's work.

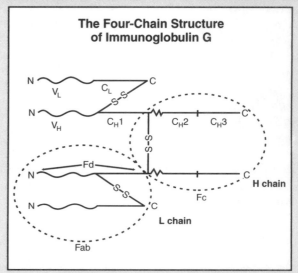

Porter and Edelman produced a Y-shaped model of the antibody immunoglobulin G (IgG). V indicates a region of variability that would permit recognition by a wide variety of antigens. (from John J. Cebra's "The 1972 Nobel Prize for Physiology or Medicine," *Science*, 1972)

Bibliography

Basic and Clinical Immunology. Daniel P. Stites, John D. Stobo, H. Hugh Fudenberg, J. Vivian Wells, eds. Los Altos, Calif.: Lange Medical Publications, 1984.

Essential Immunology. Ivan Roit. Oxford, England: Blackwell Scientific Publications, 1990.

This interest led Porter to obtain a degree in biochemistry from the University of Liverpool in 1939. During World War II, he served in the Royal Engineers. Thus, his scientific career was interrupted until his discharge in 1945.

Training on the Structure of Proteins

Porter was fortunate in the early stages of his career to have as mentors excellent biochemists, among whom were Frederick Sanger and A. J. P. Milne. Porter began his graduate studies at Cambridge University with Sanger, who taught him techniques for analyzing the structure of proteins. Later, in 1958, Sanger would accept the Nobel Prize in Chemistry for determining the structure of insulin.

As a graduate student, Porter developed a lifelong interest in the immune system initiated by Karl Landsteiner's writings advocating the chemical study of antibodies and antigens. When Porter was awarded his Ph.D. in 1948, he had already begun work on the structure of rabbit antibodies, separating the immunoglobulin G (IgG) into smaller pieces using an enzyme from papaya juice.

In 1949, Porter accepted a position at the National Institute for Medical Research in London, where he with learned chromatographic separation techniques in the laboratory of Milne, a future Nobel laureate.

The Structure of Antibodies

At the National Institute for Medical Research, Porter used his analytical skills to begin the formidable task of understanding the structure of the antibody molecule, a complicated protein system of more than 1,300 amino acids. Porter continued his studies throughout the 1950's and by 1959 published a paper on the three segments of which antibodies are composed.

At that time, Gerald M. Edelman of the Rockefeller Institute was studying the antibody molecule in a different way. He had begun by separating the four amino acid chains of the protein. By 1962, Porter, combining his work with Edelman's, developed a model of antibody structure.

During the 1960's, Edelman and Porter, who had been appointed professor of immunology at St. Mary's Hospital Medical School at London University, were major contributors in a series of informal "antibody workshops." These open meetings of interested scientists, held as often as twice a year, were a major factor in the rapid research developments in many laboratories. Together, Porter and Edelman shared the 1972 Nobel Prize in Physiology or Medicine for their important work in determining the chemical structure of antibodies.

In 1967, Porter was named Whitley Professor of Biochemistry at Oxford University. His research interests broadened to an investigation of how the body's complement system enables the reaction of antibodies to invading antigens to lead to the destruction of the antigens. The complement system involves the activation of several proteases, or protein-cleaving enzymes.

An Untimely Death

Porter was killed in an automobile accident in 1985 shortly before he was to have retired from his teaching commitments and devote his time fully to research.

Bibliography

By Porter
"The Structure of Antibodies," *Scientific American*, 1967

Chemical Aspects of Immunology, 1976

"The Proteolytic Activation Systems of Complement," *Annual Review of Biochemistry*, 1981

Biochemistry and Genetics of Complement: Proceedings of a Royal Society Discussion Meeting Held on 25 and 26 January, 1984, 1984

About Porter
"The 1972 Nobel Prize for Physiology or Medicine." John J. Cebra. *Science* 178 (1972).

Nobel Laureates in Medicine or Physiology: A Biographical Dictionary. Daniel M. Fox, Marcia Meldrum, and Ira Rezak, eds. New York: Garland, 1990.

Notable Twentieth-Century Scientists. Emily J. McMurray, ed. New York: Gale Research, 1995.

"Rodney Robert Porter." In *The Nobel Prize Winners: Physiology or Medicine*, edited by Frank N. Magill. Pasadena, Calif.: Salem Press, 1991.

(Helen M. Burke)

(The Nobel Foundation)

Ludwig Prandtl

Areas of Achievement: Physics and technology

Contribution: Prandtl was one of the founders of the modern science of aerodynamics. Many of his theories led to technical innovations that made possible modern, high-speed aviation.

Feb. 4, 1875	Born in Freising, Bavaria, Germany
1898	Graduates from the Technische Hochschule in Munich
1900	Completes a doctorate in physics at the Technische Hochschule under August Föppl
1901	Accepts a position as professor at Technische Schule in Hannover
1904	Accepts a position as head of the new Institute for Technical Physics at the University of Göttingen
1904	Reads his paper on the boundary layer to the Third International Congress of Mathematicians in Heidelberg
1909	Marries Gertrude Föppl, the daughter of his mentor
1909	Oversees the construction of the first functional wind tunnel in Germany
1918-1919	Publishes a paper on wing theory
1925	Named head of the Kaiser Wilhelm Institute for Fluid Motion Research (later called the Max Planck Institute for Fluid Mechanics)
Aug. 15, 1953	Dies in Göttingen, West Germany

(AIP Niels Bohr Library, Lande Collection)

Early Life

Ludwig Prandtl (pronounced "PRAHN-tehl") was born in Freising, Bavaria, on February 4, 1875, the only child of Alexander Prandtl, a professor of surveying and engineering at the agricultural college in Weihenstephan, and Magdalene Ostermann Prandtl. Because his mother was chronically ill, Ludwig was most strongly influenced by his father, acquiring from him an interest in natural phenomena.

In 1894, Prandtl began a course of study in engineering at the Technische Hochschule in Munich. Following his graduation in 1898, he continued his studies there, completing a doctorate in physics in 1900 under August Föppl. In 1909, he would marry Föppl's daughter, Gertrude.

Early Career

His studies complete, Prandtl took a job at the Maschinenfabrik Augsburg-Nürnberg. While working on a large vacuum for removing metal shavings, he recognized serious limitations in the contemporary understanding of how fluids flow over objects (fluid mechanics), thus kindling a lifelong interest in the subject.

In 1901, Prandtl accepted a position as professor at the Technische Schule in Hannover, where he continued to observe and study fluid mechanics. He worked in this field over the next few years, and, in 1904, he read a paper on the subject to the Third International Congress of Mathematicians in Heidelberg; it was published the next year in the proceedings of the congress. In this paper, he demonstrated that when a fluid flows past an object, the fluid on the surface of the object is stationary. This boundary layer, as it came to be known, had important implications for the flow of air over a wing and in many other applications.

Life's Work

In 1904, just before he presented the boundary layer paper, Prandtl became head of the new Institute for Technical Physics at the University of Göttingen. Under his guidance, the institute became an important center for theoretical fluid mechanics research. Prandtl, his colleagues, and his students studied and described supersonic flow, drag, and turbulence, and much of that work led to advances in aviation.

Shortly after World War I, Prandtl published a significant paper on the airflow around a wing. This work proved to be another major contribution to the technology of flight. In 1925, he was named head of the Kaiser Wilhelm Institute for Fluid Motion Research (later called the Max Planck Institute for Fluid Mechanics).

Prandtl continued his work through the 1930's and 1940's, sometimes in cooperation with Theodore von Kármán, his former student and a renowned aerodynamicist in his own right. During World War II, Prandtl managed to maintain civilian control of his work, but Adolf Hitler's emphasis on rocketry relegated Prandtl's work to the second rank.

In the closing years of his life, Ludwig Prandtl turned his attention to meteorology. He died in Göttingen on August 15, 1953.

Bibliography
By Prandtl

"Über die stationären Wellen in einem Gasstrahl," *Physikalische Zeitschrift*, 1904

"Über Flussigkeits-Bewegung bei sehr kleiner Riebung," *Verhandlungen der III Internationaler Mathematiker-Kongress*, 1905

"Die Luftwiderstand von Kugeln," *Nachrichten von der Gesellschaft der Wissenschaften zu Göttingen*, 1914

"Tragflügel Theorie, 1 und 2, Mitteilungen," *Nachrichten von der Gesellschaft der Wissenschaften zu Göttingen*, 1918, 1919

"Über die ausgebildete Turbulenz," *Proceedings*

Combining Theory and Practice

Prandtl's real accomplishment was to marry theory and practice in his work. With this approach, he made significant contributions to many disciplines, including aerodynamics, fluid mechanics, hydraulics, hydrodynamics, solid mechanics, and heat transfer.

Prandtl recognized that theory did not necessarily represent the real world and that experimental data did not necessarily represent conditions beyond the specific conditions of the experiment. He realized that a combination of the two approaches was best, and his 1904 paper on the boundary layer typified this hybrid approach. It began with general comments on the subject and eventually reached precise statements about fluid flow around certain objects. His arguments were backed up by experiments; the theory was explained and then verified with calculations and illustrations.

As a result of his approach, Prandtl's contributions proved both useful and long-lasting. His boundary layer paper was only eight pages long, yet it significantly advanced the theory of drag and was successfully applied to a wide range of aeronautical problems.

Prandtl's major accomplishment for the technology of flight was his wing theory, first published in 1918-1919 as "Wing Theory, I and II, Communications." This paper allowed a designer to predict the effect of changes in wing span, the number of wings, angle of incidence, and other features in a rational and analytical manner.

Bibliography

Aerodynamic Theory. William F. Durand, ed. 6 vols. New York: Dover, 1963.

Fluid Mechanics. David Pnueli and Chaim Gutfinger. Cambridge, England: Cambridge University Press, 1992.

Foundations of Aerodynamics: Bases of Aerodynamic Design. Arnold M. Kuethe and Chuen-Yen Chow. New York: John Wiley & Sons, 1986.

of the Second International Congress for Applied Mechanics, 1927

Hydro- und aeromechanik nach vorlesungen, 1929-1931 (*Applied Hydro-and Aeromechanics: Based on Lectures of Ludwig Prandtl*, 1934)

Abriss der Stromungslehre, 1931 (also as *Fuhrer durch die Stromungslehre*, 1942; trans. as *Guide to Flow Theory*, 1949, and *Essentials of Fluid Dynamics, with Applications to Hydraulics, Aeronautics, Meteorology, and Other Subjects*, 1952)

About Prandtl

Boundary Layer Theory. Hermann Schlicting. New York: McGraw-Hill, 1960.

Bringing Aerodynamics to America. Paul Hanle. Cambridge, Mass: MIT Press, 1986.

"Ludwig Prandtl." In *Dictionary of Scientific Biography*, edited by Charles Coulston Gillispie. New York: Charles Scribner's Sons, 1975.

The Wind and Beyond. Theodore von Kármán. Boston: Little, Brown, 1967.

(*Brian J. Nichelson*)

Vladimir Prelog

Area of Achievement: Chemistry

Contribution: Prelog has worked productively on a wide variety of chemical problems, ranging from simple carbon rings to protein enzymes. All of his studies emphasize the significance of molecular geometry.

July 23, 1906	Born in Sarajevo, Bosnia
1924-1929	Studies at the Czech Institute of Technology, Prague
1929-1935	Employed by G. J. Dríza in Prague
1935-1941	Joins the faculty of the University of Zagreb as a lecturer and advances to professor of organic chemistry
1941	Named a professor and the director of the Eidgenössiche Technische Hochschule (ETH) in Zurich, Switzerland
1950	Publishes "Newer Developments of the Chemistry of Many-Membered Ring Compounds"
1956	Publishes "Specification of Asymmetric Configuration in Organic Chemistry"
1963	Publishes "Conformation and Reactivity of Medium-Sized Ring Compounds"
1968	Publishes "Problems in Chemical Topology"
1975	Awarded the Nobel Prize in Chemistry, jointly with John Warcup Cornforth

Early Life

Born in Sarajevo in 1906, Vladimir Prelog (pronounced "PREH-lohg") was interested in science at an early age. As a boy, he imagined three noted chemists—Sir Robert Robinson,

Christopher Ingold, and Leopold Ruzicka—to be his teachers and, surprisingly, went on to work with them in later years.

Prelog was educated in typical European fashion at the Gymnasium in Zagreb and the Technological Institute in Prague, but his career plans were abruptly terminated by the worldwide economic catastrophe of 1929. Instead of pursuing a university degree, he was forced to accept an industrial position until the economic situation improved.

Chemical Variety

Prelog was to exercise his creativity in the study of carbon compounds, those found in organic or living organisms. His early work centered on the synthesis of cyclic compounds. While conceptually simple, their successful preparation is difficult. Numerous open-chain molecules with reactive atoms are found at either end, and it would seem easy to bring the ends together and cause them to react within the same molecule. That is precisely the problem, however, for the reactive atoms may instead react with the ends of different molecules. This undesirable reaction was the only product in rings of certain sizes until Prelog's work.

Prelog worked with Ruzicka on this problem in Switzerland, and the successful method that they developed remains the only practical preparation. It involves carrying out the reaction with an extremely low concentration of starting material. Under these conditions, the chance of ring formation becomes greater than that of polymer formation because of a change in the relative probability of collision. A second factor in Prelog's method is his use of a reactive metal surface as the reaction site.

Where the Paths May Lead

Prelog and Ruzicka had discovered more than a method for a particular synthesis. Further experimentation proved the existence of a number of paths that one could take and that would reveal new molecular architecture. Never content simply to make new compounds, no matter how elegant the method, Prelog thought deeply about these other possibilities.

He was especially interested in the so-called medium rings, those with eight to eleven atoms, which are very difficult to form. By study-

ing accurate models, he concluded that a structure in some remote site on the ring might influence the chemistry being studied in another part of the ring. Prelog's description of such transannular (across-the-ring) chemistry has become important in several fields, including protein chemistry.

His interest in these fine details of chemical structure also involved questions of stereochemistry. This term is applied to molecules that differ only in their arrangement of atoms in space. To study such small differences, it is necessary to separate the forms. One of Prelog's contributions involved the use of columns of a single form found in nature to purify selectively the mixtures usually found in the laboratory.

Prelog shared the 1975 Nobel Prize in Chemistry with John Warcup Cornforth for his work on chemical reactions.

Bibliography
By Prelog
"Newer Developments of the Chemistry of Many-Membered Ring Compounds," *Journal of the Chemical Society*, 1950
"Specification of Asymmetric Configuration in

(The Nobel Foundation)

Naming Chiral Compounds

In collaboration with two British chemists, Prelog developed the now universally accepted method of designating right-handed and left-handed molecules.

The basic method of naming stereochemical molecules developed by Prelog, in collaboration with R. S. Cahn and C. K. Ingold, depends on two basic conventions: an unambiguous sequence of the groups or atoms attached to the chiral atom and a specific point in space from which to view the molecule under consideration. The rules that allow clear communication among scientists are illustrated here using the most common type of chiral arrangement.

When four different atoms or groups of atoms are attached to one carbon atom, the molecule exists in two nonidentical structures related as object and mirror image. Consider the following generalized models:

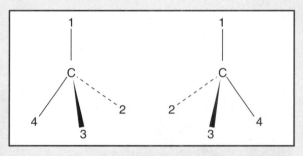

The numbers refer to the priority of the atoms as assigned largely on the basis of atomic numbers. The viewing convention is from the chiral atom along the bond to the group of lowest priority.

These structures are turned in space so that the three groups of highest priority are arranged as the spokes of a wheel.

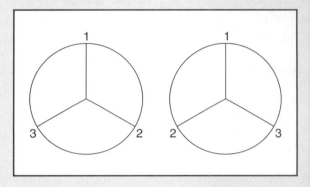

The first structure has a clockwise sequence of decreasing priority, and the second is counterclockwise. The name of the first compound contains *R* (from the Latin *rectus*, "right"), and the second contains *S* (*sinister*, "left").

Bibliography

Advanced Organic Chemistry. Francis A. Carey and Richard J. Sundberg. 3d ed. New York: Plenum Press, 1990.

Stereochemistry. O. Bertrand Ramsay. London: Heyden, 1981.

Organic Chemistry," *Experientia*, 1956 (with R. S. Cahn and C. K. Ongold)

"Conformation and Reactivity of Medium-Sized Ring Compounds," *Pure Applied Chemistry*, 1963

"Problems in Chemical Topology," *Chemistry in Britain*, 1968

"The Role of Certain Microbial Metabolites as Specific Complexing Agents," *Pure Applied Chemistry*, 1971

"Chirality in Chemistry" in *Les Prix Nobel*, 1975

"From Configurational Notation of Stereoisomers to the Conceptual Basis of Stereochemistry" in *Van't Hoff: Le Bel Centennial*, 1975 (O. Bertrand Ramsay, ed.)

My 132 Semesters of Chemical Studies: Studium chymiae nec nisi cum morte finitur, 1991

About Prelog

"The 1975 Nobel Prize for Chemistry." Ernest L. Eliel and Harry S. Mosher. *Science* 190 (1975).

"Vladimir Prelog." In *McGraw-Hill Modern Scientists and Engineers*, edited by Jay E. Greene. Vol. 3. New York: McGraw-Hill, 1980.

"Vladimir Prelog." K. Thomas Finley. In *The Nobel Prize Winners: Chemistry*, edited by Frank N. Magill. Pasadena, Calif.: Salem Press, 1990.

(K. Thomas Finley)

Joseph Priestley

Areas of Achievement: Chemistry and physics

Contribution: Priestley is credited with the discovery of oxygen, which helped overthrow the phlogiston theory.

Mar. 13, 1733	Born in Birstal Fieldhead, Yorkshire, near Leeds, England
1762	Ordained as a minister of the Congregational Church
1765	Receives an LL.D. degree from the University of Edinburgh
1766	Named a Fellow of the Royal Society of London
1767	Becomes a pastor of the Mill Hill Chapel in Leeds
1767	Publishes *The History and Present State of Electricity*
1772	Accepts a position as librarian to Lord Shelburne
1772	Shows that a gas necessary for animal life is produced by plants
1772	Discovers nitrogen monoxide and isolates gaseous ammonia
1773	Receives the Copley Medal from the Royal Society of London
1774	Discovers oxygen by heating mercuric oxide
1774	Isolates sulfur dioxide from sulfuric acid
1780	Becomes a minister of the New Meeting Chapel
1791	His chapel, home, and laboratory are destroyed by a mob
1794	Emigrates to the United States and settles in Northumberland, Pennsylvania
Feb. 6, 1804	Dies in Northumberland, Pennsylvania

Early Life

Joseph Priestley's father was a clothmaker who lived in Birstal Fieldhead near Leeds, England. Joseph's mother died in childbirth when he was six years old. Religion was a strong, life-long influence on Priestley. His grandfather was reared as a member of the Church of England but became a Calvinist dissenter through the influence of his wife. As Joseph grew older, he developed independent ideas about religion that led to his rejection of the strict Calvinist doctrines.

Since only members of the Church of England were allowed to enter English universities at the time, Priestley entered the dissenting academy at Daventry. In 1755, he left Daventry to take a position as assistant minister to a congregation in Needham Market, Suffolk. His unorthodox religious views were not well received there, and his congregation and income dwindled.

Priestley was much more successful at a position in Nantwich in Cheshire, where he started a school. Its success led to the offer of a position at the Warrington Academy. His pri-

(Library of Congress)

Oxygen and the Overthrow of the Phlogiston Theory

Priestley's discovery of oxygen was crucial to the overthrow of the phlogiston theory, which proposed that a substance was lost in all combustion reactions.

The work for which Priestley is best known was done in 1774. He had obtained a 12-inch lens that he used to focus the rays of the sun in order to achieve high temperatures. He used the lens to heat various chemicals to see if they would give off a gas. On August 1, he used his lens to heat "mercurius calcinatus" (mercuric oxide) and then collected and tested the emitted gas. It was not soluble in water, and a candle placed in it burned more brightly than in air. He also determined that mice would live longer in the gas than in an equal volume of air. Two months later, Priestley went to Paris and visited chemist Antoine-Laurent LavoisierLaurent]. He told Lavoisier of his discovery of this new gas, which is now known as oxygen.

This discovery helped discredit the phlogiston theory, chemistry's first comprehensive theory. It offered an explanation for a number of well-known chemical reactions. Its origin is attributed to the German chemist Georg Stahl in 1714. In the most familiar combustion reactions, something appears to be lost. For example, when wood is burned, only ash remains. Stahl proposed that a substance, which he called "phlogiston," is lost in all combustion reactions. Something burned until it had given off all of its phlogiston. If the burning was done in a closed vessel, it stopped when the air in the vessel was saturated with phlogiston.

The theory was extended beyond ordinary combustion reactions. When a metal was burned in air, it was thought to give up phlogiston, producing a product called a "calx." When the calx was heated with charcoal, it took up phlogiston from the charcoal and regenerated the original metal. Oxide is the modern name for a calx. Priestley was a lifelong believer in the phlogiston theory, but Lavoisier disproved it using some of Priestley's own work.

In 1772, Lavoisier determined that when burned, sulfur and phosphorus, rather than losing a substance, actually gained weight. His explanation for the increase in weight was that the phosphorus and sulfur combined with air. With Priestley's discovery of oxygen, Lavoisier was able to demonstrate that it was only the oxygen in air that combined with the material being burned. He did so by repeating Priestley's oxygen experiment using quantitative measurements.

Lavoisier weighed a sample of mercuric oxide, heated it to drive off the oxygen, and weighed the mercury produced. The weight of the collected oxygen was close to the difference between those of the mercury and the oxide. This demonstrated that when mercury was burned, oxygen must have combined with it, instead of "phlogiston" being removed.

Bibliography

Harvard Case Histories in Experimental Science. James Conant, ed. Cambridge, Mass.: Harvard University Press, 1957.

The Norton History of Chemistry. William H. Brock. New York: W. W. Norton, 1992.

The Story of Alchemy and Early Chemistry. John Stillman. New York: Dover, 1960.

mary duty was to teach languages, but while there he attended some lectures in chemistry.

Although Priestley himself had no formal science training, he believed that science should be an important part of a school's curriculum. His initial scientific interest in electricity was aroused when he met Benjamin Franklin in London in 1766. Franklin's work with electricity was well known. Priestley planned to write a detailed history of science, the first volume of which was to be devoted to electricity. Franklin encouraged Priestley to proceed with his history and gave him ideas for new experiments.

Work with Electricity

Priestley's work on his history of electricity proceeded quickly, and *The History and Present State of Electricity* was published in the fall of 1767. It was a successful work that went through five editions.

The most notable of his original observations

was that charcoal and coke are good conductors of electricity. Up to this time, it was thought that only metals and water were electrical conductors. Priestley also proposed the inverse square law for the attraction between oppositely charged bodies. This law was experimentally demonstrated by Charles-Augustin Coulomb in 1784 and now bears his name.

Initial Work with Gases

In 1767, at the age of thirty-four, Priestley assumed the position of pastor of the Mill Hill Chapel at Leeds. It is now known that air consists mainly of nitrogen and oxygen. At the time that Priestley began his work at Leeds, however, it was thought to be a single, pure substance. The word "air" was used as a general term for what is now called a gas. Common air was thought to be the only gas until Joseph Black isolated carbon dioxide, which he called "fixed air."

Soon after arriving at Leeds, Priestley began to experiment with carbon dioxide. His work produced no startling results, but it did gain for him some recognition from the prestigious Royal Society of London.

At the time, gases were routinely collected by the pneumatic method, which most high school chemistry students have used to collect oxygen and hydrogen. The gas is bubbled into a jar containing water, which is forced out by the gas. Priestley improved this gas-collecting technique by using both water and mercury as the displaced liquid. Displacement of water cannot be used to collect water-soluble gases, since the gases will dissolve in the water rather than displace it. Using his technique, Priestley was the first to isolate the water-soluble hydrogen chloride gas. He did so by heating sodium chloride and sulfuric acid.

Solutions of ammonia in water had been prepared previously, but ammonia gas had never been isolated. Priestley accomplished this task by heating ammonia water and collecting the ammonia gas driven off by mercury displacement. He knew that solutions of hydrogen chloride are acidic and that ammonia solutions are basic. He wondered if a neutral gas would be formed if they reacted together.

When he brought the two gases together, he observed the formation of a white cloud that gradually settled to form a fine powder. He identified the powder as "sal ammoniac," now called ammonium chloride. This work was done in 1772 and 1773.

In 1791, Priestley's unpopular religious and political views led to the destruction of his chapel, home, and laboratory by a mob. Three years later, he moved to the United States, where he died in 1804.

Bibliography

By Priestley

The History and Present State of Electricity, 1767

Experiments and Observations on Different Kinds of Air, 1774 (6 vols) revised 1790 (3 vols.)

Considerations on the Doctrine of Phlogiston and the Decomposition of Water, 1796

Memoirs of Dr. Joseph Priestley, to the Year 1795, Written by Himself, With a Continuation, to the Time of His Decease, by His Son Joseph Priestley, 1805

Theological and Miscellaneous Works, 1817-1831 John Towill Rutt, ed.)

About Priestley

A History of Chemistry. J. R. Partington. Vol. B. New York: St. Martin's Press, 1962.

Joseph Priestley. F. W. Gibbs. London: Thomas Nelson, 1965.

A Scientific Autobiography of Joseph Priestley, Selected Scientific Correspondence Edited with Commentary. Robert Schofield. Cambridge, Mass.: MIT Press, 1966.

(Francis P. Mac Kay)

Ilya Prigogine

Areas of Achievement: Chemistry and physics

Contribution: Prigogine significantly advanced the science of thermodynamics, which studies the interrelationships of heat, work, and energy. He also extended his ideas to the biological and social sciences.

Jan. 25, 1917	Born in Moscow, Russia
1929	Settles in Belgium
1939	Receives an M.S. from the University of Brussels
1941	Receives a Ph.D. in chemistry from Brussels
1947	Appointed a professor at the University of Brussels
1959	Named director of the Instituts Internationaux de Physique et Chimie, Solvay
1961-1966	Appointed Extraordinary Chair at the Enrico Fermi Institute for Nuclear Studies and the Institute for the Study of Metals, the University of Chicago
1967	Founds and directs the Ilya Prigogine Center for Statistical Mechanics, Thermodynamics, and Complex Systems at the University of Texas at Austin
1977	Wins the Nobel Prize in Chemistry
1979	Appointed Ashbel Smith Regental Professor of Physics and Chemical Engineering at Texas
1980	Publishes *From Being to Becoming: Time and Complexity in the Physical Sciences*
1984	Publishes *Order out of Chaos: Man's New Dialogue with Nature*, with Isabel Stengers

Early Life

Ilya Prigogine (pronounced "pruh-GAW-zhuhn") was born on January 25, 1917, in Moscow, Russia, to Roman Prigogine, a chemical engineer, and Julia Wichman Prigogine. This was a turbulent time in Russia. When Ilya was four years old, his parents joined the huge number of refugees who emigrated from the Soviet Union after the Bolshevik Revolution. The family wandered throughout Western Europe before settling in Belgium in 1929.

Prigogine's earliest interests were centered in the human sciences rather than in the physical sciences. In school, he was passionately interested in history, archaeology, and art. By chance, however, his parents had brought him to Brussels, which was a world center for research in thermodynamics, the one scientific field that does take seriously the concept of time, an idea that had always fascinated him.

Prigogine studied at the University of Brussels, where he received his master's degree in 1939 and his doctorate in 1941. In 1961, he married Marina Prokopowicz; they had two children, Yves and Pascal. Prigogine's leisure interests always included music and the arts.

In 1951, Prigogine became a professor at the University of Brussels. In 1959, he was appointed director of the Instituts Internationaux de Physique et Chimie in Solvay. From 1961 to 1966, he was a professor of chemistry at the Enrico Fermi Institute for Nuclear Studies and the Institute for the Study of Metals at the University of Chicago.

From 1967, Prigogine held the position of director of the Center for Statistical Mechanics and Thermodynamics at the University of Texas at Austin, concurrently with his professorship in Brussels; the center was later named for him. In 1979, he was appointed Ashbel Smith Regental Professor of Physics and Chemical Engineering at Texas.

Major Work

The major theme of Prigogine's work concerns the theory of dissipative structures—that is, systems that interact with their environment. Scientists have long observed that for many physical systems, there is a general tendency for the system to assume the state that is most disordered. This disorder is termed "entropy."

The phenomenon of increasing disorder is captured in the classical second law of thermodynamics, which implies that over time, physical systems increase in entropy, or chaos.

This increase in entropy occurs by means of processes that dissipate energy and that, in principle, can produce work. An important problem arises, however, concerning how a more orderly system, such as a living creature, can arise spontaneously from a less orderly system and yet sustain itself despite the tendency toward disorder. Indeed, the young Prigogine was very attracted to Erwin Schödinger's book *What Is Life?* (1944), at the end of which Schrödinger raises these same problems.

During the late 1940's, Prigogine developed mathematical models of dissipative systems—that is, systems capable of maintaining their identity only by continually remaining open to the flux and flow of their environment. These dissipative systems are therefore also called open systems, in contrast to the closed systems of classical thermodynamics. In such well-studied, closed systems, no interaction occurs between the system and its external environment. Prigogine's models show how matter and energy can interact creatively, forming complex structures (such as organisms) that can maintain themselves and even grow. Such dissipative structures exist in opposition to the increase of disorder as enunciated by the second law of thermodynamics.

Equilibrium vs. Nonequilibrium Systems

Prigogine showed that dissipative structures fall into two categories: systems that are at, or close to, equilibrium, in which order tends to be destroyed; and systems that are far from equilibrium (also called "nonequilibrium systems" or "irreversible systems"), in which order can be maintained and in which the spontaneous creation of new, complex structures occurs.

While the probability of order arising from disorder is very small, the formation of an ordered dissipative system (an open system, one that interacts with its external environment) will literally result in order out of chaos. Indeed, one of his most widely read books is titled *Order out of Chaos: Man's New Dialogue with Nature* (1984). Prigogine's ideas have been applied to many other areas, such as the origin of life on Earth, the dynamics of ecosystems, the preservation of world resources, and even the prevention of traffic gridlock.

Philosophy of Science

Prigogine's work requires scientists to rethink the nature of scientific laws. Concepts such as causal laws and fluctuations should not be treated in opposition to each other. Both types of descriptions cooperate in systems beyond a certain threshold of complexity for different physical systems.

As a whole, Prigogine's work implies that the description of nature is changing from a classically deterministic description toward a description that increasingly emphasizes the role of fluctuations, self-organization, and evolutionary patterns. Also, his work is foundational to the emerging sciences of complexity and chaos.

Prigogine's interest in time is closely associ-

(The Nobel Foundation)

Prigogine's Theory of Dissipative Structures

Prigogine developed highly advanced mathematical models to describe dissipative systems that are far from equilibrium. In such states, physical systems do not simply break down. Rather, complex new systems emerge.

Equilibrium is the state of maximum entropy in which molecules move around at random. According to the classical second law of thermodynamics, this is the state toward which the universe is heading.

If one box filled with nitrogen and one filled with hydrogen are connected by an opening, the two gases will eventually mix so thoroughly that no difference will exist in their concentrations. The system has gone to equilibrium and maximum entropy. On the other hand, if the two boxes are heated to slightly different temperatures, the gases will still mix, but not uniformly. There will be more hydrogen in one box and more nitrogen in the other. The flow of heat has produced some order. Such a system, called a near-to-equilibrium system, also displays no direction in time because it loses heat as fast as it gains heat.

It was only in far-from-equilibrium systems that Prigogine discovered the concept of "order out of chaos" and another instance of the direction (or arrow, or flow) of time. Such far-from-equilibrium systems receive considerable energy input from the outside.

One of Prigogine's favorite examples is the Bénard instability. If a pan of liquid is heated so that the lower surface is hotter than the upper surface, heat at first travels from the lower surface to the upper by conduction. The flow in the liquid is regular and smooth. This is a near-to-equilibrium state. As the heating continues, the difference in temperature between the two layers increases, and a far-from-equilibrium state is reached.

Gravity begins to pull more strongly on the upper layer, which is cooler and therefore more dense. Whorls and eddies appear increasingly throughout the liquid, which becomes increasingly turbulent until the system verges on complete disorder.

When the heat cannot disperse fast enough without the aid of large-scale convection currents, a critical bifurcation point is reached in which one of the many turbulent fluctuations becomes amplified and spreads, influencing and dominating the system. The system then shifts out of its chaotic state. The previously disordered whorls transform into a regular lattice of hexagonal currents, the so-called Bénard cells. This is a spectacular phenomenon produced by millions of molecules moving coherently.

Clearly, one very conspicuous and vitally important property of far-from-equilibrium systems is their capacity for spontaneous self-organization. Prigogine has extended this concept to other areas. For example, when termites build nests, there is no central organizer of any type. The insects roam at random picking up bits of earth and transporting these bits from one place to another. As they do so, they excrete a minute drop of chemical that attracts other termites. Randomly, higher concentrations of the chemical form in one area. The termites then head toward this area with their packets of dirt. Pillars begin to appear, and the activities of the termites become correlated until the nest is built.

Another example of self-organization can be found in vehicular traffic. A person driving on a freeway between rush hours is only minimally affected by the other vehicles. As four o'clock arrives, however, the traffic becomes heavier, and the driver begins to react and interact with the other drivers. All the drivers begin to be "driven" by the total traffic pattern. The traffic has become a self-organizing system.

All these systems are nonlinear—that is, the various components of the system react and interact with one another. The study of the laws of these open systems requires highly advanced, nonlinear mathematics.

Bibliography

Chaos: Making a New Science. James Gleick. New York: Penguin Books, 1987.

Chaos Under Control: The Art and Science of Complexity. David Peak and Michael Frame. New York: W. H. Freeman, 1994.

Complexity: The Emerging Science at the Edge of Order and Chaos. Mitchell Waldrop. New York: Simon & Schuster, 1992.

The Turbulent Mirror: An Illustrated Guide to Chaos Theory and the Science of Wholeness. John Briggs and David Peat. New York: Harper & Row, 1989.

ated with his studies in thermodynamics. Since the second law predicts that the universe is running down and will ultimately succumb to entropy, time has a direction, or "arrow." Contrary to the time reversibility so entrenched in Newtonian mechanics, physical systems in thermodynamics proceed in one direction only. According to classical thermodynamics, time is irreversible.

Prigogine showed great interest in the philosophical ramifications of his ideas. He participated in both the Eighth and the Tenth International Congresses of Logic, Methodology, and Philosophy of Science held in Moscow in 1988 and in Florence, Italy, in 1995, respectively.

Bibliography
By Prigogine
Traité de thermodynamique conformement aux méthodes de Gibbs et De Donder, 1944-1947 (3 vols.; with R. Defay; also as *Thermodynamique chimique*, 1950; trans. as *Treatise on Thermodynamics: Based on the Methods of Gibbs and De Donder*, 1954-   )
Étude thermodynamique des phénomènes irréversibles, 1947 (*Introduction to Thermodynamics of Irreversible Processes*, 1955)
Advances in Chemical Physics, 1967-1993 (various volumes as editor with Stuart A. Rice)
Thermodynamic Theory of Structure, Stability, and Fluctuations, 1971 (with Paul Glansdorff)
From Being to Becoming: Time and Complexity in the Physical Sciences, 1980
Order out of Chaos: Man's New Dialogue with Nature, 1984 (with Isabelle Stengers)
Exploring Complexity: An Introduction, 1989 (with Gregoire Nicolis)
Chaotic Dynamics and Transport in Fluids and Plasmas, 1993 (as editor)
Chaos: The New Science, Nobel Conference XXVI, 1993 (with others)

About Prigogine
The Biographical Dictionary of Scientists. Roy Porter, ed. New York: Oxford University Press, 1994.
"Ilya Prigogine." In *The Nobel Prize Winners: Chemistry*, edited by Frank N. Magill. Pasadena, Calif.: Salem Press, 1990.

(*Paul C. L. Tang*)

Margie Jean Profet

Areas of Achievement: Biology, immunology, medicine, pharmacology, and physiology
Contribution: Profet, a brilliant pioneer in the developing field of evolutionary medicine, proposed theories about human adaptations to plant toxins and infectious organisms.

Aug. 7, 1958	Born in Berkeley, California
1980	Earns a B.A. in political philosophy from Harvard University
1980-1981	Works as a computer programmer in Munich, Germany
1985	Receives a bachelor's degree in physics from the University of California, Berkeley (UCB)
1986	Presents her "pregnancy sickness" hypothesis
1989-1993	Works as a research associate at UCB
1991	Publishes "The Function of Allergy"
1992	Receives a Bosack-Kruger Foundation Grant to study evolutionary biology
1993	Publishes "Menstruation as a Defense Against Pathogens Transported by Sperm"
1993	Appointed a Fellow by the MacArthur Foundation
1994	Serves as a visiting scholar in the department of molecular biotechnology at the University of Washington
1995	Publishes *Protecting Your Baby-to-Be*
1996	Serves as a visiting scholar in the astronomy department of the University of Washington

Early Life

Margaret Jean Profet was the second of four children in a staunchly Catholic household. Both parents were trained as physicists, and her father encouraged Margie's talent in mathematics. She knew that the traditional roles of homemaker and mother were not for her, and, most of all, she feared becoming bored. Profet was committed to doing well in school and was rewarded by her admission to Harvard University.

Profet did not study science because she observed too much regimentation in classes. Instead, she majored in classical political philosophy and wrote a senior thesis entitled "Nietzsche: The Creative as Life-Affirming." After Harvard, she moved to Munich, Germany, to work as a computer programmer. From there, she visited Europe and East Africa and took a trip to Tanzania, where she climbed Kilimanjaro.

The Shift to Science

Profet's favorite questions had always been "why" questions, and she decided that physics was the best subject to assist her in this quest for knowledge. Therefore, much to her parent's surprise, she obtained a bachelor's degree in physics from the University of California, Berkeley (UCB), in 1985.

Profet, who was living in a house in San Francisco with a view of the water and local wild animals, began to read about evolutionary biology. She took advantage of Medline, a computerized database, and read everything relevant to her ideas. This period was incredibly productive and culminated in her theories on pregnancy sickness (popularly called "morning sickness") in 1986, allergies as a defense against toxins in 1987, and menstruation as part of the body's normal defenses against toxins and disease organisms in 1988.

Public Recognition

In the fall of 1988, Profet attended a colloquium by Bruce Ames, a toxicologist and professor at UCB and a recognized expert on plant toxins and natural carcinogens. She sent him some of her work, and he offered her a job in his laboratory. She preferred part-time employment so that she could continue working on her ideas, but she also published several articles compar-

---

Adaptations to Toxins and Pathogens

According to Profet, pregnancy sickness, allergic response, and menstruation are all part of the body's natural defenses against toxins and infectious organisms.

The central theme of Profet's work is that humans coevolve and adapt to pathogens and toxin-producing organisms through many kinds of defensive actions, including avoidance, evasion, and expulsion. What is unusual about her work is that she has applied this principle to what the medical community has formerly considered to be abnormalities.

For example, nausea and food aversions in early pregnancy are not simply bothersome side effects. Profet argues that pregnancy sickness is attributable to the increased sensitivity of women's bodies to toxins in foods, which protects the vulnerable embryo when limbs and organ systems are forming.

Allergies have also been assumed to be, at best, an inappropriate hypersensitivity to specific substances in one's immediate environment. Profet argues that this immunological reaction is the last line of defense in the body's array of responses to toxic substances in the environment.

Her third major proposal may be the most controversial: She suggests that menstruation cleanses the uterus and oviducts of the harmful organisms brought in by sperm.

Profet's belief that these are adaptive responses has medical implications that are being explored in the emerging field of evolutionary medicine.

Bibliography

Beauty and the Beast: The Coevolution of Plants and Animals. Susan Grant. New York: Charles Scribner's Sons, 1984.

The Blind Watchmaker. Richard Dawkins. London: W. W. Norton, 1987.

Why We Get Sick: The New Science of Darwinian Medicine. Randolph M. Nesse and George C. Williams. New York: Times Books, 1994.

ing synthetic and natural chemicals with Ames and his colleague Lois Gold, a political scientist and an expert on risk assessment.

In 1993, Profet's economic situation improved when she was recognized with an award from the MacArthur Foundation. She moved to Seattle and an office in the Department of Molecular Biotechnology at the University of Washington. In 1995, she published a popular account of her pregnancy sickness theory entitled *Protecting Your Baby-to-Be*.

What Next?
Profet advocates that pregnant women take responsibility for their nutrition within an evolutionary framework, but she has been criticized for suggesting that pregnant women avoid the foods that make them sick. Only future research will resolve this controversy.

In the meantime, Profet, who likes to change topics, shifted her sights to astronomy and the structure of space-time.

Bibliography
By Profet
"The Function of Allergy: Immunological Defense Against Toxins," *The Quarterly Review of Biology*, 1991
"Menstruation as a Defense Against Pathogens Transported by Sperm," *The Quarterly Review of Biology*, 1993
"Pregnancy Sickness as Adaptation: A Deterrent to Maternal Ingestion of Teratogens" in *The Adapted Mind: Evolutionary Psychology and the Generation of Culture*, 1992 (Jerome H. Barkow, Leda Cosmides, and John Tooby, eds.)
Protecting Your Baby-to-Be: Preventing Birth Defects in the First Trimester, 1995

About Profet
"Margie Profet." Shari Rudavsky. *Omni* 16 (1994).
"A Maverick's Menu." David L. Wheeler. *The Chronicle of Higher Education* 42 (1995).
"Profile: Margie Profet—Evolutionary Theories for Everyday Life." Marguerite Holloway. *Scientific American* 244 (April, 1996).
"Rethinking Women's Bodies." Jean Seligmann. *Newsweek* 122 (1993).

(Joan C. Stevenson)

Ptolemy

Areas of Achievement: Astronomy, cosmology, earth science, mathematics, and science (general)
Contribution: Ptolemy developed a mathematical model to explain the motion of the sun, moon, and the planets revolving around an Earth-centered universe. Although his explanation was wrong, it influenced astronomical and religious teaching for more than fifteen centuries.

| c. 100 | Born |
| c. 178 | Dies |

Life
History records very little about the life of Ptolemy (pronounced "TAHL-uh-mee"), also known as Claudius Ptolemaeus. No records of his birth or death exist. What little is known of him comes from legends and his few surviving scientific works.

Ptolemy's life is generally placed around the time period 100 to 178. He was probably born to Greek parents who lived as colonists in Egypt. Some scholars suggest that his name may be a clue to his place of birth. At that time, there was a town known as Ptolemais Hermii situated on the banks of the Nile River. It was often the custom to name children after the place where they were born. Other historians think that Ptolemy may have been born in Greece and later moved to Egypt. No one knows for certain where he was born or if he was truly a Greek.

Ptolemy flourished when Rome was at the height of its power and influence over the Mediterranean world. He lived and studied in Alexandria, Egypt, which was the center of learning in the second century. His interests were in mathematics, science, and philosophy. Astronomy was particularly interesting to him as well. It is said that he established an observatory on the top floor of a temple in order to give himself a better view of the heavens.

Ptolemy's Epicycles: A Model for Planetary Motion

Despite its failure, Ptolemy's epicycle model remained the best explanation for motion in the heavens for more than fifteen hundred years; there was no other until Nicolaus Copernicus and Johannes Kepler.

In the *Almagest*, Ptolemy begins with the belief that the earth is a perfect sphere. Since all things on Earth fall toward it, he naturally assumed that all heavenly bodies must be influenced by the force of the earth as well. If that were true, then the earth had to be the center of the universe.

The universe that Ptolemy envisioned had the Moon, Mercury, Venus, the Sun, Mars, Jupiter, and Saturn all moving about a stationary Earth in circular orbits. The stars would occupy an outer sphere that enclosed the entire universe.

Ptolemy's model of the universe was by no means flawless. Most of the time, his observations of the planets did not agree with what his explanations suggested. He believed that all the planets moved in perfectly circular motion around the earth, and at uniform speeds. This was certainly not the case, as evident in the motion of Mercury, Venus, and Mars.

In order to make his model work, Ptolemy invented complicated mathematical concepts to correct for his apparent errors. The use of "epicycles," "eccentrics," and "equants" seemed to provide the solution to planetary motion. They worked well for each planet, but, when combined as a unit, the entire model fell apart.

The basis of the motion that Ptolemy was trying to explain was founded in Aristotle's Earth-centered universe. Aristotle's logic stated that all objects in heaven must be perfect and that their motion should be perfect as well. In order for this to be true, the planet's motion had to be uniform and follow a circular path. This is what Ptolemy hoped to see in the movement of the planets, but motion centered on the earth presented a different picture. At various times, the planets changed speed and even moved backward. This created a difficult problem for Ptolemy if he were to keep the earth at the center of the universe.

Ptolemy's solution was to create a series of wheels within wheels. A planet would move within a smaller circle called an epicycle. The center of the epicycle in turn would move in its own circular path or deferent around the earth. In a final attempt to duplicate planetary motion, Ptolemy added an equant. To do so, he had to place the earth off-center in the deferent circle. The equant was the exact point opposite the earth from the deferent's center. When viewed from this point, all planets appeared to move at a constant speed. Moving all the different wheels seemed to reproduce the motion of the planets. Right or wrong, Ptolemy had created a mathematical explanation for the movement of the planets.

As convincing as it was to scholars in the second century, however, his model was wrong. Planets do not orbit the earth; they orbit the sun. Yet, even today, it is still not easy to believe that the earth is in motion because human senses simply cannot feel the direct motion of the earth. It is trust in basic scientific principles and observations of other planets and star systems that makes it believable.

Bibliography

The Exact Sciences in Antiquity. O. Neugebauer. New York: Barnes & Noble Books, 1993.

Horizons: Exploring the Universe. Michael A. Seeds. Belmont, Calif.: Wadsworth, 1995.

Technology in the Ancient World. Henry Hodges. New York: Alfred A. Knopf, 1970.

Alexandria would be Ptolemy's home during the period of his greatest writings and discoveries. His proximity to the great library there and to the many scholars who used it provided him with a creative environment. He was greatly influenced by the writings of the Greek philosophers Plato and Hipparchus.

Four Major Works

The four major works of Ptolemy that have survived the ages are commonly known as the *Almagest*, the *Geography*, the *Tetrabiblos*, and the *Optics*. The principal work for which history remembers Ptolemy is the *Almagest*, or *Mathematike syntaxis*, as it was known in Greek. Later

Arabic scholars named it the *Almagest* (literally "the great"), which clearly indicates how revered the work was to astronomers up to the time of Nicolaus Copernicus and Galileo.

In the *Almagest*, Ptolemy would be best remembered for his explanation of motion in the heavens. In his vision, he pictured the earth as the center of the universe. Around the earth moved the sun, the moon, and the planets. Surrounding everything else was a sphere of stars. To explain motion, Ptolemy introduced a complicated geometric system based on circular motion around a central and stationary earth. Many of his ideas came from the earlier works of Plato, Aristotle, and Hipparchus. He used a concept called spherical trigonometry to calculate the motion of the five known planets. The accuracy of his calculations convinced many of his fellow scientists that his view of an Earth-centered universe must be correct.

In the *Geography*, Ptolemy introduced the concept of latitude and longitude as a means of determining positions on the surface of the earth. He accepted the earth as a perfect sphere and based the system on the 360-degree geometry of a circle. On land, he reduced actual distances to degrees of a circle. Over water, he simply guessed at distances.

Latitude positions could be accurately measured by observing the sun or certain stars, but longitude could not be measured. Consequently, Ptolemy's maps were considerably off, making the world smaller than it actually was. In 1492, Christopher Columbus relied on maps based on Ptolemy's calculations. Had he realized Ptolemy's mistake, Columbus may have never attempted to sail over a much-larger earth.

The work *Tetrabiblos* describes Ptolemy's views on astrology. In his day, astrology and astronomy were closely related. Most natural phenomena were explained by supernatural causes, as the understanding of nature was limited. Ptolemy believed that some form of physical energy radiated down from heaven and influenced human lives, which represented his attempt to understand astrological concepts. *Tetrabiblos* still serves as the basic argument for the validity of modern-day astrology for those who believe in it.

The last work of Ptolemy was *Optics*, the most scientific and accurate of the four. In it, he followed a basic scientific approach to problem solving and demonstrated a few of the basic principles of optics. The concepts of reflection and refraction were discussed, and he demonstrated a certain awareness of the behavior of light.

Bibliography
By Ptolemy

Mathematike syntaxis, c. 150 (commonly known as the *Almagest*; English trans. as *Almagest*, 1948)

Geographike hyphegesis (commonly known as the *Geography*; *The Geography of Ptolemy. . .*, 1732)

Apoteles matika (commonly known as the *Tetrabiblos*; *Ptolemy's Quadripartite: Or, Four Books Concerning the Influences of the Stars*, 1701)

Opticae thesaurus, 1572 (incomplete, lost in Greek and Arabic; commonly known as the *Optics*; *Ptolemy's Theory of Visual Perception*, 1996)

(Library of Congress)

About Ptolemy

The Eye of Heaven: Ptolemy, Copernicus, Kepler. Owen Gingerich. New York: American Institute of Physics, 1993.

"Ptolemy." In *Great Lives from History: Ancient and Medieval Series*, edited by Frank N. Magill. Pasadena, Calif.: Salem Press, 1988.

(Paul P. Sipiera)

Reginald Crundall Punnett

Areas of Achievement: Biology, genetics, and zoology

Contribution: Punnett performed numerous breeding experiments that helped establish Mendelian genetics as a new field in biology.

June 20, 1875	Born in Tonbridge, Kent, England
1889	Awarded a scholarship to Caius College, Cambridge University
1899-1902	Serves as a demonstrator in natural history at the University of St. Andrews
1901	Elected a Fellow of Caius College
1902	Becomes a demonstrator in zoology at Cambridge
1902	Writes to William Bateson regarding breeding experiments
1904-1910	Conducts genetics research with Bateson
1905	Publishes *Mendelism*, the first textbook on the subject
1910	Succeeds Bateson as professor of biology at Cambridge
1910	Launches the *Journal of Genetics* with Bateson
1912-1940	Named to the new professorship of genetics (formerly biology) at Cambridge
1912	Elected a Fellow of the Royal Society of London
1922	Awarded the Darwin Medal of the Royal Society of London
Jan. 3, 1967	Dies in Bilbrook, Somerset, England

Early Life

At the age of nine, Reginald Crundall Punnett, the eldest son of a middle-class builder, suffered a bout of appendicitis. This event forced him to rest daily and read among his father's natural history books, thereby sparking a lifelong interest in the study of living things. As a medical student at Cambridge University, Punnett excelled in the natural science tripos (honors examination), particularly in zoology.

Turning from medicine to evolutionary morphology, Punnett focused on the structure of a group of marine worms called nemerteans. After several years as a University of St. Andrews natural history demonstrator, he returned to Cambridge to become a Fellow of Caius College and later a Balfour Student in zoology.

Collaboration with Bateson

Early in the twentieth century, Gregor Mendel's nineteenth century work found a receptive audience among many biologists, including Punnett. In 1902, he wrote to the foremost British advocate of Mendel's laws, William Bateson, proposing experiments involving the inheritance of coat color. Shifting the focus of his studies, Punnett enthusiastically joined Bateson's genetics research group.

Factor Interaction

Factor interactions occur when two or more factors, inherited independently, contribute to the determination of a single physical characteristic, or phenotype.

Unit characters are ones in which genetic inheritance is determined by a single pair of factors. When they segregate, each shows complete dominance. For example, Gregor Johann Mendel used clearly segregating unit characters in pea plants such as yellow or green, smooth or wrinkled, tall or short.

Yet, this pattern is not always the case. Frequently, more than one factor is involved in the expression of a phenotype. In breeding experiments with domestic fowl, Punnett and William Bateson found that more than one factor determines the inheritance of comb shape. Certain breeds of chickens have rose, pea, or single combs. Although most crosses yield familiar Mendelian ratios, Punnett and Bateson discovered that a chicken with a rose-shaped comb bred with one with a pea-shaped comb resulted in a new comb shape called walnut in all the first-generation (F_1) offspring.

Explaining the appearance of walnut-shaped combs, they conjectured that the independent inheritance of two factors determined comb shape. Hence, the presence of both dominant factors, R and P, resulted in walnut combs. The presence of only the R yielded rose combs, and the presence of only the P created pea combs. Single combs resulted from the absence of both dominant factors. Furthermore, the interaction explained why crossing chickens with walnut combs yielded a 9:3:3:1 ratio, with nine walnut combs to three rose combs to three pea combs to one single combs, in the second-generation (F_2) offspring (see figure).

The Second-Generation Cross of Chickens with Various Comb Shapes

		Male Gametes			
		RP	Rp	rP	rp
Female Gametes	RP	RRPP walnut	RRPp walnut	RrPP walnut	RrPp walnut
	Rp	RRPp walnut	RRpp rose	RrPp walnut	Rrpp rose
	rP	RrPP walnut	RrPp walnut	rrPP pea	rrPp pea
	rp	RrPp walnut	Rrpp rose	rrPp pea	rrpp single

Many other types of factor interactions occur. Bateson and Punnett extended the explanatory power of Mendelism by establishing this important concept.

Bibliography
Principle of Genetics. Eldon J. Gardner. 4th ed. New York: John Wiley & Sons, 1972.

The Science of Biology: An Introductory Study. George G. Scott. Rev. ed. New York: Thomas Y. Crowell, 1930.

Between 1904 and 1910, Bateson and Punnett collaborated on hybridization experiments with sweet peas, domestic fowl, and other animals. Confirming and extending Mendelian genetics, their research established phenomena such as factor interaction, reversion, and complementary factors. Punnett also introduced a graphical method of representing hybrid crosses, now called the Punnett square-Crundall]. Punnett's textbook *Mendelism* (1905) introduced the subject to a wider audience. Appearing in many editions, this popular book was translated into seven different languages.

Butterfly Mimicry and Poultry Genetics

Punnett's interests also included the investigation of butterfly mimicry, the notion of one species mimicking another for adaptive advantage. Between 1912 and 1914, he debated Oxford University entomologist Edward Bagnall Poulton, a firm believer in natural selection. Opposing Poulton, Punnett insisted that mimic species emerged as a result of discontinuous mutations rather than small continuous variations. Punnett's research in this subject culminated with *Mimicry in Butterflies* (1915).

Encouraging practical applications of genetics, Punnett served as an expert on poultry breeding during World War I. As wartime food shortages demanded economical measures, Punnett used sex-linked plumage colors to breed chickens of different colors according to sex. With this method, the large numbers of unwanted male chicks could be detected early and destroyed. Punnett's *Heredity in Poultry* (1923) remained the standard work on poultry genetics for several decades.

Later Work

In 1910, Punnett succeeded Bateson in the newly created Cambridge chair of biology. Two years later, this position became the Arthur Balfour Chair of Genetics, the first of its kind in Great Britain. Retiring in 1940, Punnett continued research in poultry genetics into the 1950's.

Later developments in genetic theory had little impact on Punnett's consistently Mendelian outlook. Methodologically, his work illustrates part of a broader shift in biology from descriptive fieldwork to experimental laboratory research. Although best remembered for the Punnett square, he stands among a generation of scientists who established fundamental concepts in classical Mendelian genetics.

Bibliography

By Punnett
Mendelism, 1905
Mimicry in Butterflies, 1915
Heredity in Poultry, 1923

About Punnett
"Punnett, Reginald Crundall." F. A. E. Crew. In *Dictionary of Scientific Biography*, edited by Charles Coulston Gillispie. Vol. 11. New York: Charles Scribner's Sons, 1970-   .
"Reginald Crundall Punnett." F. A. E. Crew. *Biographical Memoirs of Fellows of the Royal Society* 13 (1967).

(*Robinson M. Yost*)

Isidor Isaac Rabi

Area of Achievement: Physics

Contribution: A noted nuclear physicist who studied atomic radio-frequency spectra, magnetic moments, and energy properties, Rabi also taught many great physicists, contributed to radar and atomic bomb development, and served on many national and international committees.

July 29, 1898	Born in Rymanow, Austria-Hungary (now Poland)
1926	Awarded a Ph.D. in physics at Columbia University
1926-1929	Studies in Europe with a postdoctoral fellowship
1929	Begins to teach career at Columbia
1931	With Gregory Breit, develops a formula to determine atomic magnetic energy
1937	Publishes a means of determining nuclear magnetic moments
1940	Serves as deputy director of the Radiation Laboratory at the Massachusetts Institute of Technology (MIT)
1944	Wins the Nobel Prize in Physics
1945	Proposes the idea for an atomic clock
1946	Serves on the General Advisory Committee of the Atomic Energy Commission
1947	Helps establish the Brookhaven National Laboratory
1961	Devises a plan for a European nuclear research facility
1968	Retires from Columbia
Jan. 11, 1988	Dies in New York, New York

Early Life

Isidor Isaac Rabi (pronounced "RAH-bee"), generally known as I. I. Rabi, was born in Rymanow, in the old Austro-Hungarian Empire, on July 29, 1898. Shortly after his birth, his orthodox Jewish family immigrated to the United States. They settled in the New York City metropolitan area where Rabi's father ran a small store and Rabi attended public schools.

When Rabi was ten, he read about the Renaissance astronomer Nicolaus Copernicus. This man's accomplishments shook Rabi's orthodox Jewish faith and started his life of scientific inquiry. He tinkered with home-built radios as a teenager and worked his way through college to gain a chemistry degree from Cornell University in 1919.

Given the negative public attitudes toward Jews at that time, Rabi could not obtain work commensurate with his academic background. After a few years in low-paying jobs, he returned to Cornell to start postgraduate work in physics. He switched to Columbia University for economic reasons. For his doctoral dissertation, Rabi created a new method of determining magnetic susceptibilities in crystals.

Fellowship Study in Europe

Rabi married Helen Newmark in 1926, just after receiving his doctorate from Columbia. Still facing an unfavorable job situation in spite of his academic stature, he obtained a fellowship financial grant for physics study in Europe.

For three years, he worked with, or for, some of the greatest physicists of the time—Niels Bohr, Wolfgang Pauli, and Otto Stern, among them. While working for Stern, Rabi devised a means of determining the electromagnetic spectra in an atom's nucleus.

Columbia University

In 1929, Rabi returned to an American scientific community eager to learn of the Europeans' atomic physics discoveries, and thus he easily won a position as a professor of physics at Columbia. Throughout the 1930's, Rabi inspired graduate students and colleagues to greater discoveries in molecular beam research, which involved sending a beam of molecules through an apparatus to determine its various properties.

One notable discovery was the Breit-Rabi formula, developed jointly with Gregory Breit, which showed how the magnetic energy and moment of an atom (that is, its magnetic torque value) could vary with the strength of an external magnetic field. This finding and others, mostly published in the American physics journal *Physical Review*, enabled physicists to measure various properties of atoms. They also won for Rabi the Nobel Prize in Physics in 1944.

Government Service

Motivated in part by the German Nazis' anti-Jewish policies, Rabi was eager to help the United States government prepare for and

---

Rabi's Molecular Beam Method

In 1931, Gregory Breit and Rabi established a formula that showed how external electromagnetic fields affect energy states and orientations within an atom. They and their associates then explored the workings of molecules, atoms, and nuclei through a process known as molecular beam method.

Molecular beam method was a means of controlling the movement and electromagnetic behavior of molecules so as to determine how they work. Physicists usually used hydrogen for the process, since its molecular and atomic structures are the simplest to study. Some of their landmark findings did occur, however, with more complex materials, such as lithium, potassium, and sodium.

To start the process, the physicists drove molecules away from the chosen material, either by chemical reaction or by heat application. These freed molecules passed through a mechanical aperture, which formed their progress into a stream that could then be acted on by various electromagnetic influences. Further apertures and very precise sensors then recorded the reaction of the molecules to these influences, thereby proving or disproving theories about atomic properties.

In this way, Rabi and his colleagues were able to calculate accurately the speed of a nucleus' spin and its magnetic torque rate. They could determine the tilt of an atom's magnetic axis, as well as minute electromagnetic relationships between an atom's nucleus and its electrons. In addition, they could ascertain the effect of external electromagnetic influences on an atom's behavior. For example, an analysis of external forces pulling on a hydrogen isotope molecule revealed that even with the added attractive force of an isotope's extra nucleic particles, the electrons extended further out from their nuclei. Thus, the molecule assumed a shape not of combined spheres but of a football.

The issue of external forces also led to further avenues of study, especially those involving opposed and oscillating electromagnetic influences. In his most notable finding, Rabi accepted a colleague's challenge and hit a beam of lithium atoms with two opposed electromagnetic influences, followed by one variable oscillating influence. The result revealed that increasing the electromagnetic oscillating frequency through the Larmor frequency (a known value determining the precession of the spin of atomic particles) caused a large change in atomic axis orientation—the atoms would "topple" as the frequencies matched.

The practical effect of this research was that humans not only knew about but also could manipulate atomic processes. Rabi's experiments contributed to the development of laser, microwave, and atomic clock technology. They were also applied to medicine in the form of magnetic resonance imaging (MRI), which provides doctors with information about injured tissues.

Bibliography

The Atomic Scientists: A Biographical History. Henry A. Boorse, Lloyd Motz, and Jefferson Hane Weaver. New York: John Wiley & Sons, 1989.

"The Measurement of Nuclear Spin." Gregory Breit and I. I. Rabi. *Physical Review* 38 (1931).

"Space Quantization in a Gyrating Molecular Field." I. I. Rabi. *Physical Review* 51 (1937).

Twentieth Century Physics. Laurie Brown, Abraham Pais, and Sir Brian Pippard, eds. Vols. 1 and 2. New York: American Institute of Physics Press, 1995.

(The Nobel Foundation)

Européen pour la Recherche Nucléaire (CERN). As chair of the Science Advisory Committee of the Office of Defense Mobilization, Rabi personally advised Presidents Harry S Truman and Dwight David Eisenhower. In 1957, Rabi spurred the reorganization of this office to make it even more responsive to the president.

Man of Principle

Rabi never forgot his responsibility to society. He believed that the hydrogen bomb's extremely large-scale destructive effects made it an instrument of mass murder, and he unsuccessfully opposed its construction. He resisted the Atomic Energy Commission's 1954 removal of J. Robert Oppenheimer's security clearance, believing that this action was a mean-spirited political move instead of a legitimate attempt to protect secrets.

Throughout his government service in the 1940's and 1950's, and especially afterward, Rabi found time to teach at Columbia. In his book *Science: The Center of Culture* (1970), he pleaded for a meshing of science and humanities education to guarantee the wise use of science and technology. Rabi retired from Columbia in 1968 and died in 1988.

wage World War II. In 1940, he volunteered his services to the Radiation Laboratory at the Massachusetts Institute of Technology (MIT).

Quickly rising to a deputy director's position, Rabi made significant contributions to advances in radar technology at the laboratory. He also informally advised J. Robert Oppenheimer, the director of the Los Alamos atomic bomb research facility. As the war ended, Rabi formally proposed the idea for an atomic clock, a technology that would become the accepted means for keeping the most accurate time.

Rabi's government service continued as he served on and was later chair of the General Advisory Committee of the Atomic Energy Commission. In 1950, he spearheaded the creation of a European atomic energy research center, which became known as the Conseil

Bibliography

By Rabi

"The Measurement of Nuclear Spin," *Physical Review*, 1931 (with Gregory Breit)

"Space Quantization in a Gyrating Molecular Field," *Physical Review*, 1937

My Life and Times as a Physicist, 1960

Science: The Center of Culture, 1970

About Rabi

A Festschrift for I. I. Rabi: Transactions of the New York Academy of Science. Lloyd Motz, ed. New York: New York Academy of Science, 1977.

Rabi: Scientist and Citizen. John S. Rigden. New York: Basic Books, 1987.

Six Men out of the Ordinary. Solly Zuckerman. London: Peter Owen, 1992.

(Doug Campbell)

Sir Chandrasekhara Venkata Raman

Area of Achievement: Physics
Contribution: Raman, the product of a scientific and intellectual revival in early twentieth century India, made fundamental contributions to physics, including the discovery of the Raman effect and the study of acoustics, diffraction, and spectroscopy.

Nov. 7, 1888	Born in Trichinopoly, Madras, India
1906	Publishes his first paper in *Philosophical Magazine*
1907	Receives an M.A. with top honors from the University of Madras
1907-1917	Works at the Indian Finance Department in Calcutta
1917	Joins the University of Calcutta as Palit Chair of Physics
1921	Delivers a lecture on the theory of stringed instruments before the Royal Society of London
1924	Elected a Fellow of the Royal Society of London
1928	Discovers the Raman effect
1929	Knighted by the British government in India
1930	Wins the Nobel Prize in Physics
1930-1935	Writes series of papers on light diffraction by ultrasonic waves
1932	Resigns from Calcutta and joins the Indian Institute of Science
1935	Founds the Indian Academy of Science in Bangalore
1947	Founds the Raman Research Institute in Bangalore
Nov. 21, 1970	Dies in Bangalore, India

Early Life

Chandrasekhara Venkata Raman was born in Trichinopoly (now Tiruchchirappalli), Madras, India, on November 7, 1888.

It was a time of considerable intellectual, artistic, and creative resurgence in India. A sense of national awakening against the British colonial occupation was beginning to unite the diverse regions of the country, and the resulting nationalistic impetus manifested itself in literature, music, art, and science. Srinivasa Ramanujan, the mathematical prodigy, was born the preceding year, and the decade following Raman's birth witnessed the birth of such scientists of world stature as mathematician and physicist Satyendranath Bose and astrophysicist Meghnad Saha.

Raman was the second of eight children born to Ramanathan and Parvati Chandrasek-

(The Nobel Foundation)

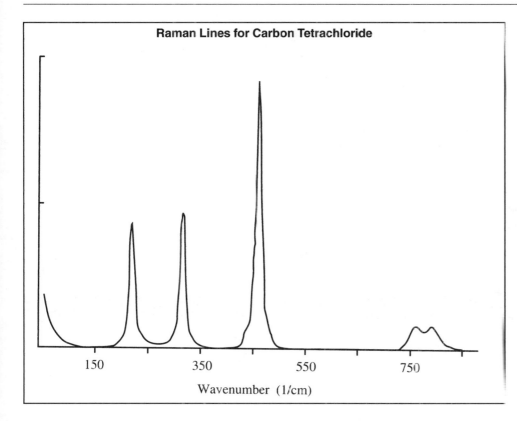

Raman Lines for Carbon Tetrachloride

Wavenumber (1/cm)

his spare time and published no fewer than thirty papers in leading journals. In 1917, he was offered the Palit Chair in Physics by Sir Asutosh Mookerjee, legendary vice chancellor of Calcutta University. Mookerjee attracted to the university exceptionally talented individuals who later went on to acquire international recognition and stature in their fields. Raman accepted the academic position despite a substantial pay cut from his government job.

During the years in Calcutta, Raman became vigorously involved in several areas of experimental research. He became an active member of the Indian Association for the Cultivation of Science, which was founded by Mahendra Lal Sircar, a nineteenth century medical doctor and philanthropist. It was in the association's laboratory that Raman later discovered the effect that came to be known by his name.

In 1921, Raman went to the British Universities Congress at Oxford to deliver a lecture on the theory of stringed instruments before the Royal Society of London Over the decade that followed, he made significant contributions to the fields of vibration and sound, musical instruments, ultrasonics, diffraction, meteorological and colloidal optics, photoelectricity, and X-ray diffraction.

har. Despite much hardship, Raman's father obtained his B.A. degree and continued his studies of literature, mathematics, and physics while teaching as a high school teacher with a modest income. Raman's early interest in physics was sparked by the ready availability of fine books in his father's library.

Raman and older brother Chandrasekhara Subrahmanyan Ayyar, the father of the astrophysicist Subrahmanyan Chandrasekhar-Subrahmanyan], received their primary education in Tamil, English, and arithmetic from their father. They attended a college in Vizagapatam of which their father was the vice principal, and both proved to be brilliant students. Raman was graduated from high school at eleven, completed college at fifteen, received his master's degree at seventeen, and earned the highest score in the All-India Competitive Examination for civil servants at eighteen.

The Palit Chair and the Calcutta Years
In 1907, Raman joined the Indian Finance Department in Calcutta as assistant accountant general, working there for ten years. During this time, he carried out extensive research in

Conflicts, Controversies, and Bangalore
Raman could be blunt. manipulative, and overbearing, and he sometimes ran into conflicts with students and peers. Significant among these is his antagonistic relationship with Saha, the eminent astrophysicist, that eventually led to Raman's resignation from the

University of Calcutta in 1932. He then joined the Indian Institute of Science in Bangalore as head of the department of physics.

Being an outstanding experimental physicist himself, Raman had little patience for those involved in theoretical research. He even derided his nephew, the distinguished astrophysicist Subrahmanyan Chandrasekhar, for "wasting his time in astrophysics, in the backwaters of science."

Raman's sincerity toward advancing scientific research in India was genuine, however, and the various research institutions that he founded or helped develop—including the Raman Research Institute in Bangalore, of which he was the first director—bear testimony to his dedication and untiring efforts. Raman died in 1970 in Bangalore at the age of eighty-two.

Bibliography
By Raman
"Dynamical Theory of the Motion of Bowed Strings," *Bulletin: Indian Association for the Cultivation of Science*, 1914

"On the Molecular Scattering of Light in Water and the Colour of the Sea," *Proceedings of the Royal Society*, 1922

"A New Type of Secondary Radiation," *Nature*, 1928 (with K. S. Krishnan)

"The Diffraction of Light by High Frequency Sound Waves," *Proceedings of the Indian*

The Raman Effect

The Raman effect is a change in the wavelength of a small fraction of the light deflected by the molecules of a transparent material.

When a light beam traverses a transparent material, most of the scattered light does not undergo a change of wavelength. A portion emerging at right angles to the original beam does change in wavelength, however, and therefore contains frequencies that are characteristic of the material. Such change is known as the Raman effect.

Raman scattering is best understood by considering that the incident light consists of particles, or photons (packets with energy proportional to frequency), striking the molecules of the sample. In most cases, the collisions are elastic—that is, the total kinetic energy remains unchanged—and, as a result, the photons are scattered without any change of energy or frequency.

In some cases, however, a molecule may either give up energy to the impinging photon or extract energy from it, thereby scattering the photon with increased or diminished energy, hence with higher or lower frequency. The amount of frequency shift is therefore a measure of the energy involved in the transition between the initial and final states of the scattering molecule.

The Raman effect is generally quite weak; the fractional intensity of the frequency-shifted light is about 1/100,000 of that of the incident beam.

The pattern of the Raman lines that are recorded from these frequency shifts is characteristic of the specific molecular species, and the scattered intensity is proportional to the number of scattering molecules in the path of the incident beam. For these reasons, Raman spectra are useful in both qualitative and quantitative analyses of optical materials.

The energies corresponding to Raman frequency shifts are associated with the transitions between different rotational and vibrational states of the scattering molecule. Pure rotational shifts are generally observed only in simple gaseous molecules; in solids or liquids, they are weak and difficult to observe. Shifts caused by vibrational transitions are larger and are readily observable in solids, liquids, and gases. Since the molecular concentration is low in gases at ordinary pressures, however, they produce very faint vibrational Raman lines.

The Raman effect has found extensive applications in laser spectroscopy, medical optics, wave mixing, stimulated scattering, and chemical analyses and measurements.

Bibliography
Introduction to the Theory of the Raman Effect. J. A. Koningstein. Dordrecht, the Netherlands: D. Reidel, 1972.

The Raman Effect. A. Anderson. New York: Marcel Dekker, 1971.

Academy of Science, 1935-1936 (with N. S. Nagendranath)

"Crystals and Photons," *Proceedings of the Indian Academy of Science*, 1941

"New Concepts of the Solid State," *Proceedings of the Indian Academy of Science*, 1942

"Floral Colours," *Proceedings of the Indian Academy of Science*, 1963

The Physiology of Vision, 1968

Scientific Papers of C. V. Raman, 1988 (S. Ramaseshan, ed.)

About Raman

Chandra: A Biography of S. Chandrasekhar. K. C. Wali. Chicago: University of Chicago Press, 1991.

Journey into Light: Life and Science of C. V. Raman. G. Venkataraman. New York: Oxford University Press, 1988.

"Sir Chandrasekhara Venkata Raman." In *The Nobel Prize Winners: Physics*, edited by Frank N. Magill. Pasadena, Calif.: Salem Press, 1989.

(Monish R. Chatterjee)

Santiago Ramón y Cajal

Areas of Achievement: Biology, cell biology, and physiology

Contribution: Ramón y Cajal applied Camillo Golgi's nerve tissue staining method in order to examine and illustrate the structure of animal nervous systems.

May 1, 1852	Born in Petilla de Aragón, Spain
1873	Receives a degree in medicine at the University of Zaragosa and enters the army
1874	Serves in Cuba, contracts malaria, and returns to Spain
1880	Marries Silvería Fanañás García
1883	Accepts a professorship at University of Valencia
1887	Accepts a professorship at University of Barcelona
1889	Publishes *Manuel de Histología normal y técnica micrográfica* (*Histology* 1933)
1892	Accepts the Chair of Histology and Pathological Anatomy at the University of Madrid
1897	Publishes the first volume of *Textura de sistema nervioso del hombre y de los vertebrados* (*New Ideas on the Structure of the Nervous System in Man and Vertebrates*, 1990)
1899	Visits the United States to give lectures at Clark University
1906	Awarded the Nobel Prize in Physiology or Medicine jointly with Camillo Golgi
1922	Retires from the university
Oct. 17, 1934	Dies in Madrid, Spain

(The Nobel Foundation)

Early Life

Santiago Ramón y Cajal (pronounced "rah-MOHN ee kah-HAHL") was born in Petilla de Aragón, in northeast Spain, on May 1, 1852. His father was a doctor who wished that his eldest son would follow in his footsteps. Young Santiago, however, was much more interested in painting and drawing. He did not excel in his early school days and was often in trouble with school officials.

Ramón y Cajal witnessed two events that turned his interest toward science. A lightning bolt struck the village church, killing the priest, and an eclipse of the sun occurred that his father had predicted. He was also fascinated by the early art of photography. He used it to record much of his own work, as well as to inspire his research on the visual system. At this time, he was apprenticed to a barber and a shoemaker, and the training that he received in using his hands and tools helped in his later career as a scientist as well.

Ramón y Cajal became serious enough about his studies to receive his degree in medicine at the University of Zaragosa. He retained his adventurous spirit, however, and he entered the army as a doctor. He volunteered to serve in Cuba, an island which Spain still controlled. He contracted malaria there and soon returned home. He did receive enough in pay to buy a microscope.

Ramón y Cajal began to study anatomy with his father, and they would occasionally slip into graveyards to obtain bones to study. Ramón y Cajal used his artistic abilities to draw anatomical details precisely and clearly. Using his microscope, he began to study and draw bodily tissues, a field known as histology. He also began to study brain tissue and used dyes to stain the cells in order to see them better.

Contributions to Science

In 1883, Ramón y Cajal accepted a professorship at the University of Valencia on the Mediterranean coast. There, he first saw a brain tissue sample stained by the Italian scientist Camillo Golgi. The sample showed individual nerve cells more clearly. The formula for the stain, accidentally discovered by Golgi, included silver, which was also used in developing photographic plates. No one knows to this day exactly why Golgi's method allows one out of hundreds of cells to be revealed.

Ramón y Cajal used the Golgi stain to produce a volume of work over his lifetime. He published more than three hundred papers and fifteen books. His primary contribution was to discover that nerve cells, called neurons, are not physically connected to one another. There are small gaps between them called synapses. He proposed that neurons communicate electrically over these gaps. This discovery was counter to the prevailing view that nerve cells were physically connected as in a network of cells and fibers, like an electrical circuit.

In 1887, Ramón y Cajal accepted a professorship in Barcelona, where he continued his work on tissue, in particular that of the nervous system. He made many contributions to the knowledge about the brain, and he began to travel to international conferences where he could more readily disseminate his ideas. At the time, none of the top brain researchers could read Spanish, and most of the work on the nervous system was written in English, German, or French.

In 1892 Ramón y Cajal accepted the position of Chair of Histology and Pathological Anatomy at the University of Madrid. His reputation was firmly established with the publication of *Textura del sistema nervioso del hombre y de los vertebrados* (1897-1904; *New Ideas on the Structure of the Nervous System in Man and Vertebrates*, 1990), which is considered a classic text in neurobiology.

Much of Ramón y Cajal's research involved not only fully developed nervous systems but also those of developing embryos. This study allowed him to see that each neuron develops an axon and that the complex connections between neurons are not random but very structured and specific.

Later Career

In 1906, Ramón y Cajal won the Nobel Prize in Physiology or Medicine together with Golgi. The two had never met, despite that fact that Ramón y Cajal owed so much to Golgi's staining method. Ramón y Cajal had improved the method and had taken the study of neurons to a higher level. In fact, Golgi was still a proponent of the network system. The two scientists never saw each other again after the Nobel Prize ceremony in Stockholm, Sweden.

The Neuron

Ramón y Cajal's work established that the neuron is an individual, well-defined cell, rather than a part of a continuous network.

There are several different types of neurons, each with a different function. Like snowflakes, however, no two individual neurons are exactly the same. The main structure of a neuron includes a cell body (also called a soma), an axon, and branchlike dendrites. A rough analogy would be to look at the neuron as a tree, with the body as the trunk, the axon as the root, and the dendrites as the branches.

Ramón y Cajal discovered small gaps between neurons called synapses. Later, it was shown that the communication between neurons is through the transmission of chemicals across these synapses, stimulated by electrical impulses in the neurons down their axons.

A human brain has about a hundred billion neurons, each of which makes approximately ten thousand connections with other neurons. Therefore, more connections exist in a single brain than the estimated total number of atoms in the universe. A human has twice as many neurons as a baby than as an adult. As babies grow, the neurons die as connections are made. By about ten years of age, the brain has stabilized.

Unlike other cells in humans and animals, neurons are not replaced when they die. When they are established, however, neurons are resilient and rarely die unless affected by injury or disease. The number of connections between neurons, however, changes constantly as an individual gains experience and learns new things. It has been shown that humans can continue learning throughout life. In fact, without such stimulation, the brain loses connections and can become less efficient, almost like a muscle that is not exercised.

Ramón y Cajal also showed that as neurons and their connections develop, they do so in a very systematic way. Just as a cell in an arm muscle "knows" where it supposed to be and what it is supposed to do, neurons are also aware of their place and function. The brain has many areas devoted to specific tasks. For example, Broca's area is responsible for a part of the speech process; certain neurons are programmed to form this area.

Ramón y Cajal traced many of the pathways of the brain, especially the visual system. By tracing the paths of individual neurons with his staining technique, he was able discover many of the specific functions of the brain.

Bibliography

"The Brain." David H. Hubel. *Scientific American* 241, no. 3 (September, 1979).

The Human Brain Coloring Book. Marian Diamond, Arnold B. Scheibel, and Lawrence M. Elson. New York: HarperPerennial, 1985.

In 1922, Ramón y Cajal retired from the University of Madrid, although he continued to work at his home laboratory. He published until his death on October 17, 1934.

Bibliography

By Ramón y Cajal

Investigaciones experimentales sobre la génesis inflamatoria, 1880

Manuel de Histología normal y técnica micrográfica, 1889

Textura del sistema nervioso del hombre y de los vertebrados, 1897-1904 (3 vols.; *New Ideas on the Structure of the Nervous System in Man and Vertebrates*, 1990)

Elementos de histología normal y técnica micrográfica, 1897 (*Histology*, 1933)

Recuerdos de mi vida, 1901-1917 (*Recollections of My Life*, 1937)

La fotografía de los colores, 1912

Estudios sobre la degeneración y regeneración del sistema nervioso, 1913-1914 (2 vols.; *Degeneration and Regeneration of the Nervous System*, 1928)

Reglas consejos sobre investigación scientifica, 1935 (*Precepts and Counsels on Scientific Investigation*, 1951)

Mi infancia y juventud, 1939

About Ramón y Cajal

Don Quixote of the Microscope. Harvey Williams. London: Jonathan Cape, 1954.

Explorer of the Human Brain. Dorothy Cannon. New York: Henry Schuman, 1949.

(Todd A. Shimoda)

John Ray

Areas of Achievement: Botany, earth science, and zoology

Contribution: Ray was the first naturalist in England to compose comprehensive descriptions of plants and animals arranged according to their resemblances to one another, rather than alphabetically by name or according to their utility to humans.

Nov. 29, 1627	Born in Black Notley, Essex, England
1648	Earns a B.A. from Trinity College, Cambridge University
1649	Elected a Fellow of Trinity College
1651-1655	Lectures in Greek, mathematics, and the humanities
1660	Publishes a flora of Cambridge
1660	Ordained in London
1662	Refuses to take an oath required by the Act of Uniformity
1663-1667	Travels in Europe and England with Francis Willughby
1667	Admitted as a Fellow of the Royal Society of London
1670	Publishes works on British plants
1672	Willughby's death leaves his study of animals unfinished
1673	Marries Margaret Oakeley
1676	Begins a prolific writing career and publishes Willughby's ornithology guide
1686	Publishes Willughby's *Historia piscium*
1686-1704	Publishes his own three-volume magnum opus on plant species
Jan. 17, 1705	Dies in Black Notley, Essex, England

Early Life

John Ray's father, Roger, was a blacksmith—an important skill when all transportation was on foot or horseback—and his mother, Elizabeth, was an herbalist and medical practitioner. John attended a local school and then Trinity College at Cambridge University, where he had a classic education, seemingly untouched by the civil war that was gripping much of England. His mastery of languages, especially Latin, later brought worldwide respect for his books, as Latin was the language of science and remains so in his chosen field of botany.

Much opposition to science existed at Cambridge. Many faculty members refused to believe Nicolaus Copernicus' theory of a sun-centered universe, and Ray could find no one at Cambridge to teach him botany, even though plants were important to medicine and there was much interest in natural history in England.

Association with Willughby

It was fortunate that Ray met Francis Willughby, a younger Cambridge student who shared his interest in natural history who was wealthy enough to fund Ray's work over the ten years that they traveled and worked together—particularly since Ray had lost his academic post after refusing, with nearly 2,000 other ministers, to take the oath of agreement with "all and everything contained in the Prayer Book."

Ray and Willughby's travels were a necessary preparation to fulfilling their grand ambition: to write a systema naturae based on first-hand observations and those of other naturalists. They became familiar with the flora and fauna of England, Wales, and Europe and with many leading experts in natural history.

Personal Life

Not much is known of Ray's personal life, except that he was kind, well liked, and respected and that he was a devout Christian who considered the study of nature a religious act. His wife had been a member of the household in one of Willughby's estates; she bore four daughters, about whom little is known, and she must have made him content at home, where he labored so intently for so many years with his books and specimens.

That Ray was accepted by the world of science is indicated by his election to the most exclusive scientific club in England, the Royal Society of London, where he had a number of friends, including Willughby.

Legacy

Ray laid the foundation of modern science in botany and zoology by questioning but not repudiating Aristotle's theories and by insisting on close observation and reasoning. Ray distrusted all speculations that could not be confirmed. He rejected all superstition and insisted that fossils were actually the remains of once-living organisms, not simply patterns in rocks.

Not all of Ray's writings were on science; he wrote a book on English words and another on English proverbs. Finally, he wrote a general text on science and religion, The Wisdom of God (1691), extolling the wonders of creation, including the solar system, geology, and human anatomy and physiology, as well as plants and animals. He published four editions, and the book became the model for literature of "natural theology" for more than 150 years.

Bibliography

By Ray

Catalogus Plantarum circa Cantabrigiam nascentium, 1660 (Ray's Flora of Cambridgeshire, 1975)

Catalogus plantarum Angliae et insularum adjacentium, 1670

Francisci Willughbeii de Middleton in agro Warwicensi, Armigeri, e Regia Societate, Ornithologia libri tres, 1676 (commonly known as Ornithologia libri tres; trans. as The Ornithology of Francis Willughby, 1678)

Methodus plantarum nova, brevitatis, et perspicuitatis causa synoptrice in tabulis exhibita, 1682 (commonly known as Methodus plantarum; revised as Methodus emendata, 1703)

Historia piscium, 1686 (with Francis Willughby)

Historia plantarum species hactenus editas aliasque insuper multas noviter inventas et descriptas complectens, 1686-1704 (3 vols.; commonly known as Historia plantarum and trans. as A Catalogue of Mr. Ray's English Herbal, 1713)

Synopsis methodica stirpium Britannicarum, 1690

The Wisdom of God, Manifested in the Works of the

Taxonomy

Ray's catalogs of flora and fauna set new standards by establishing distinctions based on shared attributes.

Ray published descriptions of 558 plants around Cambridge, England, in *Catalogus plantarum circa Cantabrigiam nascentium* (1660; *Ray's Flora of Cambridgeshire*, 1975). He then undertook a flora of all of Great Britain, traveling to most parts of the island, for *Catalogus plantarum Angliae et insularum adjacentium* (1670).

The alphabetical listing used for both works, however, became increasingly unsatisfactory. Ray's search for new principles of taxonomy led him to consider seeds as a basis for classification. In a paper on the germination of seeds, he distinguished between monocotyledonous and dicotyledonous plants, which remains a valuable distinction.

In another paper, Ray made further distinctions, dividing dicotyledons into thirty-six families and separating "imperfect" flowers such as ferns and mosses. He collected his papers into a book of general principles for botanists, *Methodus plantarum* (1682), principles that he used in revising his flora of Britain.

He defended his method in a tract and in his chief work, the three thousand-page *Historia plantarum* (1686-1704). In it, he includes descriptions of all known plants, including those recently discovered by explorers.

His colleague Francis Willughby died without publishing any of his works, and Ray felt obliged to complete them. Willughby's *Ornithologia libri tres* (1676) containing descriptions of more than 230 kinds of birds, became Ray's most popular book and the only one that he translated into English. He also completed Willughby's works on fishes, quadrupeds, and serpents. Willughby's *Historia insectorum* (1710) was left incomplete when Ray died, however, and it was published posthumously.

Bibliography

"Ray, Dillenius, Linnaeus, and the *Synopsis methodica stirpium Britannicarum*." W. T. Stearn. Introduction to the facsimile ed. of *Synopsis methodica stirpium Britannicarum*, by John Ray. London: Ray Society, 1973.

Creation, 1691; 2d. ed., enlarged, 1692; 3d. ed., enlarged, 1701; 4th ed., enlarged, 1704

Miscellaneous Discourses Concerning the Dissolution and Changes of the World, 1692 (revised as *Three Physico-Theological Discourses*, 1693, 1713)

Synopsis methodica animalium quadrupedum et serpentini generis, 1693

Historia insectorum, 1710

Synopsis avium et piscium, 1713

About Ray

Historical and Biographical Sketches of the Progress of Botany in England. Richard Pulteney. London: T. Cadell, 1790.

John Ray: A Bibliography. Geoffrey Langdon Keynes. London: Faber & Faber, 1951.

John Ray, Naturalist. C. E. Raven. Cambridge, England: Cambridge University Press, 1942.

Memorials of John Ray. Edwin Lankester, ed. London: Ray Society, 1846.

(Janet Bell Garber)

René-Antoine Ferchault de Réaumur

Areas of Achievement: Biology, botany, chemistry, earth science, genetics, invention, mathematics, physics, physiology, technology, and zoology

Contribution: Réaumur, a leading member of the Académie Royale des Sciences in Paris in the early eighteenth century, applied science to technology and made precise, innovative studies of insects.

Feb. 28, 1683	Born in La Rochelle, France
1699	Moves to Bourges to study law
1708	Made a student-geometer in the Académie Royale des Sciences
1711	Becomes a member of the Académie Royale des Sciences
1714	Elected director of the Académie Royale des Sciences for the first of eleven times
1721	Receives a pension from the government for his work on improving steel
1730	Announces his invention of a new thermometer
1734-1742	Publishes his six-volume work *Mémoires pour servir à l'histoire des insectes*
1738	Elected a member of the Royal Society of London
1744	Elected a member of the Berlin Academy
1749	Describes his invention of an egg incubator
1752	Publishes papers on digestion in birds
Oct. 17, 1757	Dies in Saint-Julien-du-Terroux, France

Early Life

René-Antoine Ferchault de Réaumur (pronounced "ray-oh-MYEWR") was born in La Rochelle, France, to parents belonging to the lesser nobility. Nineteen months after his birth, his father died, and René was reared by his mother, aunts, and uncles.

At the age of sixteen, Réaumur went to Bourges to study law. Three years later, he moved to Paris, where he joined a cousin in taking private lessons on mathematics. By 1708, his mathematical prowess was such that the great mathematician Pierre Varignon brought him into the Académie Royale des Sciences as a student-geometer.

Technological Improvement

By the time that he became a full, paid member of the Académie Royale des Sciences in 1711, Réaumur's interests had shifted away from

(Science Photo Library)

mathematics and toward other areas, especially natural history and technology. His concern with utility, evident in his later works, may have motivated this shift.

Among the technological processes that Réaumur studied in his first decade with the academy were those for making porcelain, steel, and cast iron. His work on steel was of interest to the French government, and the regent Philippe II, duke of Orléans, arranged for him to receive a special pension.

In 1730, Réaumur announced his invention of a new kind of thermometer designed to remedy the inaccuracy of traditional thermometers. Many eighteenth century scientists made use of his temperature scale.

International Renown

Réaumur became director of the Académie Royale des Sciences in 1714. All told, he would hold this position eleven times and the position of subdirector nine times. Few members of the academy were as active and dedicated. Never married and ever busy, Réaumur published papers on a wide variety of subjects.

His six-volume *Mémoires pour servir à l'histoire des insectes*, published from 1734 to 1742, won international fame for its detailed studies of insect behavior, morphology, and habitat. In addition to earning for him the respect of scientists, the series contributed to the vogue of natural history in polite culture.

Réaumur attracted correspondents and students throughout Europe and the world. Many of them furnished him with observations and specimens, and he in turn announced their discoveries to the Académie Royale des Sciences. His extensive contacts allowed him to make the Paris-based academy a truly international center for science.

Final Experiments

Although he had planned to write ten volumes on insects, Réaumur stopped publishing his *Mémoires pour servir à l'histoire des insectes* in 1742 and turned to other projects, particularly ornithology. He invented an egg incubator, collected bird specimens, and conducted experiments on digestion by making birds ingest various capsules.

Throughout his career, Réaumur championed careful observation and experimentation. He had little interest in conjecture and warned against generalizations. When French scientists became more speculative in the 1740's, Réaumur was occasionally ridiculed as being overly cautious and small-minded. His results, nevertheless, were appreciated and put to use

The Science of Bees

Using creative methods and his great skill as an experimenter, Réaumur illuminated the complexities of bee behavior and habitat.

In his studies of bees, Réaumur demonstrated the precise architecture of their cells; counted the number of workers, drones, and queens in a hive; measured the hive's temperature; and calculated how much pollen the workers could harvest in a day. Studies of insects had never before been so quantified. His hives, made with transparent walls and modular sections, gave him better access to bees than any previous structures. His technique of marking bees with colored paint was helpful in shedding light on the social structure of the hive.

Réaumur's measurements and novel experimental techniques led him to many important discoveries. For example, he proved that hives need a queen but will tolerate only one. Deprived of their queen, he showed, bees can make a new queen from a larva and will sometimes even accept a foreign one introduced in the hive.

Réaumur's work on bees was influential in the practice of beekeeping, in subsequent research on bees such as by François Huber, and in the study of insects in general.

Bibliography
The Biology of the Honey Bee. Mark L. Winston. Cambridge. Mass.: Harvard University Press, 1987.
Insect Behavior. Robert W. Matthews and Janice R. Matthews. New York: John Wiley & Sons, 1978.
The Wisdom of the Hive. Thomas D. Seeley. Cambridge, Mass.: Harvard University Press, 1995.

by many later scientists. He died in 1757 at the age of seventy-four.

Bibliography
By Réaumur
L'art de convertir le fer forgé en acier, et l'art d'adoucir le fer fondu, ou de faire des ouvrages de fer fondu aussi finis que de fer forgé, 1722 (*Réaumur's Memoirs on Steel and Iron,* 1956)

Mémoires pour servir à l'histoire des insectes, 1734-1742 (6 vols.)

Art de faire éclorre et d'élever en toute saison des oiseaux domestiques de toutes espèces soit par le moyen de la chaleur du fumier, soit par le moyen de celle de feu ordinaire, 1749 (2 vols; *The Art of Hatching and Bringing Up Domestic Fowls . . . ,* 1750)

The Natural History of Ants, from an Unpublished Manuscript in the Archives of the Academy of Sciences of Paris by René Antoine Ferchault de Réaumur, 1926

About Réaumur
"The Life and Work of Réaumur." William Morton Wheeler. In *The Natural History of Ants.* New York: Alfred A. Knopf, 1926.

Nature's Enigma. Virginia P. Dawson. Philadelphia: American Philosophical Society, 1987.

"Réaumur, René-Antoine Ferchault de." J. B. Gough. In *Dictionary of Scientific Biography,* edited by Charles Coulston Gillispie. New York: Charles Scribner's Sons, 1975.

(*Jeff Loveland*)

Walter Reed

Areas of Achievement: Bacteriology and medicine

Contribution: Reed was an Army bacteriologist and pathologist who directed the experiments which established that yellow fever is transmitted by the bite of an *Aedes aegypti* mosquito.

Sept. 13, 1851	Born in Beroi, Virginia
1869	Receives an M.D. degree from the University of Virginia
1870	Receives a second M.D. degree from Bellevue Medical College
1876	Marries Emilie Lawrence
1876-1888	Serves various posts as an Army garrison physician in the West
1889	Appointed attending surgeon and examiner of recruits for Baltimore, Maryland
1890-1891	Studies pathology at The Johns Hopkins University
1893	Assigned as curator of the Army Medical Museum
1894	Appointed professor of bacteriology at the Army Medical School
1898	Chairs a committee to investigate typhoid fever in military camps
1899	Begins to investigate yellow fever
1900	With James Carroll, submits his final report on a bacillus isolated by Giuseppe Sanarelli
1900	Establishes a research station on yellow fever in Cuba
1901	Returns to Washington, D.C., to resume his teaching duties
Nov. 22, 1902	Dies in Washington, D.C.

(Library of Congress)

Early Life

Walter Reed was born in Belroi, Virginia, in 1851. He enrolled at the University of Virginia, intending to study classics. After a brief period, however, he transferred to the medical faculty and completed his course of study in nine months. In 1869, at the age of eighteen, he received the doctor of medicine degree. He then enrolled at Bellevue Medical College in New York and earned a second medical degree.

After serving as an intern and district physician, Reed entered the U.S. Army in 1875. He served in remote outposts for many years. Reed was named the curator of the Army Medical Museum in 1893 and a professor of bacteriology in the newly established Army Medical School the following year. During the Spanish-American War of 1898, he investigated typhoid fever in military camps. The following year, he became involved in the problem of yellow fever.

The Yellow Fever Years

Yellow fever is known to be transmitted by the bite of a mosquito, which carries the virus that causes the disease. Proving this chain of events occupied the later years of Reed's life. Prior to Reed's work, the disease was thought to be transmitted by simple contact with objects such as bedding and clothing that were contaminated with yellow fever.

The Army assigned Reed and James Carroll to investigate an organism, *Bacillus icteroides*, that the Italian bacteriologist Giuseppe Sanarelli claimed to have isolated from yellow fever patients. In April, 1899, Reed and Carroll submitted their first report on the yellow fever organism. In February, 1900, they published their final report showing that Sanarelli's bacillus actually causes a variety of cholera in swine. It was only an accidental or secondary invader among individuals with yellow fever. The causative organism for yellow fever had not yet been identified.

Reed was assigned to investigate an outbreak of malaria in Havana, Cuba. After an initial review of the situation and examinations of those who were sick, he correctly diagnosed

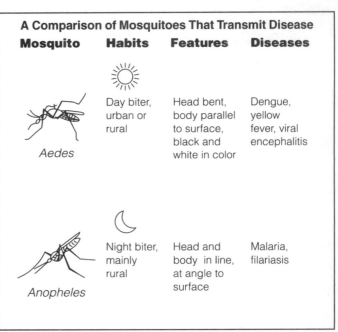

A Comparison of Mosquitoes That Transmit Disease

Mosquito	Habits	Features	Diseases
Aedes	Day biter, urban or rural	Head bent, body parallel to surface, black and white in color	Dengue, yellow fever, viral encephalitis
Anopheles	Night biter, mainly rural	Head and body in line, at angle to surface	Malaria, filariasis

(Hans & Cassady, Inc.)

The Transmission of Yellow Fever

Reed applied epidemiological principles to identify a certain type of mosquito as the vector for yellow fever and then to modify the environment in order to eliminate breeding sites for these mosquitoes.

Yellow fever is an acute viral disease characterized by a sudden onset of nausea, moderate fever, slowed heart rate, vomiting of blood, jaundice, and reduced urine output. Blood oozes from the gums, and the tongue turns strawberry red. These symptoms are followed by a severe headache and a high fever (104 degrees Fahrenheit or more). The disease has a fatality rate of up to 20 percent in untreated populations. Yellow fever has an incubation period of three to six days; the clinical disease typically lasts for two to three days. Full recovery in another two days is the rule.

In 1900, while conducting research in Cuba, Reed systematically studied a group of human volunteers over a period of a few months. He found that individuals bitten by *Aedes aegypti* mosquitoes that had previously fed on volunteers who had yellow fever became ill. Reed imported *Aedes aegypti* mosquitoes from areas that were free of yellow fever. Volunteers who were bitten by these mosquitoes did not develop the disease.

This demonstration showed that the *Aedes aegypti* mosquito was a vector responsible for spreading yellow fever. Further, Reed showed that the cause was not inherent in the mosquito but was something, most likely a microorganism, carried by it. Yellow fever could be eradicated if the mosquitoes could be exterminated. Engineering projects in Cuba to destroy the breeding grounds for mosquitoes, consisting mainly of draining swampy areas and eliminating standing water, were begun in 1901. Within three months, Havana was free of the disease.

Yellow fever is found in South America and in tropical areas of west, central, and east Africa. There are two distinct variants of yellow fever: the urban and sylvan (jungle) forms. The urban form is transmitted from person to person by the *Aedes aegypti* mosquito. The sylvan form is maintained by passage between monkeys and forest canopy mosquitoes; yellow fever is transmitted to humans when they enter the jungle. Clinically, the two varieties do not differ.

As of 1997, urban yellow fever had not occurred in the Western Hemisphere since 1954. It remained common, however, in Africa, particularly in urban centers; an average of two to three major epidemics occurred in Africa each decade since 1960. The *Aedes aegypti* mosquito breeds in small amounts of standing water such as that found in cans, tires, and puddles. Tires can transport dried eggs that hatch when water becomes available. Because of resistance to pesticides and the high price of labor, control is often difficult, and urban yellow fever was expected to return to the Western Hemisphere. Rio de Janeiro, once free of the mosquito, became reinfested.

An effective vaccine is available for yellow fever. It has been used in Asia to eliminate the disease despite the presence of *Aedes aegypti* mosquitoes. Treatment of the disease involves bed rest and the replacement of fluid and blood losses. Local measures to control yellow fever exposure include mosquito netting and repellants.

Bibliography

Control of Communicable Diseases in Man. A. S. Benenson. 16th ed. Washington, D.C.: American Public Health Association, 1995.

Yellow Fever. G. K. Strode, ed. New York: McGraw Hill, 1951

"Yellow Fever: A Medically Neglected Disease." T. P. Monath. *Review of Infectious Diseases* 9 (1987).

the disease as yellow fever. At this point, Reed decided to explore the possibility of insects spreading yellow fever as intermediate hosts. He made these suggestions in a report. The Army provided resources to conduct experiments concerning the transmission of yellow fever. The Army also noted that William Gorgas was struggling with this disease among the workers constructing a canal in Panama.

Reed established a research facility 300 miles from Havana. He recruited volunteers and systematically conducted his experiments. Under controlled situations, Reed exposed his volunteers to a variety of mosquitoes, people infected with yellow fever, and personal items that had been used by individuals who had died from the disease.

Over the next few months, Reed demonstrated that the *Aedes aegypti* mosquito transmitted the causative agent for yellow fever. Applying this knowledge, he decided to interrupt the disease cycle by eliminating the intermediate host. Within three months, Havana was free of yellow fever.

The same technology was then applied in Panama, where yellow fever was greatly slowing progress on construction of the Panama Canal. After the swamps were drained, both the mosquito population and yellow fever were eliminated.

Reed returned to Washington, D.C., from Havana and resumed his teaching duties. He died on November 22, 1902, following an operation for appendicitis.

Bibliography
By Reed
The Etiology of Yellow Fever: An Additional Note, 1902 (with James Carroll and Aristides Agramonte)

Report on the Origin and Spread of Typhoid Fever in U.S. Military Camps During the Spanish War of 1898, 1904 (with Victor C. Vaughan and Edward O. Shakespeare)

About Reed
Doctors in Uniform. Leonard N. Wood. New York: Julian Messner, 1943.

Healers in Uniform. Edwin Edelson. New York: Doubleday, 1971.

(L. Fleming Fallon, Jr.)

Ellen Swallow Richards

Area of Achievement: Chemistry

Contribution: A major contributor to the application of chemistry to practical concerns, Richards launched the fields of environmental, domestic, and sanitation chemistry.

Dec. 3, 1842	Born in Dunstable, Massachusetts
1870	Earns an A.B. from Vassar College
1871	Admitted as a special student at the Massachusetts Institute of Technology (MIT)
1873	Becomes the first U.S. woman to earn a B.S. from MIT
1873	Awarded an M.A. by Vassar
1873-1875	Conducts work in water chemistry for the Massachusetts State Board of Health
1876	Establishes the Woman's Laboratory at MIT
1879	Serves as an assistant instructor, without pay, at MIT
1882	Becomes the first woman elected to the American Institute of Mining and Metallurgical Engineers
1882	Publishes *The Chemistry of Cooking and Cleaning*
1883	Appointed Instructor in Sanitary Chemistry at MIT
1887-1897	Works as a State Board of Health water analyst
1900	Publishes *Air, Water, and Food from a Sanitary Standpoint*
1908	Elected president of the American Home Economics Association
Mar. 30, 1911	Dies in Jamaica Plain, Boston, Massachusetts

Early Life

Ellen Henrietta Swallow, the only child of Peter and Fanny Swallow, was born in rural Massachusetts and reared there and in New Hampshire. Her parents, who had both been teachers, placed an unusual emphasis on education and taught Ellen at home until she was sixteen. This early education, coupled with much hard, out-of-doors work, set important patterns for her lifelong interest in the practical application of chemistry.

Through her growing years, Ellen showed talent in both academic and practical areas. She helped her parents with their farms and stores and tutored other students. While working seriously at her studies and achieving high marks, Swallow also managed the home during her mother's frequent illnesses. She saved every available cent to reach her dreams of further education and never lost sight of her goals.

Education and Opportunity

Vassar College, Matthew Vassar's experiment in higher education for women, had only been open in Poughkeepsie for three years when Swallow entered as a special student at the advanced age of twenty-five. In 1869, only one year later, she was admitted to the senior class. Her talents in teaching, especially mathematics and Latin, provided the small amount of money necessary for minimal support.

During those two years at Vassar, Swallow discovered her love of science. The famous astronomer Maria Mitchell greatly impressed Swallow, but it was a forward-thinking male chemist, Charles A. Farrar, who completely captured her imagination. Farrar was well ahead of his times, not only in supporting education for women but also in seeing the opportunities for chemistry to solve practical problems.

The Technology Establishment

The newly opened Massachusetts Institute of Technology (MIT) in Boston had a firm policy of refusing women, but, when Swallow presented Mitchell and Farrar as references, she became "the Swallow Experiment." Her admission, as a special student, was to be without charge. While this tuition waiver appeared

magnanimous, she later learned that MIT had made the offer in order to be free of any serious involvement if she were unable to compete in an all-male environment.

She did not fail. Throughout her life, Swallow—who would change her name to Ellen Swallow Richards upon her marriage to Robert Hallowell Richards in 1875—contributed her talents to the institute, her profession, and other women looking for opportunities to make use of their intellect. In making educational opportunities available at MIT, she opened doors to scientific education and employment to succeeding generations of women. At the same time, Richards established the bases for the analytical chemistry of water, sanitation, air, and food.

Pioneering Work and Belated Recognition

Richards never doubted that women deserved an opportunity to participate in scientific work

(The MIT Museum)

Applied Analytical Chemistry

Richards sought to apply the principles and methods of chemistry to sanitation in order to promote a clean, healthy environment.

Few scientific activities have received as much attention as ecology, the study of humankind's relationship to the environment. The demand for pure water, air, and food at once raises the questions "What makes these vital substances impure?" and "How much impurity is allowable?" The unspoken assumption about what is present in pure materials is not as self-evident as might be first thought. For example, one drink of chemically pure water is enough for those who prefer mineral water, with its dissolved gases and salts.

More scientific questions concern purity itself. What does it mean when a substance is pure? Are there no atoms or molecules of another substance present? How does one know? The best one can say is that the level of impurity in a "pure" substance is less than a given method can detect.

The development of more precise analytical methods constantly engages the analytical chemist. Not only must the method determine the specific impurity, but it must function in the presence of other materials in the sample. These materials may be known or not, but the chemist must avoid false results. Even the known materials may be present in amounts and render the results unreliable.

This notion of interfering substances introduces a second important area of analytical chemistry, separation. Often, a precise analysis demands that matter be removed selectively. In dealing with the complex mixtures of the environment, analysis and separation must be studied together, with each aspect playing a role in the study of the other.

Above all, the analyst's intellectual and technical skills must be maintained at a high level. Only careful attention to detail yields reliable results. Amazingly small amounts of impurities are known to influence health. A level of 1 percent represents only one impurity in one hundred, but parts per million (ppm) or one ten-thousandth of a percent are routinely sought.

Powerful methods for such fine analyses involve electronics. The human hand and eye are replaced by an electrical signal. Such methods have revolutionized analytical chemistry, but they ultimately depend on the scientific knowledge and the technical skill of the person designing, testing, and using them.

Bibliography

Chemistry and Life. John W. Hill, Stuart J. Baum, and Dorothy M. Feigl. 5th ed. Upper Saddle River, N.J.: Prentice Hall, 1997.
Chemistry for Changing Times. John W. Hill and Doris K. Kolb. 7th ed. Englewood Cliffs, N.J.: Prentice Hall, 1995.
Chemistry in the Marketplace. Ben Selinger. 4th ed. Sydney: Harcourt Brace Jovanovich, 1989.
The Extraordinary Chemistry of Ordinary Things. Carl H. Snyder. 2d ed. New York: John Wiley & Sons, 1995.

or that social problems could be solved only through sound analysis. The homes of America demanded clean water and air for a healthy environment. Pure food, properly prepared, would lead to healthy families. Richards believed that home management by women who were scientifically trained gave hope of eliminating the worst aspects of poverty.

It was nearly seventy years after her death in 1911 before MIT finally recognized the achievements of their first female faculty member by creating the Ellen Swallow Richards Professorship.

Bibliography
By Richards
First Lessons in Minerals, 1882
The Chemistry of Cooking and Cleaning: A Manual for Housekeepers, 1882
Food Materials and Their Adulterations, 1886
Guides for Science Teaching, 1886
Home Sanitation: A Manual for Housekeepers, 1887 (with Marion Talbot)
Food as a Factor in Student Life: A Contribution to the Study of Student Diet, 1894 (with Talbot)
The Cost of Living, 1899
The Cost of Food, 1901

The Dietary Computer, 1902
Air, Water, and Food from a Sanitary Standpoint, 1900; rev. 2d ed., 1904 (with Alpheus G. Woodman)
First Lessons in Food and Diet, 1904
The Art of Right Living, 1904
The Cost of Shelter, 1905
Sanitation in Daily Life, 1907
Notes on Industrial Water Analysis: A Survey Course for Engineers, 1908
The Cost of Cleanness, 1908
Euthenics, the Science of Controllable Environment, 1910
Conservation by Sanitation, 1911

About Richards
"Ellen Henrietta Swallow Richards (1842-1911)." Mary R. S. Creese and Thomas M. Creese. In *Women in Chemistry and Physics*, edited by Louise S. Grinstein, Rose K. Rose, and Miriam H. Rafailovich. Westport, Conn.: Greenwood Press, 1993.
Ellen Swallow: The Woman Who Founded Ecology. Robert Clarke. Chicago: Follett, 1973.
The Life of Ellen H. Richards. Caroline L. Hunt. Boston: M. Barrows, 1925.

(*K. Thomas Finley*)

Charles Richet

Areas of Achievement: Immunology, medicine, and physiology
Contribution: A pioneer in organ and system physiology, Richet was awarded the Nobel Prize in Physiology or Medicine for his work on anaphylaxis, a dramatic manifestation of immunological hypersensitivity characterized by severe respiratory impairment and circulatory collapse.

Aug. 26, 1850	Born in Paris, France
1874	Studies at the Collège de France
1876	As a surgical assistant, demonstrates that gastric acid is hydrochloric, not lactic
1878	Graduated from medical school and interns at La Salpétrière Hospital
1878	Passes the *agrégation* in physiology, a competitive examination for teaching in universities
1883-1891	Lectures on physiology and studies animal heat production and its controls
1887	Appointed to the chair in physiology in the Paris Faculté de Médecine
1898	Elected to the Académie de Médecine
1900	Describes anaphylaxis
1912	Elected to the Académie des Sciences
1913	Awarded the Nobel Prize in Physiology or Medicine
1926	Awarded the Cross of the Legion of Honor
1928	Retires from teaching responsibilities
Dec. 4, 1935	Dies in Paris, France

Early Life

The son of an eminent surgeon, Charles Richet (pronounced "ree-SHAY") was born in Paris, where he conducted most of his studies and his research. He performed brilliantly in school but hesitated between a career in literature and one in medicine. He chose the latter and concentrated on experimental physiology.

Through his studies, Richet came into contact with and under the influence of eminent scientists, including Claude Bernard, the founder of experimental organ physiology; Étienne-Jules Marey, who studied muscle activity and the circulation of blood; Marcelin Berthelot, an organic chemist; and Adolf Wurtz, also a chemist. Richet's experiences as an intern stimulated his interest in hypnosis and other psychological phenomena.

Physiological Studies

As a surgical assistant, he demonstrated that stomach acid was hydrochloric acid, not lactic acid as had previously been supposed. He then turned to the control of body temperature by studying the evaporation of water from the respiratory tract and the loss of heat from the body surfaces.

Stimulated by Louis Pasteur's work on infections and immunity, Richet attempted to protect individuals against tuberculosis, unfortunately without success. An expedition to the Azores on the laboratory ship of Prince Albert I of Monaco, however, provided him with the opportunity to observe the phenomenon of anaphylaxis, in which the body's immune system becomes hypersensitive to a foreign substance (antigen), causing respiratory and circulatory failure.

Richet carried out intensive studies of anaphylaxis and related immunological problems, culminating in a monograph, published in 1911, in which he reviewed his own work and integrated it with the work of others. After receiving the Nobel Prize in Physiology or Medi-

Anaphylaxis

Richet found that immunity and hypersensitivity are related.

Richet, greatly impressed by the work of Louis Pasteur in producing vaccines and also by the problems posed by bacterial vaccines, attempted to confer passive immunity by transfusing blood from an animal that recovered from an infection to another, unexposed animal. He did indeed find that resistance to the infection could be conferred.

Encouraged by these results, Richet then extended the approach to toxic agents, such as an extract from the tentacles of the Portuguese man-of-war, a dangerous jellyfish, and from sea anemones. He found that small doses were tolerated and that larger doses killed the animals in four or five days. Extremely large doses were rapidly fatal.

When the same animals that had received the small, well-tolerated doses were given the same or even much smaller doses two or three weeks later, however, the animals died within minutes after the injections. The initial small and tolerated doses had made the animals hypersensitive to the toxic agent; they suffered respiratory impairment and circulatory collapse. This was the opposite of and contrary to protection. From this fact, the term "anaphylaxis" was coined for this reaction.

Richet had interpreted his results to indicate that some substance had formed in the animals undergoing anaphylactic reactions, making them hypersensitive. He was able to demonstrate this experimentally.

He injected the serum, the cell-free portion of clotted blood, from animals that were anaphylactic into other animals and showed that the latter would respond with an anaphylactic reaction to a challenge (the toxin) that they had never encountered before. These results established the foundations of a highly important field of clinical medicine.

Bibliography

"Anaphylaxis." Allen P. Kaplan. In *Cell Textbook of Medicine*, edited by James B. Wyngaarden, Lloyd H. Smith, Jr., and J. Claude Bennett. 19th ed. Philadelphia: W. B. Saunders, 1992.

"Immunology." Dennis J. Beer, Ross E. Kochlin, and John David. In *Scientific American Medicine*, edited by David C. Dale and Daniel D. Federman. New York: Scientific American, 1997.

(The Nobel Foundation)

Bibliography
By Richet

"Du somnabulisme provoqué," *Journal de l'Anatomie et de la Physiologie Normales et Pathologiques de l'Homme et des Animaux*, 1875

"Des propriétés chimiques et physiologiques du suc gastrique," *Journal de l'Anatomie et de la Physiologie Normales et Pathologiques de l'Homme et des Animaux*, 1878

"Des conditions de la polypnée thermique," *Comptes rendus . . . de l'Académie des Sciences*, 1887

"De l'action anaphylactique de certains venins." *Comptes rendus de la Société de Biologie*, 1902 (with Paul Portier; "The Anaphylactic Action of Certain Venoms" in *Milestones in Immunology: A Historical Exploration*, 1988, by Debra Jan Bibel)

L'anaphylaxie, 1911 (*Anaphylaxis*, 1913)

L'intelligence et l'homme Études de psychologie et de physiologie, 1927

About Richet

"Charles Richet." In *The Nobel Prize Winners: Physiology or Medicine*, edited by Frank N. Magill. Pasadena, Calif.: Salem Press, 1991.

"Prof. Charles Richet: Obituary." *Nature* 136 (1935).

"Richet, Charles Robert." Frederic L. Holmes. In *Dictionary of Scientific Biography*, edited by Charles Coulston Gillispie. New York: Charles Scribner's Sons, 1970.

(Francis P. Chinard)

cine for his studies of anaphylaxis, he expanded his fields of interest to include psychic phenomena, history, and participation in the development of one of the earliest airplanes. He was a pacifist and wrote extensively on the evils of war. He died in 1935 at the age of eighty-five.

Burton Richter

Area of Achievement: Physics
Contribution: A pioneer in the study of sub-atomic particles, Burton won the Nobel Prize in Physics for his discovery of a class of long-lived mesons.

Mar. 22, 1931	Born in Brooklyn, New York
1952	Receives a B.S. from the Massachusetts Institute of Technology (MIT)
1956	Earns a Ph.D. in physics from MIT
1956	Becomes a research associate at Stanford University
1967	Promoted to full professor of physics at Stanford
1973	Constructs a particle accelerator at Stanford and discovers new subatomic particles
1975	Receives the E. O. Lawrence Medal from the Energy Research and Development Administration
1975	Elected to the National Academy of Sciences
1976	Awarded the Nobel Prize in Physics jointly with Samuel C. C. Ting
1995	Publishes an article entitled "The Role of Science in Our Society" in *Physics Today*

Early Life

Burton Richter was born on March 22, 1931, in Brooklyn, New York. He grew up during the late years of the Great Depression and World War II. Richter earned a bachelor of science degree at the Massachusetts Institute of Technology (MIT) in 1952 and a Ph.D. in nuclear physics from the same institution in 1956.

Subatomic Particle Research

Following his graduation, Richter accepted a research position at Stanford University. He quickly advanced in rank and was elected a full professor in the department of physics in 1967. His first research efforts took the form of experiments that confirmed the validity of quantum electrodynamics at very short distances. This finding led the way to his explorations of small particles within the atom.

In collaboration with David Ritson, and with support from the Atomic Energy Commission, Richter constructed the Stanford Positron-Electron Asymmetric Ring, a colliding-beam particle accelerator that was completed in 1973. Using this elaborate apparatus, Richter discovered a new subatomic particle that he called the psi particle, the first of a new class of very massive, long-lived mesons.

It is interesting to note that a team of experimenters under the direction of Samuel C. C. Ting, working independently, and nearly si-

(The Nobel Foundation)

multaneously, at the Brookhaven National Laboratory's accelerator on Long Island, discovered the same subatomic particle, which they called the J particle. Richter and Ting jointly announced the news of their respective discoveries in 1974. In 1976, they were named cowinners of the Nobel Prize in Physics for their discoveries.

Elementary Particles

The search for the elementary, indivisible building blocks of matter is the most fundamental problem in physics.

By the mid-1990's, scientists had found approximately three hundred kinds of minute subatomic particles. It is inconceivable that all these particles are elementary particles, but it is likely that most, if not all, are composite particles made of only a few truly elementary building blocks.

In order to identify these building blocks, physicists such as Richter have tried to break protons into pieces by bombarding them with projectiles of very high energy. Unfortunately, if the energy of the projectile is large enough to crack a proton, then it is large enough to create a new particle during the collision. The creation of new particles confuses the problem, and scientists must devise ways of determining which pieces emanating from the collision are newly created particles and which are fragments of the original proton.

Collision experiments have failed to fragment protons into elementary building blocks, but somewhat more subtle experiments provide evidence that distinct building blocks do exist inside protons. At Stanford University's linear accelerator, under the direction of Richter, high-energy electrons were shot at protons. The electrons served as probes to define the interior configuration of the protons. Occasionally, the bombarding electrons were deflected as they bounced off interior surfaces within the protons, indicating the presence of a hard kernel.

Even before the electron probe experiments, theoretical physicists such as Murray Gell-Mann of the California Institute of Technology had proposed models in which subatomic particles known as baryons and mesons were constructed out of a few fundamental building blocks. According to Gell-Mann's theory, for which he won the 1969 Nobel Prize in Physics, the similarity between particles in a given family reflects the similarity of their internal construction.

Known as the quark model, his theory predicts that all particles are constructed of three kinds of fundamental building blocks called quarks. These three quarks were labeled up, down, and strange. In order to make ordinary particles out of the quarks, the quarks must be glued together in diverse ways. For example, a proton is made of two up quarks and one down quark, whereas the structure of a neutron is two down quarks and one up quark.

The three-quark model had deficiencies. For technical reasons relating to quantum mechanics laws, physicists found it necessary to postulate that each of the three quarks exists in three "color" varieties: red, green, and blue quarks. A further modification of the quark model emerged from the study of weak and electromagnetic forces. In order to produce a unified theory of such forces that fits the experimental observations, physicists had to postulate the existence of a fourth type of quark, labeled a charm quark.

The hypothesis of the charm quark received firm experimental support in 1974 when a team of experimenters under the direction of Richter at the Stanford University accelerator discovered the psi meson. His experimental data showed that these particles contain only one charm quark of a higher-than-normal mass.

By 1984, a fifth and sixth type of quark had been discovered and were labeled bottom and top quarks. All six also come in three "color" varieties. This proliferation of quarks will probably continue, raising the question of whether matter really has such a large number of elementary building blocks.

Bibliography

"Elementary Particles." H. C. Ohanian. In *Physics*. New York: W. W. Norton, 1985.

The Key to the Universe. N. Carther. New York: Viking Press, 1983.

One of the Nobel judges called their work the greatest discovery ever made in the field of elementary particles. Richter candidly admitted that even though his discovery had no immediate application, much had been learned about the structure of the universe by gaining a clearer understanding of its smallest components.

Bibliography
By Richter
Instabilities in Stored Particle Beams, 1965 (with M. Sands and A. M. Sessler)
"Two-Body Photoproduction" in *U.S. Atomic Energy Commission SLAC-PUB-501*, 1968
"Plenary Report on e(+) e(-) Hadrons" in *Proceedings of 17th International Conference on High Energy Physics*, 1974
"A Scientific Autobiography," *Stanford Linear Accelerator Beam Line*, 1976
"The Role of Science in Our Society," *Physics Today*, 1995

About Richter
The Discovery of Subatomic Particles. S. Weinberg. San Francisco: W. H. Freeman, 1983.
From X-Rays to Quarks. E. Segrè. San Francisco: W. H. Freeman, 1980.
Pioneers of Science: Nobel Prize Winners in Physics. New York: American Institute of Physics, 1980.
"The Search for New Families of Elementary Particles." D. B. Kline, A. K. Mann, and C. Rubbia. *Scientific American* (January, 1976).

(*Charles E. Herdendorf*)

Charles Francis Richter

Areas of Achievement: Earth science and physics

Contribution: A pioneer in seismology, Richter developed and refined a scale for measuring the magnitude of earthquakes and plotted earthquake-prone areas of the United States.

Apr. 26, 1900	Born near Hamilton, Ohio
1927	Begins work at the seismological laboratory at the Carnegie Institution of Washington
1928	Completes a Ph.D. in theoretical physics at the California Institute of Technology (Caltech)
1935	Creates, with Beno Gutenberg, the Richter scale for measuring the intensity of earthquakes
1935	Publishes *An Instrumental Earthquake Magnitude Scale*
1937	Returns to Caltech
1941	Publishes *Seismicity of the Earth* with Gutenberg through the Geological Society of America
1952	Promoted to full professor of seismology at Caltech
1958	Publishes *Elementary Seismology*
1959-1960	Serves as a Fulbright Scholar at the University of Tokyo
1970	Retires from the faculty at Caltech and is named professor emeritus of seismology
Sept. 30, 1985	Dies in Pasadena, California

Early Life

Charles Francis Richter was born April 26, 1900, on a farm near Hamilton, Ohio, about twenty miles north of Cincinnati. When he was nine years old, his family moved to California.

The Richter Scale

Richter and Beno Gutenberg responded to the need for a quantitative scale to measure the magnitude of earthquakes by inventing one themselves, choosing an open-ended scale that starts at zero.

Although the Richter scale has no upward limit, it is often thought of as ranging from zero to nine. No earthquake measured on this scale had registered 9.0 or higher by the mid-1990's, but a future quake certainly could. Richter and Gutenberg defined the weakest quakes that they could measure as having values just above zero. With newer, more sensitive seismographs coming into use since the development of the scale, the weakest quakes now measurable are given values with negative numbers.

The Richter scale is a logarithmic scale, meaning that each increase of one whole number on the scale represents a tenfold increase in earthquake magnitude. Therefore an earthquake measuring 5.0 on the scale is ten times more powerful than an earthquake measuring 4.0 and one hundred times more powerful than an earthquake measuring 3.0.

On the Richter scale, a 6 0 is an indication of a damaging quake. The amount of damage that a quake actually causes, however, is a factor of magnitude (measured by the scale) and vicinity of population centers, buildings, roads, or other items that can be damaged.

The scale was published in 1935 and has since been used by both scientists and news media personnel across the globe, all hungry for a way to quantify the hundreds of earthquakes reported annually.

Bibliography
Earthquakes. Bruce A. Bolt. New York: W. H. Freeman, 1993.
Earthquakes. G. A. Eiby. New York: Van Nostrand Reinhold, 1980.
Earthquakes and Geological Discovery. Bruce Bolt. New York: Scientific American Library, 1993.
Volcanoes and Earthquakes. Jon Erickson. Blue Ridge Summit, Pa.: Tab Books, 1988.
Why the Earth Quakes. Matthys Levy and Mario Salvadori. New York: W. W. Norton, 1995.

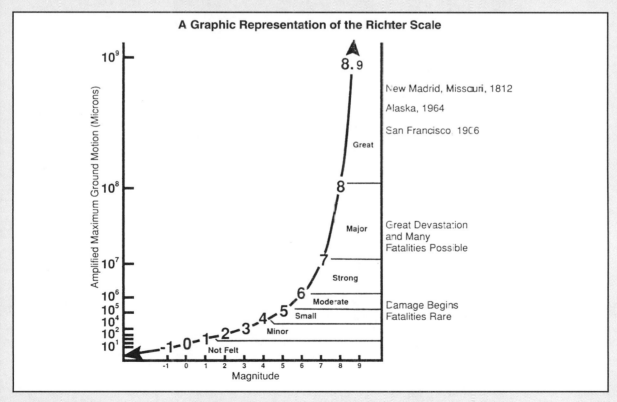

A Graphic Representation of the Richter Scale

These seismic drums record east-west, north-south, and vertical motions. (California Institute of Technology)

While Richter was in high school, his love of the outdoors manifested itself: He was a member of a natural history club and went on many hiking and camping trips in Southern California. He never lost this love and continued backpacking, often alone, well past his retirement.

In 1920, he earned an A.B. degree in physics from Stanford University. He then enrolled at the California Institute of Technology (Caltech), where he began work on a Ph.D. in physics. Before completing his doctorate, he accepted a position at the Carnegie Institution of Washington's seismological laboratory. He then changed his focus of interest from theoretical physics to geophysics, studying the forces that cause earthquakes.

The Development of the Richter Scale

When Richter began his work in seismology (the study of earthquakes), there was no quantitative means of measuring the intensity of earthquakes and therefore no way to compare earthquakes of similar intensity. The only gauge available was the qualitative Mercalli scale based on a range from I, an earthquake felt only by a few persons near the quake, to XII, a quake causing extensive damage.

Working with his colleague Beno Gutenberg, Richter devised a quantitative scale measuring the magnitude of earthquakes, which was published in 1935. Unlike the Mercalli scale, which measures the intensity of the quake at the recording station, Richter's scale measures a quake's magnitude at its epicenter (the point on the earth immediately above the focus of the quake). This calculation is done by plotting the maximum crustal movement against the distance to the epicenter.

Richter examines a seismograph. (California Institute of Technology)

Additional Work in Seismology

In 1937, Richter returned to Caltech, and he and Gutenberg continued their collaboration. Their work documented that several hundred thousand earthquakes occur worldwide each year, but that most are too small to be of major consequence. They noted that earthquakes are largely confined to four geographical areas, the largest being the circum-Pacific belt, which includes California and Alaska. Their work resulted in the mapping of earthquake-prone areas of the United States and other areas.

A major contribution of Richter was his work on a means to reduce the damage to urban areas caused by earthquakes. He was directly responsible for persuading the city of

Los Angeles to strengthen its building codes so that buildings could withstand the shaking caused by earthquakes.

After Richter retired in 1970, for many years he continued to work almost daily in the Caltech seismology laboratory while also serving as a consultant. He died in Pasadena, California, on September 30, 1985.

Bibliography

By Richter
An Instrumental Earthquake Magnitude Scale, 1935

Seismicity of the Earth, 1941 (with Beno Gutenberg)

Seismicity of the Earth and Associated Phenomena, 1949 (with Gutenberg)

Elementary Seismology, 1958

"Our Earthquake Risk: Facts and Non-facts," *Engineering and Science Quarterly*, 1965

"California Earthquakes," *Engineering and Science Quarterly*, 1967

"Our Earthquake Risk: Facts and Non-facts," *Engineering and Science Quarterly*, 1968 (with corrections and additions)

About Richter
"Richter, Charles Francis." In *Current Biography Yearbook*. New York: H. W. Wilson, 1985.

"Richter, Charles Francis." In *Larousse Dictionary of Scientists*, edited by Hazel Muir. New York: Larousse, 1994.

(Kenneth J. Schoon)

Norbert Rillieux

Areas of Achievement: Invention and technology

Contribution: Rillieux's multiple-effect evaporator revolutionized the sugar refining industry, drastically reducing fuel and labor requirements and producing sugar of much higher quality than had been possible with traditional methods.

Mar. 17, 1806	Born in New Orleans, Louisiana
1830	Teaches applied mechanics at the École Centrale in Paris
1830	Publishes a series of papers on steam engines
1830	Develops the theory behind a multiple-effect evaporator
1833	Named chief engineer at Edmund Forstall's sugar refinery in Louisiana
1834	Tries to install an evaporator at Zenon Ranson's plantation
1843	Receives his first patent for the multiple-effect evaporator
1843-1844	Installs and successfully operates an evaporator at Theodore Packwood's plantation
1845	Installs an evaporator at Judah Benjamin's plantation
1846	Packwood's and Benjamin's sugar samples win top prizes for quality at the Louisiana State Fair
1846	Receives a patent for an improved multiple-effect evaporator
1860's	Becomes headmaster at the École Centrale and publishes numerous articles in engineering journals
1891	Loses his patent for an improved sugar production process
Oct. 8, 1894	Dies in Paris, France

Early Life

Norbert Rillieux (pronounced "reel-YEW") was born in New Orleans only three years after the United States purchased the Louisiana Territory from France. Because his mother was of both African and European ancestry, Rillieux was assigned the racial and legal status of "quadroon libre" (free quadroon).

His father, recognizing Norbert's unusual intelligence and aptitude for engineering, sent him to France to study mechanical engineering. By 1830, Rillieux was teaching applied mechanics at the École Centrale in Paris and had begun to design a multiple-effect evaporator for processing sugar cane.

A Difficult Road to Acceptance

From the early 1830's to 1846, Rillieux perfected his invention. He designed it to solve two problems at once: the high fuel and labor costs involved in evaporating water from sugar cane juice, as well as the danger of scorching the syrup during the evaporation process.

Unable to interest French manufacturers in his invention, however, Rillieux returned to Louisiana in 1833. He left a position as chief engineer at Edmund Forstall's sugar refinery after his father and Forstall quarreled. Later, Forstall used his power in the state legislature to award directorship of Rillieux's own drainage plan to another engineer.

In 1834, Rillieux's attempt to install and operate his invention at Zenon Ranson's plantation failed when the death of his instructor interrupted the work. Rillieux had difficulty persuading other planters to try his evaporator, perhaps because many had suffered severe financial losses after experimenting with a different innovation in 1830.

Success in Louisiana

In 1843, Rillieux received a patent for his multiple-effect evaporator and was hired by Theodore Packwood to build one on his plantation. The monetary savings and the quality of sugar produced persuaded Judah Benjamin to install the evaporator on his plantation in 1845. In 1846, the Louisiana Agriculturalists' and Mechanics' Association awarded Packwood's and Benjamin's sugar top prizes for quality and devoted several pages of its annual report

(The Louisiana State Museum)

to analyzing the increased profits that Rillieux's invention created.

Rillieux patented an improved version in 1846. For the next ten years, he installed the evaporator at plantations across Louisiana. His invention eventually became a standard part of the sugar production process.

Return to Paris

Increasingly severe restrictions had been placed on free African Americans after the Louisiana Purchase; by 1855, they were not allowed to walk down the streets of New Orleans without permission or to visit the city without a white sponsor. Rillieux returned to France around that time, perhaps considering these laws intolerable.

In Europe, Rillieux's reputation as an engineer had been damaged after German-manufactured evaporators, built from a stolen and badly understood copy of his design, failed to work well.

Rillieux accepted a position as headmaster at the École Centrale and published articles in

Multiple-Effect Evaporation

Rillieux devised a process for using the latent heat of the vapor produced in an initial stage of evaporation to fuel multiple stages of evaporation.

When a liquid is heated, its molecules begin to move faster, colliding with other molecules, until, at the boiling point, some break through the surface of the liquid and escape as a gas.

This process of evaporation is one stage in producing raw sugar from sugar cane or sugar beets. Water in the plant juices is separated from the sucrose through evaporation, leaving a concentrated syrup. The syrup is then heated until sugar crystals form.

Rillieux's multiple-effect evaporator used the latent heat of the vapor produced in an initial stage of evaporation to evaporate the water in the remainder of the liquid in additional stages. In the first stage, steam heat passes through coils in the bottom of a chamber holding plant juice, making the juice boil. Water escapes from the juice as vapor (the first effect) into the chamber's open space.

This vapor then passes through a tube into coils in the second chamber, while the liquid moves through a separate tube into the chamber itself. The boiling point of the liquid is reduced by using a vacuum to lower the air pressure in the chamber. This feature compensates for the slight loss of heat energy that occurs from one stage to the next. Each succeeding chamber is maintained at a higher vacuum. The number of chambers may vary; triple- effect or quadruple-effect evaporators are most common.

Whereas one pound of heating steam will evaporate one pound of liquid in a single-effect evaporator, the same pound of steam will evaporate two pounds of liquid in a double-effect evaporator, three in a triple-effect, and so on.

The fuel savings alone significantly lowered production costs, and labor requirements were lower as well. The lowered boiling points reduced losses of sugar from scorching and produced sugar of higher quality. The size of the chambers also allowed much more syrup to be processed.

Since Rillieux's evaporator made production of mass quantities of cheap, high-quality sugar possible, it is credited with changing sugar from a luxury product for elites to a common household item.

Multiple-effect evaporators based on Rillieux's invention are widely used today in making paper, sugar, soap, condensed milk, and many other products.

Bibliography

The Discovery of Specific and Latent Heats. Douglas McKie and Niel S. H. de V. Heathcote. London: Edward Arnold, 1935.

Fundamentals of Engineering Thermodynamics. Michael J. Moran and Howard N. Shapiro. 3d ed. New York: John Wiley & Sons, 1995.

Heat and Thermodynamics: An Intermediate Textbook. Mark W. Zemansky and Richard H. Dittman. 6th ed. New York: McGraw-Hill, 1981.

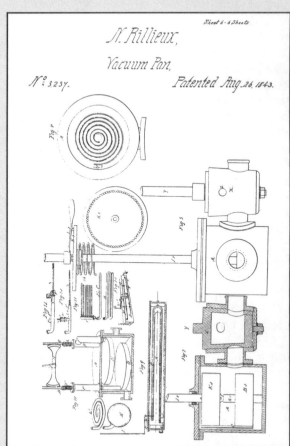

A diagram of Rillieux's vacuum pan, which was part of his sugar evaporation process. (U.S. Patent Office)

engineering journals. He engaged in Egyptology for a time but returned to engineering in 1881, when he refined the initial stages of sugar production to produce a thinner, more easily heated juice. He lost the patent for this process in 1891, however, when French experts refused to recognize it as an invention.

His lifelong friend, P. Horsin-Devon, wrote that Rillieux died at the age of eighty-eight of the disappointment brought by this last setback. Nevertheless, according to J. G. McIntosh in *The Technology of Sugar* (1903), modern sugar refiners around the world recognized Rillieux as "one of the greatest benefactors of the sugar industry."

Bibliography

By Rillieux

"For Evaporating Sugar Solutions: Two Howard Vacuum Pans Connected in Multiple Effect," 1843 (U.S. Patent 3,237)
"For Evaporating Sugar Solutions in Vacuo," 1846 (U.S. Patent 4,879)

About Rillieux

"Degas and the 'Black World.'" Stanley Kauffman. *The New Republic* 215, no. 17 (October 21, 1996).
Eight Black American Inventors. Robert C. Hayden. Reading, Mass.: Addison-Wesley, 1972.
"A Negro Scientist of Slavery Days." George P. Meade. *The Scientific Monthly* 57 (January-June, 1946).

(Ann Binder)

Richard Roberts

Areas of Achievement: Cell biology, invention, and physics

Contribution: Roberts discovered radioisotope beryllium 7 and delayed neutrons from fission, was a key designer of the proximity fuse, determined the biosynthesis of *Escherichia coli* (*E. coli*), and studied the basis of long-term memory.

Dec. 7, 1910	Born in Titusville, Pennsylvania
1936	Graduated from Princeton University with a Ph.D.
1936	Begins work at the Carnegie Institution's Department of Terrestrial Magnetism (DTM)
1938	Uses a Van de Graaff accelerator to study reactions of lithium and discovers beryllium 7
1939	Verifies uranium fission and discovers delayed neutrons
1939	Serves as a member of President Franklin D. Roosevelt's Uranium Committee
1939	Shows placental permeability using radioactive sodium 24
1940	Helps initiate development of the proximity fuse, which becomes an important Allied weapon
1946	Returns to DTM
1947	Awarded the Presidential Medal of Merit
1947	Helps start biophysics work at DTM
1955	Reaches the culmination of his *E. coli* studies
1955	Begins studies of the brain
Apr. 4, 1980	Dies in Washington, D.C.

Early Life

Richard Brooke Roberts was born in Titusville, Pennsylvania, to Erastus Titus Roberts, a banker. He attended private schools in Princeton, New Jersey, and in New York City and was graduated from Princeton University with a Ph.D. in 1936. He joined the research in nuclear physics led by Merle Tuve at the Carnegie Institution's Department of Terrestrial Magnetism (DTM), where he later became a staff member and remained for his entire career, except for wartime work.

Work with Fission

At DTM, Roberts conducted a series of experiments in which separated isotopes of lithium were bombarded by beams of protons and deuterons from the DTM's Van de Graaff accelerators. From one of these experiments, Roberts discovered the radioisotope beryllium 7, which was found to play an important role in the nuclear reactions of the sun. It was also the second example of decay by electron capture, a process unknown in natural radioactivity.

Public news of uranium fission came at a meeting in Washington, D.C. in January, 1939. Roberts and his coworkers verified the sensational phenomenon and demonstrated it to notables from the meeting. Within a few days, Roberts completed an experiment showing that a small fraction of the neutrons from fission are emitted after delays of a few seconds. Without delayed neutrons, it would be possible to construct a bomb but not a reactor.

Weapons Research

Owing to his experience with fission, Roberts served with Tuve on a committee to advise the government about the potentialities of this reaction. Both saw other defense problems to be more pressing and set about designing an artillery fuse with a small radio that would detonate the device if the fuse came within about 20 meters of an aircraft. This invention changed antiaircraft fire from an inaccurate to an extremely effective defensive weapon.

Isotopes Discovered and Used

Roberts studied nuclear reactions and identified isotopes, research that he applied to biological processes through the use of radioactive tracers.

Roberts found that the bombardment of lithium 6 by deuterons yields the unknown isotope beryllium 7 plus a neutron in the following reaction:

deuteron + lithium 6 → neutron + beryllium 7

The beryllium isotope is radioactive and decays, with a half-life of fifty-three days, in a process whereby the nucleus captures an atomic electron and emits a neutrino. Such decay is observable only through the X ray—in this case, an extremely weak one—that results when an electron fills the vacancy left by the captured electron. About 10 percent of the beryllium 7 nuclei, however, are left in an excited state and decay by emitting an easily observable gamma ray.

A uranium nucleus has a much greater proportion of neutrons relative to protons than do isotopes in the middle of the periodic table, and, when one splits through fission, a few neutrons are immediately released. A very small fraction of the fission fragments release neutrons after beta decay.

Accelerators and reactors made possible the creation of hundreds of radioisotopes from throughout the periodic table that were quickly used by scientists for tracing chemical and biological processes, as their radioactivity allows them to be identified at any stage of such processes. For example, the isotope sodium 24 allowed Roberts and Louis Flexner to observe the transfer of maternal material to the fetus through the placenta, and carbon 14 allowed his research group to understand the metabolic processes of the bacterium *Escherichia coli* (*E. coli*), which was found to behave like a miniature chemical factory whose output can be controlled.

Bibliography

"Nuclear Physics." Lawrence Wilets. *Encyclopedia of Physical Science and Technology*. New York: Academic Press, 1987.

Radioactive Tracers

After this work was completed at the newly established Applied Physics Laboratory, Roberts returned to DTM and joined two other nuclear physicists, Philip Abelson and Dean Cowie, in studying biology using radioactive tracer isotopes. Roberts had been a pioneer in this research in a 1939 experiment that demonstrated the transfer of material in fetal circulation. The new group's great achievement in their first years was detailing the methods of synthesis of the bacterium *Escherichia coli* (*E. coli*) by use of the tracer carbon 14. They published a book that remains the standard reference on *E. coli*.

Roberts became interested in the chemical aspects of how memory is achieved in the brain and studied the effects of stimulants and inhibitors of protein synthesis on the memories of trained mice. It was a line of research that he followed until his death in 1980. In addition, his knowledge of weapons and his concerns about their use led him to become an organizing member of a committee that evolved into the Arms Control and Disarmament Agency.

Bibliography

By Roberts

"The Delayed Neutron Emission Which Accompanies Fission of Uranium and Thorium," *Physical Review*, 1939 (with L. R. Hafstad, R. C. Meyer, and P. Wang)

"The Measurement of Placental Permeability with Radioactive Sodium," *American Journal of Physiology*, 1939 (with Louis Flexner)

Studies of Biosynthesis in Escherichia coli, 1955 (with Philip Abelson, Dean Cowie, Ellis Bolton, and Roy Britten)

About Roberts

"Richard Brooke Roberts." Roy Britten. *Biographical Memoirs*. Washington, D.C.: National Academy Press, 1993.

(Louis Brown)

Sir Robert Robinson

Area of Achievement: Chemistry

Contribution: Robinson contributed to the modern electronic theory of organic reactions. He is best known for the structure determination and chemical synthesis of natural products, especially alkaloids, plant pigments, and steroids.

Sept. 13, 1886	Born on Rufford Farm, near Chesterfield, Derbyshire, England
1912-1930	Serves as an organic chemistry professor at several universities
1920	Elected a Fellow of the Royal Society of London
1930-1955	Named Waynflete Professor of Chemistry at Oxford University
1939-1941	Elected president of the Chemical Society
1939	Knighted
1942	Receives the Copley Medal of the Royal Society of London
1945-1950	Serves as president of the Royal Society of London
1947	Wins the Nobel Prize in Chemistry and the U.S. Medal of Freedom
1949	Included in the Order of Merit
1953	Receives the Priestley Medal from the American Chemical Society
1955	Elected president of the British Association for the Advancement of Science
1955	Becomes director and consultant for Shell Chemical Company
1958-1959	Elected president of the Society of Chemical Industry
Feb. 8, 1975	Dies in Grimm's Hill Lodge, Great Missenden, Buckinghamshire, England

(The Nobel Foundation)

Early Life

Robert Robinson was born in England at Rufford Farm near Chesterfield, Derbyshire. He was the eldest of five children of William Bradbury and Jane (Davenport) Robinson. The family also included the seven surviving children of William's previous marriage to Elizabeth Lowe, who died in 1871. When Robert was three, they moved to Field House in nearby New Brampton, where his father was a prominent Congregationalist and manufacturer of surgical dressings and boxes for ointments and pills.

Robinson's early education was in Chesterfield until the age of twelve, when he was enrolled in Fulneck School, run by the Moravian Church, at Pudsey Greenside near Leeds. He entered Manchester University in 1902 to study chemistry, earning a B.Sc. degree with first-class honors in 1905 and remaining as a University Fellow (1906) and 1851 Exhibition Scholar (1907-1909) to acquire a doctor of science degree in 1910 under William H. Perkin,

Robinson, Sir Robert   1099

Jr., who (together with Arthur Lapworth) greatly influenced Robinson's lifelong research interests.

A Diverse Academic Career

Robinson was an assistant lecturer and demonstrator while at Manchester, from 1909 to 1912 and then traveled to Australia to become the first professor of organic chemistry at the University of Sydney. In 1915, he returned to England to accept the newly created Heath Harrison Chair of Organic Chemistry at the University of Liverpool, which he left in 1920 to serve as the research director of British Dyestuffs Corporation.

Robinson subsequently held chairs of organic chemistry at St. Andrews University in Scotland, Manchester University, and University College of London. He succeeded his mentor Perkin as the Waynflete Professor of Chemistry at Magdalen College of Oxford University in 1930 and remained there until his retirement in 1955.

He founded the international journal of organic chemistry *Tetrahedron* in 1957 and continued research on alkaloids and the composition and origins of petroleum in a small laboratory at Egham, where he was a consultant for the Shell group of chemical companies until his death in 1975.

The Foremost Natural Products Chemist

Robinson studied the chemical constituents from natural sources as diverse as the royal jelly of bees, the dyes from brazilwood (brazilin and brazilein) and logwood (hematoxylin), and numerous plant alkaloids. He investigated the chemical basis for genetic variations in flower color, devised small-scale tests to establish which pigments give a flower petal a

---

The Natural Products Chemistry of Alkaloids

Robinson investigated the chemical structure and synthesis of alkaloids.

The traditional definition of an alkaloid as a basic, pharmacologically active, and nitrogen-containing heterocyclic organic compound from plants has been broadened to include about ten thousand naturally occurring nitrogenous secondary metabolites of vegetable, microbial, or even animal origin. Many exhibit pronounced physiological activity on humans and animals as medicines, cardiac and respiratory stimulants, tranquilizers and muscle relaxants, analgesics, psychedelics, or poisons.

Alkaloidal natural products are designated by the ending "-ine" in their chemical name. The nitrogen of most alkaloids resides in a heterocyclic ring. Examples include caffeine from coffee beans, nicotine from tobacco, morphine from the opium poppy, cocaine from coca leaves, quinine from cinchona bark, atropine from deadly nightshade, coniine from poison hemlock, and strychnine from *Strychnos nux-vomica*. Alkaloids with exocyclic nitrogen include ephedrine from several *Ephedra* species, mescaline from peyotyl cactus, and other biogenic amines.

The natural products chemist isolates a pure alkaloid using extraction, crystallization, and chromatography, then determines its structural formula with chemical reactions, spectroscopy, or X-ray diffraction. Total chemical synthesis provides ultimate proof of the molecular structure and is often an incentive to discover new chemical reactions in organic chemistry.

Bibliography
"Alkaloids." David R. Dalton. In *Kirk-Othmer Encyclopedia of Chemical Technology*. Vol. 1. 4th ed. New York: Wiley-Interscience, 1991.
Bioactive Natural Products: Detection, Isolation, and Structure Determination. Steven M. Colegate and Russell J. Molyneux. Boca Raton, Fla.: CRS Press, 1993.
Chemistry of the Alkaloids. S. W. Pelletier, ed. New York: Van Nostrand Reinhold, 1970.
Dictionary of Alkaloids. I. W. Southon and J. Buckingham, eds. 2 vols. London: Chapman and Hall, 1989.
Introduction to Alkaloids: A Biogenic Approach. Geoffrey A. Cordell. New York: Wiley-Interscience, 1981.

particular hue, and synthesized the group of anthocyanin (blue-red) and anthoxanthin (yellow) pigments.

Robinson also made major contributions to establishing the molecular structure of penicillin and to the synthesis of the female hormone estrone and more powerful artificial steroid hormones (stilbestrol, hexestrol, and dienestrol) used for oral contraception and cancer therapy.

Many of Robinson's synthetic procedures, such as his annulation to close five- and six-membered rings, were reported in more than seven hundred scientific publications. His chemical syntheses and biosynthetic speculations were aided by his development of a qualitative electronic theory for organic reactions, from which the modern concepts of mechanistic "curly arrows" and aromatic sextet are derived.

Bibliography

By Robinson

"A Theory of the Mechanism of the Phytochemical Synthesis of Certain Alkaloids," *Journal of the Chemical Society*, 1917

An Outline of an Electrochemical (Electronic) Theory of the Course of Organic Reactions, 1932

"Synthesis in Biochemistry," *Journal of the Chemical Society*, 1936

The Building of Molecules, 1937

"The Red and Blue Colouring Matters of Plants," *Endeavour*, 1942

"The Development of Electrochemical Theories of the Course of Reactions of Carbon Compounds," *Journal of the Chemical Society*, 1947

"Some Polycyclic Natural Products" in *Les Prix Nobel en 1947*, 1949

The Chemistry of Penicillin, 1949 (as editor, with Hans T. Clarke and John R. Johnson)

The Structural Relations of Natural Products, 1955

"The Origins of Petroleum," *Nature*, 1966

The Art and Science of Chess: A Step-by-Step Approach, 1973 (with Raymond Edwards)

"Sixty-five Years' Discovery," *Chemistry in Britain* 10 (1974)

An Introduction to Organic Chemistry: Aliphatic and Alicyclic Compounds, 1975 (with Eric D. Morgan)

Memoirs of a Minor Prophet: Seventy Years of Organic Chemistry, 1976

About Robinson

"A Centenary Tribute to Sir Robert Robinson." Special issue of *Natural Product Reports* 4 (February, 1987).

"Robert Robinson." Lord Todd and J. W. Cornforth. *Biographical Memoirs of Fellows of the Royal Society* 22 (1976).

"Robert Robinson." Martin D. Saltzman. In *Nobel Laureates in Chemistry: 1901-1992*, edited by Laylin K. James. Washington, D.C.: American Chemical Society, 1993.

Robert Robinson: Chemist Extraordinary. Trevor I. Williams. Oxford, England: Clarendon Press, 1990.

"Sir Robert Robinson: A Contemporary Historical Assessment and a Personal Memoir." A. J. Birch. *Journal and Proceedings of the Royal Society of New South Wales* 109 (1976).

(Martin V. Stewart)

Wilhelm Conrad Röntgen

Areas of Achievement: Chemistry and physics

Contribution: Röntgen's careful study of cathode emissions led to his discovery of an entirely different radiation that he called X rays. He also studied the nature of gases, fluids, light, magnetism, and electricity.

Mar. 27, 1845	Born in Lennep, Prussia (now Remscheid, Germany)
1869	Completes a Ph.D. at the Swiss Polytechnic Institute in Zurich
1872	Marries Anna Bertha Ludwig
1875	Appointed a professor of physics and mathematics at Hohenheim University in Württemburg
1876	Named a professor of theoretical physics at the University of Strasbourg
1879	Appointed a professor of physics at the University of Giessen in Hesse
1888	Becomes a professor of physics and the director of the new Physical Institute at the University of Würzburg
1895	Announces his discovery of X rays
1896	Demonstrates X rays at the court of Kaiser Wilhelm II and is decorated with the Order of the Crown
1900	Named head of the Philosophical Faculty at the University of Munich
1901	Awarded the first Nobel Prize in Physics
1920	Retires from Munich
Feb. 10, 1923	Dies in Munich, Germany

Early Life

Wilhelm Conrad Röntgen (pronounced "REHNT-guhn") was born in Lennep, Prussia, in 1845. His father was a cloth merchant, and his mother was from the Netherlands; Wilhelm was their only child. The family moved to Apeldoorn, the Netherlands, when Röntgen was only three. He attended local public schools there until the family moved later to Utrecht. He was a bright, active child, who loved to roam the fields and hills near his home.

Röntgen continued his education in the Netherlands until 1865, when he enrolled in the mechanical engineering program at the Polytechnic Institute in Zurich, Switzerland. At the institute, he studied with two famous physicists: Rudolf Clausius, who formulated the second law of thermodynamics, and August Kundt, who became Röntgen's mentor. After Röntgen earned his Ph.D. from the Swiss Polytechnic Institute, he stayed on as Kundt's assistant and then followed Kundt as an assistant to several universities in Germany.

A productive researcher and writer, Röntgen had already published forty-eight scientific papers by 1895, the year that he discovered X rays.

The Discovery of X Rays

Many scientists working in the nineteenth century had been studying the flow of electric current in the environment of glass vessels from which air had been at least partially evacuated. As air was being removed from the tube, other gases would be introduced. Electrodes would be mounted inside the tube, permitting electric sparks to leap through the gas. In this manner, a glow was observed in the vicinity of one of the metal elements called the cathode.

Sir William Crookes, a British physicist, thought that the glow was caused by the collision of cathode rays with solid objects in their path. He speculated that the cathode rays were electrical particles and traveled in straight lines, unless deflected by a magnetic field.

One evening in late November, 1895, Röntgen was working alone in a darkened laboratory, investigating the cathode rays described by Crookes. He was repeating a well-known experiment in which high-voltage current is applied to a vacuum tube. Röntgen had covered the tube with black cardboard in order to eliminate extraneous light.

When he activated the device, he noticed that a paper shield coated with barium platino-cyanide crystals began to glow. When he cut off the current, the paper stopped glowing. The paper glowed even when moved farther away from the tube. He learned that the emissions from the tube traveled through paper, wood, and even his own hand.

Röntgen concentrated feverishly during the next few weeks on observing the tube emissions, which he called X rays, to emphasize their unknown nature. When he found that X rays could affect photographic paper, he realized that he could offer pictorial proof of the existence of the rays and show how they penetrate various objects placed in their path. Using X rays, he produced photographic images of the interiors of metal objects and the bones of his wife's hand.

Röntgen knew that he was on the track of a major scientific discovery. He wanted to be sure that his observations were accurate and defensible, but he was anxious to publish his findings. Seven weeks after his initial observation of X rays, Röntgen submitted his conclusions to a Würzburg scientific journal. He also sent letters and photographs to the scientists whom he knew. His discovery was noted quickly in the journals of other countries and in the press. Röntgen regretted the notice that he received in the immediate aftermath of publication, saying that the uproar distracted him from work.

Röntgen's experiments were verified quickly by others. More than a thousand scientific papers related to X rays were published in 1896. The medical application of X rays was seen early, and they were used immediately to produce medical images and to treat various maladies. Unfortunately, the dangers to people of being exposed to X rays were overlooked in the rush to investigate, resulting in burns, excruciating pain, loss of limbs, cancer, and even death. Investigators soon learned, however, that good results could be obtained from limited and low-level emissions.

Röntgen's Observations Unlock the Mysteries of an Invisible Ray

Many scientists before Röntgen had produced X rays with the equipment that they used in their investigations. He was the first, however, to recognize X rays as a specific emission that differed from the rays streaming from the cathode element.

At the time of Röntgen's discovery of X rays, physics was gleaning more from the observation of puzzling phenomena and the application of experimental techniques than from abstract theorizing. Investigation was facilitated by creating improved devices, such as better air pumps used to remove the air from glass vessels and electrodes that could be integrated more effectively with glass vessels. This technology enabled scientists to see how electric current would behave in partial vacuums and in the presence of introduced gases.

Röntgen's careful and comprehensive examination of X rays made him able to describe the phenomena clearly and effectively. He speculated that X rays are electromagnetic in nature but at wavelengths so short that they are invisible to the human eye. Unlike cathode rays, Röntgen claimed, X rays could not be deflected by electric or magnetic fields, and, unlike light waves, they could not be refracted by a lens.

Röntgen's work stimulated the growth of careful observation and comprehensive experimentation. Other physicists drew on Röntgen's work, which helped them extend their own studies and make significant contributions. All of this set the stage for physicists to improve markedly their understanding of the nature of atomic structure and energy.

Bibliography

McGraw-Hill Encyclopedia of Science and Technology. Sybil Parker, ed. 7th ed. New York: McGraw-Hill, 1992. Pp. 251-254.

The New Book of Popular Science. Lawrence Lorimer, ed. Danbury, Conn.: Grolier, 1994. Pp. 251-254.

Van Nostrand's Scientific Encyclopedia. Douglas Considine, ed. 8th ed. New York: Van Nostrand Reinhold, 1995. Pp. 3357-3364.

(Library of Congress)

Awards

Röntgen received many honors in the years immediately following his discovery, including the Order of the Crown from Kaiser Wilhelm II of Germany, in 1896, and the first Nobel Prize in Physics, in 1901. He died in 1923 at the age of seventy-seven.

Bibliography

By Röntgen

"Über die Bestimmung des Verhältnisses der spezifischen Wärmen bei der Luft," *Annalen der Physik und Chemie*, 1870

"Über fortführende Entladungen der Elektrizität," *Annalen der Physik und Chemie*, 1874

"A Telephonic Alarm," *Nature*, 1877

"Über die elektromagnetische Drehung der Polarisationsebene des Lichtes in den Gasen," *Annalen der Physik und Chemie*, 1879 (with August Kundt)

"Über die elektromagnetische Drehung der Polarisationsebene des Lichtes in den Gasen: 2. Abhandlung," *Annalen der Physik und Chemie*, 1880 (with Kundt)

"Über die thermo-, aktino, und piezo-elektrischen Eigenschaften des Quarzes," *Annalen der Physik und Chemie*, 1883

"Über eine neue Art von Strahlen," *Sitzgsber. physik.-med. Ges. Würzburg*, 1895 (also in *Annalen der Physik und Chemie*, 1898)

"Eine neue Art von Strahlen: 2. Mitteilung," *Sitzgsber. physik.-med. Ges. Würzburg*, 1896 (also in *Annalen der Physik und Chemie*, 1898)

About Röntgen

Dr. W. C. Röntgen. Otto Glasser. 2d. ed. Springfield, Ill.: Charles C Thomas, 1958.

From X-Rays to Quarks: Modern Physicists and Their Discoveries. Emilio Segrè. San Francisco: W. H. Freeman, 1980.

The Mysterious Rays of Dr. Röntgen. Beverly Gherman. New York: Macmillan, 1994.

Wilhelm Conrad Röntgen and the Discovery of X Rays. Bern Dibner. New York: Franklin Watts, 1968.

(Russell Williams)

Sir Ronald Ross

Areas of Achievement: Medicine and zoology

Contribution: Ross was awarded the 1902 Nobel Prize in Physiology or Medicine for his demonstration that malaria is transmitted to humans through the bites of infected mosquitoes.

May 13, 1857	Born in Almora, India
1865	Moves to England to begin his education
1874	Receives medical training at Saint Bartholomew's Hospital, London
1881	Enters the Indian Medical Service
1888-1889	On leave in England, earns a doctorate in public health
1894-1895	On second leave in England, meets Patrick Manson
1897	Sees malaria parasites in mosquitoes for first time
1898	Publishes his proof of the mosquito transmission of malaria
1899	Returns to England as a lecturer at the Liverpool School of Tropical Medicine and retires from the Indian Medical Service
1901	Made a Companion of the Bath
1902	Awarded the Nobel Prize in Physiology or Medicine
1911	Made a Knight Commander of the Bath
1912	Named physician of tropical diseases at King's College Hospital, London
1926	Appointed director of the Ross Institute and Hospital for Tropical Diseases, Putney
Sept. 16, 1932	Dies in Putney, London, England

Early Life

Ronald Ross was born in India in 1857 as the son of a British army officer. He made his first trip to England at the age of eight in order to begin his education. Although Ross had a passionate interest in the arts, as is evidenced by his lifelong output of poetry, he entered medical school in 1874. He failed in his first attempt to obtain the qualification necessary for the Indian Medical Service. After a brief stint as a ship's surgeon, he passed the appropriate examination and entered the service in 1881.

Ross initially showed little interest in medical research, and, during his first tour in India, he continued to cultivate his artistic talents. After obtaining a doctor of public health degree during his first leave in England, Ross returned to India and carried out some brief malaria studies.

Parasites had been seen in the blood of infected patients, but from these early studies Ross believed that these parasites were not the cause of malaria. During his second leave in England, he met Patrick Manson, a physician who had recently propounded the mosquito theory of malaria transmission.

(The Nobel Foundation)

The Transmission of Malaria

Ross showed that malaria is transmitted to humans via the bite of an infected mosquito.

Malaria is a protozoal infection for which an insect host is required. This discovery, made simultaneously by Ross and the Italian scientist Giovanni Battista Grassi, was remarkable as two different variables complicated the matter. First, only certain species of *Anopheles* mosquito transmit the parasite. Second, the *Plasmodium* parasite within human and mosquito hosts follows a complex life cycle, which means that not all forms are visible at all times.

When mosquitoes of the proper species bite an infected person, parasites living in human blood cells are ingested along with the blood. The parasites develop through several stages and ultimately settle in the mosquito's salivary glands. When the infected mosquito bites its next victim, it injects an anticoagulant at the site of the bite in order to prevent blood from clotting too quickly. Parasites from its salivary gland pass into the host along with this anticoagulant, and a new cycle of infection is initiated.

Ross's discovery, which was hailed by the scientific community, suggested a strategy for eradicating malaria through destruction of the mosquitoes or their breeding grounds. Although this strategy was successful in the United States,

A Comparison of Mosquitoes That Transmit Disease

Mosquito	Habits	Features	Diseases
Aedes	Day biter, urban or rural	Head bent, body parallel to surface, black and white in color	Dengue, yellow fever, viral encephalitis
Anopheles	Night biter, mainly rural	Head and body in line, at angle to surface	Malaria, filariasis

(Hans & Cassady, Inc.)

at the end of the twentieth century malaria remained one of the leading infectious disease killers in the world.

Bibliography

Bruce-Chwatt's Essential Malariology. Herbert M. Miles and David A. Warrell. 3d ed. Boston: Edward Arnold, 1993.

Malaria: The Biography of a Killer. L. Warshaw. New York: Rinehart, 1949.

Malaria Studies

Upon his return to India, Ross devoted himself to solving the malaria problem. After a series of arduous studies, he finally demonstrated on August 20, 1897, that the parasites seen in human patients are also found in the gut of certain mosquitoes. He could not conduct confirming human experiments, but he soon discovered that a similar parasite causes malaria in birds.

In the summer of 1898, Ross demonstrated the life cycle of this new parasite in mosquitoes and was able to infect healthy birds via the bite of infected mosquitoes.

Return to England

Ross's discovery made him famous, and he was invited back to England as a lecturer at the Liverpool School of Tropical Medicine in 1899. Awards and honors followed. Topping the list were the second Nobel Prize in Physiology or Medicine, awarded in 1902, and knighthood bestowed on him by King George V in 1911.

After his return to England, Ross devoted much of his energy to eradicating malaria, particularly in British colonial possessions. He participated in numerous surveys of malarial districts and published a range of material, often addressed to members of the general public to inform them of steps to take to protect themselves against the disease. He also served as a consultant on malaria to the British government during World War I.

Ross did not abandon his other interests, and, during this period, he published numerous mathematical papers as well as the bulk of his impressive literary output. He died in 1932 at the institute founded in his name.

Bibliography

By Ross

Edgar: Or, The New Pygmalion; and the Judgement of Tithonus, 1883

The Child of Ocean, 1889

The Deformed Transformed, 1890

The Spirit of Storm: A Romance, 1896

"On Some Peculiar Pigmented Cells Found in Two Mosquitoes Fed on Malarial Blood," *British Medical Journal*, 1897

Report on the Cultivation of Proteosoma, Labbé, in Grey Mosquitoes, 1898

Instructions for the Prevention of Malaria, 1899

Malarial Fever: Its Cause, Prevention, and Treatment, 1902

Mosquito Brigades, and How to Organise Them, 1902

In Exile, 1906

Fables, 1907

The Prevention of Malaria, 1910

Philosophies, 1910

The Setting Sun, 1912

Psychologies, 1919

The Revels of Orsera, 1920

Memoirs, with a Full Account of the Great Malaria Problem and Its Solution, 1923

Studies on Malaria, 1928

Memories of Sir Patrick Manson, 1930

About Ross

The Malaria Capers: More Tales of Parasites and People, Research and Reality. Robert S. Desowitz. New York: W. W. Norton, 1991.

The Mosquito Man: The Story of Sir Ronald Ross. John Rowland. London: Butterworth Press, 1958.

Sir Ronald Ross: Discoverer and Creator. R. L. Mergoz. London: G. Allen & Unwin, 1931.

(James G. Hanley)

Carl-Gustaf Arvid Rossby

Area of Achievement: Earth science

Contribution: A pioneer in the science of meteorology, Rossby studied atmospheric turbulence and discovered waves in the jet stream that influence weather on Earth.

Dec. 28, 1898	Born in Stockholm, Sweden
1919	Joins the Geophysical Institute at Bergen, Norway
1921	Studies at the Geophysical Institute of the University of Leipzig
1921	Works at the Prussian Aerological Observatory at Lindenberg
1921	Enters the Swedish Meteorological and Hydrological Service
1925	Earns the equivalent to a Ph.D. from the University of Stockholm
1926	Wins a one-year fellowship with the U.S. Weather Bureau
1927	Becomes chair of the Committee on Aeronautical Meteorology of the Daniel Guggenheim Fund for Promotion of Aeronautics
1931-1939	Serves as an associate professor of meteorology at the Massachusetts Institute of Technology
1939	Appointed assistant chief of the U.S. Weather Bureau
1941-1950	Serves as chair of the meteorology department at the University of Chicago
1950	Organizes the International Meteorological Institute, Sweden
1950	Joins the faculty of the University of Stockholm
Aug. 19, 1957	Dies in Stockholm, Sweden

Early Life

Carl-Gustaf Arvid Rossby, the son of Alma Charlotta Marelius and Arvid Rossby, a construction engineer, was born in Stockholm on December 28, 1898. He studied mathematics, mechanics, and astronomy at the University of Stockholm and hydrodynamics at the University of Leipzig, eventually earning the equivalent of a Ph.D. at Stockholm in 1925.

In 1919, Rossby began his work at the Geophysical Institute at Bergen, Norway, and was greatly influenced there by Vilhelm Bjerknes, the developer of the polar-front theory of cyclones. Two years later, he returned to Stockholm and joined the Swedish Meteorological and Hydrological Service. In 1926, he accepted a one-year fellowship with the U.S. Weather Bureau.

Administrative Work

In 1927, Rossby accepted the chair of the Committee on Aeronautical Meteorology of the Daniel Guggenheim Fund for Promotion of Aeronautics. As chair, he was able to establish a weather service in California for the develop-

ing airline industry that became a model for many subsequent programs. He remained in the United States for twenty-four years.

Rossby joined the faculty at the Massachusetts Institute of Technology (MIT) in 1928. MIT created the first department of meteorology in the United States, and, as its head, Rossby was instrumental in establishing a course of study for meteorologists.

In 1939, the year that he obtained American citizenship, he was appointed assistant chief of the U.S. Weather Bureau. In the two years that he was with the bureau, he helped to refocus its mission toward greater efforts in scientific research.

Just before the outbreak of World War II, Rossby became head of the new department of meteorology at the University of Chicago. During the war, Rossby coordinated the establishment of a military meteorology program with courses needed by the armed forces for weather forecasting. Rossby also helped reorganize the American Meteorological Society and established the *Journal of Meteorology*.

In 1950, he accepted a request by the Swed-

Rossby Waves

Rossby waves are long, horizontal meanders in the jet stream that greatly influence surface weather conditions. These waves are slow moving and aid in the transfer of heat from the low latitudes toward the poles.

Jet streams are fast-moving air currents with wind speeds that are usually higher than 65 miles per hour. They are located in the upper troposphere above regions most characterized by warm and cold fronts. One of the jet streams is the polar front jet, which is found above the boundary between polar and mid-latitude air masses. Jet streams are found closer to the equator in the winter and closer to the poles in the summer.

Rossby did much research of air flow and turbulence. He discovered that certain weather features at the surface of the earth were accompanied by wavelike meanders in the jet stream. When these waves, now called Rossby waves, are of great enough amplitude, masses of air become detached and become the low-pressure and high-pressure cells that produce much of the

weather in the middle latitudes.

Rossby discovered that there are generally three to five such waves in each hemisphere. After much observation and calculation, he was able to postulate dynamic theories describing their behavior. The Rossby equation describes their propagation speed. An understanding of Rossby waves aids considerably in being able to forecast the weather.

Bibliography

The Atmosphere and the Sea in Motion: Scientific Contributions to the Rossby Memorial Volume. Bert Bolin. New York: Rockefeller Institute Press, 1959.

Calculating the Weather: Meteorology in the Twentieth Century. Frederik Nebeker. San Diego: Academic Press, 1995.

Dynamics of Atmospheric Motion. John A. Dutton. New York: Dover, 1995.

Mid-Latitude Weather Systems. Toby N. Carlson. New York: HarperCollins Academic Press, 1991.

ish government to return to his native country and organize the International Meteorological Institute. He joined the faculty at the University of Stockholm that same year. Rossby died in 1957 at the age of fifty-eight.

Theoretical Research

Among Rossby's early research topics was atmospheric turbulence. While at MIT, he designed the Rossby diagram for the identification of air masses and their processes of formation.

He investigated the long "Rossby waves" of the jet stream and realized that these waves influence surface weather conditions. His development in 1939 of the

(AP/Wide World Photos)

Rossby equation, which determines the propagation speed of these waves, was one of the most important advancements of meteorological research of the twentieth century.

Rossby's later work centered on the interactions of atmospheric and oceanic circulation and of the effects of chemicals in the air. Once computers with sufficient memory and speed became available, much of his theoretical work was used in programming them so that they could be used for weather prediction.

Bibliography

By Rossby

Airplane Transportation, 1929 (with James Woolley, Earl Hill, and William MacCracken)

A Generalization of the Theory of the Mixing Length with Applications to Atmospheric and Oceanic Turbulence, 1932

Thermodynamics Applied to Air Mass Analysis, 1932

The Layer of Frictional Influence in Wind and Ocean Currents, 1935 (with R. B. Montgomery)

Dynamics of Steady Ocean Currents in the Light of

Experimental Fluid Mechanics, 1936

On the Momentum Transfer at the Sea Surface, 1936

"Planetary Flow Patterns in the Atmosphere," *Quarterly Journal of the Royal Meteorological Society*, 1940

"The Scientific Basis of Modern Meteorology" in *Climate and Man*, 1941 (U.S. Department of Agriculture)

Kinematic and Hydrostatic Properties of Certain Long Waves in the Westerlies, 1942

Boundary-Layer Problems in the Atmosphere and Ocean, 1943

About Rossby

"Rossby, Carl-Gustav Arvid." In *Dictionary of Scientific Biography*, edited by Charles Coulston Gillispie. New York: Charles Scribner's Sons, 1980.

"Rossby, Carl-Gustav Arvid." In *Larousse Dictionary of Scientists*, edited by Hazel Muir. New York: Larousse, 1994.

(Kenneth J. Schoon)

Peyton Rous

Areas of Achievement: Biology, genetics, and virology

Contribution: Rous was the first to demonstrate that cancer in animals can be caused by viruses. His discovery resulted in his being awarded the 1966 Nobel Prize in Physiology or Medicine

Oct. 5, 1879	Born in Baltimore, Maryland
1900	Earns a B.A. at The Johns Hopkins University
1904-1906	Serves as resident house officer at The Johns Hopkins Hospital
1905	Awarded a medical degree from Johns Hopkins
1906-1908	Becomes an instructor in pathology at the University of Michigan
1909	Accepts a position as an assistant member at the Rockefeller Institute for Medical Research
1910	Demonstrates that sarcomas in chickens are caused by a "filterable agent"
1920-1945	Named a member in pathology and bacteriology at the Rockefeller Institute
1920-1970	Serves as editor of the *Journal of Experimental Medicine*
1927	Elected to the National Academy of Sciences
1945	Named member emeritus of the Rockefeller Institute
1957-1970	Serves on the board of consultants at the Sloan-Kettering Institute
1966	Awarded the Nobel Prize in Physiology or Medicine
Feb. 16, 1970	Dies in New York, New York

Early Life

Francis Peyton Rous (pronounced "rows") was born in Baltimore to Charles and Frances Rous. His father died when Peyton was eleven, and his mother decided to remain in Baltimore to take advantage of the educational opportunities. It was there that Rous grew to adulthood.

Rous demonstrated an early interest in science. In his late teens, he authored a "flower of the month" column for the *Baltimore Sun*. Interest in biology led him to enroll at the nearby Johns Hopkins University, from which he was graduated in 1900. Rous then entered the medical school there, earning his M.D. in 1905.

During his residency at the hospital, Rous decided that his interests lay in research, rather than in the treatment of illness. In 1906, he began a period of study on blood cells with Aldred Walthin at the University of Michigan, followed by a summer of study in Germany. Returning to the United States in 1909, Rous contracted tuberculosis and was forced to recuperate in an Adirondacks sanatorium.

(The Nobel Foundation)

The Rockefeller Institute

In 1909, Simon Flexner, the director of the recently established Rockefeller Institute for Medical Research, asked Rous to come to New York and carry out cancer research. Rous would remain associated with the institute (later Rockefeller University) until his death.

Shortly after Rous joined the institute, a chicken with a large breast tumor was brought to him. Rous prepared cell-free filtrates from the tumor and demonstrated that these filtrates would cause similar tumors when injected into healthy chickens. This work, published in the *Journal of Experimental Medicine* in 1910, was the first to demonstrate that cancer in animals is transmissible.

Difficulties in repeating his work when studying other forms of mammalian tumors, however, resulted in Rous abandoning this line of research in 1915. During World War I, he was instrumental in developing a means to preserve and transfuse blood. He traveled to France and created the first blood bank, using blood donated by soldiers.

The study of blood represented a new area of research for Rous. Following the war, his interests entered the area of physiology, reflected in the variety of projects with which he became associated: capillary permeability in muscles, gallstone formation, and the function of the gallbladder.

In 1933, Richard Shope of the Rockefeller Institute discovered a virus that caused warts (papillomas) in rabbits. Rous soon established that the papilloma was actually a tumor. He would continue to study this topic for most of the remainder of his career.

Awards and Recognition

Understanding of the significance of Rous's 1910 discovery of what would be known as the Rous sarcoma virus was a long time in coming. Eventually, the role of viruses in some forms of cancer would be recognized; Rous received the Nobel Prize in Physiology or Medicine in 1966 as a result of his contributions.

Rous was awarded nine honorary degrees over the course of his career. Among the other major honors bestowed on him were the John Scott Medal in 1927, the Walker Prize from the Royal College of Surgeons in 1942, the Kovalenko Medal in 1956, the Lasker Award in 1958, and the National Medal of Science in 1966. He died in 1970.

The Isolation of Tumor Virus from Animals

Rous's isolation of a tumor virus from chickens in 1910 represented the first demonstration that cancer can be caused by a virus.

At the beginning of the twentieth century, the concept of viruses was still unclear; they had never actually been seen, and the possibility that they could cause cancer was not even considered.

A local farmer brought a Plymouth Rock chicken with a large breast tumor to the Rockefeller Institute. Rous determined that the tumor was a sarcoma, a type of cancer associated with connective tissue. He prepared an extract from the tumor and passed the material through a filter to remove any cells or bacteria. When he injected the cell-free filtrate into other chickens, they too developed sarcomas.

Rous's conclusions were not initially accepted by much of the scientific community. The feeling was that the work had been sloppy, that either bacteria or tumor cells had also passed through the filter. Rous also proved unable to repeat the work using mammalian tumors, and he eventually moved into other areas of research.

The isolation of other tumor viruses some decades later would vindicate Rous. His initial isolate became known as the Rous sarcoma virus and would play a key role in the study of genes associated with cancer.

Bibliography

Genes and the Biology of Cancer. Harold Varmus. New York: W. H. Freeman, 1993.

"The Molecular Genetics of Cancer." J. Michael Bishop. *Science* 235 (1987).

Racing to the Beginning of the Road. Robert Weinberg. New York: Harmony Books, 1996.

Bibliography

By Rous

"A Transmissible Avian Neoplasm (Sarcoma of the Common Fowl)," *Journal of Experimental Medicine*, 1910

"A Sarcoma of the Fowl Transmissible by an Agent Separable from the Tumor Cells," *Journal of Experimental Medicine*, 1911

"The Preservation of Living Red Blood Cells in vitro: I. Methods of Preservation," *Journal of Experimental Medicine*, 1916 (with J. Turner)

"The Preservation of Living Red Blood Cells in vitro: II. The Transfusion of Kept Cells," *Journal of Experimental Medicine*, 1916 (with Turner)

The Modern Dance of Death, 1929

"A Virus-Induced Mammalian Growth with the Characters of a Tumor," *Journal of Experimental Medicine*, 1934 (with J. Beard)

About Rous

A Notable Career in Finding Out: Peyton Rous, 1879-1970. New York: Rockefeller University Press, 1971.

Notable Twentieth-Century Scientists. Emily J. McMurray, ed. Detroit: Gale Research, 1995.

"Peyton Rous." In *The Nobel Prize Winners: Physiology or Medicine*, edited by Frank N. Magill. Pasadena, Calif.: Salem Press, 1991.

(Richard Adler)

F. Sherwood Rowland

Area of Achievement: Chemistry
Contribution: Rowland was the first to recognize that chlorine atoms released by the decomposition of chlorofluorocarbons in the stratosphere could seriously damage the protective ozone layer of the earth.

June 28, 1927	Born in Delaware, Ohio
1952	Receives a Ph.D. in chemistry from the University of Chicago
1952	Takes a faculty position at Princeton University
1956	Appointed a professor of chemistry at the University of Kansas
1964	Becomes the first chairperson of the chemistry department at the University of California, Irvine
1974	Publishes a paper on the destruction of the ozone layer by chlorofluorocarbons
1976	Receives the Tolman Medal of the American Chemical Society
1981	Receives the Humboldt Senior Scientist Award
1986	Publishes a paper explaining the formation of the ozone hole over Antarctica
1987	Receives the Charles A. Dana Award for Pioneering Achievement in Health
1995	Awarded the Nobel Prize in Chemistry jointly with Mario Molina and Paul Crutzen

Early Life

Frank Sherwood Rowland was born in Delaware, Ohio, in 1927. His undergraduate studies were done at Ohio Wesleyan University, where he played on the baseball and basketball teams. After earning his degree, he entered the University of Chicago to study for his doctorate. While there, Rowland conducted research on radiochemistry under Willard F. Libby, who was awarded the 1960 Nobel Prize in Chemistry for his development of carbon 14 dating.

Rowland's first teaching position was at Princeton University. After four years, he moved to the University of Kansas, where his research in radiochemistry earned him an international reputation. In 1964, he became the first chairperson of the newly formed chemistry department at the University of California, Irvine.

Atmospheric Research
In the 1970's, Rowland began to think about expanding his research to areas with different challenges. Chlorofluorocarbons (CFCs) had become popular as spray can propellants in the 1960's. Rowland became intrigued by the question of what happened to the CFCs in the atmosphere. When Mario Molina joined Row-

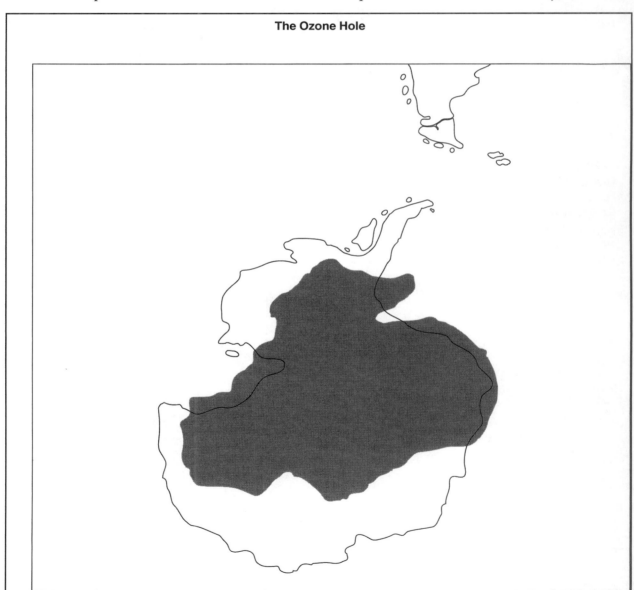

The Ozone Hole

In the mid-1980's, scientists studying the atmosphere over Antarctica first observed a hole in the ozone layer (shown in gray) predicted by Rowland and Mario Molina's theories about CFCs and ozone destruction.

Rowland (left) receives a Japan Prize in environmental science and technology in 1989. (AP/Wide World Photos)

land's research group for postdoctoral work in 1973, Rowland suggested that they study this topic.

CFCs are very stable chemicals and so are long-lived in the atmosphere. This finding raised the probability that the CFCs would eventually rise into the stratosphere, where a layer of ozone (O_3) between 25 and 30 kilometers above the surface protects life on Earth by absorbing damaging ultraviolet (UV) light from the sun.

Rowland and Molina discovered that the UV light in the atmosphere has enough energy to break a chemical bond in CFCs, releasing a chlorine atom. Chlorine atoms are very reactive and will attack and destroy ozone. Their studies indicated that CFCs could produce a 7 to 13 percent decrease in the ozone layer. This seemingly small reduction would result in a very significant increase in skin cancer rates and could also drastically effect weather patterns. Rowland and Molina called for a ban on the production of CFCs.

The Antarctic Ozone Hole

Unbeknownst to Rowland and Molina, Joseph Farman had been making measurements of the ozone level in the atmosphere for the British Antarctic Survey. He found a drastic decrease in the ozone level at the beginning of the Antarctic spring (October in the Southern Hemisphere). Between the 1960's and 1985, the October ozone levels fell by a third.

Rowland and Molina were able to explain the large seasonal drop in ozone. Around the end of August, the sun begins to appear again,

The Fight to End the Production of Chlorofluorocarbons

Rowland was convinced that continued contamination of the atmosphere with CFCs could produce an ecological disaster.

By the 1970's a large industry had been built up around the production and use of CFCs. They were used as propellants in aerosol cans and as a refrigerant in air conditioners and refrigerators. In the United States, the value of the entire CFC industry was eight billion dollars. Despite warnings from Rowland and other scientists about the environmental dangers associated with these chemicals, the industry resisted a ban on their production.

In 1976, a report of a study panel of the National Academy of Sciences confirmed Rowland's predictions of an ozone loss of 7 to 13 percent. Within a year, the Environmental Protection Agency (EPA) and the Food and Drug Administration (FDA) ordered an end to the production of CFCs for nonessential uses in aerosols in the United States. Nevertheless, while Rowland continued to press for a complete ban, the production of CFCs for other uses continued to expand rapidly.

The 1985 announcement of the discovery of a hole in the ozone layer over Antarctica stimulated the analysis of new and existing data on ozone levels by the Ozone Trends Panel of the National Aeronautics and Space Administration (NASA) and the World Meteorological Organization. They confirmed the ozone depletion in March, 1988.

The DuPont Company responded to these new results by announcing that it would quickly cease production of CFCs, and other U.S. manufacturers quickly followed DuPont's lead. At an international meeting in Montreal, an agreement to cease all production of CFCs on January 1, 1996, was reached.

Bibliography

Between Earth and Sky. Seth Cagin and Philip Dray. New York: Pantheon Books, 1993.

Ozone Crisis. Sharon Roan. New York: John Wiley & Sons, 1989.

ending the long Antarctic night. At the same time, very cold stratospheric clouds are still overhead containing tiny ice crystals. These crystals provide a surface on which the ultraviolet rays of the sun catalyze ozone-destroying chemical reactions.

For his research into the effects of CFCs and the state of the ozone layer, Rowland shared the Nobel Prize in Chemistry with Molina and Paul Crutzen in 1995.

Bibliography

By Rowland

"Stratospheric Sink for Chlorofluoromethanes: Chlorine Atom-Catalyzed Destruction of Ozone," *Nature*, 1974

"Ozone Depletion: Twenty Years After the Alarm," *Chemical and Engineering News*, 1994

About Rowland

Notable Twentieth-Century Scientists. Emily J. McMurray, ed. Detroit: Gale Research, 1995.

(Francis P. Mac Kay)

Carlo Rubbia

Area of Achievement: Physics
Contribution: Rubbia led a team of a hundred scientists who designed, constructed, and used one of the world's largest superconducting supercolliders.

Mar. 31, 1934	Born in Gorizia, Italy
1958	Earns a doctoral degree in physics at the University of Pisa
1960	Marries Marissa Romé
1961	Works as a researcher for the Conseil Européen pour la Recherche Nucléaire (CERN), the European Organization for Nuclear Research
1970-1988	Serves as Higgins Professor of Physics at Harvard University
1984	Awarded the Nobel Prize in Physics, jointly with Simon van der Meer, for his proof of the existence of W^+, W^-, and Z^0 particles
1985	Receives the Ledlie Prize
1986	Awarded the Jesolo d'Oro
1987-1996	Serves as chair of the board of Sincrotrone Triest and operates a 2 million-electronvolt synchrotron, a large device for accelerating particles and directing them toward targets
1989-1994	Acts as director general of CERN
1993	Proposes the construction of an energy amplifier, a tool for producing neutrons and introducing them into atomic fuel

Early Life

Carlo Rubbia was born on March 31, 1934, into the family of Silvio and Bice Liceni Rubbia. Carlo was an outgoing boy and a good student. He was admitted to the Scuola Normale Superiore in Pisa—the same school that another famous atomic physicist, Enrico Fermi, had attended. From this high school, Rubbia moved to the University of Pisa, where, in 1958, he earned a doctorate at the age of twenty-four. His studies were marked with boundless energy and enthusiasm, qualities that would continue into his adult life

In 1960, Rubbia married Marissa Romé; two daughters, Laura and Andrea, completed the family. The year after his marriage, Rubbia began work as a researcher for the Conseil Européen pour la Recherche Nucléaire (CERN), the European Organization for Nuclear Research, where he stayed for thirty-three years.

Building Colliders

As the 1980's began, several large laboratories were in competition to find the next particles of

(The Nobel Foundation)

which atoms are composed. To do so, it was necessary to build increasingly powerful tools. In Europe, CERN had large machines near Geneva, Switzerland, built so that large electromagnets generate energy in pieces of atoms (such as protons) that are put into them.

The more powerful the magnets and the weaker the friction in the machines, the more energy the pieces gather and the faster they go as they travel many miles inside the machines. The faster the particles are made to go, the more pieces they break into when they collide with targets or with other parts of atoms. Some of the pieces of atoms combine with other pieces or have their masses change to energy in very short times—in a millionth or a trillionth of a second. These accelerators have very sensitive measuring devices to detect these particles before they disappear.

The challenge facing these scientific centers in the 1980's had originated in 1967, when Steven Weinberg proposed a theory that the weak nuclear force and electromagnetism could be explained using the same umbrella of mathematical equations. One needed to imagine, however, three more subatomic particles that worked as exchange particles, as particles involved in changing one kind of particle into another.

Weinberg's arithmetic suggested that the three new particles had a relatively large mass, at least a hundred times the mass of a proton.

Searching for Subatomic Particles

Rubbia directed the construction and use of a large collider, a tool to direct very small particles at high energy levels and release them to smash into other small particles or into targets. In this way, he discovered several subatomic particles.

Two kinds of scientists often team to make scientific discoveries. Theoretical scientists create mathematical and sometimes computer models and propose theories about nature. Experimental scientists study these theories and look for experiments to test them. Rubbia is an experimental scientist working with particles of matter and energy that are smaller than atoms.

In 1967, Steven Weinberg had predicted the existence of three particles, bigger than protons, but with very short lives. He called them W^+, W^-, and Z^0. Finding these three particles would support Weinberg's theory that combined two of the universe's forces under one set of mathematical equations. It would be another giant step in scientists' efforts to explain the universe mathematically.

In 1982, Rubbia began a number of experiments in Geneva, Switzerland, to find signs of Weinberg's three particles. What particles and what sorts of collisions might produce evidence of these particles, which existed for only a billionth of a second? Rubbia decided on a number of possibilities and changed the existing tools on his supercollider to detect the three particles. In one year, he obtained 140,000 signs of particle events using his large, powerful machine. Five of these events suggested the presence of the W^- particle, and only one suggested the W^+ particle.

Weinberg's arithmetic also predicted the sizes of these particles. Bigger particles required more energy to move through the collider, just as more energy is needed to move a train than an automobile. Rubbia's team measured the energy of the moving particles. From these measurements, they could determine the mass of each particle. Each particle, W^- and W^+, seemed to have the mass predicted by Weinberg.

Rubbia needed to increase the power of his supercollider in order to find the third particle, Z^0, since it was, by Weinberg's estimate, heavier than the others. Rubbia announced his discovery of the W particles in January, 1983, and then continued to change his machine and conduct new tests. In May of that year, he and his team found signs of the Z particle. Scientists began to believe that they had found all the different particles that make up the universe. Rubbia's proof of the Weinberg-Salam theory of universal forces was a giant step toward working out a unified theory.

Bibliography
Atom: Journey Across the Subatomic Cosmos. Isaac Asimov. New York: E. P. Dutton, 1991.
The Key to the Universe. Nigel Calder. New York: Viking Press, 1977.

(The new particles are large when compared to other subatomic particles, but all bits that compose atoms are much too small to see.) Researchers were accustomed to machines that produced enough energy to hurl about neutrons, neutrinos, and protons. It would take a hundred times that amount of energy to break materials and find the three new particles.

As one of his duties at CERN—he divided his energy between CERN and Harvard University—Rubbia teamed with Simon van der Meer to produce the more powerful accelerator needed to test Weinberg's theory, among other uses. Electric generators had to be more powerful in order to speed up larger particles and smash them against other particles or targets. New methods had been discovered to cool the electric coils to very low temperatures at which there was almost no resistance to the flow of electricity.

Success at CERN

Even if the new generators succeeded and the new particles were given off, they would combine with other particles or otherwise disappear within a millionth of a second. In that short time, they would not be visible. Other tools needed to be created to detect the new particle formation.

Rubbia provided the leadership and van der Meer the engineering skills for this task. Together, they directed a team of a hundred scientists at CERN, the first laboratory to reach the new electrical strengths. More than 100 million electronvolts were generated by giant magnets to speed up particles and hurl them against other particles.

Pieces of the original particles fly off in all directions—the direction guided in part by the electrical charges that each particle has. A particle with a negative charge flies off in one direction, and one with a positive charge flies off in another. In addition, according to their masses, the particles fly off at different angles. The detecting devices that Rubbia built into the machine printed a pattern of particle flight and circles of various sizes where they collided with targets. Teams of scientists led by Rubbia could then measure angles, sizes of impact circles, and other indications of particle movement.

The Energy Amplifier

In 1993, Rubbia and his team of scientists proposed to build an energy amplifier. This machine would use an accelerator to crash neutrons, the particles in atomic nuclei that have no electric charge, into radioactive materials in a bed of shielding material such as lead. The neutrons would break other nuclei, releasing energy that could be converted to electricity for houses and businesses.

The energy amplifier would be safer than existing nuclear power plants because the occurrence of any problem could be made to shut off the accelerator and the flow of neutrons. In addition, much less radioactive waste material would be created; the energy amplifier would produce more than a thousand times less plutonium, for example, than the usual nuclear power plants.

Rubbia used different arrangements of already-known equipment to conduct his tests on the amplifier. His design was very inefficient—a much more powerful accelerator was needed. Nevertheless, scientists in Los Alamos, New Mexico; Brookhaven, New York; Japan; and Russia began to experiment with the energy amplifier for a number of uses: to destroy waste, to break down plutonium for safe use, and to produce tritium, an element needed by military units throughout the world.

Bibliography
By Rubbia
Il Dilemma nucleare, 1987 (with Nino Criscenti)
Edoardo Amaldi: Scientific Statesman, 1991

About Rubbia
"Carlo Rubbia." In Current Biography Yearbook. New York: H. W. Wilson, 1985.
"Carlo Rubbia." In The Nobel Prize Winners: Physics, edited by Frank N. Magill. Pasadena, Calif.: Salem Press, 1989.
"Rubbia Leaves Italian Synchrotron." Science (October 18, 1996).

(George Wilson)

Vera C. Rubin

Areas of Achievement: Astronomy and physics

Contribution: Rubin's study of the movement and rotation of galaxies provided evidence for the existence of the Local Supercluster, the Great Attractor, and dark matter.

July 23, 1928	Born in Philadelphia, Pennsylvania
1948	Earns a bachelor's degree from Vassar College
1950	Presents paper to the American Astronomical Society
1951	Earns a master's degree from Cornell University
1954	Awarded a Ph.D. from Georgetown University
1955	Begins work at Georgetown as a research associate
1959	Promoted to lecturer
1962	Promoted to assistant professor
1963-1964	Conducts research with Margaret and Geoffrey Burbidge at the University of California, San Diego
1965	Begins work at the Department of Terrestrial Magnetism
1972-1982	Serves as associate editor of the *Astronomical Journal* and then of the *Astrophysical Journal Letters*
1979-1987	Serves on the editorial board of *Science* magazine
1981	Elected to the National Academy of Sciences
1990-1992	Serves on the visiting committee of the Space Telescope Scientific Institute
1993	Awarded the National Medal of Science

Early Life

Vera C. Rubin was born Vera Cooper in Philadelphia, Pennsylvania, on July 23, 1928. Her parents were Philip Cooper, an electrical engineer, and Rose Applebaum Cooper. In 1938, the family moved to Washington, D.C.

Vera developed an interest in astronomy at an early age. She attended Vassar College in Poughkeepsie, New York, earning her bachelor's degree in 1948. She was encouraged by the example of Maria Mitchell, the first American woman to become a noted astronomer, who had been a professor at Vassar in the late nineteenth century. In 1948, Cooper married Robert Rubin, a graduate student in physical chemistry at Cornell University in Ithaca, New York. She attended Cornell with her husband, earning her master's degree in 1951.

Vera Rubin presented her first paper, "Rotation of the Universe," to the American Astronomical Society in December, 1950. In it, she offered findings that supported the idea that galaxies in different regions of the universe were moving away from the earth at different speeds that could not be explained fully by the general expansion of the universe. Her paper was soundly rejected by most astronomers, but she was vindicated in 1956 when French astronomer Gérard de Vaucouleurs used her work to support his concept of the Local Supercluster, a vast conglomerate of many clusters of galaxies, including the Milky Way.

The Georgetown Years

Rubin obtained her Ph.D. from Georgetown University in Washington, D.C., in 1954. Her doctoral thesis on the uneven distribution of galaxies in the universe anticipated the work of other astronomers by about fifteen years. After teaching mathematics and physics for a year at Montgomery Junior College in Takoma Park, Maryland, she returned to Georgetown as a research associate in 1955. She was promoted to lecturer in 1959 and assistant professor in 1962.

While still employed by Georgetown, Rubin spent a year at the University of California, San Diego from 1963 to 1964, where she worked with astronomers Margaret and Geoffrey Burbidge on determining the rotation of the Andromeda galaxy. She also spent time making observations at Kitt Peak National Observatory, near Tucson, Arizona, and other large observatories. She was the first woman officially allowed to make observations at Mount Palomar Observatory near San Diego. (Margaret Burbidge had been unofficially allowed to make observations there because she was married to Geoffrey Burbidge.)

The Great Attractor and Dark Matter

In 1965, Rubin left Georgetown to work at the Department of Terrestrial Magnetism at the Carnegie Institution in Washington, D.C. The department was originally founded in the early twentieth century to promote the study of the earth's magnetic field, but its goals expanded to include research on a variety of astronomical topics. Rubin began a collaboration with physicist W. Kent Ford that led to her most important discoveries.

At first, Rubin worked on quasars, newly discovered objects that are extremely distant but extremely bright. She soon tired of the intense competition among astronomers over this new topic, however, and returned her attention to the movement of galaxies. Rubin found evidence that local galaxies are moving in a way that cannot be explained by simple expansion. Her observation, known as the Rubin-Ford effect, led later astronomers to theorize the existence of a distant massive concentration of galaxies known as the Great Attractor that pulls local galaxies in its direction with gravitational force.

Disappointed by the initial skeptical reaction to the Rubin-Ford effect, Rubin turned to the rotation of galaxies. She repeated the studies that she had made of the Andromeda galaxy with the Burbidges, this time using more sensitive equipment. She then studied the rotation of several other galaxies. Her results indicated that these galaxies contain large

Rubin stands before a photograph of a spiral galaxy at the Carnegie Institution of Washington. (R. T. Nowitz/Photo Researchers)

amounts of unseen material. Perhaps as much as 95 percent of a galaxy might be made up of this invisible mass, known to astronomers as dark matter.

Editing and Awards

Rubin was also active in editing scientific journals. She served as associate editor of the *Astronomical Journal* from 1972 to 1977, then as associate editor of the *Astrophysical Journal Letters* from 1977 to 1982. From 1979 to 1987, she served on the editorial board of the prestigious journal *Science*.

Among her many awards were several honorary degrees from major universities. She was also awarded the National Medal of Science from President Bill Clinton in 1993.

Bibliography

By Rubin
"Dark Matter in Spiral Galaxies," *Scientific American*, 1983
"Women's Work," *Science*, 1986
Large-Scale Motions in the Universe: A Vatican Study Week, 1988 (as editor, with George V. Coyne)

Dark Matter

Rubin's measurements of the rotation of galaxies provided evidence that they contain large amounts of unseen mass known as dark matter.

Galaxies are made up of billions of stars held together by gravity. These stars rotate around the center of the galaxy, just as the planets in the solar system rotate around the sun. Astronomers can measure the speed at which these stars rotate by making use of the Doppler effect.

The Doppler effect, named for the nineteenth century Austrian physicist Christian Doppler, causes light from objects that are approaching the observer to appear more blue and light from objects receding from the observer to appear more red. When a galaxy rotates, in most cases part of it will be moving in such a way that it is approaching the earth, while another part of it will be receding from the earth. By measuring how far the light from these parts of the galaxy are shifted toward the blue and red ends of the light spectrum, astronomers can tell how fast the galaxy is rotating.

Before astronomers made careful measurements of the rotation speeds of galaxies, they assumed that they would follow a simple relationship known as Kepler's third law, first announced by German astronomer Johannes Kepler in 1618. This law states that the further an object is from the center of mass around which it rotates, the more slowly it will move. For example, the planet Pluto, which is distant from the sun, moves much more slowly than Mercury, which is near the sun. In a galaxy, Kepler's third law would mean that stars far from the bright center of the galaxy should move more slowly than those near to it.

When Rubin made her observations, she discovered that the expected results did not occur. Instead, the stars at the edge of the galaxy moved as quickly or even slightly more quickly than those nearer the center. This result implies that the majority of mass is not located at the bright center, but that there must be some unseen mass surrounding the galaxy. Measurements revealed that this unseen mass, called dark matter, makes up as much as 95 percent of the mass of a galaxy.

Rubin's work implied that astronomers had ignored most of the matter in the universe. The exact nature of dark matter became one of the most active areas of research. Some possibilities suggested to explain this unseen mass include small, dim stars; large, planetlike bodies; black holes; neutrinos, assuming that these subatomic particles are shown to possess mass; and hypothetical gravity particles or magnetic particles.

Bibliography

The Fifth Essence: The Search for Dark Matter in the Universe. Lawrence Maxwell Krauss. New York: Basic Books, 1989.
Modern Cosmology and the Dark Matter Problem. D. W. Sciama. Cambridge, England: Cambridge University Press, 1993.
Through a Universe Darkly: A Cosmic Tale of Ancient Ethers, Dark Matter, and the Fate of the Universe. Marcia Bartusiak. New York: HarperCollins, 1993.

The Local Supercluster

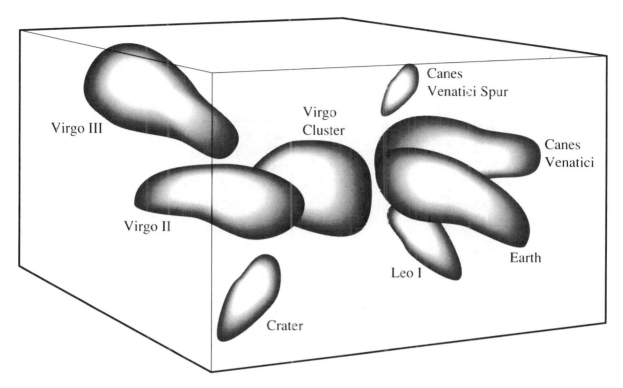

Rubin's work on the movement of galaxies away from the earth provided evidence for the existence of the Local Supercluster. The illustration shows the relative positions of the galaxy clusters that form this structure.

About Rubin

A Hand Up: Women Mentoring Women in Science. Deborah C. Fort, ed. Washington, D.C.: Association for Women in Science, 1993.

Lonely Hearts of the Cosmos: The Scientific Quest for the Secret of the Universe. Dennis Overbye. New York: HarperCollins, 1991.

Origins: The Lives and Worlds of Modern Cosmologists. Alan Lightman and Roberta Brewer. Cambridge, Mass.: Harvard University Press, 1990.

(Rose Secrest)

Benjamin Rush

Areas of Achievement: Chemistry, medicine, and psychiatry

Contribution: Rush was the most prominent physician and medical educator in colonial America and the early United States. He has been called the founder of American psychiatry.

Jan. 4, 1746	Born in Byberry, Pennsylvania
1768	Earns an M.D. at the University of Edinburgh
1769	Begins his medical practice in Philadelphia
1769	Accepts a position as professor of chemistry at the College of Philadelphia
1770	Publishes *A Syllabus of a Course of Lectures on Chemistry*
1776	Becomes a member of the Continental Congress
1776	Signs the Declaration of Independence
1777	Takes the position of surgeon general of the central department of the Continental Army
1786	Establishes the first free dispensary in the United States
1792	Becomes a professor of the Institute of Medical and Clinical Practice at the University of Pennsylvania
1797	Accepts an appointment as treasurer of the U.S. Mint
1812	Publishes *Medical Inquiries and Observations upon the Diseases of the Mind*
Apr. 19, 1813	Dies in Philadelphia, Pennsylvania

Early Life

Benjamin Rush was born twelve miles north of Philadelphia in Byberry Township in 1746. His father was a farmer and gunsmith who died when Benjamin was five years old. His mother supported her seven children by operating a grocery store in Philadelphia. At the age of eight, Rush was enrolled in the Nottingham Academy, a boarding school south of Philadelphia.

In 1756, Rush entered the College of New Jersey, which later became Princeton University. His original intention was to study law, but his interest shifted to medicine. At the age of fifteen, he left the college to live as an apprentice with Dr. John Redman, a very successful physician.

After a five-year apprenticeship, Rush enrolled in the medical program at the University of Edinburgh, Scotland. While there, he studied under William Cullen, an outstanding medical educator, and Joseph Black, an eminent chemist. His doctoral dissertation involved a study of the human digestive processes. After his graduation, he visited factories in England in order to study the chemical manufacturing process being used. He also went to France and visited prominent chemists to familiarize himself with research being conducted there.

An Educator and Physician

On August 1, 1769, Rush was appointed professor of chemistry at the College of Philadelphia, which today is the University of Pennsylvania. During the same year, he started a private medical practice. He did little chemical research, and what he did was of little significance. As a teacher, however, he fostered a strong interest in chemistry in many of his students.

Rush continued in the position of professor of chemistry until 1789, when he assumed a position as professor of the theory and practice of medicine. He published works on a wide range of medical topics, including Indian medicine, geriatrics, dentistry, and veterinary medicine. Although none of his publications involved significant advances, he was generally recognized as being the leading physician in the new United States.

An Educator and Innovator

Rush is not well known because of significant scientific work that he did in the areas of chemistry and medicine. His fame is the result of his political involvements and his pioneering work in medicine and education.

At the time of the American Revolution, science in America was at a primitive state. The only well-known American scientist at the time was Benjamin Franklin. Rush deserves credit for his part in establishing the foundation from which American science could develop.

Estimates are that up to three thousand students attended Rush's chemistry classes during the twenty years that they were offered. The course was based on the highly successful one that Joseph Black had developed in Edinburgh, Scotland, and that Rush had attended. The first chemistry textbook published in America consisted of Rush's lectures.

Other American firsts attributed to Rush include offering a series of lectures on chemistry to the public, opening a free clinic in Philadelphia, and developing a chemistry course for women. Rush believed that the development of the country required educated women.

In 1787, Rush was given charge of the mental patients at the Pennsylvania Hospital. A common belief of the time was that mental illness was a punishment from God for evil deeds. Rush argued that the causes of mental illness were in the physical environment and that such illness was curable.

Bibliography

"Benjamin Rush, Chemist." *Chymia* 4 (1953).

The Pursuit of Science in Revolutionary America, 1735-1789. Brooke Hincle. 1956. Reprint. New York: W. W. Norton, 1974.

Three Early Champions of Education: Benjamin Franklin, Benjamin Rush, and Noah Webster. Abraham Blinderman. Bloomington, Ind.: Phi Delta Kappa Educational Foundation, 1976.

A Patriot and Revolutionary

Much of Rush's fame is attributable to his involvement in politics, which began slowly in 1773 and escalated as the revolutionary spirit developed in the colonies. As his involvement grew, he worked closely with George Washington, John Adams, Patrick Henry, Thomas Paine, and others involved with the revolutionary cause. On July 20, 1776, he was chosen as one of Pennsylvania's eight members of the Continental Congress. Shortly thereafter, he became a signer of the Declaration of Independence. A year later, Rush was appointed surgeon general for the middle department of the Continental Army. He treated the dying and wounded on the battlefields of Trenton and Princeton during the American Revolution.

Rush went on to become treasurer of the U.S. Mint, in 1797. He died in Philadelphia in 1813 at the age of sixty-seven.

(Library of Congress)

Bibliography

By Rush

A Syllabus of a Course of Lectures on Chemistry, 1770

An Account of the Effects of the Stramonium or Thorn Apple, 1771

An Oration, Delivered Before the American Philosophical Society, held in Philadelphia on the 27th of February, 1786: Containing an Enquiry into the Influence of Physical Causes upon the Moral Faculty, 1786

Medical Inquiries and Observations upon the Diseases of the Mind, 1812

About Rush

Benjamin Rush, Philosopher of the American Revolution. Donald J. D'Elia. Philadelphia: American Philosophical Society, 1974.

Benjamin Rush, Physician and Citizen, 1746-1813. Nathan G. Goodman. Philadelphia: University of Pennsylvania Press, 1934.

Benjamin Rush: Revolutionary Gadfly. David F. Hawke. Indianapolis: Bobbs-Merrill, 1971.

(Francis P. Mac Kay)

Henry Norris Russell

Areas of Achievement: Astronomy and physics

Contribution: Russell studied the composition, structure, and dynamics of stars, discovering a fundamental relationship among their size, temperature, and intrinsic brightness that clarifies the process of stellar evolution.

Oct. 25, 1877	Born in Oyster Bay, New York
1897	Graduates insigne cum laude from Princeton University
1899	Earns a Ph.D. in astronomy from Princeton
1902-1905	Studies at Cambridge University
1905	Appointed an instructor of astronomy at Princeton
1911	Promoted to professor of astronomy
1911	Publishes *Determination of Stellar Parallax*
1912	Becomes the director of Princeton's observatory
1914	Publishes "Relations Between the Spectra and Other Characteristics of the Stars" in the journal *Nature*
1918-1919	Works as an engineer for the Army Aviation Service
1921	Works as a research associate at Mount Wilson Observatory
1927	Appointed C. A. Young Research Professor at Princeton
1933	Elected president of the American Association for the Advancement of Science
1934-1937	Serves as president of the American Astronomical Association
Feb. 18, 1957	Dies in Princeton, New Jersey

The Hertzsprung-Russell Diagram

This diagram plots the relation between a star's temperature and its intrinsic brightness, providing information about its size and stage in stellar evolution.

The Hertzsprung-Russell diagram, derived independently by Russell and Danish astronomer Ejnar Hertzsprung, classifies stars by size, brightness, and temperature. It is a graph whose vertical axis gives the absolute magnitudes of stars and whose horizontal axis gives their surface temperatures.

Absolute magnitude measures how bright stars would look if they were all at the same distance from Earth. The graph places the dimmest stars at the bottom and the brightest stars at the top. Since large stars have more surface area from which to broadcast light, they are at the top of the graph, and smaller stars are found at the bottom. Astronomers can deduce surface temperature from a star's spectrum—its light separated into its colors, like a rainbow. The horizontal axis orders the temperatures from the hottest at the right to the coolest at the left.

About 90 percent of stars fall on a gentle, elongated S-curve from the top left of the graph to the bottom right. This curve is known as the main sequence of stars. Three groups of stars are found away from the main sequence: Cool supergiant and giant stars are above it, and hot dwarfs are beneath it.

Bibliography

The Life and Death of Stars. Donald A. Cooke. New York: Crown, 1985.

One Hundred Billion Suns: The Birth, Life, and Death of Stars. Rudolf Kippenhahn. New York: Basic Books, 1983.

Stars. James B. Kaler. New York: Scientific American Books, 1992.

Early Life

Born in Oyster Bay, New York, in 1877, Henry Norris Russell grew up in a well-educated, cultured family of Scottish descent. Alexander G. Russell, his father, was a Presbyterian minister; Eliza Norris, his mother, was a gifted amateur mathematician, as was her mother. They taught Henry at home until he was twelve years old, developing his own considerable mathematical talent.

In 1889, the family moved to Princeton, New Jersey. Russell later studied at Princeton University, being graduated with the highest possible honor, insigne cum laude, in 1897. In 1899, he earned a doctorate from Princeton as well, having already published articles on what was to become a major focus of his scientific career, binary stars.

Stellar Parallax

Russell went to Cambridge University in England for postgraduate studies in 1901. There, he became the research assistant of Arthur R. Hinks at the Cambridge Observatory. They used photographs of stars to measure the shift in position of nearby stars as seen from different vantage points in the earth's orbit, a technique called stellar parallax.

In 1908, Russell married Lucy May Cole, with whom he had three daughters and a son. In 1908, he also became an assistant professor of astronomy at Princeton, where he had served as an instructor since 1905. In 1911, he became a full professor, and he was named director of the university's observatory the next year.

Measuring Stars

Russell devoted much of his career to studying binary star systems in which the stars eclipse each other. He analyzed the varying light intensity from these eclipsing binaries and the shapes of their orbits. His findings supplied methods for determining the density of stars and for calculating their mass.

Russell is best known, however, for discovering the relation between a star's absolute magnitude and its spectral type, which he announced in a 1913 lecture. The relation contradicted the prevailing theory describing the evolution of stars and inspired him to publish his own theory. He proposed that stars change

(AP/Wide World Photos)

in appearance, shrinking when they heat up or expanding when they cool down. Although briefly influential, the theory was later discarded.

Spectra and Atomic Structure

Russell also studied the spectra of stars extensively to infer their chemical composition. Turning his attention to the sun, he astonished his colleagues by claiming, correctly, that hydrogen is the most common solar element. He also used detailed spectral analyses of elements to infer how electrons absorb and emit light.

Throughout his long career, Russell wrote popular articles on astronomy for *Scientific American*, as well as one for the *Encyclopedia Britannica*. By the time that he retired in 1947, Russell was popularly regarded as the dean of American astronomy. He was also laden with honorary doctorates and gold medals from scientific societies. He served as president of the American Association for the Advancement of Science and was a member of the National Academy of Sciences. Russell died in 1957.

Bibliography
By Russell
"On the Origin of Binary Stars," *Astrophysical Journal*, 1910

Determination of Stellar Parallax, 1911

"On the Determination of the Orbital Elements of Eclipsing Variable Stars," *Astrophysical Journal*, 1912

"Relations Between the Spectra and Other Characteristics of the Stars," *Nature*, 1914

Astronomy: A Revision of Young's Manual of Astronomy, 1926-1927 (2 vols.; with Raymond Smith Dugan and John Quincy Stewart)

Fate and Freedom, 1927

"On the Composition of the Sun's Atmosphere," *Astrophysical Journal*, 1929

The Solar System and Its Origin, 1935

The Masses of the Stars, with a General Catalog of Dynamical Parallaxes, 1940 (with C. E. Moore)

About Russell
"Henry Norris Russell (1877-1957)." Katherine G. Kron. *Vistas in Astronomy* 12 (1970).

The History of Astronomy from Herschel to Hertzsprung. Dieter B. Herrmann. Cambridge, England: Cambridge University Press, 1984.

The Norton History of Astronomy and Cosmology. John North. New York: W. W. Norton, 1995.

(Roger Smith)

Ernest Rutherford

Areas of Achievement: Chemistry and physics

Contribution: Among Rutherford's accomplishments was the identification of radioactivity as a process in which the emanation of radioactive particles results in the transmutation of the element. He also discovered the nucleus of the atom.

Aug. 30, 1871	Born in Spring Grove (later Brightwater), near Nelson, New Zealand
1887	Enters Canterbury College in Christchurch, New Zealand
1895	Receives a scholarship to Trinity College, Cambridge University
1897	Distinguishes alpha and beta radiation from uranium
1898	Becomes a professor of physics at McGill University, Canada
1902	Explains the nature of radioactivity
1902	Becomes a Fellow of the Royal Society of London
1904	Receives the Rumford Medal of the Royal Society of London
1907	Named a professor of physics at the University of Manchester
1908	Wins the Nobel Prize in Chemistry
1909	Describes the alpha particle
1911	Discovers the atomic nucleus
1914	Knighted
1919	Becomes Cavendish Professor of Physics at Cambridge
1919	Detects protons in the nucleus
1931	Named Baron Rutherford of Nelson
Oct. 19, 1937	Dies in Cambridge, England

Early Life

Ernest Rutherford was born in a rural area near Nelson, New Zealand When he was fifteen, his family moved to Pungarehu, where his father raised flax and ran a mill.

Rutherford won a scholarship to Canterbury College in New Zealand and then another to the Cavendish Laboratories at Cambridge University in England. The director of the laboratory was the great physicist Sir J. J. Thomson, the discoverer of the electron. Rutherford was twenty-four when he arrived at Cambridge in 1895.

The Transformation of Elements

At around that same time, two discoveries were made on the continent of Europe that determined the course of Rutherford's research at Cambridge. Wilhelm Röntgen discovered X rays in 1895, and Antoine-Henri Becquerel discovered radioactivity in 1896. Thomson invited Rutherford to join him in studying these two new phenomena.

(The Nobel Foundation)

In his experiments with uranium, Rutherford observed two different kinds of radioactive emanations, which he called alpha radiation and beta radiation. Paul Villard, a French scientist, is credited with the discovery of the third kind of radioactive emanation, gamma radiation. Work by others showed that beta rays are electrons and gamma rays are electromagnetic radiation.

The nature of alpha particles was determined later by Rutherford. In working with the radioactive element thorium, he observed that it gave off a gaseous substance, also radioactive, that he called thorium emanation. He enlisted the aid of a brilliant chemist, Frederick Soddy, to isolate and identify it.

Soddy was able to demonstrate that thorium emanation was a gas that was chemically unre-

The Nucleus and the Structure of the Atom

Rutherford's discovery of the nucleus prompted the suggestion of a planetary model for atomic structure.

At the time that Ernest Marsden and Hans Geiger did their experiment bombarding a gold foil with alpha particles, Sir J. J. Thomson's theory of the structure of the atom was dominant. The proton had not yet been discovered, so there was no reason to believe that the atom contained positive particles. Thomson proposed that the atom consisted of a jellylike mass of positively charged material, with the electrons embedded in it in a definite arrangement.

Rutherford followed his discovery of the nucleus with a planetary model for the atom, in which electrons orbit the nucleus just as the planets orbit the sun. Even those who advanced the model, however, recognized that it had a serious flaw. The laws of electrodynamics state that a moving electric charge must constantly give off energy. As the electron orbited the nucleus, its energy would steadily decrease. This means that it should spiral down into the nucleus as it lost energy, resulting in the collapse of the atom.

Niels Bohr spent the first half of 1912 in Rutherford's laboratory in Manchester, so he was quite familiar with Rutherford's model. He was also familiar with the ideas of Max Planck on the quantization of energy. Bohr was able to combine the two to solve the problem of the collapse that would occur with the Rutherford model.

Bohr applied the quantization hypothesis to the atom by proposing that the electron could occupy only certain orbits around the nucleus. Each orbit would have a definite energy depending on its distance from the nucleus. Since the electron can have only certain energies, it could not steadily lose energy as it orbits. It could only change its energy by single jumps between orbits.

Using concepts of classical Newtonian physics and the quantum hypothesis, Bohr was able to calculate the energies of the orbits in the hydrogen atom. These energies correlated very well with the experimentally determined atomic spectrum of hydrogen that had previously been determined. With this verification of its validity, the Bohr-Rutherford model for the atom gained quick acceptance.

Since its development in 1869, chemists had been using the concept of the periodic table developed independently by Dmitry Mendeleyev and Julius Lothar Meyer to systematize and predict the reactivity of the chemical elements. No basic understanding existed, however, of why the elements in groups in the periodic table had similar properties and chemical reactivities. When the electrons in elements were assigned to the energy levels in the Rutherford-Bohr model, it was found that the outer electrons were in parallel energy levels. It then became apparent that the reactivities of the elements were determined by their outer electron configurations.

This focus on the electrons as the determinants of chemical reactivity led to enormous growth in the field of mechanistic studies of chemical reactions. The greater understanding of how chemical reactions occur has facilitated the development of materials such as polymers and pharmaceuticals that are so important in modern life.

Bibliography
Explaining the Atom. Selig Hecht. New York: Viking Press, 1964.
The World of the Atom. Henry Boorse and Lloyd Motz, eds. 2 vols. New York: Basic Books, 1966.

active, just like the recently discovered family of inert gases. The gas that was called thoron is now known to be an isotope of radon with a mass of 220. In giving off its radiation, thorium is converted into a different element, radon. In radioactive disintegration, nature does spontaneously what chemists had thought impossible.

Rutherford then set out to determine the nature of alpha particles. The charge-mass ratio of the alpha particle had led him to suspect that it was a doubly positively charged helium atom. He confirmed this hypothesis by collecting alpha particles and condensing the resulting gas. The atomic spectrum of the gas confirmed that it was helium.

The Nucleus of the Atom

Rutherford's next two major discoveries involved the use of alpha particles. When a beam of alpha particles was passed through a thin gold foil, the image of the beam on a detection screen appeared to be fuzzy. This result seemed to indicate that something was producing small deflections of the alpha particles as they passed through the atoms in the gold foil. Careful follow-up work by Hans Geiger and Ernest Marsden gave a surprising result. For one in every eight thousand alpha particles, the deflections were not small but exceeded ninety degrees.

Rutherford calculated that a charge greater than one hundred times that of the electron would be needed to produce so great a deflection of the charged alpha particles. It took him two years to arrive at a model that would explain this entirely unexpected result. The atom had to have a very tiny nucleus that contained all of its positive charge.

At this time, the nature of the positive charge in the atom was not known. No positive particle corresponding to the electron had been discovered. Additional experiments using alpha particles led to Rutherford's last great achievement, the discovery of the proton.

When he passed alpha particles through nitrogen gas, he was able to detect the presence of protons, positively charged hydrogen atoms. Since there was no hydrogen gas present to account for the production of the protons, Rutherford concluded that the nucleus of the nitrogen atom must contain protons. The collision of the very energetic alpha particle with the nitrogen nucleus resulted in the expulsion of a proton.

Rutherford realized that this nuclear reaction resulted in the conversion of nitrogen to oxygen. He was therefore the first to carry out the artificial transmutation of an element. This was the last work that Rutherford did at the University of Manchester.

In 1919, he succeeded Thomson as Cavendish Professor of Physics at Cambridge. Rutherford died on October 19, 1937. He is buried in Westminster Abbey close to the grave of Sir Isaac Newton.

Bibliography
By Rutherford
Radioactivity, 1904
Radioactive Transformations, 1906
Radioactive Substances and Their Radiations, 1913
The Newer Alchemy, 1937

About Rutherford
Lord Rutherford. Norman Feather. London: Priory Press, 1973.
Rutherford. David Wilson. Cambridge, Mass.: MIT Press, 1983.

(Francis P. Mac Kay)

Johannes Robert Rydberg

Areas of Achievement: Mathematics and physics

Contribution: Rydberg discovered the fundamental pattern for spectral lines.

Nov. 8, 1854	Born in Halmstad, Sweden
1873	Completes the Gymnasium at Halmstad and enters the University of Lund
1875	Receives a bachelor's degree in philosophy from Lund
1879	Receives a Ph.D. in mathematics from Lund
1880	Appointed a lecturer in mathematics at Lund
1882	Becomes lecturer in physics at Lund
1890	Publishes "Recherches sur la constitution des spectres d'émission des éléments chimiques" (research on the constitution of emission spectra of chemical elements)
1892	Promoted to assistant at the Physics Institute
1901	Appointed provisional and then permanent professor of physics at Lund
1906	States for the first time the rule that two, eight, and eighteen elements are found in the first three periods of the periodic table
1913	Expands his rule regarding the periodic table to include the rare earths
1919	Elected a foreign member of the Royal Society of London
Dec. 28, 1919	Dies in Lund, Sweden

Early Life

Johannes Robert Rydberg (pronounced "RIHD-behr"), a Swedish physicist, was born in Halmsted in 1854 and was educated at the Gymnasium there. In 1873, he began his studies at the University of Lund, where he spent the rest of his career.

After defending his dissertation on the construction of conic sections, Rydberg was awarded a doctorate in mathematics. He was appointed lecturer in mathematics and later lecturer in physics at the University of Lund.

Dmitry Mendeleyev's periodic table of elements greatly fascinated the young Rydberg. He believed that the periodicity in the table could be used to explain atomic spectra and ultimately the structure of the atom itself. He dreamed of one day using it to explain the properties of the elements.

Atomic Spectral Formula

Rydberg's most important contribution was his formula for atomic spectral lines. At the time he began his work, voluminous spectral data were available in the scientific literature,

(AIP Niels Bohr Library, W. F. Meggers Collection)

Atomic Spectra

Rydberg was the first person to devise a universal empirical formula for the wavelengths of the spectrum of the elements in the periodic table.

When a gas of a particular element is excited by applying a high voltage, the gas emits light of a characteristic color. When this light is analyzed with a spectroscope, a series of discrete lines is observed. This series of lines is called an emission spectrum. Each element has a unique spectrum that acts like a fingerprint, making it possible to determine which elements are present in a gas mixture.

Rydberg devised a universal empirical formula for the spectra of elements in the periodic table. His formula expresses the wave number, the reciprocal of the wavelength, as a difference between two spectral terms and contains what is called the Rydberg constant. Later, Niels Bohr showed that the Rydberg constant can be written in terms of fundamental physical constants.

Bohr also offered a physical reason for the regularities in a spectrum. When electrons make a transition from a higher to a lower energy state, they emit radiation of a certain wavelength that depends on the difference in energy between the two levels. Since each atom has its own set of energy levels, it is able to make only certain transitions—hence, the uniqueness of a given spectrum.

Although Rydberg never understood why the spectral lines he saw formed the patterns that he identified, his formula contains most of the basic properties of spectral series. Rydberg's formula proved useful in determining the electronic shell structure of the elements.

Bibliography

Fundamentals of Physics. R. M. Eisberg. New York: John Wiley & Sons, 1964.

Modern Physics. Paul A. Tipler. New York: Worth, 1978.

Spectroscopy and Molecular Structure. Gerald W. King. New York: Holt, Rinehart and Winston, 1964.

but it was unclear how spectral lines were related to one another. Despite the imprecise data at his disposal, Rydberg saw hidden regularities.

He noted that atomic spectral lines fall into three categories: strong, persistent lines, which he called "principal"; weaker but well-defined lines, which he called "sharp"; and broader lines, which he called "diffuse." He also noticed the regular behavior of the wave number of these spectral lines.

With this information, he devised a formula that could be used to find the wavelengths of all series and all elements. Spectral lines could be predicted before they were seen.

The Periodic Table

In 1897, Rydberg correctly suggested that elements in the periodic table should be organized by atomic number rather than by atomic weight. He did not realize at the time that the atomic number corresponds to the number of protons in the atom. In 1906, he also noted that there were two, eight, and eighteen elements in the first three periods of the periodic table. By 1913, he showed that the fourth period could also be included in this pattern. This observation proved useful in understanding the electronic shell structure of the elements.

Not all of Rydberg's ideas were correct. Because of the way in which he organized the elements of the periodic table, it seemed to him that two elements in the first period were still undiscovered. He suggested the names "nebulium" and "coronium" for the missing elements which he thought were responsible for spectral lines that are present in nebulas and in the solar corona. These elements were later identified as ionized oxygen and nitrogen and highly ionized iron.

Although Rydberg failed to fulfill his dream, he was able to devise a simple universal relationship for atomic spectra. This formula has greatly impacted the understanding of atomic structure. Rydberg died in Lund, Sweden, in 1919 at the age of sixty-five.

Bibliography

By Rydberg

"Recherches sur la constitution des spectres d'émission des éléments chimiques," *Kungliga Svenska vetenskapsakademiens handlingar*, 1890

"On the Structure of the Line-Spectra of the Chemical Elements," *Philosophical Magazine*, 1890

"Contributions à la connaissance des spectres linéaires," *Ofversigt af K. Vetenskapsakademiens förhandlingar*, 1893

"The New Elements of Cleveite Gas," *Astrophysical Journal*, 1896

"The New Series in the Spectrum of Hydrogen," *Astrophysical Journal*, 1897

"On the Constitution of the Red Spectrum of Argon," *Astrophysical Journal*, 1897

"La Distribution des raies spectrales," *Rapports présentés au Congres international de physique*, 1900

Elektron, der erste Grundstoff, 1906

"Untersuchungen über das System der Grundstoffe," *Acta Universitatis lundensis*, 1913

"The Ordinals of the Elements and the High-Frequency Spectra," *Philosophical Magazine*, 1914

About Rydberg

Proceedings of the Rydberg Centennial Conference on Atomic Spectroscopy. Bengt Edlen, ed. Lund, Sweden: C. W. K. Gleerup, 1955.

"Rydberg: The Man and the Constant." Sister St. John Nepomucene. *Chymia* 6 (1960).

Swedish Men of Science, 1650-1950. Sted Lindroth, ed. Trans. by Burnett Anderson. Stockholm: Almquist & Wiksell, 1952.

(Kathleen Duffy)

Florence Rena Sabin

Areas of Achievement: Bacteriology, cell biology, immunology, and medicine

Contribution: Sabin studied the anatomy of the brain, the development of blood cells and lymph vessels, the immune system, and the tuberculosis bacterium. She also greatly improved the quality of public health in Colorado.

Nov. 9, 1871	Born in Central City, Colorado
1884-1889	Attends Vermont Academy
1889-1893	Attends Smith College, earning a bachelor's degree
1893-1895	Teaches mathematics at Wolfe Hall, a boarding school in Denver, Colorado
1895-1896	Teaches zoology at Smith
1896-1900	Attends The Johns Hopkins University, in Baltimore, Maryland, earning an M.D.
1901	Serves an internship at Johns Hopkins
1902	Employed as an assistant in anatomy at Johns Hopkins
1903-1905	Works as an associate in anatomy at Johns Hopkins
1905-1917	Promoted to associate professor
1917-1925	Serves as a professor of histology at Johns Hopkins
1925-1938	Joins the Rockefeller Institute
1938	Retires to Colorado
1944-1947	Becomes head of the Subcommittee on Public Health of the Colorado Post-War Planning Committee
1947-1951	Serves as manager of the Denver Health and Welfare Department
Oct. 3, 1953	Dies in Denver, Colorado

Early Life
Florence Rena Sabin was born in Central City, Colorado, on November 9, 1871. Her father, George Kimball Sabin, lacking funds to pursue a medical education, had moved from Vermont to Colorado in 1860 to work as a mining engineer. Her mother, Serena Miner Sabin, also from Vermont, had moved to Colorado in 1867 to become a teacher.

When her mother died, Sabin and her sister were sent to Wolfe Hall, a boarding school in Denver, Colorado. The sisters later lived with an uncle in Chicago and with grandparents in Vermont. After attending the Vermont Academy, in Saxtons River, from 1884 to 1889, Sabin entered Smith College, in Northampton, Massachusetts, where she earned a bachelor's degree in 1893.

Years at Johns Hopkins
After teaching mathematics at Wolfe Hall from 1893 to 1895 and zoology at Smith from 1895 to 1896, Sabin entered the medical school of The Johns Hopkins University in Baltimore, Maryland. She earned an M.D. there in 1900. While still a student, she constructed a three-dimensional model of the brain that was adapted into a popular textbook in 1901.

Sabin served an internship at Johns Hopkins in 1901 and became the school's first female faculty member in 1902, when she was made an assistant in anatomy. She was promoted to associate in anatomy in 1903, to associate professor in 1905, and to professor of histology in 1917. Her most notable research at Johns Hopkins involved the development of lymph vessels in embryos and the origins of blood cells.

New York and Colorado
Sabin left Johns Hopkins in 1925 to join the Rockefeller Institute for Medical Research in New York City. While at the institute, she organized its department of cellular studies. She conducted research into the immune system's response to the tuberculosis bacterium and the role of white blood cells in immunity.

Sabin retired from the institute in 1938 and returned to Colorado to live with her sister. She remained active on several national advisory boards. In 1944, she was appointed head of the Subcommittee on Public Health of the Colorado Post-War Planning Committee. In 1947, the passage of laws that she had promoted transformed Colorado's outdated and ineffective public health system into one of the nation's best. As manager of the Denver Health

The Origin of Lymph Vessels in Developing Embryos

Lymph vessels were once believed to originate in the tissues of developing embryos and grow toward the veins. Sabin discovered that they originate in the veins and grow toward the tissues.

Lymph is a fluid that surrounds body tissues. It transports proteins and fluids from the tissues to the blood in order to maintain fluid balance. The white blood cells found in lymph remove bacteria, viruses, and other foreign objects.

The white blood cells in lymph consist of macrophages and lymphocytes. Macrophages ingest foreign objects. Lymphocytes bind to foreign objects and carry them to lymph nodes. Lymph nodes contain large numbers of cells that destroy foreign objects by engulfing them or by releasing antibodies.

Lymph is carried from the tissues to the veins by lymph vessels. It is moved through these ves-

sels by the normal activity of the body's muscles, which squeeze the vessels and cause the lymph to flow.

The exact manner in which lymph vessels develop within embryos was unknown until the beginning of the twentieth century. They were formerly believed to originate in tissues and develop toward veins. By injecting the lymph vessels of pig embryos with a dye, Sabin proved that they originate from veins and develop toward tissues.

Bibliography
The Developing Human. Keith L. Moore. Philadelphia: W. B. Saunders, 1973.
Human Embryology. William J. Larsen. New York: Churchill Livingstone, 1993.
Lymph and the Lymphatic System. Hymen S. Mayerson, ed. Springfield, Ill.: Charles C Thomas, 1968.

(Library of Congress)

and Welfare Department from 1947 to 1951, she made similar reforms in the city's public health system. For her work in public health, she won the Lasker Award from the Albert and Mary Lasker Foundation in 1951.

Sabin died of a heart attack on October 3, 1953. Buildings were named in her honor at Smith College and the medical school of the University of Colorado. A statue of Sabin was placed in the U.S. Capitol among a group of statues representing two outstanding individuals from each state.

Bibliography
By Sabin
An Atlas of the Medulla and Midbrain, 1901
"The Origin and Development of the Lymphatic System" in *Manual of Human Embryology*, 1912 (Franz Kiebel and Franklin P. Mall, eds.)
Franklin Paine Mall: The Story of a Mind, 1934

About Sabin
Florence Sabin: Colorado Woman of the Century. Eleanor Bluemel. Boulder: University of Colorado Press, 1959.
The Story of Dr. Florence Sabin: Probing the Unknown. Mary K. Phelan. New York: Thomas Y. Crowell, 1969.
Women in Science: Antiquity Through the Nineteenth Century. Marilyn Bailey Ogilvie. Cambridge: MIT Press, 1986.

(Rose Secrest)

Carl Sagan

Areas of Achievement: Astronomy, biology, cosmology, and physics

Contribution: Sagan's greatest contribution to science came from his ability to communicate astronomical concepts to the general public. He participated in many space missions as a consultant.

Nov. 9, 1934	Born in Brooklyn, New York
1959	Becomes involved with the U.S. space program
1960	Awarded a doctorate in astronomy and astrophysics from the University of Chicago
1960-1962	Named Miller Resident Fellow in Astronomy at the University of California, Berkeley
1962-1968	Becomes an assistant professor of astronomy at Harvard University
1968	Named an associate professor of astronomy at Cornell University
1969	Wins NASA's Apollo Achievement Award
1972	Given NASA's Exceptional Scientific Achievement Award
1973	Publishes *The Cosmic Connection*
1977	Becomes David Duncan Professor of Astronomy and Space Sciences at Cornell
1978	Wins a Pulitzer Prize for *The Dragons of Eden*
1980	Publishes the book *Cosmos*, based on his popular television series
1983	Publishes predictions concerning the effects of "nuclear winter"
1991	Receives the Mazursky Award from the American Astronomical Association
Dec. 20, 1996	Dies in Seattle, Washington

Early Life

Carl Edward Sagan was born in Brooklyn, New York, on November 9, 1934, to Samuel and Rachel Sagan. At the age of five, Carl boldly announced that he hoped to be an astronomer some day. This wish developed from his early fascination with the stars and later from reading science fiction. Among his favorite books was a series of novels that described various heroic adventures that took place on Mars; they were written by Edgar Rice Burroughs, the creator of Tarzan. The images of Mars that Burroughs created would stay with Sagan forever.

Sagan's childhood took place during World War II. It was a time of rapid technological change. The war demanded new technology, and scientists produced faster airplanes and more powerful rockets. After the war, many of those who had created the weapons of war turned their attention to the heavens. The first rockets were reaching the edge of space, and a huge astronomical telescope had been built in California. The universe was opening itself up to human exploration, and Sagan was ready to join in.

A Life of Science

In the early 1950's, many notable scientists either taught at or were associated with the University of Chicago. Among the more famous scientists there were Hermann Joseph Muller, Joshua Lederberg, and Harold C. Urey, all Nobel Prize winners. It proved to be an irresistible environment for Sagan, and he went on to complete all of his academic degrees at the University of Chicago.

He achieved an A.B. degree in 1954, a B.S. in 1955, an M.S. in physics in 1956, and a doctorate in astronomy and astrophysics in 1960. His doctoral dissertation was entitled "Physical Studies the Planets." His adviser was the astronomer Gerard Peter Kuiper. No doubt it was Kuiper who galvanized Sagan's interest in the planets, and it was Lederberg who encouraged him to become involved in the United States' growing space program.

A Rising Star

Sagan's professional career began after his 1960 graduation from the University of Chicago. He accepted a position as a resident fellow in astronomy at the University of California, Berkeley (UCB), that would last from 1960 to 1962. From UCB, it was on to Harvard University, where he accepted an assistant professorship. He would remain at Harvard from 1962 to 1968.

After Harvard, it was on to Ithaca, New York, to become an associate professor of astronomy at Cornell University. Later, he was promoted to professor and made associate director of the Center for Radiophysics and Space Research. In 1977, he was named the David Duncan Professor of Astronomy and Space Science.

An Award-Winning Career

It was the extremely successful Mariner 9 mission to Mars that propelled Sagan into prominence. Up to this time, he had been involved in the planning stages of several planetary probes and had worked with the results of those missions for the National Aeronautics and Space Administration (NASA). He had established himself as a respected scientist. The photographs of volcanoes and huge canyons on Mars caught the public's attention.

People wanted to know more about the planets, and science needed a spokesperson. Sagan was chosen to appear in several educational films that described the Mars discover-

Mariner 9 returned pictures of Mars that were used to create this mosaic view of the planet, with the north pole at the center. (National Aeronautics and Space Administration)

Exploration of the Planet Mars

Prior to 1965, the planet Mars was first believed to be very Earth-like, and then the Mariner 4 spacecraft showed it to be similar to Earth's moon in appearance. All that changed when the Mariner 9 probe revealed huge canyons, giant volcanoes, and a system of river channels. Scientists such as Sagan quickly realized that Mars was a unique world unto itself.

For centuries, Earth-based astronomers studied the planet Mars and observed dramatic color variations that were believed to represent changing seasons. The reddish surface would apparently turn green as the polar ice caps melted during the martian summer. It was believed that melted water from the ice caps would nourish plant life. Some astronomers such as Percival Lowell imagined a system of canals conveying water from the polar regions to the dry equatorial zones. All of this fired the imagination of Earth-bound astronomers and science-fiction writers alike.

The first three spacecraft to Mars—Mariners 4, 6, and 7—all showed a surface terrain very similar to the moon. The planet appeared to be covered by craters of all sizes, and there was no evidence of the rivers, forests, or large bodies of water for which scientists had hoped. For all practical purposes, Mars could have been just another moon. The unfortunate thing about these three Mariner missions was that they were designed to take a series of pictures as they flew by the planet. As luck would have it, they each flew over some of the least interesting terrain on Mars. It would be left up to Mariner 9 to show the real Mars.

Mariner 9 reached Mars in 1971 and photographed the surface from orbit. During its operational lifetime, it discovered a volcanic region populated by four huge volcanoes. The largest, Olympus Mons, is thought to be the largest volcano in the solar system. It is a basaltic volcano similar to the Hawaiian Island volcanoes on Earth, but twice their size. Nearby, an enormous canyon system named Valles Marineris stretched across the equatorial region. In length, Valles Ma-

rineris is approximately ten times the size of the Grand Canyon, in Arizona.

Perhaps the most significant discovery made by the Mariner 9 was the presence of long river channels resembling those of the largest river systems on Earth. The only difference was that the ones on Mars are totally dry. Apparently, water has not flowed across the surface of Mars for millions of years.

Following the successful Mariner 9 mission, Project Viking landed two robot spacecraft on Mars in 1976. Their primary mission was to answer one of the fundamental questions about Mars: Is life present? Throughout his life, Sagan had asked this question, and he hoped that Viking would provide the answer. Unfortunately, the Viking experiments provided no conclusive evidence for life, but they did not rule it out either.

Mars was Sagan's best hope for finding evidence of extraterrestrial life during his lifetime. His search for life did not end with Mars; he looked to the moons of Jupiter and Saturn for possible evidence. As for intelligent life, Sagan joined with fellow Cornell scientist Frank Drake to develop the Search for Extra Terrestrial Intelligence (SETI) Project, a radio search. At the time of Sagan's death in 1996, scientists thought that they had found evidence of a fossil life form in a meteorite believed to have come from Mars. It may not have been conclusive proof, but it certainly fired the imagination of Carl Sagan.

Bibliography

Exploring the Planets. W. Kenneth Hamblin and Eric H. Christiansen. New York: Macmillan, 1990.

Mars: The Story of the Red Planet. Peter Cattermole. London: Chapman & Hall, 1992.

The Planets: A Guided Tour of Our Solar System Through the Eyes of America's Space Probes. Nigel Henbest. London: Viking Press, 1992.

Space Probes. Nigel Henbest. London: Viking Press, 1992.

ies. His mannerism and delivery worked well and led to many appearances on television talk shows. Sagan quickly became the public's expert on astronomy and space issues. He was in great demand.

In 1973, Sagan's book *The Cosmic Connection* was published. In this book, he conveyed his philosophy about the universe and humanity's place in it. It was an instant success, and several other books would follow. His book *The Dragons of Eden* (1977) won a Pulitzer Prize in 1978. Perhaps Sagan's most influential work was the television series *Cosmos*, which ran on public television in 1979. Millions of people heard about everything from the origin of life to the detection of black holes in space. In each episode, Sagan's personality captivated the audience. It is estimated that, by the mid-1990's, more than 600 million people had viewed the *Cosmos* series.

Throughout his career, Sagan received numerous awards for his work in both science and literature. Perhaps his greatest recognition came from the people whom he inspired to go into careers in science. He promoted science for the average person and made it enjoyable. Although many of his colleagues argued that he presented scientific speculation as fact, he certainly inspired people's imaginations. Without a scientist such as Sagan, millions of people would never have experienced the wonders of astronomy.

Sagan died in 1996 at the age of sixty-two. In July, 1997, after the Mars Pathfinder mission successfuly reached the surface of that planet, the lander for the Sojourner rover was officially christened the Sagan Memorial Station in his honor.

Bibliography
By Sagan

Intelligent Life in the Universe, 1966 (with I. S. Shklovskii)

The Cosmic Connection, 1973

The Dragons of Eden, 1977

Broca's Brain: Reflections on the Romance of Science, 1979

Cosmos, 1980

Contact: A Novel, 1985

A Path Where No Man Thought: Nuclear Winter and the End of the Arms Race, 1990 (with Richard Turco)

(Library of Congress)

Pale Blue Dot: A Vision of the Human Future in Space, 1994

About Sagan

"Carl Edward Sagan: Astronomer and Popularizer of Science." A. R. Hogan. *Ad Astra* 3 (1991).
"In the Valley of the Shadow." Carl Sagan. *Parade Magazine*. March 10, 1996.
"A Man Whose Time Has Come." Rian Ridpath. *New Scientist* 63 (July 4, 1974).
"Shadows of Forgotten Ancestors." Roger Lewin. *New Scientist* 137 (January 16, 1993).
The Visible Scientists. Rae Goodell. Boston: Little, Brown, 1975.

(Paul P. Sipiera)

Abdus Salam

Area of Achievement: Physics
Contribution: Salam formulated a theory that encompasses both the electromagnetic and the so-called weak interaction of elementary particles. In addition, he carried out fundamental work on the renormalization theory of mesons and the concepts of supersymmetry and superspace.

Jan. 29, 1926	Born in Jhang-Maghiana, Punjab, India (now in Pakistan)
1946	Attends St. John's College, Cambridge University, England
1952	Receives a Ph.D. in physics and mathematics from the Imperial College of Science and Technology in London
1955	Attends United Nations Atoms for Peace conference
1957	Appointed a professor of theoretical physics at the Imperial College of Science and Technology
1963-1975	Serves as a member of the United Nations Advisory Committee for Science and Technology
1964	Founds and directs the International Center for Theoretical Physics in Trieste, Italy
1965-1969	Independently develops the electroweak theory with Steven Weinberg and Sheldon L. Glashow
1979	Awarded the Nobel Prize in Physics with Glashow and Weinberg
1988	Delivers the Dirac Memorial Lecture on the unification of fundamental forces
Nov. 21, 1996	Dies in Oxford, England

Early Life

Abdus Salam (pronounced "saw-LAWM") was born in Jhang-Maghiana, Punjab, India (now in Pakistan), on January 29, 1926. He attended the Government College at Lahore and received a baccalaureate degree in mathematics. A scholarship from the government of India in 1946 enabled him to attend St. John's College at Cambridge University in England. At Cambridge, Salam took the mathematics and physics tripos and came out a Wrangler by receiving a first-class degree.

Even though tripos firsts were expected to conduct experiments, Salam realized that he lacked the qualities required for experimental work. As a result, he decided to concentrate on quantum electrodynamics, a relatively new field at the time. Following the suggestion of Paul Matthews, a fellow student at Cambridge,

(The Nobel Foundation)

Salam began research on an unsolved problem in quantum electrodynamics and developed the theory of renormalization of mesons in only five months, which became his doctoral dissertation.

Lahore and Cambridge

In 1951, Salam returned to the Government College at Lahore (now in Pakistan) as a professor of mathematics and taught there for three years. The research atmosphere was dismal, however, with no journals, no tradition for postgraduate work, and no possibility of attending any conferences.

Faced with this dilemma, Salam returned to Cambridge as a lecturer in mathematics. In 1957, he was appointed a professor of theoretical physics at the Imperial College of Science and Technology in London and threw himself passionately into physics. Over the next ten years, he invented the two-component theory of the neutrino and worked on particle symmetries and gauge theories with the intent of unifying the weak and electromagnetic forces.

An International Center for Physics

In 1960, Salam conceived the idea of setting up the International Center for Theoretical Physics (ICTP), with funds from the international community, such as from the United Nations. Despite the indifference of the developed countries, Salam's persistence was finally rewarded in 1964 when the ICTP was established, with Salam as its director, in Trieste, Italy.

The Electroweak Theory

In the period between 1965 and 1969, Salam worked on the problem of unifying the theories of the weak forces and the electromagnetic forces associated with subatomic particles. The early work was carried out independently by Sheldon L. Glashow in the United States and Salam and John Ward in England.

This research culminated toward the end of the 1960's with the development of the so-called electroweak theory independently by Salam and Steven Weinberg, a theoretical physicist from the United States. Many of the postulates of the theory have been subsequently verified. In addition, the theory led

The Electroweak Theory

The electroweak theory encompasses both the electromagnetic interaction and the weak interaction of elementary particles. The weak force, a million times weaker than the electromagnetic force, acts only across distances smaller than the atomic nucleus, while the electromagnetic force can extend across substantial distances.

The electroweak theory arose out of efforts to develop a self-consistent theory for the weak force, analogous to the successful quantum theory of the electromagnetic force called quantum electrodynamics (QED) developed in the 1940's. There are two basic requirements for the theory. First, it should be gauge invariant; in other words, it should behave the same way at different points in space and time. Second, it should be renormalizable; in other words, it should not contain any nonphysical infinities.

The strong force binds particles together: By binding quarks within protons and neutrons, it helps form nuclei. Nuclei can, however, break apart naturally in the process known as radioactivity. The most basic beta decay involves the transmutation of a neutron into a proton, accompanied by the release of an electron for charge balance. In 1930, Wolfgang Pauli showed that the neutron also emits a neutral, massless particle called a neutrino.

The rates of nuclear decay indicate that the force involved in beta decay is weaker than the force that binds nuclei together. The physicist Hideki Yukawa originally tried to explain both phenomena—weak decays and strong bindings—with the exchange of a single type of particle.

In 1934, Enrico Fermi incorporated the neutrino particle into his theory for beta decay, drawing on an analogy with QED as did Yukawa. Fermi, however, regarded the emission of the neutrino and electron by a neutron as analogous to the emission of a photon by a charged particle, and he did not invoke a new exchange particle. Fermi's theory successfully described nuclear beta decay and received additional support with the subsequent discoveries of the pion and the muon.

The nature of the weak force began to be revealed in 1956, when Tsung-Dao Lee and Chen Ning Yang discovered that the decay of the strange particles could be explained if one assumed that the weak nuclear force does not respect a symmetry property called parity.

This parity violation and a universal form of weak interaction were combined in 1958 by Murray Gell-Mann and Richard P. Feynman. They discovered the vector minus axial (V-A) vector theory, which proved successful at relatively low energy interactions. It was clear, however, that the theory might go wrong at high interaction energies. The problems with V-A theory were related to a basic requirement of quantum field theory—the existence of a gauge boson, or messenger particle, to carry the force.

Early in the 1960's, Sheldon Glashow in the United States and Salam and John Ward in England began working with a combination of two symmetry groups. This requires four spin 1 messenger particles, two electrically neutral and two charged. The theory still required the messengers to be massless, which was acceptable for photons but not for the messengers of the weak force.

Near the end of the 1960's, Salam and Steven Weinberg independently realized how to introduce massive messenger particles into the theory while preserving gauge symmetry. The answer was based on the concept of hidden symmetry discovered by Peter Higgs. In 1971, Gerard van't Hooft[Henricus] proved that the Salam-Weinberg theory was renormalizable, and the electroweak theory became acceptable.

By the late 1970's, enough evidence had been gathered to confirm both charged and neutral current interactions, two processes essential for the validity of the electroweak theory.

Bibliography

Unification of Fundamental Forces: First 1988 Dirac Memorial Lecture. Abdus Salam. Cambridge, England: Cambridge University Press, 1990.

to the discovery in 1983 of so-called charged W and neutral Z particles.

Scientific Research in Developing Countries

In addition to his research activities, Salam was active in his efforts to upgrade the educational, scientific, and development policies of Pakistan and other developing countries. To this end, he founded the Third World Academy of Sciences and served as the president of the Third World Network of Scientific Organizations.

Salam died on November 21, 1996, in Oxford, England, at the age of seventy.

Bibliography

By Salam

"The Path-Integral Quantization of Gravity" (with J. Strathlee) in *Aspects of Quantum Theory*, 1972 (Salam and Eugene P. Wigner, eds.)
Supergravities in Diverse Dimensions, 1989 (as editor, with Ergin Sezgin)

About Salam

"Abdus Salam." In *The Nobel Prize Winners: Physics*, edited by Frank N. Magill. Pasadena, Calif.: Salem Press, 1989.
Conference on Highlights of Particle and Condensed Matter Physics. Singapore: World Scientific Publications, 1994.

(Monish R. Chatterjee)

Jonas Salk

Areas of Achievement: Immunology, medicine, and virology
Contribution: Salk developed the first effective vaccine used for the prevention of poliomyelitis. His earlier research also contributed to an understanding of influenza infection.

Oct. 28, 1914	Born in New York, New York
1934	Graduated from the City College of New York
1939	Receives a medical degree from the New York University School of Medicine
1942	Given a National Research Fellowship at the University of Michigan
1947-1964	Appointed head of the Virus Research Laboratory at the University of Pittsburgh
1952	Tests his first prototype vaccine against poliomyelitis at the Watson Home for Crippled Children, reporting his results in *Journal of the American Medical Association*
1954	Nationwide field trials of the Salk vaccine are conducted
Apr. 12, 1955	The success of vaccine field trials is announced
1963	Appointed director of the Salk Institute for Biological Studies in La Jolla, California
1972-1973	Publishes *Man Unfolding* and *The Survival of the Wisest*
June 23, 1995	Dies in La Jolla, California

Early Life

Jonas Edward Salk was born in New York City in 1914, the eldest of three sons of Daniel and Doris Salk. Soon after his birth, the family moved to an apartment in the Bronx, where Salk attended school.

Salk showed early promise in the sciences, attending Townsend Harris High School, which specialized in teaching students with exceptional potential. At the time, Salk was more interested in a law career. After enrolling in City College, however, at the age of fifteen, he observed the beauty and intricacies of science and decided to make medicine his career.

After his graduation from City College in 1934, he enrolled in the New York University (NYU) School of Medicine. Salk received his medical degree in 1939.

Research in Virology

During Salk's first year in medical school, he was awarded a fellowship for studies in protein chemistry, learning techniques that he would use in his vaccine studies in later years. He also had the opportunity to meet Thomas Francis, Jr., a prominent bacteriologist who had recently arrived from the Rockefeller Institute. Francis was interested in the production of vaccines, particularly one against influenza (flu). In this manner, Salk was introduced both

(National Archives)

to the concept of immunology and to the intricacies of virus replication.

One summer, working in a laboratory at Woods Hole, Massachusetts, while in medical school, Salk met Donna Lindsay, a student in the School of Social Work at NYU. They married in 1939, the day after Salk's graduation. Although the marriage ended in divorce in 1968, they had three sons. In 1970, Salk married painter François Gilot, a former companion of artist Pablo Picasso and the mother of two of Picasso's children.

Salk had hoped to remain in New York and sought a residency at various hospitals, but the anti-Semitic attitude that was pervasive at the time prevented any such appointment. Instead, when Salk was awarded a National Research Council Fellowship in 1942, he joined Francis in Michigan. During this period, he perfected his techniques of vaccine production, developing with Francis several commercial flu vaccines. The work was considered as an important contribution to the war effort during World War II.

The Fight Against Poliomyelitis

In 1947, Salk joined the staff at the University of Pittsburgh as director of virus research. He also changed the emphasis of his work from influenza to the study of poliomyelitis (polio).

An ancient disease, paralytic polio was a devastating illness. Striking seemingly without warning, polio could leave a child paralyzed for life, or even dead. In the early decades of the twentieth century, polio epidemics came with increasing regularity; in 1952, 58,000 cases and 3,000 deaths were reported in the United States alone.

A Polio Vaccine

Salk turned his attention to vaccine production in 1949. First, he inactivated the virus by treating it with formalin. Once the logistics were worked out, Salk was ready to test a preliminary vaccine on children. After determining its safety by first injecting himself and his family, Salk tested the prototype vaccine at the Watson Home for Crippled Children in 1952. It proved successful.

In 1954, Salk began nationwide field studies of his vaccine. The trials were coordinated

A Polio Vaccine

Salk developed the first effective vaccine that would immunize persons against poliomyelitis.

Although several attempts had been made before Salk to develop a vaccine to combat poliomyelitis (polio), none were both safe and effective. As the twentieth century progressed, the disease struck with increasing frequency. As many as 50,000 persons, mostly children, were being diagnosed with the illness.

It was against this background that Salk began his work. The initial problem was that of organization. Research into the disease and its cause was disjointed. It was only in the early 1940's that the fecal-oral method of transmission became understood. By the late 1940's, it was still unclear exactly how many strains of the virus even existed; some estimates placed the number in the hundreds.

Such background research was important. As early as 1931, Frank Macfarlane Burnet had shown that monkeys which were immune to one type of the virus could still be infected by other strains. Funded through the National Foundation for Infantile Paralysis, often referred to as the March of Dimes, Salk and other scientists became part of a team to determine how many varieties of the virus existed.

Salk and his coworkers began his typing study in 1949. By the end of the year, much of the confusion had been cleared up; Salk had found that despite dozens of minor varieties, there were likely only three strains of the virus.

The problem of varieties was now manageable. Instead of dozens of vaccines, Salk would only have to find a way to grow and inactivate the three major strains of virus. The critical problem here was the necessity that in order to produce millions of doses of vaccine, one had to first have a means to grow the virus. Since the polio virus would only grow in primates, much research required the use of live monkeys.

Other scientists solved the problem. At the same time that Salk was perfecting his viral techniques with Thomas Francis, Jr., John Enders at Harvard had developed a method for growing the polio virus in laboratory cells. Salk availed himself of this technique, growing large quantities of the virus in monkey kidney cells in laboratory vessels.

Once Salk had his virus, he extensively tested inactivation procedures using the chemical formalin. Carried out correctly, the procedure resulted in a vaccine composed of dead virus that could still immunize people effectively.

Although Salk's killed vaccine has been largely replaced by an attenuated form developed by Albert Sabin, its use in the 1950's and 1960's saved the lives of thousands of children. By the 1990's, poliomyelitis had been eradicated in the Western Hemisphere.

Bibliography
Margin of Safety: The Story of Poliomyelitis Vaccine. John Wilson. London: Collins, 1963.

Polio and the Salk Vaccine. New York: Public Affairs Committee, 1955.

Polio and the Salk Vaccine: What You Should Know About It. Alton Blakeslee. New York: Grosset and Dunlap, 1956.

through the University of Michigan. Some 1.8 million children would participate.

On April 12, 1955, Salk announced the results of the field trials at a press conference held in Ann Arbor, Michigan. The vaccine worked. Its efficacy became clear in subsequent years, as the number of new polio cases dropped sharply each year.

A Hero to the Public
Salk became a household name to the public. Although nominated, he was never named a Nobel laureate, but among his honors were a Presidential Citation in 1955, a Congressional Gold Medal in 1955, the Albert Lasker Award in 1956, the Mellon Institute Award in 1969, and the Presidential Medal of Freedom in 1977. He received the Robert Koch Medal from Germany, while France named him a Chevalier de la Legion d'Honneur. His greatest reward was the knowledge of being instrumental in the eradication of a terrible disease.

In 1963, funded in part through the March of Dimes, the Salk Institute for Biological Studies

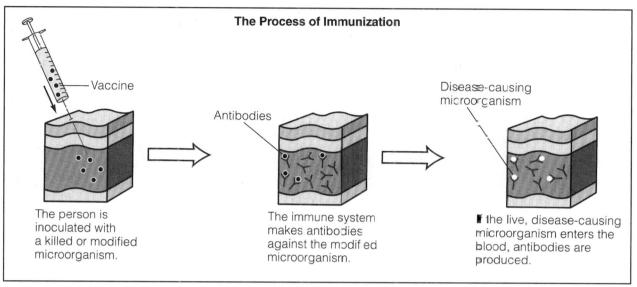

The Process of Immunization

Vaccine

The person is inoculated with a killed or modified microorganism.

Antibodies

The immune system makes antibodies against the modified microorganism.

Disease-causing microorganism

If the live, disease-causing microorganism enters the blood, antibodies are produced.

(Hans & Cassady, Inc.)

was built in La Jolla, California, a suburb of San Diego. Salk became its first director.

The Salk Institute

Salk had long hoped for an institute where outstanding scientists could gather for research on topics important for humanity. The creation of the Salk Institute was the fulfillment of a lifetime dream. Situated on land overlooking the Pacific Ocean, the institute became a magnet for many important scientists.

During his later years, Salk carried out research on a variety of subjects such as cancer and acquired immunodeficiency syndrome (AIDS). He also found more time to relax with his hobbies: poetry and painting. Weakened by congestive heart failure, Salk died on June 23, 1995.

Bibliography
By Salk
"A Simplified Procedure for Titrating Hemagglutinating Capacity of Influenza Virus and Corresponding Antibody," *Journal of Immunology*, 1944
"Studies in Human Subjects on Active Immunization Against Poliomyelitis: 1. A Preliminary Report of Experiments in Progress," *Journal of the American Medical Association*, 1953

"Considerations in the Preparation and Use of Poliomyelitis Virus Vaccine," *Journal of the American Medical Association*, 1955
"Persistence of Immunity After Administration of Formalin-Treated Poliovirus Vaccine," *Lancet*, 1960
"A Review of Theoretical, Experimental, and Practical Considerations in the Use of Formaldehyde for the Inactivation of Poliovirus," *Annals of New York Academy of Sciences*, 1960 (with J. Gori)
Man Unfolding, 1972
The Survival of the Wisest, 1973
"Control of Influenza and Poliomyelitis with Killed Virus Vaccines," *Science*, 1977 (with Darrell Salk)
"Noninfectious Poliovirus Vaccine" (with Jacques Drucker) in *Vaccines*, 1988 (Stanley Plotkin and Edward Mortimer, Jr., eds.)

About Salk
Breakthrough: The Saga of Jonas Salk. Richard Carter. New York: Trident Press, 1966.
A History of Poliomyelitis. John Paul. New Haven, Conn.: Yale University Press, 1971.
The Polio Man: The Story of Dr. Jonas Salk. John Rowland. New York: Roy, 1961.

(Richard Adler)

Allan Rex Sandage

Areas of Achievement: Astronomy and cosmology

Contribution: Sandage continued Edwin Hubble's work using the 200-inch telescope on Mount Palomar to map the distances to galaxies, in order to determine the rate of expansion of the universe and the decrease in that rate over time. He did important work in theoretical cosmology, putting it into a form that can be verified by observations.

June 18, 1926	Born in Iowa City, Iowa
1944	Enters Miami University, Ohio, in physics
1945	Drafted into the U.S. Navy
1948	Receives an A.B. degree in physics from the University of Illinois
1952	Joins the staff of Mount Wilson Observatory
1953	Receives a Ph.D. in astronomy from the California Institute of Technology (Caltech)
1958	Given the Helen Warner Prize from the American Astronomical Society
June 8, 1959	Marries Mary Lois Connelly
1960	Becomes the first person to identify a quasar
1961	Publishes a paper suggesting that the universe began from a "big bang"
1963	Awarded the Eddington Medal of the Royal Astronomical Society
1973	Wins the Russell Prize of the American Astronomical Society
1991	Awarded the Crafoord Prize, astronomy's equivalent to the Nobel Prize

Early Life

Allan Rex Sandage was born in Iowa City, Iowa, on June 18, 1926. His father was the son of a farmer and was the first in his family to go to high school; from there, he went on to college and then to the University of Iowa for a Ph.D. Sandage's mother was born in the Philippines, where her father was the commissioner of education. Upon their return to the United States, Sandage's grandfather became president of Graceland College, the church school of the Reorganized Church of Latter-day Saints.

Neither of Sandage's parents were particularly interested in science. Sandage first became interested in the subject when he was in the fourth grade, living in Philadelphia. His friend had a telescope, and Sandage soon was spending his weekends at the Franklin Institute and the planetarium. James Stokely, then head of the Fels Planetarium, became his hero. From that time, Sandage felt compelled to be an astronomer, reading astronomy texts and teaching himself.

Sandage began college at Miami University, in Ohio, where his father was a professor in advertising. He studied physics as a route to astronomy. Ray Edwards, his physics professor, was inspirational to Sandage and very demanding. Not naturally analytical, Sandage found that physics did not come easily.

In 1944, he was drafted by the U.S. Navy and served for two years repairing electronic equipment. Afterward, Sandage attended the University of Illinois, where he received his bachelor's degree in physics in 1948. For his junior and senior theses, he worked for Robert Baker, the only astronomer at Illinois at that time. Baker taught him observational techniques that would later prove invaluable to Sandage.

Sandage entered the California Institute of Technology (Caltech), in Pasadena, California. That year, an astronomy program was begun, and he became one of the first class of astronomy graduate students, receiving his Ph.D. in 1953. In the summer of 1950, he worked for Edwin Powell Hubble observing a bright, variable star. When Hubble suffered his first heart attack, in 1952, Sandage took a position at the Mount Wilson Observatory, overlooking Pasadena, as a research assistant to Hubble.

The Big Bang

Sandage's work supported the theory that the universe began with a "big bang," in which all the matter now existing exploded outward from a single point to create galaxies.

Cosmology is the study of the structure and evolution of the universe. The foundation of this field is based on two assumptions: The universe is homogeneous, having the same composition everywhere, and the universe is isotropic, appearing the same in any direction. These two assumptions form the cosmological principle.

It was assumed until the twentieth century that the universe was also infinite in extent and unchanging in time. If this is true, and assuming the cosmological principle holds, then the universe should be uniformly populated with galaxies filled with stars. No matter where one looks, one should see a star. The night sky should be as bright as the surface of the sun. That it is not, a situation known as Olbers' paradox, implies that either the universe is finite or it changes over time.

In 1912, Vesto Melvin Slipher discovered that almost every spiral galaxy has a redshifted spectrum. This shift of the spectra toward lower frequencies indicates that the galaxies are moving away from Earth, just as the sound of a siren shifts to a lower pitch as the source moves past the observer. In the 1920's, Edwin Powell Hubble began plotting the recessional velocities of the galaxies versus their distances from Earth and noticed a relationship. Called Hubble's law, it states that velocity is directly proportional to distance, where the constant of proportionality is called Hubble's constant:

velocity = Hubble's constant × distance

Considerable work has been done to determine Hubble's constant accurately, since it is a fundamental quantity. Using the simple definition of velocity, the time taken for the galaxies to reach their present distances from Earth is as follows:

$$time = \frac{distance}{velocity}$$
$$= \frac{1}{Hubble's\ constant}$$

Using the accepted value for Hubble's constant, this time is about 13 billion years. The implication of Hubble's law is important: The universe is expanding. The fact that the time of expansion is the same for all galaxies implies that at some time, all the galaxies were at the same place. It is believed that about 13 billion years ago, everything—matter and radiation—was confined to a single point that exploded, flying apart at high speeds in all directions. This gigantic explosion is called the big bang.

The big bang theory helps resolve Olbers' paradox. Whether the universe is infinite or finite does not matter since it is finite in age. One can only see a finite part of the night sky, since the light from any object more than 13 billion light years away has not reached Earth yet. The idea that everything seems to expand from a single point seems to violate homogeneity. The only explanation is that the big bang is an expansion of the universe itself, much like a balloon inflating.

To understand the idea of the entire universe shrinking to a point requires general relativity, the idea that the presence of matter causes a curvature of space. This curvature of space implies that there are three possible futures for the universe: It can continue to expand forever at a constant rate, it can expand for a while and then start to deflate, or it can expand forever but at a decreasing rate. The correct alternative depends on the density of the universe, which determines the gravitational attraction between objects. Unfortunately, the determination of the universe's density is not an easy task.

Will the universe end as a small, dense point as it began, or will it expand forever? The task of present-day astronomers is to determine the answer to this question.

Bibliography

Astronomy Today. Eric Chaisson and Steve McMillan. Englewood Cliffs, N.J.: Prentice Hall, 1993.

Encyclopedia of Physics. Rita G. Lerner and George L. Trigg, eds. New York VCH, 1990.

The Left Hand of Creation: The Origin and Evolution of the Expanding Universe. John D. Barrow and Joseph Silk. New York: Basic Books, 1983.

Red Giants and White Dwarfs. Robert Jastrow. New York: W. W. Norton, 1990.

Mount Wilson

Although his dissertation had been in the area of stellar evolution, Sandage felt compelled to carry on the work of Hubble, since there was no one else to do it. He undertook the measurement of the speeds and distances to galaxies. This information is necessary to determine the rate of expansion of the universe and the rate of deceleration of that expansion. Although an observational astronomer by training and inclination, Sandage taught himself cosmology (the study of the structure and origin of the universe) in order to carry on this work.

In 1960, Sandage, along with radioastronomer Thomas Matthews, optically identified a distant, starlike object as the source of the radio waves being emitted from that part of the sky—the first identification of an individual object that was a radio source. This very unusual object, which was not identifiable as a star or a galaxy, became known as a quasi-stellar object, or quasar.

In 1961, Sandage presented a paper that summarized his and Hubble's work into a theoretical cosmology that could be verified by observations. He described the universe as made of dynamic galaxies that are moving away from Earth at velocities proportional to their distances. This motion, he claimed, was most likely caused by some primordial "big bang."

Honors

Sandage's contributions have been widely recognized. He received numerous awards from astronomical societies around the world. His greatest award came from the Royal Swedish Academy when it bestowed on him the Crafoord Prize. Astronomy is not a science honored with a Nobel Prize; the Crafoord Prize is considered to be astronomy's equivalent.

Although Sandage spent his entire career at Mount Wilson and Palomar Observatories, visiting lectureships and fellowships took him around the world. A dedicated Christian, Sandage maintained that "life is not a dreary accident." His childlike awe of the universe was replaced by "the awe of the enormous complication and order of the world of physics."

Bibliography

By Sandage

"The Color-Magnitude for Globular Cluster M3," *Astronomical Journal*, 1953

The Hubble Atlas of the Galaxies, 1961

"The Ability of the 200-inch Telescope to Discriminate Between Selected World Models," *Astrophysical Journal*, 1961

"The Light Travel Times and the Evolutionary Correction to Magnitudes of Distant Galaxies," *Astrophysical Journal*, 1961

"The Change of Redshift and Apparent Luminosity of Galaxies Due to the Deceleration of Selected Expanding Universes," *Astrophysical Journal*, 1962

"Evidence from the Motions of Old Stars that the Galaxy Collapsed," *Astrophysical Journal*, 1962 (with O. J. Eggen and D. Lynden-Bell)

"Cosmology: A Search for Two Numbers," *Physics Today*, 1970

A Revised Shapley-Ames Catalog of Bright Galaxies, 1981 (with G. A. Tammann)

(California Institute of Technology)

Atlas of Galaxies: Useful for Measuring the Cosmological Distance Scale, 1988 (with John Bedke)

About Sandage

Lonely Hearts of the Cosmos: The Story of the Scientific Quest for the Secret of the Universe. Dennis Overbye. New York: HarperCollins, 1991.

Origins: The Lives and Worlds of Modern Cosmologists. Alan Lightman and Roberta Brawer. Cambridge, Mass.: Harvard University Press, 1990.

(Linda L. McDonald)

Frederick Sanger

Areas of Achievement: Chemistry and genetics

Contribution: Sanger was the first person to receive two Nobel Prizes in Chemistry. The first was awarded for his determination of the complete amino acid sequence of the protein insulin. Sanger's role in the development and use of a novel method to sequence deoxyribonucleic acid (DNA) resulted in a second Nobel Prize.

Aug. 13, 1918	Born in Rendcombe, Gloucestershire, England
1939	Graduated from St. John's College, Cambridge University
1943	Earns a Ph.D. from St. John's College
1944-1951	Awarded a medical research fellowship at Cambridge
1951	Joins the Medical Research Council
1953	Determines the entire amino acid sequence of insulin
1958	Begins work on sequence determination for DNA
1962-1983	Serves as head of the Medical Research Council Laboratory of Molecular Biology
1976	Awarded the William Hardy Prize of the Cambridge Philosophical Society
1977	Deduces the entire DNA sequence of bacterial virus Phi X 174
1977	Awarded the Copley Medal by the Royal Society of London
1980	Wins the Nobel Prize in Chemistry for his work with nucleic acids
1984	Elucidates the entire DNA sequence of the Epstein-Barr virus

Early Life

Frederick Sanger was born in Rendcombe, Gloucestershire, England, on August 13, 1918. The son of a physician, he spent his early education at Bryanston School. Sanger attended Cambridge University for his entire university education, earning first a bachelor of arts degree in 1939 and then a doctorate in 1943 through St. John's College at Cambridge. He continued his biochemistry research at Cambridge as a research fellow until 1951, at which time he joined the staff of the Medical Research Council.

Tools to Study Proteins

During the 1940's and 1950's, much chemical research focused on the hereditary molecule

---

Determining the Amino Acid Sequence of a Protein

The amino acid sequence of a protein gives vital information about its function. This sequence can be determined by the degradation and separation of the protein's components.

In order to understand the function of important proteins, it is critical to know their chemical makeup. Sanger summoned his formidable scientific skills to tackle the task of determining that makeup.

Proteins consist of subunits called amino acids, of which there are twenty different types in human beings. Sanger chose to use the protein hormone insulin, which was isolated from the pancreatic tissue of cattle, as his first subject.

Sanger had discovered a particular chemical called 2,4-dinitrofluorobenzene (later known as Sanger's reagent) that binds to one end of a chain of amino acids. Using an enzyme, a type of protein that cuts other proteins between amino acids, Sanger cut the insulin molecule into small pieces. He labeled one end with Sanger's reagent, then cut the fragments into even smaller, single amino acid pieces with the enzymes.

The individual amino acids from one labeled section were separated by a process called paper chromatography. The amino acid mixture was placed in a solvent, and the end of a strip of paper was placed in the solvent and amino acid mixture. Capillary action drew the solvent mixture up along the length of the paper, and the amino acids were separated according to their size and charge. Based on the distance of migration, the chemically labeled amino acids could be identified.

After repeating this time-consuming and tedious process literally hundreds of times, with long and short pieces, Sanger was able to fit together the puzzle of information into a cohesive picture that revealed the linear sequence of amino acids. It took Sanger and his collaborators eight years to map the fifty-one amino acids of insulin. The results of this monumental undertaking were published in 1953, and Sanger was awarded the Nobel Prize in Chemistry for this work in 1958.

In addition, Sanger was able to determine that there were small but significant sequence differences between insulin derived from pigs, horses, sheep, and whales. This finding had particular significance for human beings, for when human insulin was sequenced, it was found to differ slightly from that of pigs. For many years, individuals suffering from insulin-dependent diabetes had only insulin derived from pigs as a source of medicine. The systems of many individuals rejected the pig insulin because of these differences.

Sanger's methods led to the rapid sequencing of many other proteins, including enzymes of important biochemical pathways. His work paved the way for the first artificial synthesis of a protein, insulin, by 1964. His perseverance and scientific insight have led to the sequencing and synthesis of many proteins and a means to explore their functions.

Bibliography

Biology. Neil Campbell. 4th ed. Redwood City, Calif.: Benjamin/Cummings, 1996.

Genetics: The Mystery and the Promise. Francis Leone. Blue Ridge Summit, Pa.: McGraw-Hill, 1992.

Molecular Biology of the Gene. James D. Watson et al. 4th ed. Menlo Park, Calif.: Benjamin/Cummings, 1987.

Molecular Design of Life. Lubert Stryer. New York: W. H. Freeman, 1989.

The Process of Sequencing DNA

Deoxyribonucleic acid (DNA) is made of a linear sequence of four different subunits called nucleotides. The sequence can be determined by complex biochemical methods.

DNA is made of repeating chemical subunits called nucleotides. The four nucleotides—adenine, cytosine, guanine, and thymine—differ by the type of organic base attached. With the advent of recombinant DNA technology in the mid-1970's, it became critical to determine the nucleotide base sequences of the DNA that makes up genes. A chemical degradation method existed soon afterward, but it was a slow process entailing months to sequence a single gene.

Sanger and his colleagues developed a method that revolutionized DNA sequencing. In a test tube, a single strand of DNA, along with all the chemical components to synthesize a complementary strand, was mixed with a radioactively labeled nucleotide. Also included were nucleotides that would halt the DNA synthesis at one of the four types of nucleotides. After millions of molecules were replicated, the newly synthe-

sized DNA strands were separated by gel electrophoresis. The gels were then exposed to X-ray film, which indicated the location of the radioactive tags and the lengths of DNA fragments.

Sanger's sequencing method was adapted to become automated, so that the sequence of thousands of bases could be determined in a single day. This development had a major impact on the swiftness of sequencing. It has facilitated the sequencing of the entire human genome—a formidable three billion nucleotides—through the Human Genome Project of the National Institutes of Health and the Department of Energy.

Bibliography

An Introduction to Genetic Engineering. Desmond S. T. Nicholl. Cambridge, England: Cambridge University Press, 1994.

Molecular Biology of the Gene. James D. Watson et al. 4th ed. Menlo Park, Calif.: Benjamin/Cummings, 1987.

Molecular Design of Life. Lubert Stryer. New York: W. H. Freeman, 1989.

The Four Nucleotides Found in DNA

deoxyribonucleic acid (DNA) and proteins, the products of DNA. Sanger's primary research interest at this time was in determining the exact amino acid sequence of a protein.

In the early 1940's, he experienced a significant breakthrough toward that end. In 1945, he devised a method to use the chemical 2,4-dinitrofluorobenzene, later known as Sanger's reagent, to label one end of the protein chain. Sanger could then use acid to break up the protein into smaller fragments.

Other scientists had designed a method to separate the individual amino acids from a mixture called paper chromatography. Sanger planned to break down the sequence of amino acids partially, attach his reagent to one end, break these labeled fragments down to individual amino acids, and separate them using paper chromatography. In this way, he could identify which amino acid was labeled. By painstakingly repeating this procedure many times, he could generate overlapping fragments of the protein and then, as if working a jigsaw puzzle, deduce the order of the amino acids.

Insulin

The protein hormone insulin had been isolated some twenty-five years earlier and was known to consist of two connected chains of fifty amino acids. Sanger chose this protein, which he obtained from the pancreatic tissue of cattle, for his sequence experiment.

For eight years, Sanger repeated the finely detailed, meticulous, and somewhat tedious work of the sequencing procedure. When he had deduced the sequence of many short fragments of insulin, he put together a map of how they fit together in longer fragments and then finally the intact molecule. The results of his stunning achievement were published in 1953.

The scientific community acknowledged this major breakthrough by awarding to Sanger the Nobel Prize in Chemistry in 1958.

Sequencing Nucleic Acids

In the late 1950's, the direction of Sanger's research turned toward sequencing DNA, the chemical molecule that specifies the amino acid sequence of proteins, and ribonucleic acid (RNA), which is an intermediate between DNA and proteins. James D. Watson and Francis Crick had elucidated the three-dimensional structure of DNA in 1953, and by this time many enzymes that interact with DNA had been identified. Sanger combined these fields to develop methods to sequence nucleic acids.

Sanger first worked on RNA, which occurs in relatively short lengths. He then moved on to DNA, which can have up to one hundred million base units per chain. For experimental tools, Sanger used a combination of enzymes that cut or extend DNA, radioactive labeling, and separation of DNA bases on gels, a procedure called electrophoresis.

By 1977, Sanger and his colleagues had obtained the complete sequence of the bacterial virus Phi X 174, which is composed of more than 5,400 DNA bases. Carried on by this success, they soon were able to sequence the DNA of human mitochondria (cellular organelles), which are more than 17,000 bases long, followed by the relatively huge human virus known as Epstein-Barr, with 150,000 bases. In 1980, Sanger was awarded a second Nobel Prize for his nu-

(The Nobel Foundation)

cleic acid work, jointly with Paul Berg and Walter Gilbert. Sanger became the first person to receive two Nobel Prizes in Chemistry and one of the elite few to receive two awards.

Legacy
The fundamental principles discovered by Sanger stimulated many areas of research. The sequences of a tremendous number of proteins and genes are now known. Many proteins essential for human life can be synthesized or produced through recombinant DNA technology. The methods that he developed greatly accelerated research in the fields of medicine and physiology, and the fruits of this research will continue to have a major impact for generations to come.

Bibliography
By Sanger
"The Amino Acid Sequence in the Glycyl Chain of Insulin: The Identification of Lower Peptides from Partial Hydrolysates," *Biochemical Journal*, 1953 (with E. O. P. Thompson)
"A Rapid Method for Determining Sequences in DNA by Primed Synthesis with DNA Polymerase," *Journal of Molecular Biology*, 1975 (with A. R. Coulson)
DNA Sequencing with Chain-Terminating Inhibitors," *Proceedings of the National Academy of Sciences*, 1977 (with S. Nicklen and Coulson)
"Nucleotide Sequence of Bacteriophage λ DNA," *Journal of Molecular Biology*, 1982 (with Coulson, G. F. Hong, D. F. Hill, and G. B. Petersen)
Selected Papers of Frederick Sanger, with Commentaries, 1996 (as editor, with Margaret Dowding)

About Sanger
The Eighth Day of Creation. Horace Freeland Judson. New York: Simon & Schuster, 1979.
"Frederick Sanger." In *The Nobel Prize Winners: Chemistry*, edited by Frank N. Magill. Pasadena, Calif.: Salem Press, 1990.
Frederick Sanger: The Man Who Mapped Out a Chemical of Life. Alvin Silverstein. New York: John Day, 1969.

(Karen E. Kalumuck)

Horace Bénédict de Saussure

Areas of Achievement: Botany and earth science

Contribution: Saussure was a pioneer in the scientific study of the structure and physical environment of mountains.

Feb. 17, 1740	Born at Conches, near Geneva, Switzerland
1759	Receives a degree in philosophy from the Academy of Geneva
1760	Travels to Chamonix to collect plants for Albrecht von Haller
1762	Appointed a professor at the Academy of Geneva
1765	Marries Albertine Amélie Boissier
1768-1769	Goes on a Grand Tour and meets French and British scientists
1771-1773	Journeys to Italy, touring Mount Vesuvius, climbing Mount Etna, and revising his theory of mountain uplift
1774-1776	Serves as rector of the Academy of Geneva
1779	Publishes the first volume of *Voyages dans les Alpes*
1787	Ascends to the summit of Mont Blanc and carries out scientific measurements there
1788	Elected a foreign member of the Royal Society of London
1791	Named a foreign member of the French Académie des Sciences
1794	Partially paralyzed by a stroke
1796	Publishes the third and fourth volumes of *Voyages dans les Alpes*
Jan. 22, 1799	Dies in Geneva, Switzerland

Early Life

Horace Bénédict de Saussure (pronounced "soh-SEWR"), the son of a patrician intellectual, was born at Conches, his father's estate near Geneva, Switzerland. From childhood, he was fascinated by the views of the Alpine peaks, dominated by the distant Mont Blanc, the highest peak in the Alps. By the time that he was eighteen, he had climbed most of the mountains in the vicinity of Geneva and was determined to explore and study the higher peaks.

Saussure studied philosophy and natural history at the Academy of Geneva (later the University of Geneva), being graduated in 1759 with a dissertation on the heat of the sun. He was encouraged in his study of natural history by his uncle, naturalist Charles Bonnet, and by the noted physician and botanist Albrecht von Haller. In 1760, Saussure traveled to Chamonix, at the base of Mont Blanc, to collect Alpine plants and birds for von Haller. That year, he offered a reward to the first person to climb Mont Blanc. His treatise on the leaves and petals of plants helped him obtain a professorship at the academy in 1762.

Travels in the Alps and Abroad

Saussure made several trips to Chamonix, attracted by the vast glaciers of the valley. His attempts to understand the movement of glaciers and the complex Alpine formations awakened his interest in geology. In 1767, he again toured the Mont Blanc region, making observations on magnetism and atmospheric conditions using instruments that he devised himself.

Saussure was exposed to new ideas when he and his wife toured France, England, and Scotland in 1768-1769. He discussed the origin of basalt with French geologists, and, in London, he met Benjamin Franklin and members of the Royal Society of London. From 1771 until 1773, he was in Italy, where he studied marine sediments and climbed Mount Vesuvius and Mount Etna.

A Passion for Mountains

From 1774 to 1789, Saussure made the major expeditions that he described in his classic four-volume work *Voyages dans les Alpes* (1779-1796). He found mountain climbing exhilarating but was mainly occupied in examining details of structure and taking detailed field notes on the exposed beds of tilted and distorted stratified rocks. He hoped to develop a comprehensive theory of Earth's evolution.

In 1787, the year after two mountaineers finally reached the top of Mont Blanc, Saussure made the climb with eighteen guides and much equipment. He was watched from Chamonix by everyone who had a telescope. Saussure spent more than four hours at the summit on August 3, 1787, making many meteorological observations with a hygrometer, an

(National Library of Medicine)

Mountain Structure: Key to Earth's History

Saussure applied precise methods of observation and measurement to his studies of the Alps. He paved the way for future geologists who developed a more comprehensive theory of mountain uplift.

Saussure recognized that the vertical strata of mountain peaks had originally been laid down horizontally in the ocean, then uplifted by unknown forces, possibly volcanic and seismic action. To explain some of the complicated S-shaped and C-shaped folds, he introduced the idea of horizontal compression.

In *Voyages dans les Alpes* (1779-1796), he wrote of the effects of torrential streams in shaping valleys and in moving large rocks long distances. James Hutton used long passages from Saussure's work in his influential *Theory of the Earth* (1795) to illustrate the principle of uniformitarianism—that the earth is shaped by known processes acting over long periods of time.

Saussure invented the hair hygrometer to measure humidity. With this and other instruments, he accurately measured the atmospheric conditions that affect the earth. He was one of the first geologists to experiment on granite and other rocks to see if they could be melted or fused. He also popularized the term "geology."

Although he did not achieve the grand theory of the earth for which he had hoped, Saussure published an "Agenda" in the last volume of *Voyages dans les Alpes* outlining further work to be done.

Bibliography
The Earth and Its Mountains. Raymond A. Lyttleton. New York: John Wiley & Sons, 1982.
Geology in the Nineteenth Century: Changing Views of a Changing World. Mott T. Greene. Ithaca, N.Y.: Cornell University Press, 1982.

anemometer, a thermometer, and other instruments. This ascent gained for him an international reputation.

Last Years
Through membership on various civic councils, Saussure tried to introduce educational reforms and promote a more democratic government for Geneva. During the French Revolution, he lost much of his fortune invested in French securities. In 1794, at the age of only fifty-four, he was partially paralyzed by a series of strokes and died five years later.

Bibliography
By Saussure
Observations sur l'écorce des feuilles et des pétales des plantes, 1762

Essais sur l'hygrométrie, 1783
Relation abrégée d'un voyage à la cîme du Mont-Blanc, 1787
Voyages dans les Alpes, précédés d'un essai sur l'histoire naturelle des environs de Genève, 1779-1796

About Saussure
Founders of Geology. Archibald Geikie. 2d ed. 1905. Reprint. New York: Dover, 1962.
"Horace Bénédict de Saussure." Albert V. Carozzi. In *Dictionary of Scientific Biography,* edited by Charles Coulston Gillispie. New York: Charles Scribner's Sons, 1975.
The Life of Horace Bénédict de Saussure. Douglas W. Freshfield. London: E. Arnold, 1920.

(Peggy Champlin)

Arthur L. Schawlow

Areas of Achievement: Physics and technology

Contribution: A pioneer in the field of spectroscopy, Schawlow, with his colleague Charles H. Townes, was the first to propose a theory of operation and a structure for the laser.

May 5, 1921	Born in Mount Vernon, New York
1949	Earns a Ph.D. in physics from the University of Toronto
1949	Given a fellowship as a research associate at Columbia University
1951	Becomes a research physicist at Bell Telephone Laboratories
1958	With Charles H. Towne, conceives the laser
1960	Becomes a visiting associate professor at Columbia
1961	Appointed a professor of physics at Stanford University
1962	Awarded the Franklin Institute's Ballantine Medal
1963	Wins the Thomas Young Medal and Prize from the British Institute of Physics
1964	Receives the Liebman Memorial Prize from the Institute of Electrical and Electronic Engineers
1976	Given the Optical Society of America's Frederick Ives Medal
1977	Becomes a Marconi International Fellow
1981	Wins the Nobel Prize in Physics
1991	Awarded the National Medal of Science
1991	Named Emeritus Professor of Physics at Stanford

Early Life

Arthur Leonard Schawlow was born in Mount Vernon, New York. He was the son of immigrant parents—his mother was a native of Canada, his father of Latvia. Arthur grew up in Toronto and received a physics scholarship to the University of Toronto, where he not only distinguished himself in his studies but also found time to play jazz clarinet.

Schawlow received his bachelor's degree a few months before the United States entered World War II. During the war, he taught physics to military personnel at the University of Toronto. After the war, Schawlow continued his graduate work at the university, receiving his Ph.D. in physics in 1949.

Association with Townes

After receiving his doctorate, Schawlow was awarded a research scholarship at Columbia

(The Nobel Foundation)

Lasers

A laser is a light amplifier emitting a monochromatic, unidirectional, coherent beam with exceptionally high optical power density. Any material, if pumped hard enough, can "lase."

The individual atoms and molecules of ordinary incoherent light sources emit their radiation independently and spontaneously in a random manner. Because spatial and time relationships are not defined and predictable in incoherent light, it has an average intensity and a predominant wavelength based on the laws of probability. Coherent laser light has a predictable wavelength and color. Its intensity is high because all atoms of the material are stimulated to resonate in the same direction and in phase.

Schawlow and Charles H. Townes proposed building a laser using a resonant cavity bounded on two ends by parallel mirrors that could bounce light waves back and forth. One of the mirrors has a small transparent hole, allowing the amplified laser light to emerge when a certain energy threshold is passed. Cavity material and mirror spacing specify laser frequency.

An external energy source raises the energy levels of the electrons, stimulating photon emission. With each round trip through the cavity, a continuously amplified traveling wave is generated. Laser light is capable of attaining an intensity several orders of magnitude greater than the sun.

Bibliography
Advances in Laser Spectroscopy. F. T. Arecchi et al., eds. New York: Plenum Press, 1983.

Introduction to Lasers and Their Applications. D. C. O'Shea et al. Reading, Mass.: Addison-Wesley, 1977.

The Principles of Nonlinear Optics. Y. R. Shen. New York: John Wiley & Sons, 1984.

University, where he met Charles H. Townes, who was seven years Schawlow's senior. They began a long association in the measurement and analysis of radiation emitted by materials when stimulated by electromagnetic radiation. So close was this collaboration that Schawlow married Townes's sister in 1951.

In the same year that he married, Schawlow accepted a position with Bell Telephone Laboratories in northern New Jersey, but he continued to collaborate with Townes, who had worked for Bell during the war. In 1955, they published a fundamental text in the field of spectroscopy, *Microwave Spectroscopy*.

In 1958, Schawlow and Townes published their seminal paper, "Infrared and Optical Masers," describing the physical principles and structure of the laser (which stands for "light amplification by stimulated emission of radiation"). Using these principles, a fellow physicist, Theodore Maiman, successfully constructed the first laser device in 1960.

Stanford University
Schawlow left Bell Telephone Laboratories in 1961 to become professor of physics at Stanford University, where he was a zealous researcher who collaborated with nearly one hundred scientists in studying and writing about the atomic structure and chemical kinetics of all matter. By the 1990's, he had written more than two hundred papers on atomic molecular and solid-state spectroscopy and on lasers and quantum electronics. He became a world authority in laser spectroscopy, the use of the laser to probe and measure the basic properties of matter, and in the reactions and changes that occur within the atomic structure of a material.

A Teacher and Science Advocate
Schawlow was honored not only for his research skills but also for the positive influence that he exerted in promoting scientific ideas and attitudes among his students. His warm humor and obvious enthusiasm for scientific discovery proved inspirational to his students and to the general public. Through his television appearances and organizational work, he helped educate the public about the nature of physics.

Schawlow was formally recognized with the 1981 Nobel Prize in Physics, which he shared with Nicolaas Bloembergen and Kai M. Siegbahn. Townes, his longtime collaborator, had himself shared the 1964 Nobel Prize in Physics for his work with the maser ("microwave amplification by stimulated emission of radiation"). Many of Schawlow's colleagues considered his greatest achievement, however, to be the role of a humane teacher who instilled confidence into inexperienced and insecure graduate students and postdoctoral researchers.

Bibliography

By Schawlow

Microwave Spectroscopy, 1955 (with Charles H. Townes)

"Infrared and Optical Masers," *Physics Review*, 1958 (with Townes)

"Optical Resolution of the Lamb Shift in Atomic Hydrogen by Laser Saturation Spectroscopy," *Nature*, 1972

"From LASER to MASER" in *Impact of Basic Research on Technology*, 1973 (Behram Kursunoglu and Arnold Perlmutter, eds.)

"The Spectrum of Atomic Hydrogen," *Scientific American*, 1979 (with Theodor W. Hänsch and George W. Series)

About Schawlow

A History of Engineering and Science in the Bell System: Physical Sciences (1925-1980). S. Millman. Vol. 4. Edited by M. D. Fagen. New York: AT&T Bell Laboratories, 1983.

Lasers, Spectroscopy, and New Ideas: A Tribute to Arthur L. Schawlow. W. M. Yen and M. D. Levenson. New York: Springer-Verlag, 1987.

"The 1981 Nobel Prize in Physics." Boris P. Stoicheff. *Science* (November 6, 1981).

(Philip N. Seidenberg)

Matthias Jakob Schleiden

Areas of Achievement: Biology, botany, and cell biology

Contribution: A pioneering microscopist, theorist, and popularizer, Schleiden helped to unify the biological sciences and focus them on cellular processes.

Apr. 5, 1804	Born in Hamburg, Germany
1824-1826	Studies law in Heidelberg
1827-1831	Practices as an attorney
1831	Suffers a mental crisis and attempts suicide
1833	Gives up law to study botany
1838	First formulates his cell theory
1839	Moves to the University of Jena, where he receives his Ph.D. and a position as instructor
1842	Publishes a textbook elaborating his cell theory
1843	Receives an honorary degree in medicine and is elected to several scientific academies
1846	Promoted to professor of medicine
1848	Becomes involved in politics after the Revolutions of 1848
1850	Teaches botany and directs the botanical gardens at Jena
1862	Resigns from the University of Jena
1863	Teaches anthropology at the University of Dorpat
1864	Resigns from Dorpat and continues to write popular books on science and history
June 23, 1881	Dies in Frankfurt am Main, Germany

Early Life

Matthias Jakob Schleiden (pronounced "SCHLI-dehn") grew up in Hamburg, Germany, where his father was a prominent doctor. As a young man, he studied law and then practiced from 1827 until 1831.

Schleiden was unhappy and unsuccessful as a lawyer. He became depressed and ended his legal career by shooting himself in the head. Schleiden survived to begin a new life in science by going to Berlin in 1833 to study with physiologist Johannes Müller.

Cell Theory

Using the compound microscopes that had become available in the 1830's, Schleiden observed how plants grow and take form and realized the importance of cells. He discussed his findings with Müller's assistant, Theodor Schwann, who did similar work on animals, and together they developed the cell theory.

Schleiden's version of the theory appeared in the paper "Beiträge zur Phytogenesis" (1838). Translated into French in 1839 and into English in 1841 as "Contributions to Phytogenesis," it established his international reputation.

Jena

In 1839, Schleiden moved to the University of Jena in the German state of Saxe-Weimar, where he received his Ph.D. and began to teach. There, he wrote his textbook *Grundzüge der wissenschaftlichen Botanik* (1842; *Principles of Scientific Botany as an Inductive Science*, 1849), in which he discussed cell theory, microscopy, and scientific method. In this and other writings, he attacked or ridiculed anyone who did not live up to his methodological standards.

Even though he insulted some leading scientists, Schleiden received an honorary degree in medicine and was elected to scientific academies all over Europe in the 1840's. By 1850, he was full professor of botany and director of the botanical gardens at Jena and had the title of court counselor to the grand duke of Saxe-Weimar.

After the Revolutions of 1848, Schleiden was active in the moderate party, mediating between the citizens and the court at Weimar. His interest in research began to wane, and he concerned himself increasingly with science education and popularization. His books, magazine articles, and public lectures about botany,

---

The Cell Theory and Scientific Botany

The cell theory considered the cell to be the basic unit of life and the common building block of all plants and animals. For Schleiden, it was the key to a new, theoretical approach to botany.

The development of improved compound microscopes and their adoption by biologists in the 1830's and 1840's allowed a closer view of plant and animal anatomy than ever before and revealed the importance of cells. Schleiden, Theodor Schwann, and other microscopists found cells in every organism that they examined, and they discovered that even such noncellular structures as xylem in plants or cartilage in animals are produced by cells.

In the cell theory, Schleiden and Schwann stated their conclusion that the cell was the universal building block of plants and animals, as well as the fundamental unit of life. The theory helped to unify the biological sciences by identifying an important common feature of all living things. It also initiated a research program to explain the form and function of organisms by the activities of individual cells.

In Schleiden's words, traditional botany had overemphasized "hay collecting"—gathering and describing plants and organizing them in gardens and herbaria—and had neglected scientific explanation. Under the influence of Schleiden's compelling ideas and combative personality, botanists began to explain plant form and function in modern, scientific terms instead of merely describing them.

Bibliography

Biology in the Nineteenth Century. William Coleman. Cambridge, England: Cambridge University Press, 1977.

History of Botanical Science. Alan Morton. London: Academic Press, 1981.

medicine, agriculture, and human biology were very successful.

While at Jena, Schleiden also married, in 1844, and had three daughters. His wife died in 1854, and he remarried the following year.

Dorpat and After

In 1862, Schleiden resigned unexpectedly from the University of Jena. In 1863, he accepted a position at the University of Dorpat in Russia (now Tartu in Estonia), where his lectures filled the main auditorium to overflowing. He was resented by other professors, however, and his views on Darwinism and human evolution provoked controversy. He left Dorpat after only a year and returned to Germany, where he lived on the money from his popular writings and a pension granted by the czar.

Schleiden then wrote his best-selling works, including books on roses, salt, and marine biology. He also wrote articles about the Jews and their importance for European culture that were unusual in their time for their philo-Semitism.

During the last years of his life, Schleiden suffered severely from asthma, which weakened him progressively. He died on June 23, 1881.

Bibliography

By Schleiden

"Beiträge zur Phytogenesis," *Archiv für Anatomie, Physiologie, und wissenschaftliche Medicin*, 1838 ("Contributions to Phytogenesis," *Scientific Memoirs*, 1841)

Herr Dr. Justus Liebig in Gießen und die Pflanzenphysiologie, 1842

Offenes Sendschreiben an Herr Dr. Justus Liebig in Gießen, 1842

Grundzüge der Wissenschaftlichen Botanik, 1842-1843

(*Principles of Scientific Botany as an Inductive Science*, 1849)

Beiträge zur Botanik: Gesammelte Aufsätze, 1844

Schelling's und Hegel's Verhältniß zur Naturwissenschaft, 1844

Die neueren Einwürfe gegen meine Lehre von der Befruchtung, 1844

Grundriß der Botanik, zum Gebrauch bei seinen Vorlesungen, 1846

Beiträge zur Kenntniß der Sassaparille, 1847

Die Pflanze und ihr Leben: Populäre Vorträge, 1848 (*The Plant: A Biography*, 1848)

Die Physiologie der Pflanzen und Thiere und Theorie der Pflanzencultur: Für Landwirthe bearbeitet, 1850

(Library of Congress)

Handbuch der medicinisch-pharmaceutischen Botanik und botanischen Pharmacognosie, 1852-1857

Studien: Populäre Vorträge, 1855

Zur Theorie des Erkennens durch den Gesichtssinn, 1861

Das Alter des Menschengeschlechts, die Entstehung der Arten und die Stellung des Menschen in der Natur, 1863

Ueber den Materialismus der neueren deutschen Naturwissenschaft, sein Wesen und seine Geschichte, 1863

Das Meer, 1867

Für Baum und Wald, 1870

Die Rose: Geschichte und Symbolik in ethnographischer und kulturhistorischer Beziehung, 1873

Das Salz: Seine Geschichte, seine Symbolik und seine Bedeutung im Menschenleben, 1875

"Die Bedeutung der Juden für Erhaltung und Wiederbelebung der Wissenschaften im Mittelalter," *Westermanns Monatshefte*, 1877

Die geognostischen Verhältnisse des Saalethales bei Jena, 1846 (with E. Schmid)

Ueber die Natur der Kieselhölzer, 1855 (with Schmid)

About Schleiden

History of Biology. Erik Nordenskiöld. New York: Tudor, 1935.

"Schleiden, Matthias Jakob." Isaac Asimov. In *Isaac Asimov's Biographical Encyclopedia of Science and Technology*. New York: Doubleday, 1972.

(Sander J. Gliboff)

Maarten Schmidt

Areas of Achievement: Astronomy and cosmology

Contribution: Schmidt conducted research on the structure, dynamics, and evolution of the Galaxy. He is best known for his discovery of quasars, which are highly energetic quasi-stellar objects at great distances from the Milky Way.

Dec. 28, 1929	Born in Groningen, the Netherlands
1949	Receives a B.A. degree from the University of Groningen
1956	Receives a Ph.D. in astronomy from the University of Leiden
1956	Begins working at the Leiden Observatory
1956	Becomes a Carnegie Fellow in Pasadena, California, at Mount Wilson Observatory
1959	Moves to the United States and joins the astronomy department of the California Institute of Technology (Caltech)
1960	Takes up the work of Rudolph Minkowski upon his retirement from Mount Wilson Observatory
1963	Notices a shift toward the red end of the spectrum for two stellar objects, later identified as quasars
1964	Wins the Warner Prize of the American Astronomical Society
1968	Awarded the Rumford Award of the American Academy of Arts and Sciences

Early Life

Maarten Schmidt was born on December 28, 1929, in Groningen, the Netherlands. It was Schmidt's uncle, an amateur astronomer, who introduced him to the joys of observing the skies. One summer at his grandfather's house in the country, Schmidt found a large lens, which he then combined with an eyepiece, using a toilet paper roll as a spacer, to make a telescope. His uncle told him to try to resolve a double star to test his telescope. Schmidt had to get a book on astronomy to look up the location of the star and became interested in what the book had to say.

Although concerned about his prospects in this field, since there were few positions in astronomy in the Netherlands at that time, Schmidt's parents were always supportive and encouraged his interest in astronomy. Schmidt became an avid stargazer; the blackout conditions of World War II were perfect for making observations. As a result of this early experience, Schmidt later became known to his colleagues as a "good eye," someone who worked a telescope well—a talent that would later pay off.

Research on the Galaxy

When Schmidt entered the University of Groningen in 1946, he knew that he wanted to study astronomy. His interest at first lay in the study of the Milky Way. His initial area of study was an observation of one of the spiral arms. For his thesis, he prepared a mass model of the Galaxy.

In 1956, he accepted a Carnegie Fellowship at Mount Wilson Observatory in Pasadena, California. Schmidt published a mass model of the galaxy M_{31}, which was an extension of the work that he had done on the Milky Way. He also became interested in the consequences of the change of gas density in the Galaxy as a consequence of star formation.

Quasars

After a brief visit to the Netherlands, in 1959 Schmidt returned to Mount Wilson in a permanent position. In 1960, he investigated the helium abundance in the center of M_{31}. He found that the abundance of helium did not follow the distribution of a metal as expected. This discovery was later explained by the idea that the helium had been produced primordially in the big bang.

Quasars

In 1963, Schmidt observed spectral (light) readings from two stellar objects unlike any seen before. These objects were later identified as quasars.

In the 1950's, radioastronomers, who observe emissions in the radio region of the electromagnetic spectrum, began locating new objects. They needed visual analysis of the objects' light in order to tell if they were stars or galaxies. Increasingly powerful telescopes were able to look farther out than ever before. At the edges of the observable universe, they found very different objects. They are rather faint and starlike, are extragalactic, emit radiation (which is usually polarized) at all frequencies, show a large redshift, and are usually largely variable over short time periods. These objects became known as quasi-stellar objects, or quasars.

These characteristics paint a strange picture. The variation in their brightness over short periods indicates that quasars are quite small, no more than twice the diameter of the solar system. Their great distances and small size mean that in order to be seen at all, they must be at least a hundred times brighter than anything else previously observed. The extreme redshift of the quasars indicates that they are moving away from Earth at very high speeds and are very far away.

No completely satisfactory model for a quasar yet exists. They exhibit all of the properties of active galaxies, which has led to a theory that quasars lie at the center of galaxies. Their energy source, however, is still unknown. The most commonly accepted theory is that quasars have a black hole at their cores. As the black hole exhausts its fuel, it begins to feed on passing galaxies, a concept that has been observed.

Bibliography

Astronomy Today. Eric Chaisson and Steve McMillan. Englewood Cliffs, N.J.: Prentice Hall, 1993.

Encyclopedia of Physics. Rita G. Lerner and George L. Trigg, eds. New York: VCH, 1990.

Voyage Through the Universe: Galaxies. Editors of Time-Life Books. Alexandria, Va.: Time-Life, 1988.

A 48-inch Schmidt telescope. (California Institute of Technology)

(California Institute of Technology)

Rudolph Minkowski and Walter Baade had been using the 200-inch telescope at Mount Wilson Observatory for the past decade in an attempt to identify radio sources optically. When Minkowski retired in 1960, Schmidt took up this work, since there seemed to be no one else to do it. Two interesting objects, 3C48 and 3C273, were starlike objects that could not be identified as either a galaxy or a star. The most baffling part of the problem was their spectra; they were totally different from those of any star.

In 1963, Schmidt noticed in the spectrum of 3C273 the distinctive spacing of four hydrogen lines that had been highly redshifted. This large shift in the spectral lines toward the red end of the spectrum indicated that 3C273 was receding from the Galaxy at a high rate of speed and was a huge distance away. Given its distance and small size, this meant that 3C273 had to be about a hundred times brighter than any other luminous radio source identified thus far. A similar analysis was possible for 3C48. Both objects seemed to be too far, too small, and too powerful for anything previously observed. They were named quasi-stellar radio sources, or quasars.

Bibliography
By Schmidt
"A Model of the Distribution of Mass in the Galactic System," *Bulletin of the Astronomical Institutes of the Netherlands*, 1956

"The Distribution of Mass in M31," *Bulletin of the Astronomical Institutes of the Netherlands*, 1957

"The Rate of Star Formation," *Astrophysical Journal*, 1959

"The Rate of Star Formation: II. The Rate of Formation of Stars of Different Mass," *Astrophysical Journal*, 1963

"3C 273: A Star-like Object with Large Redshift," *Nature*, 1963

"Optical Spectra and Redshifts of Thirty-one Radio Galaxies," *Astrophysical Journal*, 1965

"Space Distribution and Luminosity Functions of Quasi Stellar Radio Sources," *Astrophysical Journal*, 1968

About Schmidt
"Beacons in Time: Maarten Schmidt and the Discovery of Quasars." R. Preston. *Mercury* 17 (1988).

Origins: The Lives and Worlds of Modern Cosmologists. Alan Lightman and Roberta Brawer. Cambridge, Mass.: Harvard University Press, 1990.

(Linda L. McDonald)

Erwin Schrödinger

Area of Achievement: Physics

Contribution: Through a study of the wave properties of matter, Schrödinger developed wave mechanics, with which he found the solution to a number of problems in atomic physics.

Aug. 12, 1887	Born in Vienna, Austria
1898	Enters the Academische Gymnasium
1910	Earns a Ph.D. in physics from the University of Vienna
1910-1914	Works at the Second Physics Institute at Vienna
1914-1918	Serves in the Imperial Army during World War I
1918-1921	Teaches in Vienna, Jena, Stuttgart, and Breslau
1920	Marries Annemarie Bertel
1921-1926	Teaches at the University of Zurich
1927-1933	Teaches theoretical physics at the University of Berlin
1933	Flees Germany for Oxford, England, upon the coming to power of the Nazi Party
1933	Wins the Nobel Prize in Physics
1936-1938	Serves as a professor at the University of Graz, Austria
1939	Flees Austria upon the German annexation of that country
1939-1956	Teaches theoretical physics at the Institute for Advanced Studies in Dublin, Ireland
1944	Publishes *What Is Life?*
1956	Accepts a position at the University of Vienna
Jan. 4, 1961	Dies in Vienna, Austria

Early Life

Erwin Schrödinger (pronounced "SHROY-dihng-ur"), an only child, was born to Rudolf Schrödinger and Georginer Bauer, a daughter of Rudolf's chemistry professor. Schrödinger's father, the owner of a successful oil cloth factory, was a highly gifted man with a broad education and broad interests that he pursued throughout his life. The young Erwin was first educated at home, taking lessons twice a week from a visiting elementary school teacher.

He attributed his interest in scientific, literary, and philosophical matters to his father, however, whom he would later describe as "his friend, teacher, and tireless partner in conversation." At the age of eleven, Schrödinger entered the Academische Gymnasium and he studied mathematics and physics, as well as classical languages and German poetry.

In 1906, he entered the University of Vienna, where he followed Friedrich Hasenohrl's lectures on theoretical physics five days a week for eight successive semesters. Schrödinger also studied mathematics and experimental physics. During his studies at Vienna, he acquired a mastery of eigenvalue problems in the physics of continuous media—the foundation for his future great work.

Foundational Work

After his graduation in 1910, Schrödinger stayed on as an assistant at the university's Second Physics Institute until the outbreak of World War I, when he was mobilized into the Imperial Army. He spent the three years following the war studying and teaching in Vienna, Jena, Stuttgart, and Breslau. Shortly after his arrival in Breslau in 1921, he accepted an offer from the University of Zurich to assume the professorship formerly held by Albert Einstein and Max von Laue.

Schrödinger remained in Zurich for six years, enjoying the friendship of his colleagues—among whom were the mathematician Hermann Weyl and the physicist Peter J. W. Debye—and pursuing a number of problems in theoretical physics. He wrote papers dealing with specific heats of solids, problems of thermodynamics from a statistical point of view, and atomic spectra. He also studied the theory of color vision and wrote a paper on color blindness. His great discovery, Schrödinger's wave equation, was made at the end of this period, during the winter of 1925-1926.

Nobel Prize Work
Concerned with problems in Niels Bohr's orbit theory of atomic structure and dissatisfied with the solutions then proposed, Schrödinger argued that atomic spectra should be determined by some kind of eigenvalue problem.

His pursuit of that idea led him to his wave theory of atomic phenomena, for which he was awarded the Nobel Prize in Physics in 1933, jointly with Paul A. M Dirac.

Later Studies
In 1927, Schrödinger succeeded Max Planck as professor of theoretical physics at the University of Berlin, then a center of great scientific activity. Later worried by the Nazi regime and

The Emergence of Wave Mechanics

Schrödinger developed equations for the motions executed by the electrons and their interactions that define them as waves, providing a solid foundation to the theory called quantum mechanics.

When, in the early 1920's, Schrödinger involved himself in the study of the atom, he found the existing state of knowledge "fairly desperate." The model proposed by Niels Bohr in 1913 and further developed by Arnold Sommerfeld was being defied by various anomalous effects found in experiments. In order to make it work, new postulates, the so-called quantum conditions and quantum postulates, had to be added ad hoc.

For Schrödinger, the way out lay in the possibility of attributing to the classical mechanical principles in the interior of the atom the operation of a wave mechanism, on which the point-mechanical processes are essentially based.

The point of departure in developing this idea was Louis de Broglie's theory of matter. De Broglie had raised the question in 1924 that if waves show corpuscular character, should not particles also show wave character? He assumed that they should and that the waves associated with a particle have a wavelength given by Planck's constant (h), divided by its momentum, as in the case of a light quanta, or photons. De Broglie then pictured an electron inside an atom as an undulatory movement. Those orbits where resonance occurs—that is, where the number of wavelengths is a whole number—are the "permitted" orbits in the sense of Bohr's model.

Schrödinger went a step further. Since the electrons are the seat of outgoing waves, he thought that it should be possible to find a wave equation

for the motions executed by the electrons and their interactions that would define these waves in the same way as the wave equation that determined the propagation of light. From the solution of this wave equation, one should be able to select those oscillations that are feasible for the motions within the atom.

He eventually succeeded in establishing his famous wave equation, a second order differential equation which, when applied to the hydrogen atom, yielded the results of Bohr and de Broglie.

Schrödinger was also successful in determining wave equations for a series of different motions of the electron. These equations give finite solutions only when the energy of the system has specific discrete values, determined by Planck's constant. In Bohr's theory, these discrete energy values of the electron paths were only hypothetical, but, in Schrödinger's theory, they appeared as completely determined by the form of the wave equation.

The theory developed by Schrödinger soon became known as wave mechanics. He also showed that his theory is mathematically equivalent to matrix mechanics, the quantum theory proposed by Werner Heisenberg about the same time. His work gave a solid foundation to the new quantum theory, called quantum mechanics.

Bibliography
The Conceptual Development of Quantum Mechanics. Max Jammer. New York: McGraw, 1966.
Twentieth Century Physics. L. M. Brown, A. Pais, and B. Pippard, eds. Vol. 2. New York: AIP Press, 1995.

(The Nobel Foundation)

its treatment of scientists after Adolf Hitler came to power in 1933, Schrödinger left for Oxford, England.

More homesick than cautious, however, he accepted a position at the University of Graz, Austria, in 1936. When Germany annexed Austria in 1938, he was in immediate danger, since his earlier flight from Germany was considered an unfriendly act. Through the efforts of Eamon de Valera, the president of Ireland who was himself a mathematician, Schrödinger found his way to Dublin, where he assumed a position at the new Institute for Advanced Studies.

Schrödinger's seventeen-year residence in Dublin was a productive period during which he continued to pursue a variety of philosophical and scientific topics. In 1944, he published a book entitled *What Is Life?* in which he defended his idea that the biological process of growth could also be understood on the basis of quantum theory. This analysis exerted a notable influence on both physicists and molecular biologists.

In 1956, he returned to his homeland to teach at the University of Vienna. One year later, he suffered from an illness that weakened him considerably. He died on January 4, 1961, at the age of seventy-three.

Bibliography
By Schrödinger
Abhandlungen zur Wellenmechanik, 1927
What Is Life?, 1944
Science and Humanism: Physics in Our Time, 1951
Nature and the Greeks, 1954
Mind and Matter, 1958
Meine Weltansicht, 1961 (*My View of the World*, 1964)
The Interpretation of Quantum Mechanics: Dublin Seminars (1949-1955) and Other Unpublished Essays, 1995

About Schrödinger
"Erwin Schrödinger." Armin Hermann. In *Dictionary of Scientific Biography*, edited by Charles Coulston Gillispie. Vol. 12. New York: Charles Scribner's Sons, 1975.
Erwin Schrödinger: An Introduction to His Writings. William T. Scott. Amherst: University of Massachusetts Press, 1967.
Schrödinger, Life and Thought. Walter Moore. Cambridge, England: Cambridge University Press, 1989.

(Rosa Alvarez Ulloa)

BIOGRAPHICAL ENCYCLOPEDIA
of
SCIENTISTS

Index

In the following index, volume numbers appear in **bold face** type and page numbers appear in normal type. The names of scientists who are profiled in the encyclopedia are shown in **bold face**.